The Company We Keep

50 Years of Arkansans Creating Just Communities

Ruth D. Shepherd

BUTLER CENTER BOOKS

The Butler Center for Arkansas Studies
Central Arkansas Library System
100 Rock Street
Little Rock, Arkansas 72201
www.bultercenter.org

First Printing: April 2013

ISBN (13) 978-1-935106-54-8

Book and cover design: H. K. Stewart

Library of Congress Cataloging-in-Publication Data
Shepherd, Ruth D.
 The company we keep : fifty years of building just communities / Ruth D.
Shepherd.
    pages cm
 Includes bibliographical references and index.
 ISBN 978-1-935106-54-8 (pbk. : alk. paper)
 1. Civic leaders~Arkansas~Biography. 2. Community development~
Arkansas~History. 3. Multiculturalism~Arkansas~History. 4.
Arkansas~Biography. I. Just Communities of Arkansas. II. Title.

HN79.A83C6596 2013
307.1'40922767~dc23
                                        2013003111

Printed in the United States of America
This book is printed on archival-quality paper that meets requirements of the
American National Standard for Information Sciences, Permanence of Paper, Printed
Library Materials, ANSI Z39.48-1984.

The publishing division of the Butler Center for Arkansas Studies
was made possible by the generosity of Dora Johnson Ragsdale and
John G. Ragsdale Jr.

The Company We Keep

Contents

Dedication

The *Company We Keep* is lovingly dedicated to the memory of Dave Grundfest Sr., who served as chair for the first National Conference of Christians and Jews (NCCJ) Brotherhood Dinner in 1964. Grundfest, along with other commu- nity leaders, understood the importance of recog- nizing those outstanding individuals who were working for a just commu- nity, and the honoree that first year was the Honor- able Brooks Hays, who be- cause of his courageous actions during the 1958 school desegregation crisis had lost his Fifth District seat in the U.S. Congress.

What Grundfest Sr. and the other NCCJ lead- ers couldn't have known then is that they were es- tablishing a tradition that would live and grow to become an important an- nual opportunity for Arkansans to honor our most visionary leaders. At first, the annual din- ner brought together a mostly white group of Christians (including Catholics) and Jews. In 1970, NCCJ honored its first African American, Dr. Lawrence Davis, chancellor of the Agricultural, Mechanical, and

Normal College (AM&N), now University of Arkansas at Pine Bluff (UAPB). Former *Arkansas Democrat-Gazette* High Profile editor Phyllis Brandon says that the Arkansas NCCJ, now Just Communities of Arkansas (JCA), Humanitarian Dinner was the first racially integrated social event in Central Arkansas. In 2013, it is difficult to imagine that a social event in Central Arkansas would not welcome guests of all races. Perhaps that is partially a result of the foresight of Dave Grundfest Sr.

In 1965, the second Brotherhood Dinner was chaired by E. Grainger Williams, and the honoree was Dave Grundfest Sr. Shockingly, that dinner was cut short by a bomb threat. Today, a dinner celebrating the commonality of people from different religious traditions or races is hardly seen as controversial, but at the time such a dinner was a bold statement by forward thinking leaders of our community. Many years later in 2006, Jack Grundfest, grandson of Dave Grundfest Sr., and his wife, Kathy, served as dinner chairs when the Honorable Joyce Elliott, Dr. Dean Kumpuris, and Mary Steenburgen were honored with the Humanitarian Award.

The tradition has continued, year after year and generation after generation, and we are hopeful that another fifty years from now, Just Communities of Arkansas will have equally wise and prescient leaders who will honor our past as they celebrate, and even create, the possibilities of our future *where every person is valued, where every voice is heard, and where everyone has a fair chance to succeed.*

Thank you for your leadership, Dave Grundfest Sr.

Introduction

The *Company We Keep* is a love story. It's about mostly ordinary people who, because of their love for others, have been able to do extraordinary things. The common theme is the amazing capacity of human beings to care about others. We see it in the parents, mentors, teachers, coaches, and friends who influenced our subjects. We see it in the compassion of the subjects themselves. Most of them have had challenges, but they've also had vision. They imagine a better world, and they've worked to bring it about for those they hold close and for those they've never met. A few of these individuals were born to privilege; most were not; and some were born into poverty. What they had in common was a belief in themselves, and others who believed in them. Their stories are heartwarming, sometimes funny, and most of all inspiring. As I met and interviewed each person, I found hardly any pretention, but a lot of pride. I found some remorse, but more often gratitude. I found ambition, not just for themselves but for a better community.

In 1927, the National Conference of Christians and Jews (NCCJ) was organized "for the advancement of justice, amity and peace." In 1964, the Arkansas regional office was opened; at its height, NCCJ had sixty-five regional offices across the United States. In the mid-1990s, the organization changed its name to the National Conference for Community and Justice (still NCCJ) to better reflect its mission and to recognize the growing diversity in our country. In 2005, NCCJ moved from a unitary structure of governance to independent, autonomous regions. Shortly thereafter, the national office was closed, and NCCJ of Arkansas became Just Communities of Arkansas (JCA).

Since 1964, Arkansas NCCJ/JCA has recognized 135 individuals, and we are fortunate to include all of them with the exception of former President Bill Clinton and former Secretary of State Hillary Clinton, whose worldwide travels made interviews with them impossible during the compilation of the book. However, you can find excellent biographies of each in *The Encyclopedia of Arkansas History and Culture*. Published by the Central Arkansas Library System, the online encyclopedia was an invaluable resource in doing the research for this project. (Because we are so much a part of each other's stories in Arkansas, you will find many mentions of both Bill and Hillary Clinton throughout the biographies.)

The original working title for this book was *Amazing Arkansans*. However, as I began to do the interviews, I realized how fortunate we are in our "wonderful small state" to be interconnected and familiar with so many of our illustrious leaders, so the title became *The Company We Keep*. That is one of the loveliest benefits of being an Arkansan. I doubt that there is any other state where a poor girl from Oklahoma could have gained access to these remarkable, and very busy, people.

These stories, told mostly in their own words, will make you feel proud to be a member of our human family. They certainly made me feel that way. My one regret is that I was unable to visit with those of our honorees who had died. How I would have loved to have heard their stories firsthand, also. Unless otherwise indicated, biographies were adapted from tributary remarks delivered at the Father Joseph H. Biltz and Humanitarian Awards presentations.

Much of the work that we do at Just Communities of Arkansas to build a community *where every person is valued, where every voice is heard, and where everyone has a fair chance to succeed* is built on taking the risk of sharing our own story, of telling our own truth. When people share their stories, they give us a gift. When we really hear their stories, we return that gift with gratitude.

Thanks

There are many people to thank for making this love story possible. As my friend Chancellor Joel Anderson once pointed out, "If you are on a country road and you see a turtle atop a fence post, you can bet that turtle didn't get there by itself."

There are two people who can claim just as much ownership of this book as I do. Kerri Sernel, development and marketing director of JCA, read every biography and every other section of this book, making suggestions that helped me improve those first drafts every time. Katherine Whitworth, program coordinator at the Winthrop Rockefeller Institute, upon hearing about the project, volunteered to be the editor. Her skill and insight brought further refinement, continuity, and a professional quality to each biography. This is a much better book because of Kerri and Katherine. My gracious thanks to each of them.

JCA staff members Elizabeth Akama-Makia and Andrea Gómez kept the "home fires" of JCA burning, and actually increased our programming reach, while I concentrated in large measure on this book for practically a year. And members of the JCA board of directors were supportive throughout the process. Our intern, Perry Smith, did the yeoman's work of keeping more than 130 stories organized, scanning photos, and helping with every tedious task asked of him. JCA's good friend, Doris Krain, contributed her photos from the annual dinner and Gathering of Friends for the past ten years.

David Stricklin, head of the Butler Center for Arkansas Studies, was supportive from the very beginning. In fact, his vision and influence increased the scope of this project in a way that I had not even dreamed. And then he delivered me into the capable hands of Rod Lorenzen and H. K. Stewart. That was my good fortune, for sure. It's great to work with professionals who know exactly what needs to be done at every step of the way.

And there were legions of people along the way who either helped me find photos, get appointments, or steered me to the right place to find the perfect tribute for those honorees who had died. Those include: Philip S. Anderson, Tisha D. Arnold, Kathleen Atkins, Julie Baldridge, James Bankhead, Patty Barker, Mary Biondo, Cathy Bozynski, Justice

Robert L. Brown, Joyce A. Campbell, Madalyn Dortch, Vivan Flowers, Jeane Hamilton, Carolyn Hardie, Richard D. Hardie III, Melea Hargett, Johnny Hasan, Garbo and Dr. Archie Hearne, Christopher Hervey, Holly Hiett, Reverend Ray Higgins, Henry Jones Jr., Shareese Kondo, Cal Ledbetter, Theba Lolly, David Margolick, Mack McLarty, Gwen Moritz, Anne Bradford Mourning, Sheffield Nelson, Irene Palnick, Lynn Parker, Pat Patterson, Jim Pfeifer, Skip Rutherford, Hillis Schild, Stephanie Sims, David L. Speer, Stephanie Streett, David Ware, Ann Wedaman, Alfred Williams, and Brooks Wolfe.

Frank Fellone and Lynn Hamilton of the *Arkansas Democrat-Gazette* were gracious in their support by giving permission to use "whatever from their archives" that we needed to make this book complete. And Jim Pfeifer provided access to the Temple B'nai Israel archives. Thanks to each of them for taking a special interest in making this the best remembrance possible.

Jack Grundfest (the grandson of Dave Grundfest Sr.) graciously, and miraculously, supplied me with an audio copy of the "speech the bomb threat delayed." However, that doesn't begin to enumerate the many ways in which Jack and the Grundfest/Bauman family have lent their support, not only to this book, but to the work of JCA over its history. I, and this organization, owe the Grundfest/Bauman family a great debt.

Gracious thanks to all the honorees and dinner chairs from the past fifty years. Without their commitment to the mission of Just Communities, there would be no book.

Finally, I thank my husband, Steve, my best friend and biggest cheerleader, who always believes in me even when I have doubts. I also must thank our children, Stephanie and Paul, both now grown up and making successful lives for themselves. But, they learned at an early age to leave a written note on my calendar if they needed something special like a poster board for a class project. They also learned how to pack their own lunches, select their own clothes, and solve most of their own problems, which gave me enormous room to grow as an individual even when my primary role was being a mother to them. I also want to thank our daughter-in-law, Laura-Rose, who was a role model for me when, the first time I met her, she said, "I am a writer." I thought that was awfully gutsy at the time, but her self-confidence was one of the things that gave me the heart to begin this project.

We Arkansans have much to celebrate, and we are certainly blessed by *the company we keep.*

The Biographies

Annie McDaniel Abrams
Father Joseph H. Biltz Award, 2004

Visiting with Annie McDaniel Abrams is like sitting in on a college level history class. With more than fifty years of activism on her résumé, Annie's "been there, done that" when it comes to racial and social justice issues.

Born during the depression in Arkadelphia, she left her home to attend the segregated Dunbar Senior High School in Little Rock and graduated there in 1950. Her bachelor of science degree was earned at Philander Smith College, and she began her paid employment as a teacher in Marianna.

It's her volunteer résumé, however, that makes one breathless with appreciation for all that she has accomplished. We know her best for her local service, but she has served in numerous national roles, such as board service for the Young Women's Christian Association (YWCA), president of the National Council of Negro Women, and delegate to the White House Conference on Aging.

It's difficult to select Annie's most important contributions—there have been so many. One significant role was serving as the first African-American president of the Central High School Parent Teacher Student Association (PTSA). In fact, the Little Rock School District (LRSD) has Annie's handprint all over it: She was a charter member of Volunteers in Public Schools and chair of the LRSD Biracial Committee, she helped name Fulbright and Rockefeller Schools, and she even helped select a superintendent along the way.

Annie also helped establish the Central High Museum. Rett Tucker, who served with her to establish the museum, says Annie always had a keen understanding of the historical importance of the work they were doing and would admonish them to keep everything: minutes, drawings, even napkins with notes. When Annie expressed her opinion, in the middle of a history lesson, Rett called her talks, "Annie's sermons." Mayor Jim Dailey also cites Annie's grandmotherly authority, which makes her a force to reckon with.

Presently Annie works as a Commissioner for Fair Housing, on the boards of Habitat for Humanity and the Martin Luther King Jr. Commission, and in the Democratic Party and Democratic Black Caucus, along with serving in the PTA (still) and neighborhood groups. We've heard that her next volunteer job is going to be "executive director of the world." And that might be a very good thing.

Annie was married to Orville Abrams until his death in 1999; she has eight children, twenty grandchildren, and six great-grandchildren, one of whom lives with her.

Through Annie's tireless efforts and sometimes not-so-gentle prodding, we are a better people and a better community, culturally richer, learning from our history.

Dr. Sunny Anand
Father Joseph H. Biltz Award, 2007

At seventeen years old, Sunny Anand graduated from high school in Indore, India. Instead of the equivalent of going to Myrtle Beach to celebrate, he and seven friends went to live and work for twelve days in a village of untouchables. Their aim was to build a road to the village, which had been inaccessible before. They delivered medicines, sang with the children, and worked on the road. Around the eighth or ninth day, the villagers began to trust them and help them, and by the eleventh day, a mobile ambulance came to the village on the new road bringing the first two doctors the villagers had ever seen.

Sunny was raised as a Sikh, a religion based on belief in One God and recognizing the equality of all human beings. Sunny's father had been born into a poor farm laborer's family. He was a self-made man, and he and his wife taught their children to respect all persons and all religious faiths. When explaining that concept, Sunny says, "Water is called by many names." The Sikh faith teaches that we should help those who are less fortunate, another practice that is clearly a part of Sunny's life.

Educational opportunity and political unrest in his Indian homeland conspired to put Sunny on a path to residence in the United States. He and his wife, Iti, have three children: daughter Amrit, son Tej, and their adopted son Dhiraj, who now lives in Memphis. The Anands have lived in Little Rock since 1997, and Sunny holds impressive titles at Arkansas Children's Hospital and the University of Arkansas for Medical Sciences (UAMS) and has been recognized internationally for his research on pediatric pain relief.

But we recognize Sunny for his constant work at building interfaith understanding and working for those less fortunate. When he and Iti arrived in Little Rock and found there was no Gurudwara or temple, they established a prayer room in their own home that is open every Friday for singing and prayer. As those who gathered on that first Friday night in 1997 left the upstairs room, they found that sacred ash had manifested spontaneously on the photos of Sri Sathya Sai Baba that hung in the stairwell. Clearly this was a holy place. Members of all faith groups are welcomed, and even when the Anands must be out of town, the prayer room is open to all for the Friday gatherings.

Following 9/11, Sunny says their group often met every night to pray together. It was a time of great collective hurt that needed great collective healing. Some of the activities that came after were the Celebrating Universal Values program, which was held for several years. They've held a light vigil to celebrate American heroes who served as police officers, fire fighters, and emergency-response paramedics. And since 2004, they have held an Easter weekend spiritual retreat, which up to 200 people of all faiths attend. These are just some of the activities they have undertaken to promote healing.

In his modest way, Sunny often forgets to mention the work he's done to help establish the Harmony Health Clinic. Partners include the Arkansas Interfaith Alliance and attorney volunteers Matt House and Amy Johnson. During 2007, the Harmony Clinic elected their board and got their 501(c)3 status approved. Sunny is serving as president of the board, and when it opens, Harmony Clinic will provide medical care, dental care, a pharmacy, and mental health services, all completely free to the patients.

Clearly the road that Sunny helped build at seventeen years old is still leading him to help others.

Dr. Joel E. Anderson
Humanitarian Award, 2008

Chancellor Joel Anderson explains that he and the University of Arkansas at Little Rock (UALR) have grown up and come of age together. During his more than thirty years at UALR, he finds much to be proud of, and picking just one thing would be similar to picking one's favorite child... not easily done.

Joel was raised on a farm in Northeast Arkansas, where he played basketball at Swifton High School, was active in 4-H, and church, and spent autumns picking cotton. He graduated from Harding University, where he met his wife, Ann, and they have three sons and two granddaughters. Joel earned a master's degree from American University, and when he left Arkansas to pursue his PhD at the University of Michigan, he didn't expect to return.

However, in 1969, Little Rock University (LRU) became UALR, and an editorial in the *Arkansas Gazette* touted the important and bright future of this new University of Arkansas institution. Joel was intrigued and got an interview with Dr. Cal Ledbetter, who hired Joel as an assistant professor of political science in 1971. As UALR grew and prospered, Joel Anderson became a key leader on campus and in the community.

Among other accomplishments and leadership roles, Joel has been acting chair of the Department of Political Science and Criminal Justice, served as coordinator for the College of Liberal Arts in the Center for Urban and Governmental Affairs, and established UALR's Graduate School, serving as the dean from 1977 through 1984. In 1984, Joel became the provost and vice chancellor for academic affairs, the second-ranking university officer. In December of 2002, Joel was named the eighth chancellor of UALR.

The constant theme of Joel's leadership has been that UALR should serve in partnership with the community, and he has established this partnership through many endeavors. In the early 1990s, Joel championed keeping our two public radio stations (KUAR and KLRE) as a public service. Later he led the university task force on the LRSD, releasing the nationally recognized report "Plain Talk: The Future of Little Rock's Public Schools" in 1997. In 2000, he led the university task force that issued the report "Water for Our Future: Overcoming Regional Paralysis." Joel said almost everyone was shocked when the cities adopted all of the recommendations in this report, which led to the merger of the Little Rock and North Little Rock water utilities and won for UALR the Jack Evans Regional Leadership Award from Metroplan.

As chancellor, Joel has led the university to purchase and renovate the University Plaza Shopping Center and is leading the efforts to restore Coleman Creek to become a recreational area and natural laboratory for study.

Of special significance to constituents of Just Communities of Arkansas is an annual survey of racial attitudes in Pulaski County that Joel initiated based on his belief that "you have to face it to fix it." The university's strategic plan, UALR Fast Forward, made seven pledges to the community. One was: "UALR pledges to be the keeper of the flame on the subject of race." The five subsequent yearly surveys have shown that race remains a foremost barrier to social and economic progress. Through its leadership, UALR is insisting that our community face this controversial issue.

All of us who care about racial equality and justice have come to rely upon UALR's annual survey to legitimize and inform our work. To introduce one year's survey, Joel said,

> A survey provides good information as a foundation for community discussion of a sensitive issue. Each survey is a mirror that permits us to see ourselves as a diverse community more clearly.... The

first challenge is to develop a community understanding that something needs to be done. The problem of race in our community is, after all, a community problem that will require a community solution. I hope and expect that the university surveys will be the starting point for the framing of a fresh community agenda on race, developed with broad participation and pursued arm-in-arm."

In 2004, another important initiative of the university's strategic plan was begun: the first Annual Regional Summit, "Solutions Big Enough to Fit the Size of the Problems." In his keynote address Joel said, "Seeds...are small, modest beginnings. But in time they grow. They can mature into something a thousand times greater. I am confident that the small seeds planted here today will in time give the people of our region more prosperous, healthy, and livable communities." Through the seeds of Joel's leadership, just as the University of Arkansas at Little Rock has grown, we are indeed growing a better community.

Honorable Jim Argue Jr.

Father Joseph H. Biltz Award, 2000
Humanitarian Award, 2007

After college graduation in 1973, Jim Argue became a banker. He must have been pretty good at it, because he was tapped for the executive management training program and began to learn all aspects of the business. He served as a branch manager for eight years and later became head of the marketing department at Commercial National in Little Rock. But in what Jim calls a premature mid-life crisis, he wanted something else, and friends were able to recruit him in 1981 to head the fledgling United Methodist Foundation, which had only $67,000 in assets at the time. "It was tough, and it took forever to raise the first million," according to Jim. "But for the first five years, the lay leaders who served on the board of the foundation delivered everything I asked for." Jim credits his six-person staff and those loyal board members with the incredible success of the foundation, which now boasts a permanent charitable fund of over $102 million to support good works in the name of the United Methodist Church. Jim says that leading the foundation has given him a chance to serve a church he loves, and he feels that the Spirit was at work when he accepted the job.

Jim's next big career step occurred in 1990 as he watched the Arkansas legislature fail to provide adequate resources for public education, especially for the neediest children. His good friend Stacy Sells got tired of his complaining and said, "Why don't you do something about it and run for office?" In 1991, Jim was elected to the Arkansas House of Representatives for the first of eight terms in public office. By his second term, he joined the Education Committee and there found the opportunity to focus on what he felt really mattered.

For Jim, public education reform is a spiritual issue, and he feels that it is immoral to fail to give children all that they need to learn in school and to build successful lives. In addition, he points to Arkansas's low standing on economic scales as one result of a less-than-adequate system of public education. Therefore, unlike many others, Jim welcomed the November 2002 Lakeview ruling, which forced the Arkansas legislature to find ways to improve schools and school facilities across the state.

In a bipartisan spirit, Jim and then-governor Mike Huckabee joined forces to accomplish the first-ever forced consolidation of school districts that served fewer than 350 students. Jim and his legislative colleagues created state funding for high quality pre-kindergarten programs for children from low-income homes. Additionally, Jim was diligent in his call for school improvements leading to a twenty-six percent increase in teacher salaries, mandatory high school curriculum standards, academic and financial accountability standards, and increased per-student funding for our most challenged students. Jim says that even he has been amazed at how quickly these actions have resulted in higher test scores on national student assessments.

Jim is quick to point out that his is only one of 135 votes, and he credits the will and courage of his colleagues for the many education reform measures now in place. In his final legislative session, in 2012, Jim continued to champion education reform and high standards for all schools, and he is hopeful that future legislators will understand the urgency and continue to make public schools a priority.

During the 2007 legislative session, Jim also spoke out against a bill that would have barred gay or lesbian individuals from serving as foster or adoptive parents even to children from their own families. Jim co-authored the Arkansas Senate's Code of Ethics and calls himself "the resident idealist." As a legislator, Jim has consistently voted his conscience rather than worry about his re-election, and his integrity has been rewarded by those re-elections.

Jim is a graduate of Hendrix College, and in 1980 he spotted an attractive new alto in his church choir. He and Elise Carey were married four months later. They have two daughters, Sarah and Emily.

Jim loves Arkansas and feels honored and blessed to have been able to represent his neighbors at the Capitol. He says his community has been good to him. We'd say, "Right back at ya', Jim Argue!"

Kay Kelley Arnold

Humanitarian Award, 1999

(Interview conducted August 2, 2012)

If you want to see Kay Kelley Arnold get animated, ask her about what an adobe brick-making machine can do for a small Central American village.

It all started when President Bill Clinton appointed her to the board of the Inter-American Foundation. Kay was subsequently re-appointed by President George W. Bush and served as both vice chair and chair of the board. When her second term on the board ended in early 2012, she joined the IAF Advisory Council, which she serves as vice chair. The Inter-American Foundation is an independent agency of the U.S. government that funds development projects undertaken by grassroots groups in Latin America and the Caribbean. It was created through the Foreign Assistance Act of 1969 as an experimental alternative to traditional foreign assistance, and Kay is convinced that the experiment has been a success.

Take, for example, the brick-making machine. A small village had been totally washed away by the combination of a hurricane and monsoon rains. The residents wanted to re-build, so they asked for an adobe brick-making machine grant. The twelve families began to make bricks and then built twelve houses. They didn't select their houses until after they were built, so they all worked to make each house equally sturdy. The houses had concrete floors, running water, and tin roofs. Once the houses were built, they constructed a school and a community center. Next they planted gardens. They had rebuilt their entire village with the gift of one machine. Kay says that she learned that communities know what they need. She was gratified to be a small part in helping this community rebuild not only their homes but their lives.

With that kind of attitude, it's easy to see why Kay has been tapped as vice president of public affairs for Entergy Corporation. Dividing her time mostly between Little Rock and Washington DC, Kay manages the corporate foundation, the civic and social responsibility activities, the political action committees, and the grassroots and low-income programs—all the things that Entergy does to be a good citizen itself and to promote civic involvement by its employees. She's been preparing for this job all her life.

As a girl growing up in Heber Springs, Arkansas, she watched her parents, Henry Clay and Tommie Lou Kelley, take leadership roles in the community. They instilled in her that giving and participating in the life of the community is critical to being a good citizen. She says, "I learned a whole arm's length of values from them that continue to guide my life to this day: the value of education, independence, giving back, loyalty, everything I know."

Kay attended the University of Arkansas at Fayetteville for her undergraduate and master's degrees in communications. To help with expenses, she tended bar and waited tables at the D-Lux on Dickson Street. What she learned there was to always leave a generous tip.

After Fayetteville, Kay had some great opportunities, such as being Governor Bill Clinton's liaison to the Departments of Arkansas Heritage and Parks and Tourism. She worked at the Arkansas Arts Council and for the Arkansas Legislative Council. She later served as director of the Department of Arkansas Heritage and was the founding director of The Nature Conservancy's Arkansas office. She loved working with people throughout the state who welcomed her into their homes and worked hard within their communities to make good things happen. She also got her law degree and passed the bar in 1981. She went to work for Arkansas Power & Light (now Entergy) in 1988 as the general manager of corporate communications.

On the day of Bill Clinton's inauguration in 1979, she was introduced to Richard Sheppard Arnold, whom she married in September of that year. Richard Arnold served as a judge of the U.S. District Court and was appointed by President Jimmy Carter to the Eighth Circuit Court of Appeals. Kay and Richard were soul mates who shared common interests in history, literature, government, and the law. Richard died on September 23, 2004. Kay says that being married to a federal judge was always interesting and that her husband's position afforded them many opportunities. Two presidents (Nixon and Clinton) considered appointing Arnold to the Supreme Court, and it has been said that Richard Arnold will be remembered as "perhaps the best judge never to serve on the Supreme Court." In May 2002, the U.S. Courthouse in Little Rock was renamed in Judge Arnold's honor.

Kay's list of community commitments is long and lately includes the Winrock International Advisory Board, the Conservation Fund, the National Wildlife Foundation President's Council, and the Lyon College Board of Trustees. She's just completing a second term on the Bill and Hillary Clinton National Airport Commission. She talks about how much fun her service has been, how much she has learned, and how gratified she feels when she is able to give back—just like her parents taught her.

Kay has also been recognized with many awards and honors, most notably for her work in conservation and environmental public policy.

As a child back in Heber Springs, Kay also learned a love of reading from her mother and a favorite English teacher, Ms. Alice Andrews. She recalls her favorite book was To Kill a Mockingbird, and she couldn't decide whom she most wanted to be, Atticus or Scout. Turns out she's a bit of both: She's an attorney with a strong sense of justice like Atticus, and she's tender-hearted and compassionate like Scout.

Bishop Steven M. Arnold

Humanitarian Award, 2003

Steven Arnold's fundamental principle for living is that God wants us to demonstrate the love of God by our love for others and our behavior toward others. For Arnold, love is a verb, not a noun. Through his ministry, especially as senior pastor at St. Mark Baptist Church, he has consistently put this belief into action. For example, St. Mark provides 160 food baskets each month to the elderly or single-parent families from throughout Pulaski County. The church also sponsors three mission trips each year to third-world countries, where volunteers build schools and churches. Since 1994, St. Mark has given out $170,000 in college scholarships. Locally, church members also build Habitat for Humanity homes; provide a tutoring program, a youth enrichment summer camp, a prison ministry, and an addiction support group; and participate in Sharefest with other local congregations.

Through Bishop Arnold's leadership, St. Mark has grown in membership from 300 to over 5,000 and added an 8 a.m. Sunday service and a Sunday service in Jacksonville. The church also has retired its building debt, completed a $1 million renovation project, and implemented a television ministry, *Light of the World*, which is broadcast in more than 20 states.

Bishop Arnold attended Northeast High School in North Little Rock where he was named an All-State and All-American in football and track. He received his BA from Philander Smith College.

Bishop Arnold has served the larger community in numerous ways, including as Chaplain for the University of Arkansas at Pine Bluff (UABP) football team, as a member of the Baptist Health and Bank of the Ozarks boards, and as a member of the Philander Smith College Business Advisory Board. He also is chairman of the board of Eastwind Community Development Council. In 1998, he founded the Fellowship of Christian Churches (FCC), an interdenominational organization that provides a spiritual foundation for other ministries and churches. As Presiding Bishop of the FCC, he oversees and mentors thirteen churches in a three-state area.

Annie Mae Johnson Bankhead

Humanitarian Award, 1976
(December 16, 1904–January 28 1989)
Provided by James Bankhead

On December 16, 1904, in Brooksfield, Mississippi, Daniel Webster and Thamer (White) Johnson were blessed with the first of six children, Annie Mae. Two siblings died as infants. The other siblings, Solomon, John Anthony, and Ida completed the Johnson family. The Johnson children received their early education in Mississippi.

The family moved from Mississippi to Southeast Missouri and remained there for a short period of time. The family moved to College Station, Arkansas, on January 16, 1926. On February 2, 1926, they united with the Pilgrim Rest Missionary Baptist Church. Annie Mae served in many capacities. Out of all her religious accomplishments, the two that she cherished most were her roles as teacher in the Baptist Training Union and president of the Mission Society. She began her community endeavors two months after the family arrived. During this period in her young life, at age twenty, she began to realize the many needs of College Station and its citizens.

She completed her formal education as a graduate of Little Rock Dunbar High School in 1931. She later was united in holy matrimony with R. B. Bankhead. This union was blessed with one daughter, Annie B., and three sons, Joe, Augustus, and James. One other daughter was born to this union. However, she only lived a short time.

Annie Mae began to give her time and energy to help the people in College Station and to make it a better place to live. In 1946, as a lone crusader, she went door to door encouraging citizens to buy a poll tax and register to vote. This venture would be the beginning of a long career of volunteerism in civic and humanitarian service.

Although she had many accomplishments, many of her contributions continue to benefit the community to the present time. In 1960, she was one of the organizers of the College Station Progressive League, which remains the governing body of College Station. She served as President for more than twenty years and led many improvement initiatives during her tenure. She led the successful efforts of College Station residents to secure running water, electricity, natural gas, paved streets, a health clinic, and to establish a credit union.

Her work in College Station received state and national recognition. In 1965, she served on President Lyndon Johnson's National Poverty Program Advisory Committee and represented Arkansas for two years. In 1969, she received the Woman of Conscience Award from the National Council of Women. In 1971, she was the *Arkansas Democrat* Woman of the Year. She won the National Brotherhood and Humanitarian Award from the NCCJ in 1976 and the Distinguished Citizen's Award from the Governor's Office on Volunteerism and Channel 4 in 1980. In July 1986, a street was dedicated to her and named Annie M. Bankhead Drive.

On December 13, 1976, Annie Mae was one of the six presidential electors who met to cast Arkansas's six electoral votes for President-Elect Jimmy Carter and Vice-President-Elect Walter Mondale. She was believed to have been the first black Presidential Elector from Arkansas at the time.

In all of her endeavors, Annie Mae remained anchored in her Christian faith, humble, and committed to her belief in her fellow man.

Annie May Bankhead was the first African American woman to be honored by the Arkansas Affiliate of the National Conference of Christians and Jews with the National Humanitarian Award.

Daisy Bates

Humanitarian Award, 1991
(November 11, 1914–November 4, 1999)

Funeral for Bates honors life spent on social causes
By Shareese Kondo, November 10, 1999
Reprinted with permission from the Arkansas Democrat-Gazette

Dignitaries in dark suits streamed along-side Daisy Bates's white coffin, as well as those dressed in sweat socks, house dresses, and blue jean jackets. And in the nearly full gymnasium where her funeral was held Tuesday, some of them wanted to honor her for the work she did for social causes, civil rights, and education. Others wanted to be there for the historical figure she repre-sented. "She's the queen mother," said Hashim Mustafa, a Little Rock auto salesman, who thought Bates's funeral should have been held in the auditorium of Central High School in Little Rock. "There should be something over there for her. I think it would have been big enough."

Bates died Thursday at Baptist Medical Center. She was eighty-four. Her funeral was held in the family life center of her family's church, Full Counsel Christian Fellowship in North Little Rock. Bates's funeral was hailed as a "homecoming celebration" with more than 1,000 people estimated in attendance.

Yet, obviously absent were the nine people she became nationally known for helping attend Central High School in 1957. The first black students to attend the school forty-two years ago were being honored in Washington DC on Tuesday with the Congressional Gold Medal. Ernest Green, the first black student to graduate from Central, represented the nine students Monday by visiting Bates's body that lay in state at the

Capitol. He issued a statement from the group at that visit praising Bates's contributions to the nation's civil rights movements.

Bates embodied the American Dream and what it means to commit to a community and a purpose, said U.S. Transportation Secretary Rodney Slater, the president's official representative at the funeral. "Just before the service I talked to the president and he reminded me of a time when we were all together in Memphis at the opening of the Civil Rights Museum," Slater said to a swarm of reporters after the service. It was one of those special moments he said he had reflected on over these past few days when "we have all come to recognize that she is no longer with us in body, but clearly is with us in spirit, because it is the spirit of America."

During the funeral, letters from President Clinton, Rosa Parks, and Coretta Scott King were read, as well as a resolution from Julian Bond, chairman of the board of the National Association for the Advancement of Colored People (NAACP), Kweisi Mfume, executive director of the organization, and Dale Charles, president of the Arkansas chapter. In a statement read by Elaine Steel, a caretaker of Rosa Parks, Parks called Bates her "sister in the movement." She said she will miss her "lovely smile and minute attention to detail." Parks lauded Bates's nephew, Cleotis Gatson and his wife, Sharon, for taking care of her in Bates's later days. She also regarded herself and Bates as the "old guard who passed the torch to the new guard" of civil rights activism who should continue to work to end racial segregation. "Mrs. Bates was one of those courageous pioneers of the African-American struggle for racial justice and equality and a most beloved leader of the American Civil Rights Movement," King wrote in her tribute to Bates. "Her unrelenting commitment was an inspiration to me personally, and to everyone who had the privilege of working with her in the movement. I pray that her vibrant spirit will live on in the hearts of all those she touched."

Bates was born on Nov. 11, 1914, in Huttig. In 1941, she married the late L. C. Bates, publisher of the *Arkansas State Press*. For eighteen years they ran the paper as outspoken voices for civil rights who attacked politicians and policies that promoted racial segregation. Slack advertising revenues forced them to close the paper in 1959.

Bates is best known to Arkansans as the former president of the Arkansas chapter of NAACP during the school desegregation efforts in 1957. She was viewed as a mentor and adviser to the Central High students who were photographed meeting and eating meals at her home.

Bates worked in Washington DC for the Democratic National Committee and for anti-poverty programs in the Lyndon B. Johnson administration. She suffered a stroke in 1965 and returned to Arkansas.

She recorded her version of the Central High School events in her memoir *The Long Shadow of Little Rock*. Her husband died in 1980.

In the remarks Clinton sent to be read at the funeral, he called Bates a leader and mentor for the nation. "I deeply regret that she won't be here to see when I finally have the privilege to present Congressional Medals to the nine people who braved the storm there in 1957."

Local and national television crews filmed the service from the balcony. Deborah Robinson, a Nashville, Tennessee, independent television journalist, said she spent the past six years filming interviews with Bates for a documentary of Bates's life. Robinson, a Central High graduate, said her video crews captured the "final chapter" of the Bates story. She said the film's narrators, Ossie Davis and Ruby Dee, will tell about Bates's accomplishments and struggles in the documentary scheduled to air on Thanksgiving.

"There are so many people who still don't know who she was," Robinson said. "I started working on this in 1993, and Mrs. Bates, in her true form, gave me permission to do the project because she thought it would help me. She was truly a woman who lived her life for others and that's what this documentary will show. Today just marks the closing chapter of her dynamic life."

Bates was buried in the Haven of Rest Cemetery. Honorary pallbearers included John H. Johnson, publisher of *Ebony* and *Jet*; attorney John Walker; Dr. Jerry Jewell; and the staff of Full Counsel Ministries.

First Lady Ginger Beebe
Humanitarian Award, 2013

When Ginger Beebe was a little girl, she dreamed of being a Radio City Rockette or an airline stewardess, both glamorous possibilities in her mind. However, she was too short, despite the fact that she tried to stretch herself by hooking her feet under the bed frame and straining to be taller. Alas, she ultimately had to settle for being one of Arkansas's most beloved first ladies as wife of Mike Beebe, the forty-fifth governor of Arkansas.

Ginger always knew that she was a lucky little girl. She was adopted by Buell and Virginia Croom when she was four years old. They had earlier adopted another baby girl, and Ginger thought more than once, "What if they hadn't wanted another girl?" Ginger and her sister, Jean Loyd, along with their extended families, enjoy gathering in the big kitchen at the Governor's Mansion where everyone helps cook Thanksgiving dinner each year.

Buell Croom owned the American Oil bulk plant in Searcy, which provided gasoline to service stations there. Virginia Croom volunteered at the hospital, the school, the church, and anywhere else she saw a need. Ginger learned by example what a difference one person can make when he or she is willing to lend a hand. She also learned the importance of non-partisanship, when her father counseled her mother, "Don't forget, both Democrats and Republicans buy gas from us."

Another important role model for Ginger was her home-economics teacher, Mrs. Charlotte Morgan. Mrs. Morgan was tastefully dressed every day, calm in her demeanor, and accomplished at sewing and cooking. Ginger today still emulates Mrs. Morgan, taking a personal and hands-on approach to life in the Governor's Mansion. Her tastes are evident in the works by Arkansas artists that are displayed on a rotating basis, in the seasonal décor, and in the lovely events and parties that are hosted frequently by the Beebes for non-profit and educational groups. The mansion belongs to the people of Arkansas; that's why the governor and first lady refer to it as "the people's house."

Ginger's first real job was working through the summer of 1966 for an Arkansas gubernatorial candidate, Frank Holt. Holt was one of seven Democratic candidates who decided to run when Governor Orval Faubus decided not to seek another term. Holt made the run-off but lost to Jim Johnson, who later lost to Winthrop Rockefeller in the general election. Ginger said she worked in an office at the Mayfair Hotel, in Searcy, mostly answering phones, and she loved this introduction to politics. At the end of the summer, she took all her earnings ($25) and bought a suit, a black corduroy skirt and jacket with yellow, orange, and red flowers on the lapel.

Ginger got married during her first year in college, had two children, David Powell and Tammy Powell Taylor, and had settled in Searcy by the time she was divorced in 1976. Following in her mother's footsteps, she was very active in the Jaycettes, the women's auxiliary of the Jaycees, and that's how she met Mike Beebe, when they were working on Jaycee projects together. They were married in 1979, and the day after their wedding, a moving van arrived at her home to move her, the children, and their belongings to their new home, which Mike Beebe had bought six months earlier. They delayed their honeymoon until the following summer. Ginger and Mike later had one son, Kyle Beebe, and they are now the proud grandparents of seven grandchildren, ages ranging from two to twenty-two years old. Ginger has been particularly grateful to all Arkansans and the media who allow them to balance their public responsibilities while maintaining their privacy.

Because of her personal history, Ginger is focused on the needs of women and children, and she is actively involved in doing all that she can, both as an individual and as first lady, to improve the prospects for women and children in Arkansas. She has served on the advisory board of Women and Children First, and was honored as its Woman of the Year in 2011. She has served as the honorary chair of the Natural Wonders Partnership Council, an Arkansas Children's Hospital group that addresses the health needs of children. She is working with other leaders to promote First Lady Michelle Obama's "Let's Move" initiative, and she advocates the importance of maintaining a healthy diet and regular exercise when she visits with school children. She also serves on the board of the Women's Foundation of Arkansas and the Arkansas Discovery Network, a collaboration of museums that promotes inquiry learning.

Ginger has a special commitment to fostering mental health, and in 2007, she conducted a listening tour with families whose children suffer from mental illness. She has also served for several years as chair of the NAMI Walk (National Alliance on Mental Illness) which raises awareness and funds to support families who are dealing with mental illness.

Ginger created a special audio tour of the Governor's Mansion herb garden for use by blind and visually impaired visitors. She glows when she talks about watching visually impaired children use the tour to experience the herb garden. When she asks children what they think about when they smell the oregano plant, they invariably say, "Pizza." She laughs when she explains that the audio has to be updated each season because sometimes one of the herbs just doesn't grow that year.

Ginger's advice to someone who wants to make a difference: just get out there and do it. She says that as first lady, she has become aware of a wider array of needs throughout our state, and she believes there is a cause for every Arkansan where they can make a real difference. She recalls helping provide food and toys to a needy family when she was a Jaycette in Searcy. That particular family had no electricity and only mattresses on the floor, and the Jaycettes helped them for several years. Years later, when Ginger's aunt had cancer, the visiting nurse said to Ginger one day, "You don't remember me, but you helped my family. Because

of support from you and others like you, I was able to get my education
and today I am a nurse. Thank you!"

Being first lady is a big job, and Ginger takes her responsibilities
very seriously. She got some good advice from her husband when they
embarked on their life of public service together. He said, "Just be yourself, and everyone will love you." And we do.

Governor Mike Beebe
Humanitarian Award, 2009
Biography provided by Matt DeCample of Governor Beebe's staff

With Mike Beebe, what you see is what you get. There's nothing phony about him; he's the genuine article. He's very bright, pragmatic, and upbeat. He is a leader and a man with a positive outlook on life. He's excited to go to work every day, and he's personally involved in the hands-on, day-to-day work of running state government smoothly, efficiently, and fairly.

Mike was born in the tiny town of Amagon, Arkansas, and spent part of his younger years in places as diverse as New Mexico and Michigan, before his mom settled in Newport. He is the only child of a single mother who worked long hours as a waitress to support them through the tips she received. The caring people of Newport opened their homes and their hearts to Mike, and he felt always welcome and well-loved in that close-knit community. He learned, firsthand, the importance of mentors in his life, and he carefully listened to the wise counsel of these strong figures. Family members, friends, and mentors taught him a set of values and beliefs that he followed despite what others may have thought, and he always had a passion to succeed at any endeavor he felt was important. His first job was sacking groceries, where he learned a lot about people and the value of hard work. At the age of ten, Mike decided he wanted to be a lawyer or an FBI agent.

Mike's mother had one overriding goal for her son: a good education. She was not fortunate enough to go to college herself, and that fact had always kept her from furthering her ambitions. He chose to attend Arkansas State University in Jonesboro, where he became interested in the structure of campus government and local politics, and where he became inspired by the words of Robert Kennedy and the legacy of John F. Kennedy. Soon, he realized that a legal career was his calling.

He also realized the importance of a good education and of giving back so that others might have the same advantages he had. He wanted to help the people of Arkansas and our country achieve the same American Dream that he had been able to live. After completing law school at the University of Arkansas, while serving his country in the U.S. Army Reserves, he clerked for a small law firm and became fascinated by the legal and judicial process.

A leader in the Arkansas Senate for twenty years, and attorney general for four years before being elected governor, Beebe consistently works to reach across party lines and to solve problems. He believes that public service is a noble calling and that serving others can only make our world a better place.

Since taking office in 2007, Governor Mike Beebe has made improving education, expanding Arkansas's economy and cutting taxes his top priorities. Under Beebe's leadership, Arkansas was one of only four states to enter the past two fiscal years without a projected budget shortfall. Arkansas has avoided the massive cuts in services and tax increases suffered by other states, while achieving more than $1.2 billion in tax relief during the Beebe administration.

Governor Beebe's education policies and initiatives have garnered nationwide attention, and Arkansas now ranks fifth in overall K-12 education. To build a better-trained workforce, Governor Beebe has worked to match colleges and universities with local businesses and has led changes in the way schools teach math, science, engineering, and technology. All of these efforts have made Arkansas an attractive place for business investment, and the state was recently named the second-easiest place in America to start a small business.

The parents of three adult children, Governor Beebe and his wife, Ginger, have worked together to improve children's health and literacy throughout the state and have been recognized for their leadership in fighting childhood hunger.

Raymond V. Biondo, MD, MS

Father Joseph Biltz Award, 1989
(June 13, 1936–December 7, 2008)
Biography provided by Mary Biondo

Ray was born in New York City and grew up in Atlantic City, New Jersey. He served in the U.S. Air Force until 1958. Ray received his BA from University of Northern Colorado and his MS and MD from the University of Arkansas for Medical Sciences. Ray served an internship at the University of Cincinnati Medical Center and completed his residency in Dermatology at UAMS. Ray was a volunteer professor in the department of dermatology at UAMS. Ray maintained a solo private practice of dermatology in North Little Rock from 1971 until his retirement in 1990.

Professionally, Ray was a fellow of the American Academy of Dermatology and the Academy of Psychosomatic Medicine; he was a member of the American Medical Association, the Arkansas Medical Society, the Pulaski County Medical Society, the Arkansas and Memphis Dermatological Societies, the Society for Investigative Dermatology, the South Central Dermatological Congress, and the Arkansas Caduceus Club.

Ray was a volunteer with the Boy Scouts of America for more than thirty years. He worked directly with young people as a unit leader, with adult volunteers in district and local council positions, and on the regional and national levels. At each of these levels he earned all of Scouting's highest honors.

Ray was the only Arkansas recipient of the Leadership Award given by the U.S. Department of Veterans Affairs for Voluntary Service. Ray was program chairman of the National Museum of American Jewish

Military History in Washington DC and a founder and past post commander of the Arkansas Jewish War Veterans Post 436.

In 1990, Ray received the Father Joseph H. Biltz Award from the Arkansas Council of National Conference for Community and Justice. His résumé of local, national, and international volunteer work includes participation in programs that provide free health and dental care for the uninsured, Red Cross work in Israel and serving on its National Council, volunteer medical research, training managers in the non-profit sector through the American Humanics program at UALR, and tutoring Russian immigrant families. He furthered international brotherhood as a member of American Physicians Fellowship for Medicine in Israel by bringing to Arkansas representatives of Israeli Scouting.

He was a member of Congregation B'nai Israel, where he served on the board. Ray was also a member of the Jewish Federation of Arkansas.

Sister Margaret Vincent Blandford

Humanitarian Award, 1985

(October 27, 1920–December 8, 1996)

Nun who rose to lead medical center dies

By Larry Ault, December 9, 1996

Reprinted with permission from the Arkansas Democrat-Gazette

Sister Margaret Vincent Blandford, a driving force for four decades in the rise of Little Rock's St. Vincent Infirmary Medical Center, died December 8, 1996.

Sister Margaret Vincent rose from nursing supervisor at St. Vincent Infirmary in 1954 to chief executive officer and board chairman of the medical center. She retired in 1988 and moved to Lexington, Kentucky, where she died of natural causes at seventy-six.

"All of us at St. Vincent Infirmary Medical Center are deeply saddened by Sister Margaret Vincent's death," said Diana T. Hueter, St. Vincent's president and chief executive officer. "Under her leadership, St. Vincent became recognized as one of Arkansas's premier medical centers," Hueter said.

"Sister Margaret brought a unique perspective to health care, because she was able to bring the spiritual aspect of health care to St. Vincent's," said William E. Clark, St. Vincent's board chairman. "She was always able to keep the board focused on this part of our mission. She was a terrific lady."

St. Vincent's has grown to a 717-bed hospital of about 3,000 employees that provide health care to patients statewide.

At her death, Sister Margaret Vincent was serving on the boards of four Sisters of Charity of Nazareth hospitals, and the St. Vincent

Development Foundation Board. "I now have more time for relaxation, reading, travel, and especially daily prayer," she said in a recent interview. "I am active in my religious congregation in future planning and other functions."

Sister Margaret Vincent was transferred to St. Vincent's on December 8, 1954, by the Sisters of Charity of Nazareth, Kentucky. She began as nursing director and a year later was appointed as the hospital's administrator. "The first few years were difficult," Sister Margaret Vincent recalled in a 1987 interview with the *Arkansas Democrat*. "We were unable to make the payroll the first year and a half. During six years, I learned a lot and the hospital grew. We were able to start new construction."

In 1961, Sister Margaret Vincent left the hospital after she was elected by the general congregation of Sisters of Charity to coordinate ten hospitals run by the order.

In 1971, she returned as a full-time board member. From 1972 until 1986, her title was president and chief executive officer of St. Vincent's. From 1986 through 1987, she was chief executive officer and chairman of the board of directors. She retired from her duties at the medical center on January 1, 1988.

During Sister Margaret Vincent's tenure, the hospital had considerable growth in its medical technology, staff, and the number of hospital beds it maintains.

The decade of the '70s was a time of phenomenal growth for St. Vincent's. Sister Margaret Vincent, as president and chief executive officer, and A. Jack Reynolds, administrator, worked together in attracting new physicians, adding new services, and enlarging the plant, hospital officials said Sunday. Improvements were made in the radiology, pathology, surgery, emergency department, intensive care, and coronary areas.

In the 1980s, Sister Margaret Vincent oversaw the expansion of outpatient services through which more than 113,981 patients were treated in the past fiscal year. A new oncology wing was opened to accommodate the growing number of cancer patients.

In a farewell interview, the Tennessee native said she was "peaceful" with the decision to leave St. Vincent's. "I was able to prepare for it with the last two years," she said. She said she felt "sad in leaving so many friends who have strengthened and supported me while I have served her."

She was born October 27, 1920, to John and Lydia Blandford in rural Tennessee near Lebanon. Sister Margaret Vincent said the quiet confidence attributed to her derived from her home in Tennessee, where her parents were "very kind, strong in their religious beliefs." "They not only talked about it, they lived it out. They also gave us a belief that we were put here on earth to do good to others, and the type of work we went into was important," she said. "I had a mother and father who in-stilled in me a healthy respect for myself," she said.

Sister Margaret Vincent went to Catholic schools and graduated from high school in 1938. She became a registered nurse in 1941. She entered Sisters of Charity of Nazareth convent at Nazareth in 1942 and took her vows in 1946. She received her hospital administration certifi-cates from Cornell University in 1962 and St. Louis University in 1964.

"I always felt that I may have a calling to the religious life, but I wanted to be sure," she said. "I got some spiritual guidance from a priest. I had difficulty with it, because naturally, there was a part of me that wanted something else. Marriage was a beautiful thing. I loved chil-dren. I liked nice clothes. But I had an interior felling that I was being called," she said.

In 1942, she entered a period of self-study to determine whether she wanted to be a nun and whether the order found her to be fit. She entered the Mother House at Nazareth. "We were separated from any relationship to the world," she said. "It was a period of great withdrawal for me, after being so active as a nurse. I found the confinement of being in one place very difficult. At that time, you weren't always treated as an adult able to make decisions for yourself."

There were rigid rules. No visits from or to parents. Silence at meals. Strict rules of visitation to others. "When you went out for any reason, there always had to be two of you." For the first six months, she was a "postulant," wearing a type of dress that "set you aside, and it was a period of preparation to receive the habit."

In 1946, Sister Margaret Vincent and others took the three-fold "perpetual" vows of the Sisters of Charity of Nazareth—poverty, chastity, and obedience. "It isn't all rosy and easy, always to be poor, never to be married and have children, and always to obey the Mother General of the order," she said.

But Sister Margaret Vincent lived to earn the equivalent of the salary of any chief executive officer of a major Little Rock corporation. The check, however, was made out to the Sisters of Charity of Nazareth and went to the Mother House. She received the same stipend as any nun in the order.

Sister Margaret Vincent also remained active in the community. She was honored by the NCCJ; named Greater Little Rock Woman of the year; named Citizen of the Year by the Arkansas Chapter, March of Dimes Foundation; received the A. Allen Weintraub Award, Arkansas Hospital Association; presented an Honorary Doctor of Humane Letters from the University of Arkansas at Little Rock; awarded the Arkansas Professional Women of Distinction Award, Worthen Bank and Trust Company and the William F. Rector Memorial Award, Fifty for the Future; and was a Paul Harris Fellow, Rotary Foundation of Rotary International.

She was a fellow of the American College of Healthcare Executives; past member of the board of directors and past chairman of the American Health Congress; past member of the Arkansas Hospital Association; past president of the Metropolitan Hospital District; past member of U.S. Catholic Health Conference; past American Hospital Association delegate and American Hospital Association Regional Advisory Board member; and West Little Rock Rotary Club.

She also served on the boards of the former Worthen Bank and Trust Co., Little Rock; United Way of Pulaski County; Arkansas State Chamber of Commerce; Central Arkansas Radiation Therapy Institute

(CARTI); the Arkansas chapter of the NCCJ; Central Arkansas Health Systems Agency; Greater Little Rock Chamber of Commerce; executive advisory committee of Sisters of Charity of Nazareth Health Corp.; and Conway County Hospital in Morrilton.

William H. "Bill" Bowen

Humanitarian Award, 1992
(Interview conducted July 16, 2012)

We know William H. Bill Bowen as "The Boy from Altheimer" who has left his mark on Arkansas and far beyond. In 2005, President Bill Clinton described Bill Bowen this way: "Besides his time as my chief of staff, Bill was a U.S. Navy fighter pilot during World War II, a tax attorney, president of a major bank, chief executive officer of a health maintenance corporation, dean of the law school that now bears his name, and a fine family man."

Bill Bowen was the middle child of five brothers and one sister, Lois Rhene, who died just before her fourth birthday during the influenza pandemic in 1918. The population of Altheimer was 498, and there was only one paved road. The boys worked alongside their dad at their general store, on the farm, and at the cotton gin. During their free time, they roamed the bayous and even built a boat out of flooring from their front porch. (That first boat promptly sank, but their next attempt was more successful.) For such a tiny community, they had a first-class school due to the leadership of the superintendent, Ms. Ruth Pipkin Suits. After school they played six-man football and other sports.

Bill's parents always stressed the importance of education. After his high school graduation in 1941, he worked all summer at the Kroger grocery in Pine Bluff to save enough money to enter Henderson State Teachers College (now Henderson State University) that fall. He continued to work throughout his time at Henderson, doing jobs such as waiting tables and driving an ambulance. During his third semester, Pearl Harbor was bombed. Bill soon joined the U.S Navy to train as a fighter pilot.

The pilot training was challenging—and dangerous. Only twenty-five percent of his class remained by the end of the instrument training segment. And according to one of his fellow pilots, during training in Florida in 1944, one dive-bomber pilot died every day. Bill's biggest disappointment was that after two years of training, he missed actually flying combat during World War II, which officially ended on August 15, 1945, when Japan surrendered.

Upon his return to Arkansas, Bill attended the University of Arkansas on the GI Bill. There he met his wife, Connie, also a student at the university, who worked in the registrar's office. Bill completed law school in 1949, and they moved to Washington DC. Their first child, Cynthia Ruth, was born in 1951. Children Scott and Patty soon completed their family. In Washington, Bill worked for the government and gained an expertise in tax law. When they returned to Little Rock in 1954, Bill was well situated to build a tax law practice on behalf of clients. After twenty years in law, with several banks as his clients, Bill accepted the position of President of Commercial National Bank in 1971, thus beginning his successful career in banking. During the twenty years that Bill led the bank, Commercial National merged with First National to become First Commercial Bank, and through other acquisitions grew from the fourth-largest bank in Arkansas to the largest. First Commercial was ultimately bought by Regions Bank in 1998.

During the early 1960s, Little Rock was still feeling the aftershocks of the desegregation crisis in 1957. When Bill drove to work at the bank each day, he saw a moribund community, and he was determined to do something about that. Bill made working to improve the community a priority, and several of his accomplishments were significant.

Bill Bowen was involved, sometimes leading the effort, in persuading the House Ways and Means Committee, chaired by Representative Wilbur Mills, in making the Eighth Street Expressway (now Interstate 630) a part of the federal interstate highway system; in bringing Little Rock University (now UALR) into the University of Arkansas system; in getting the Arkansas Arts Center onto firm financial ground, which included hiring Townsend Wolfe, who served as AAC director from 1968 to 2002; in developing the Governor's Distinguished Scholars program, which provides college scholarships for Arkansas students who get their post-secondary education in Arkansas; in getting the Arkansas tax code rewritten to be more business friendly in 1987; in establishing the Aerospace Education Center; in proposing changes in the LRSD's desegregation plan to win court approval; in raising capital campaign funds for building improvements on the Philander Smith Campus; and in the merger of the Little Rock and North Little Rock water systems.

Supreme among Bill Bowen's accomplishments was his founding and leadership of the First Commercial Bank National Advisory Board in 1971. This august body of Arkansans, "made up primarily of native Arkansans who had become major successes outside the state, with a few acknowledged in-state business leaders," met yearly to discuss and make recommendations regarding the most pressing issues facing our state. It could be called Arkansas's Think Tank, and its work over twenty-seven years informed a number of policies and projects. It was disbanded when First Commercial was bought by Birmingham-based Regions Bank.

In the meantime, UALR chancellor Charles Hathaway appointed Bill Bowen to be dean of the Law School, where he served from 1995 to 1997. The law school was later named the William H. Bowen School of Law.

When Governor Bill Clinton decided to seek the presidency in 1991, knowing that he would be absent from the state a good bit of time for the campaign, he asked his longtime friend Bill Bowen to serve as his gubernatorial chief of staff. In the foreword to Bill's biography, *The Boy from Altheimer*, Clinton said, "Bill agreed to become my chief of staff, leaving Commercial National Bank and turning his life upside down so that I would always know the state government was in good hands in my absence. He took an hour to think it over before accepting. If you knew how decisive he usually is, you'd know that one hour is an unusually long time for Bill Bowen to make up his mind."

Bill recalls that during his junior year in high school, the Works Progress Administration built a new gymnasium at the Altheimer high school. Over the boys' locker room door was a banner that read:

> For when the One Great Scorer comes
> To write against your name,
> He marks—not that you won or lost—
> But how you played the game
> (Grantland Rice).

Bill Bowen surely took that advice to heart throughout his storied life.

Robert L. Brown Sr.

Humanitarian Award, 1994
(May 11, 1926–November 6, 2001)

Executive assisted many a TV career

By Parker Conrad, November 8, 2001

Reprinted with permission from the Arkansas Democrat-Gazette

By the time of his death on Tuesday at age seventy-five, Robert L. Brown Sr. had served as a mentor to many people in Arkansas's television industry.

"There are a lot of people who owe their careers to that man—in local broadcasting, but also nationally, and in sales," said Anne Jansen, anchorwoman for Little Rock station KTHV-TV, Channel 11.

Brown's wife, Linda, said he died of a heart attack. While his health had been declining—he had two heart bypass operations in recent years—it had nothing to do with his lifestyle, his wife said. Brown is also survived by five children, four grandchildren, and two great-grandchildren.

Brown, who ran both KTHV and KARK-TV, Channel 4, during his career as a local television executive, started out as an elevator operator at a radio station in Denver. He was always eager to give other people their big break.

As the general manager of KARK, Brown hired Ann Sawyer, the first black person and the first woman to report or anchor for an Arkansas news show. Sawyer was working as a singer in Al Porter's Jazz Trio when Brown, impressed by her stage presence, invited her to the station for an interview.

"He was the one who taught me the TV business," says Bud Northern, an advertising salesman for KARK. "He taught me how to meet people—I was a very green salesman—and he opened a lot of doors for me to meet people he knew that eventually became clients of mine."

Brown even met with newscasters at competing television stations to help them with their job searches.

"The day I left Channel 7 he called me and said let's get together," says B. J. Sams, currently an anchorman for KTHV. Brown helped him film an audition tape at Channel 4's studios and sent the tape to a friend of his in Denver, who hired Sams as an anchorman in Hawaii.

As a boss, Brown was easygoing and approachable.

"He listened to his employees," says Joe Quinn, who used to work as an anchorman under Brown and is now spokesman for the state Department of Human Services. "You could always sit down and talk to him about what was going on in the news. It was very different than the corporate button-down approach today."

As a businessman, Brown was superb.

At KBTV in Denver, he built out the nascent television advertising market, bringing companies on board a new broadcast medium with an unproven track record.

"People thought [television] wasn't going to last, that it was just a fad," said his wife of twenty-seven years, the former Linda Pitts. "But Bob had such charisma; he could just talk to anybody."

But friends and colleagues say Brown was most impressive in service to the public.

Brown was renowned for using a television station's resources to help the surrounding community, giving local charities free airtime for their telethons while most TV stations around the country would charge.

"He was always extremely generous with the airtime of the station he managed for local charities," said Tom Bonner, who worked with Brown as an anchorman at KARK and now works as a senior vice president at Arkansas Children's Hospital. "He lived by the philosophy that the TV station that is a strong, nurturing presence in the community is going to win in the long run."

Dr. Thomas A. Bruce
Humanitarian Award, 2007

Look up "modesty" in the dictionary and it will likely say: "see: Tom Bruce." For a man who has had several distinguished careers, modest is still the best descriptor. Tom grew up in Mountain Home, Arkansas, during the Depression, when all 500 residents were still poor. His father, who came from a long line of blacksmiths, joined the U.S. Corps of Engineers to help build the Norfork Dam in the early '40s and went on assist with most of the big dams along the White River in Northern Arkansas.

Tom said that his childhood teachers always expected the best from him because his mother taught school. He excelled in school and dreamed of becoming a concert pianist. He smiles when he tells about how he auditioned for a college scholarship by playing a selection of "showy, masculine, and dramatic" piano pieces. He was dissuaded from that path by one of the judges, who questioned whether he had *really* thought about being a professional musician. She went on to suggest that plumbing or carpentry or almost any other job might be a more remunerative career.

Tom instead chose to enroll in pre-med, thinking that he would be a small-town physician; he ended up in cardiology. His training began at Fayetteville, but he also studied in Little Rock; Durham, North Carolina; New York City; Dallas; and London. He also completed the Health Systems Executive Program at Harvard Business School. As a doctor in Detroit and then Oklahoma City, Tom not only cared for patients, but was also an assistant dean, teacher, and researcher. He developed experimental medical curricula and helped plan for a new outpatient teaching facility.

In what might be considered his second career, Tom became dean of the University of Arkansas for Medical Sciences, a post he held from 1974 to 1985. He then was recruited by the W. K. Kellogg Foundation to begin a third career in Michigan, where for twelve years his focus was improving rural health systems. At Kellogg, he helped create new grantmaking initiatives and directed projects in health, leadership, and rural development.

Tom and his wife, Dolores, returned to Little Rock in the late '90s, primarily to look after his elderly parents. Soon after his return, he was recruited by then-chancellor Harry Ward to chair the search committee for a dean for the brand new UAMS College of Public Health. Part way into that process, Ward looked at Tom and said, "Will you be the first dean and help us establish this school?" Tom agreed, and says about his two years in that position, "It was fun! Everyone wanted to be a part of this exciting initiative." When Dean James M. Raczynski was hired in 2001, he asked Tom Bruce to remain as a senior advisor. Tom was next recruited by UA System chancellor Alan Sugg to help establish the Clinton School of Public Service. In 2007, Tom retired from his role at the Clinton School as associate dean for academic affairs.

And all along the way, Tom has given countless hours of volunteer service ... some as a leader, a strategist, a recruiter of volunteers, and fund-raiser, and some as a gardener. Tom learned to garden in Michigan at the Battle Creek Botanical Garden, and he has been a principal in the development of the gardens at Wildwood Park, which opened the weekend he moved back to Little Rock. Other non-profit groups that have benefitted from Tom's commitment include Arkansas Community Foundation, Garvan Woodland Gardens, Watershed Community Development Agency, and Heifer Project International. He has received numerous awards and recognitions for his contributions both professionally and personally.

Tom's life experiences have taught him that we must serve others in a way that helps them to build their own capacity. Simple charity is not the answer. Through Tom Bruce's example, we are all learning how to truly help others.

Tom and Dolores have two children and four grandchildren.

Betty Bumpers

Humanitarian Award, 1974
(Interview conducted August 17, 2012)

Once when Betty Bumpers had traveled to Moscow for a Peace Links event, she heard a knock on her hotel room door in the middle of the night. A little frightened, even though she knew there were guards in the hall, she opened the door to find a young woman with her child standing there. Betty had met the young woman at an earlier event, but this time, the mother and child had traveled 300 miles to meet with Betty again. Betty says, "Shortly, we all crawled into bed to get some sleep, because she had been traveling for three days." Surely this was an example of how right Betty had been in her belief that real conversations and relationships with women from around the world, based upon a shared concern for the well-being of children and families, would help promote peace. Betty has been right about a number of things, and she has seldom been hesitant to speak up. She quite often says that she "shamelessly" used her position as first lady of Arkansas and as a senator's wife to work on causes she felt were important.

Betty Flanagan was born in 1925, to Herman (Babe) Flanagan and Ola Callan Flanagan. The Babe Flanagan family, just like everyone else, had a difficult time during the depression, but Babe was resourceful, "a genius at trading anything for something else and coming out a little ahead," according to Dale Bumpers in his autobiography, *The Best Lawyer in a One-Lawyer Town.* When Babe began selling butchered meats in Fort Smith, Arkansas, Ola insisted that the family move there. Next, Babe figured out how to transport Jersey cows from Arkansas to Iowa, where the cows were in demand for their rich milk. He enlisted his daughters Maggie and Betty to help. Only in their mid-teens, the girls would travel between Arkansas and Iowa with the cows, work the auction ring, and sometimes even sleep in the sale barns to make sure the cows were cared for and ready for the next day's sale.

By the time the Flanagan family moved back to Charleston, Betty was entering her senior year in high school. Dale Bumpers writes, "Betty was in blue jeans, cowboy shirt, boots, and hat the first time I saw her. She was with her brother, Callans, and they had obviously been working cattle .... No woman ever looked quite as authentic, I thought, or as glamorous as Betty did that morning .... I had the sinking feeling that her lifestyle in Fort Smith ... put her beyond my reach. Even so, I knew I was going to try." After several years of friendship, courtship, and passing each other on trains as college and World War II intervened, Betty and Dale Bumpers were married in September of 1949. After Dale finished law school in 1951, they returned to Charleston, Arkansas, where Dale began his law career and bought the hardware store that his father and a partner had once owned. Betty became a third-grade teacher, but when she became pregnant with their first child, she had to quit teaching because of school-district rules.

Betty and Dale had three children, Brent, Bill, and Brooke, and the Bumpers family appreciated all the good things about raising children in a small town. They had observed their own parents taking care of others, and they found the same kind of community. "Since we knew everyone in town," Betty explains, "we knew who you could depend on to head a project or fund drive." Betty says that even though they moved to the Governor's Mansion in 1971, she never let the children feel that their father was anybody special other than just being their dad. The biggest challenge came when Dale was elected to the U.S. Senate in 1974, and Brooke had to attend a new school in the middle of her seventh-grade year. Betty called that a difficult time, but explains that Brooke learned how to make new friends and ultimately did fine.

Because of her role as a mother, it is easy to understand Betty's immediate positive response when the Centers for Disease Control (CDC) asked her, as first lady, to help educate Arkansans about vaccines. Along with her friend Nell Balkman, who was head of the Arkansas League of Nursing, they enlisted Public Health, the Cooperative Extension Service, and the National Guard to immunize "Every Child in 1974" against preventable childhood diseases. Using existing agencies, they immunized more than 350,000 Arkansas children on one Saturday. They were so successful that the CDC used their program as a national model, and Betty traveled to other states to assist them in developing similar immunization programs. After moving to Washington, Betty teamed up with First Lady Rosalynn Carter to change the law in every state to provide that every child must be immunized in order to enter school. Later realizing that some parents were waiting to get their children immunized until they were ready to enter school, the Bumpers-Carter team started a national program, "Every Child by 2," traveling to every state to build coalitions. Betty proudly notes that the immunization rate for children from birth to two years old is now ninety percent.

A conversation with her daughter, Brooke, got Betty thinking about what she could do to promote world peace. Brooke had asked her one day what their family plan was in case there was a nuclear war. Betty asked other friends and learned that their children were also frightened by the same question. Betty rallied nearly 200 congressional and gubernatorial women and started Peace Links in 1981. In no time, Peace Links had 30,000 participants, from forty states, Europe, and the USSR, who also cared about the future of our human family. The premise was that ordinary American women could develop lasting relationships with women in the Soviet Union, and thereby help solve our global conflicts without a nuclear war. Peace Links held discussions on peace-related issues, organized rallies in cities across the United States, published educational materials for teaching peace, and established cultural exchanges for Soviet women to visit the United States and for American women to visit the USSR. Dale Bumpers recounts that on one trip when he accompanied Betty to Moscow, where she was to be honored for her work,

"She was greeted by a packed auditorium as if she were a rock star. It was amazing how many people knew and loved Betty." In an online publication, "Legendary Women of Causes," Betty Bumpers's entry is titled, "First Lady of Peace."

In recognition of Betty's leadership, in 1999, the National Institutes for Health, with Congressional approval, named the new vaccine research center "The Dale and Betty Bumpers Vaccine Research Center." It is a joint venture of the National Cancer Institute and the National Institute of Allergy and Infectious Diseases and addresses immunology, virology, and HIV research.

Arkansans are justly proud to claim Betty Bumpers. Not many governors' or senators' wives have used their unique position so "shamelessly"—or successfully—to make such a profound difference for human beings worldwide.

Honorable Dale Bumpers

Humanitarian Award, 1974
(Interview conducted August 17, 2012)

Dale Bumpers is quick to explain that his going into politics was motivated by a combination of ego, naiveté, plain foolishness, and his father's confidence that his children could be anything they wanted to be. Therefore, the senator's only regret is that his father died before seeing his younger son serve as governor of Arkansas and in the U.S. Senate.

Dale was twelve years old when his father took him and his older brother, Carroll, to Booneville, Arkansas, to see President Franklin Delano Roosevelt. The president was making a whistle stop train trip across the country, stopping in Arkansas to endorse Senator Hattie Caraway, the first woman ever elected to the U.S. Senate. In his book, *The Best Lawyer in a One-Lawyer Town,* Bumpers relates, "Dad was determined that his sons would actually gaze not just upon a president, which would have been awesome enough, but upon Franklin Roosevelt, into whose arms we would fly when we died—or so we had been taught." On the way home, Dale's dad, William Rufus (W. R.) Bumpers, explained to his boys that FDR had to be helped to walk and stand as a result of contracting polio at thirty-nine years old. W. R. then said, "Now, you boys should let that be a lesson to you. If a man who can't even walk and carries twelve pounds of steel on his legs can be president, you boys have good minds and good bodies, and there isn't any reason you can't be president."

The Bumpers family lived in Charleston, Arkansas. Born in 1925, Dale was the youngest child of William Rufus and Lattie Jones Bumpers. Just four years later came the Great Depression, and times were hard on everyone. Dale's dad and a partner owned a funeral home, and one of Dale's jobs as a youngster was to "...fan the flies off the open casket and, after the funeral, return the family to their miserable existence." Although Dales's family was poor, just like everyone else during those years, he realized that some families had even less, and hardly any chance to improve their lot.

As a senator, Dale was recognized for his oratorical skill. He credits his English and American literature teacher, Miss Doll Means. As a matter of course, Miss Doll called upon students to read aloud in class. After reading several paragraphs of Beowulf in class one day, Dale looked up at Miss Doll, wondering why she had allowed him to read longer than the other students. She said, "Doesn't he read well? And doesn't he have a beautiful voice? And wouldn't it be a tragedy if he didn't take advantage of those talents?" Dale later said, "She did more for my self-esteem in a few seconds than anyone before or since."

Dale interrupted his undergraduate college years to serve in World War II, then returned to graduate from the University of Arkansas at Fayetteville in 1948. During his first year in law school, in 1949, he lost both of his parents in a car accident caused by a drunk driver. In September of that same year, he married Betty Lou Flanagan. After he graduated in 1951 from law school at Northwestern University in Evanston, Illinois, he and Betty returned to Charleston to make their home. There they raised their three children, Bill, Brent, and Brooke, and Dale worked as a lawyer in addition to running his father's hardware store and operating a 350-acre Angus cattle ranch. As an attorney, he lost only three jury cases.

As a community leader, Dale was asked his advice about how the Charleston schools should respond to the 1954 Supreme Court decision that had found school segregation based on race to be unconstitutional. Dale advised the school board to comply with the decision, and, consequently, in the fall of 1954, the Charleston School District was the first in all the eleven states of the old Confederacy to integrate their schools.

Dale's first political race in 1962, which was for the Arkansas House seat once held by his father, ended in defeat. However, in 1970, Dale ran for governor, beginning with one percent statewide name recognition, and defeated seven other Democratic candidates, including former governor Orval Faubus. He then beat incumbent Republican governor Winthrop Rockefeller, who was seeking a third term. By his own admission, Dale never really enjoyed serving as governor, saying, "I spent an inordinate amount of time trying to prevent bad things from happening, more time than I spent trying to make good things happen." But a lot of good things did happen during his two two-year terms, among them a reorganization of state government, reducing the number of agencies reporting to the governor, and an increase in income taxes to provide better pay for teachers. He expanded the state park system, created a consumer protection division in the attorney general's office, made improvements in social services, created a state-supported kindergarten program, and provided free textbooks for high school students. He also led a major construction program at the state's public colleges.

It was not an easy decision to run against U.S. Senator J. William Fulbright in 1974. Dale had been a supporter of Fulbright and considered him a great senator and a friend. The polls said that Fulbright was vulnerable, and Dale wrote in his autobiography, "I didn't want to oppose him; on the other hand, I would never forgive myself if he was defeated by someone whose views were anathema to me." When Dale defeated Fulbright, becoming a U.S. Senator from Arkansas, he obviously found his true calling and proved his father's wisdom and faith in him.

As a senator from 1975 to 1998, Bumpers was widely respected, and not just by Arkansans. He supported environmental legislation and the National Park System. He supported efforts to reduce the national debt and was often critical of increased military spending. He was not afraid to vote his conscience, alienating some constituents with his support of the Panama Canal treaties, which returned control of the canal to Panamanians, and his vote that reportedly killed a labor law reform bill in 1978. Troubled by President Ronald Reagan's militaristic stance toward the Soviet Union, Dale supported his wife's work for the organization Peace Links, even though at the time he thought it might cause him to lose his office. And perhaps most notably, Bumpers voted against every constitutional amendment that was introduced during his tenure, including one that would have allowed prayer in public schools.

Dale Bumpers is well known for his sense of humor, and he often used it to his advantage, particularly with political opponents. For example, when someone questioned Betty's Peace Links work during a re-election campaign, he quipped, "Anyone who loves nuclear war and whooping cough should definitely vote against me." That ended that conversation.

Dale Bumpers's last speech to the Senate came shortly after his retirement when he was asked by President Bill Clinton to make the closing defense argument in Clinton's impeachment trial. That speech was widely hailed as making the difference in the Senate voting to acquit Clinton of the impeachment charges. Miss Doll, his high school teacher, was prescient in her estimation of Dale Bumpers's speaking skills.

Arkansans recognize Dale Bumpers as one of the greatest statesmen of our times. But he probably describes himself as a politician. He says, "Dad never wavered in the honest conviction that there was nothing as exhilarating as a political victory and nothing as rewarding or as honorable as being a dedicated, honest politician who actually made things better and more just." Dale Bumpers's life has shown that his father, W. R. Bumpers, was prescient, too.

Bob Cabe
Humanitarian Award, 2005

It would be difficult to find a more modest or more competent man than Bob Cabe. Everyone who has ever worked with Bob says the same thing. Other adjectives abound, too: discreet, wise, sensitive, caring, committed, influential, respected, quiet, intellectual ... oh, and did we mention, nice?

After growing up in Benton, Arkansas, Bob graduated with a BA in business and economics from Hendrix College in just three years. He then earned his law degree from Duke University School of Law and returned to Little Rock to join the Wright, Lindsey & Jennings Firm, later becoming a partner in that firm and serving as chair of its labor law department. During the '80s he continued to practice law with other partners and was then hired as vice president and general counsel of Arkansas Blue Cross and Blue Shield in 1988. Bob retired as executive vice president, of legal, governmental relations and communication services from Blue Cross. His co-workers consistently praise his quiet leadership there.

Bob's extraordinary career would have been enough, but fortunately for our community and state, Bob also chose to be involved as a volunteer. At the very young age of twenty-nine, Bob was named to the board of trustees at Hendrix College. He served there from 1971 to 1986, and was the board's chair for six of those years. Because of his leadership ability he was also tapped to chair the search committee that named Dr. Joe Hatcher as Hendrix President.

Because of his interest in education and the needs of children and youth, Bob has also served on the Arkansas State Board of Higher Education (1988 to 1994) and the Technical Education Enhancement Study Committee (1989), and he chaired the Quality Higher Education

Study Committee (1983 to 1984) and the search committee for the LRSD superintendent in 1981.

Most residents of Central Arkansas know Bob best for his faithful leadership as a board member of the Arkansas Repertory Theatre, Arkansas Symphony Orchestra Society Foundation, Arkansas Symphony Orchestra, Arkansas Museum of Science and History, (now the Museum of Discovery), and the Winthrop Rockefeller Foundation. In every organization, Bob is recognized as being the leader who understands the critical difference in roles of board members and staff, for his thorough understanding of board governance issues, and his ability to lead a non-profit organization through change and growth. Bob is also treasured because he is not only able but willing to raise money for non-profit causes.

The Arkansas Region of NCCJ has been fortunate to have Bob as a board member since 2002. He has chaired our strategic planning initiative and continues to serve as chair of the board governance and development committee. It's a cliché, but when Bob Cabe speaks, we all listen.

Bob is a member of the Quapaw Quarter United Methodist Church, where he also serves on the finance team. He is married to Julie, and he has two children. Matthew is an architect who lives in Fayetteville. Meredith is an attorney married to Peter Hutchins, and she has retired to be a full-time mother to Bob's granddaughter, Eva Elizabeth.

Elijah E. Coleman
Father Joseph Biltz Award, 1999
(September 3, 1924–February 25, 2000)

Elijah Coleman was an educator who worked throughout his life to build understanding and to lift up his students "for the better things the South will offer," as he wrote in an essay contest sponsored by Lion Oil Company. With that essay, Elijah earned a scholarship for advanced study, having already earned a bachelor's and a master's degree.

Elijah was born in Chidester, Arkansas, the son of Lloyd and Mable Carter Coleman. He earned a BA degree in drama from Philander Smith College in 1949 and an MEd from the University of Arkansas at Fayetteville in 1954. He began his professional career as principal of Immanuel High School, in Almyra, Arkansas, serving from 1949 to 1954. Following that he served as principal of the new Townsend Park High School in Almyra.

In 1966, he became the director of the Arkansas Council on Human Relations, which was organized in December 1954, and incorporated and staffed in 1955, as a voluntary non-profit, non-political organization. It was associated with the Southern Regional Council. The purpose of the ACHR was to seek improved human relations by working to secure equal opportunity for all people. According to University of Arkansas at Little Rock professor John A. Kirk, the council "effectively used the white community's embarrassment over the national spotlight on Little Rock to begin, in the early 1960s, focusing on integrating businesses and public facilities while devoting attention to bolstering black activism." The council merged with the Little Rock chapter of the Urban League in 1974.

One year before the merger, in 1973, Elijah became director of the Arkansas Voter Registration program; in 1975, he returned to public secondary education, serving as principal and later as superintendent of the Tucker Plum Bayou School District until his retirement in 1984.

Elijah was a life member of the NAACP and Omega Psi Phi fraternity; he served as president of the Arkansas Teachers' Retirement Association and of the Arkansas Black Republican Party. He was a board member of the NCCJ, and a member of the Advisory Committee of the U.S. Commission on Civil Rights.

In addition to the Father Joseph H. Biltz Award from NCCJ, he received the Philander Smith Alumna of the year award in 1988 and the Arkansas Teachers' Award in 1986. Elijah was also included in a compilation of biographies and photos by D. J. Albritton, PhD, retired professor from the University of Arkansas at Pine Bluff, titled, "The Black Men of Pine Bluff, Of High Quality Character, Outstanding Community Leadership and a Positive Outlook On Life," which was given to the Arkansas History Commission in 1983.

At his death in 2000, Elijah was survived by his wife, Dr. Viralene Johnson Coleman, children Ronald Andrew Coleman and Sandra Rayfus Henry, and two grandchildren, Jamillah and Ronald Andrew Coleman, Jr.

Reverend Stephen Copley
Father Joseph H. Biltz Award, 2006

Ask Stephen Copley where he got his commitment to helping those less fortunate or where he learned his values, and he is quick to say, "My mom." It was just the two of them, and Mary Copley was clearly the most important influence in his life.

Steve was born in Lawton, Oklahoma, and they moved to Gentry, Arkansas, when he was barely five years old. He graduated from high school in Gentry in a class of forty-eight, where he excelled at sports including football, basketball, baseball, and track. During his senior year, he was third in the state discus, for example. But even in high school Steve was interested in politics, too, and he remembers getting very excited when Jimmy Carter was elected president in 1976.

Steve went to college at the University of Central Arkansas (UCA) with several possibilities in mind: he could be a coach, he might attend law school, and he began to explore the call he felt for the ministry. With an undergraduate degree in history and a minor in philosophy, he attended Emory in Atlanta in a joint theology and law program. Steve married Judi in 1984, and he began his career as a Methodist minister as a circuit preacher in Georgia.

A pivotal point for Steve occurred when a guest speaker at Emory, William Gowland, talked about Luton Industrial College in England. As a result of hearing Gowland, Steve decided to go to serve a church at Manchester in Prestwich. While serving there, Steve learned more about industrial mission, which sought to understand how faith relates to economics, and there Steve found his ultimate calling. After a brief return to the states, Steve and Judi returned to England, where Steve served as assistant director of Luton Industrial

College serving England, Wales, and Northern Ireland. At one point, they tore a church down and built an eight-story building where they established lay and clergy-led seminars on how to make the church relevant to the ordinary folk who had become separated from the church. They began to look at the issues of wages, for example. After three years there, they returned to Horatio, Arkansas, and Steve has led churches in Arkansas since then.

However, Steve has never been just a minister. During all this time, Steve also served as a state officer of the Young Democrats in Georgia and finished a Master of Divinity degree from Southern Methodist University. He secured a grant from the Winthrop Rockefeller Foundation to set up a micro-economics program designed to move people out of poverty. And recently (in 2003), he earned a law degree from UALR. So in all practical ways he has pursued each of his dreams. He is the senior pastor for First Methodist Church in North Little Rock, has earned a law degree, and serves as a "coach" to several teams of people who have joined him in working on critical social issues in Arkansas.

Most recently, Steve chaired the alliance that campaigned for and won a $1.10 raise in the minimum wage for Arkansans. He characterizes that fight as not about "issues" but about people who are trying to support their families. And he describes feelings of joy when he realizes what a difference that will make for some Arkansas families.

The most frequent description of Steve's role in any group is president, chair, leader, or maybe coach. To name a few of those groups in which he serves:

- Arkansas Interfaith Alliance
- Coalition to Abolish the Death Penalty
- Hunger Task Force, of the Arkansas Hunger Coalition
- Justice for our Neighbors Program
- United Methodists National Immigration Law Program

If there is an identified human need, you best try to involve Steve Copley in helping meet that need.

And if you want to see Steve get animated, just ask him about what he's working on now, and what his dreams for the future are.

One important project is the Statewide Fuel Fund, which is part of the Arkansas Energy Network. Through this program the Network hopes to help low-income people in paying their energy bills by setting up a network of existing funds, finding what else is needed, and meeting those needs.

Another exciting project is called the Benefit Bank. Volunteers are trained to help low-income folks learn about available federal programs through online databases placed in accessible locations such as churches or food banks. The volunteers can quickly determine if a person is eligible and then help the client fill out the needed application forms.

In a way, you might call Steve Copley a liberal or a radical...especially if those descriptors indicate someone who thinks all Arkansans should have a living wage for their honest work, a chance to become a citizen if they follow the law, a warm and safe home, and enough food to feed their family. He's constantly working for all those things.

Gerald Cound
Father Joseph H. Biltz Award, 2010

Gerald Cound is a gardener. Often he is
digging in the dirt to raise plants, but even
more often, he is cultivating people and organizations. It takes a lot of attention and
patience to be a gardener, and the patience
he has learned in the garden he is using to
build community. As he builds rock walls,
one rock at a time, he transfers that practice
to the community to work with each organ-

ization, family, or individual in support of community.

Gerald was born into what he describes as a transplanted Texas
family looking for work. His dad was a railroad man but his parents were
divorced when he was very young. His mother remarried, and they settled on a farm in Gillham, Arkansas, where he spent nights catching
chickens while his mother worked on the line in a chicken plant to help
pay the bills. He lost his mother, who was ninety-three years old, in
January of 2010. Gerald credits her with a very important legacy. He
says, "She could see the beauty in small things. She didn't consider race
or class and could always see the good in others."

Gerald left home before he graduated from high school, lived on
his own, and ended up hitchhiking the Talimena Trail to attend Eastern
Oklahoma A&M Junior College. Although he was, at best, an average
student those first two years, he excelled as an athlete in baseball, basketball, and track and field. Running, which was to become his passion,
captivated him almost by accident. During the break in a double-header
baseball game in which he was playing shortstop, he wandered over to
watch the track and field events. The school needed a half-miler: he entered the race and won. He lost few races after that during his racing career, which lasted until he was thirty years old.

After his two years at A&M, he worked a short stint in a chicken plant, but decided that wasn't a good life plan, hitchhiked to Arkansas State Teacher's College (now UCA) in Conway, enrolled a week late, was a walk-on in basketball, and ended with a basketball scholarship. Again he gravitated to running, and he became a national champion half-miler. In the last week of his senior year, he ran in the National Amateur Athletic Union (AAU) track meet, graduated from college, married his sweetheart Bitsy Spinks, and went into the Peace Corps.

After PC training, Gerald and Bitsy were sent to Venezuela, where they worked with state and national athletic teams. Their next homes were on a Navajo Reservation in New Mexico as teachers and then in Oregon where Gerald taught social studies, coached, and competed in track and field for the Portland Track Club. He was lured back to Arkansas to head the Baptist Student Group at the University of Arkansas at Monticello in the late '60s. In this capacity he led a number of creative mission trips. On one in particular that he remembers, he and Bitsy took twenty-one college students and their two children (ages two and four) and worked hoeing sugar beets and picking beans with migrant families in Idaho and Oregon. He credits these experiences with raising his consciousness about justice. He saw firsthand the challenges lower socioeconomic groups and different races have trying to live reasonable, equitable, and quality lifestyles.

In 1969, he was hired as a track coach at Hendrix, and eventually became dean of student life. He left Hendrix in 1975 for a short stint of coaching at UCA, and then he bought into Camp Ozark. At that time, Camp Ozark was an all-male baseball camp, and for the next five years Gerald served as director and made major changes to bring girls into the camp. When he left education, he went to work at Systematics and Alltel for twenty years as director of corporate facilities. During this period of corporate life he continued to be busy in the community: activities included building an international learning trail at the Heifer Ranch, creating a landscape garden at Camp Aldersgate, and setting up a program for excess furniture to be given to non-profits throughout Central Arkansas. Among many other community involvements, he served on the original Habitat for Humanity board in Central Arkansas, served on the board of Our House Shelter for the Homeless, and taught Bible school in the prison.

During his time at Systematics and Alltel, he lost Bitsy and his youngest son Jerry, who, despite his heart disease, became the world champion in the 100 and 200 meters in the Transplant Olympic Games in Vancouver. This is one of Gerald's most important memories. The transplant national awards are now given in Jerry's name. Gerald's surviving children are a great source of pride for him: Mike is one of the top sports agents in the U.S. for women's basketball, and Chela is a cardiac nurse and mother of four in Florida. He has eight grandchildren, and is married to Sharon, who for the past fourteen years has been a wonderful mate and supporter of his garden and his community activities.

So once Gerald retired from the corporate world, and was no longer *racing* around, what did he spend his time doing? Just to name a few of his projects: He served on the Pulaski Heights United Methodist Church staff to set up recreation and youth programs; he was director of facility services and project building manager for the International Heifer Headquarters; he was project manager for the recent Camp Aldersgate improvements, including the swimming pool and a new medical center; and he served as the project coordinator for the Arkansas Foodbank headquarters and a new CASA Women's shelter in Pine Bluff.

The bottom line for Gerald is that he believes that all of us need to give a small part of our lives weekly and monthly to our communities, as we would to any garden. For that reason he, along with a number of friends, has put together a non-profit to support grassroots needs for our greater community. Village Commons, housed on South Main Street in Little Rock, raises awareness of community through education and programs on sustainable living. Village Commons works with all people—

especially those in underserved communities—to secure healthy and sustainable futures through training for individuals and organizations. Their programs include Sustainable Urban Gardening, Project Healthy Communites, justice initiatives, community clean-up and recycling activities, and Green Organization Mentoring.

He believes strongly that we need more soul involvement in our community endeavors, that by working together to provide quality "commons," we will have increased quality of soul for all of us, which in turn will support making the community a better place for all.

Yes, Gerald is gardening again, and he invites you to grab a hoe and join him in improving our commons and, consequently, our communities.

Dr. William Dale Cowling

Humanitarian Award, 1976
(January 27, 1924–April 9, 2006)
Obituary reprinted with permission from Roller Chenal Funeral Home

Our Merciful Father took Dr. Dale Cowling, of Little Rock, home April 9, 2006. Dr. Cowling was pastor of Little Rock's Second Baptist Church for twenty-five years, presiding over one of the city's influential downtown churches. He was one of a few leading clergymen who stood against the tide of unreason that swept Arkansas in the late 1950s in the celebrated Little Rock school crisis.

Cowling had come to the pastorate in Little Rock at the age of twenty-eight, after receiving degrees at Ouachita Baptist College and Southwestern Seminary and after working two years as head of students for the Arkansas Baptist Convention. In 1957, when Governor Orval E. Faubus put Arkansas in the spotlight in the confrontation at Central High School, Cowling had to choose between falling silent, as many preachers did, or taking a stand on the issue of racial segregation.

It was a time of terrible tension, for majority opinion was behind the governor. On the Thursday before Faubus called out the National Guard in defiance of court orders, Cowling went down to his little family farm at Mineral Springs and, in prayer, he was inspired to speak out. He returned to Little Rock to deliver a sermon declaring that segregation was wrong and the rule of law must prevail.

His congregation listened in stunned silence, for, Cowling estimated, ninety percent of his members were against what he said.

What surprised him was that no one spoke out against him in the sanctuary and whatever the deacons thought, there was no move to fire him. He was gratified that he kept his pulpit and was allowed to continue his advocacy of Christian principle.

Later, blacks came to Second Baptist's services and, in time, joined the church. Cowling had given explicit instructions to his ushers to welcome everyone. Today, Second Baptist has been integrated for decades even though as late as the 1960s the president of the Southern Baptist Convention was calling for segregation in the churches.

After Faubus called out the National Guard and President Eisenhower federalized the Guard to support the federal courts, Little Rock schools were closed for a year. Second Baptist Church opened its own school in its educational building to help fill the void left by Faubus's action. The public schools reopened after segregationist board members were defeated in the next election.

Dr. Cowling was later awarded the Second Baptist Church's Annual Brooks Hays Award, named after the congressman who was defeated for re-election after he tried to mediate the school crisis. He also was an honoree of The National Conference of Christian and Jews, based on his race-relations endeavors.

In later years of his tenure at Second Baptist, he resisted suggestions that Second Baptist join other downtown churches in moving to the suburbs. He did not propose to move to fashionable neighborhoods but felt that the church should stay in the heart of the city. He prevailed.

In Dr. Cowling's time at Second Baptist, the church accomplished three major enterprises in community service.

The Albert Pike Hotel, a downtown landmark near the church, was acquired and turned into a residential hotel for the elderly. Cowling put out word of the church's interest in the hotel, and a retired school teacher, Marcia Tillman, walked into his office to present a check for $156,000 (anonymously at the time) to buy and refurbish the hotel and give it a new life and a new purpose.

Success with the Albert Pike caught the attention of a New Orleans dentist, Horace Buffington, who visited the hotel and church. He returned to New Orleans to rewrite his will and underwrite the construction of another residential hotel across the street for the Albert Pike. Buffington died a few days later. Buffington Towers was erected in fulfillment of the vision that he and Cowling shared.

Earlier, ten members of Second Baptist Church had put up $20,000 each to acquire Lake Nixon in western Little Rock and establish a summer camp and recreation center, which serves children and youth of the city.

Cowling was a dedicated and fiercely resolute believer in the church as an instrument of public service. After his retirement from Second Baptist, he spent years preaching and strengthening churches at Mineral Springs and nearby communities. He was particularly engaged in encouraging young preachers.

At Ouachita, he met and married Olive Blackwood of Rector. She preceded him in death in March 2005. They had three daughters, Rebecca; Sue-Carol, her husband, Mike, their son, Michael; Kriste Dale, her husband, Lonnie, and their daughter, Amanda. "Grand daddy" recently said that although he wouldn't be able to see Michael and Amanda grow all the way up, he had the feeling the good Lord would allow him to know what they would ultimately become in His plan.

Anna Cox
Father Joseph H. Biltz Award, 2012

Anna Cox has worked with Mother Teresa and studied with His Holiness the Dalai Lama, but it was probably her mother who set her life's path. When the little girl Anna was distressed by some injustice that she saw, her mom would often say, "When you grow up, you can do something to change people's lives!"

Anna grew up in Connecticut and moved to Fort Smith, Arkansas, before her senior year in high school. She says civic engagement was a constant in her home, and her mother, accompanied by other women, both black and white, often drove to Little Rock to work for equal rights.

During Anna's college years, the issues of the day were integration and women's rights. Anna describes herself then as young and impassioned but not very skilled. After the dormitory for black women students at University of Arkansas burned down for a second time, she naively decided to circulate a petition in her all-white dorm asking that the black girls be allowed to live there, too. She walked down the hall, petition in hand, only to find empty rooms. All the girls had gathered in one room where they not only refused to sign her petition but bombarded her with angry questions such as, "Would you want a Negro girl to use your hairbrush?" She remembers feeling very vulnerable and alone.

Anna married a kindred spirit activist, and together they moved to Little Rock because they couldn't find jobs in Fayetteville to pay for school. She earned her degree in sociology and psychology from UALR, had a baby, and continued her activist work. She worked on George McGovern's campaign, protested the war in Vietnam, and continued to support racial integration and women's rights. She remembers attending the public memorial service for Dr. Martin Luther King Jr. hosted by Governor Winthrop Rockefeller on the Capitol steps in Little Rock in 1968. Anna says, "I was deeply touched by Governor Rockefeller's courage and energized by the diverse crowd. It felt like we Arkansans were developing a template of how to think in grand and inclusive ways about our future."

Over the years, Anna worked in the Arkansas State Hospital and the Little Rock Public Schools. After earning her master's in clinical social work, she entered private practice. Following her own near-death experience in a medical procedure, Anna began to practice meditation. In 1979, Anna traveled to India where she served in Mother Teresa's Kali Ghat home for the dying in Calcutta. Through feeding, bathing, and cleaning the wounds of those who were dying, Anna learned of the profound connection that is possible when we accompany someone through the transition from life into death. From Mother Teresa she also learned that those who have little in the way of material goods are not necessarily suffering. Anna witnessed families living on the sidewalks with hardly any possessions who were rich beyond measure in the emotional and spiritual gifts of family and intimacy.

Returning from her first trip to India, she was invited by friends to join them in Madison, Wisconsin, to help prepare for a visit of His Holiness the fourteenth Dalai Lama. Between preparing meals and ironing robes for the monks, Anna was able to sit in the temple with the Dalai Lama as he prepared himself for the services, and Anna knew then she had found her spiritual home. Upon her return to Little Rock, she began to practice as a Vajrayana Buddhist. Along with others, Anna founded the Ecumenical Buddhist Society, which has provided a place for meditation, retreats, classes, and social events since the early 1990s.

Anna was drawn to begin her non-profit, Compassion Works for All, in the 1990s, after she met and got to know Frankie Parker, a death-row inmate and fellow Buddhist, who contacted Anna to help him prepare for his impending death. While visiting Frankie, Anna met other death-row inmates, and helped them through their grief following Frankie's execution. After Frankie's execution received national news coverage, Anna began to hear from prisoners from across the country. Anna gained accreditation as a certified religious advisor so that she could visit with more than one prisoner at a time. She's inordinately proud of those in prisons who have developed insight and compassion for themselves, and who in turn have reached out to support others as mentors and guides—especially to the youngest among them. What began as prison visits to a few has grown into offering a self-help newsletter for over 4,000 across the country in jail or prison with a prison home-study curriculum on finding hope and meaning in one's life, and even learning to read. Anna refers to her inspirational and self-help videos as "piddly," but they now number 150 and are available on the Internet and have been viewed by countless people. She regularly receives thanks from soldiers in war zones or parents far from Little Rock, Arkansas.

Anna and a small band of dedicated board members and volunteers, including her husband of twenty-five years, Jim Rule, believe in the "drop and ripple" theory of change. Through Compassion Works for All, they are daily providing the drops of compassion. The ripples are evident, traveling farther and wider than any of us will ever know.

Fred K. Darragh Jr.

Humanitarian Award, 1979
(November 13, 1916–March 20, 2003)

State's ACLU founder Fred Darragh dies at 86

By Reid Forgrave, March 25, 2003

Reprinted with permission from the Arkansas Democrat-Gazette

Fred Darragh, a founding member of the Arkansas chapter of the American Civil Liberties Union, died Thursday, March 20, 2003, in Little Rock. He was eighty-six.

Darragh was one of the first to fly "The Hump," the treacherous trek over the Himalayas into India during World War II. It was in India that the travel bug bit him and where he heard the words of Mahatma Gandhi.

Friends remembered Darragh as the man who traveled to more than 150 countries as an "old impassioned liberal." "He had a great sense of adventure, and that kind of pulsated from him," said former U.S. senator David Pryor. "I've never met a more intriguing, more generous man."

Darragh's life adventure included founding the Arkansas chapter of the American Civil Liberties Union. He stood for free speech and diversity and hated conservatism.

"As he used to say, the journey is the destination," said Fred Poe of Little Rock, one of Darragh's best friends who traveled with him to places such as Vietnam and Antarctica.

In 1957, Darragh stood with Daisy Bates at the Central High School desegregation crisis, one of few white men who spoke out.

"He was absolutely fearless as far as speaking his mind," said Bobby Roberts, director of the Central Arkansas Library System.

Later in life, Darragh became a benefactor for libraries around Arkansas, having the Darragh Center for Intellectual Freedom named for him at the Main Library in Little Rock. He liked to say illiteracy was the most evil thing in society.

"He would say the written word would set people free," Poe said.

Darragh is survived by his sister, Louisa Preston of Richmond, Virginia, his brother, Ted Darragh and wife, Babs, of Little Rock; and seven nieces and nephews.

In addition to the featured obituary by Reid Forgrave, the family and Ruebel Funeral Home submitted the following information, which is reprinted with permission.

Fred K. Darragh, age 86, of Little Rock, died March 20, 2003

Retired chairman of the board of Darragh Company Agribusiness, Fred attended the University of Pennsylvania, and the Wharton School, class of 1938.

He was also on the board of directors of J.B. Hunt Transport Inc. and Skyway Commuter Airlines until its sale to Midwest Airlines.

He was an Episcopalian, having served on the Vestry of Christ Episcopal, St. Mark's Episcopal and St. Michael's where he was once senior warden.

He also was on the board of Camp Mitchell and the Standing Committee of The Episcopal Diocese of Arkansas, and was a member of World Mission Committee and deputy to the General Convention of the Episcopal Church, South Bend, Louisville, and Houston.

Of all of the many civic offices held, he was most proud of his military experience, which included being one of the pilots that flew "The Hump" during World War II.

A major in the Army Air Corps, he received the Distinguished Flying Cross, and in 1988 presented a pair of Pilot Wings from the

Chinese Air Force.

In 1962, he was honored as Pilot of The Year by the National Pilots Association, and in 1999 he was inducted into the Arkansas Aviation Hall of Fame.

Other honors bestowed Fred included the Humanitarian Award of the Arkansas Council of The National Conference of Christians and Jews, Arkansas Civil Libertarian of the Year by the ACLU, and the Fred Darragh Center of Intellectual Freedom at the Central Arkansas Library System, which is a meeting room at library named for Fred, with endowed yearly lectures.

Dr. Lawrence Arnette "Prexy" Davis Sr.

Humanitarian Award, 1970
(July 4, 1914–June 5, 2004)
Reprinted courtesy of the University Museum and Cultural Center, University of Arkansas at Pine Bluff

Lawrence Arnette Davis Sr. was born at McCrory, Arkansas, July 4, 1914, as the only child of the late Virgil and Pawnee Davis. He received nurturing and support from his late grandmother Mrs. Emma Janie Brown, with whom he lived most of his young life.

A man of notable athletic ability, he played baseball with adults in the Negro league at the age of twelve. When he was fourteen, he moved to Pine Bluff to complete his secondary education at Merrill High School, where he graduated as valedictorian. He earned a BA degree in English at AM&N College, a master's degree in English at the University of Kansas, and a doctorate in higher education administration at the University of Arkansas at Fayetteville. He continued study at various educational institutions across the country and abroad. He has several honorary degrees to his credit as well as appointments to presidential commissions under the administrations of Presidents Truman, Johnson, and Nixon.

After being appointed president of AM&N College in 1943 at the age of twenty-eight, he was the youngest college president in the country. During his tenure the college flourished in enrollment growth, physical plant expansion, and received its first North Central Association accreditation. His dreams for AM&N were realized with support from then-governor Sidney "Sid" McMath for whom he had much admiration and respect.

He served as president of AM&N for thirty years and as the first chancellor of the University of Arkansas at Pine Bluff (UAPB) for one year. His impact on students was so profound during his era that they affectionately referred to him as "Prexy," which became synonymous with his name to everyone. After his tenure at UAPB, he served as a president of Laney College at Oakland, California, for seven years. He enjoyed working with senior citizens as a consultant for the city of Oakland after his retirement at Laney College.

While all of his organizational affiliations and recognitions are too numerous to mention, some of them include Omega Psi Phi Fraternity, Inc., Sigma Pi Phi Boule, Prince Hall Masons, Order of the Elks, and the Twentieth Century Club. A recognition for which he is well noted is his honor as Arkansas Man of the Year in 1967. He has been awarded many plaques, citations, and honors for his educational, civic, community, and organizational leadership and service. As part of his civic responsibility, he worked to acquire needed funding to complete the Pine Bluff Civic Center, and assisted with the plans for construction of the Pine Bluff Convention Center. His additional contributions to the development of the city of Pine Bluff are numerous.

A prolific writer, orator, and avid reader, he kept a sharp mind until the end of his life. He continued to enjoy solving crossword puzzles, watching the Chicago Cubs baseball games, reading, discussing national and international events, and watching news shows on cable television. He remained the patriarch of the Davis family and spent the last three years of his life close to his children in Pine Bluff.

His legacy leaves five sons, Lawrence, Jr., Larnell, and Michael (Pine Bluff, Arkansas); Ronald (Grady, Arkansas); Lauren (Ann Arbor, Michagan) and four daughters, Janice Kearney (Pine Bluff, Arkansas) Gail Thigpen (Peoria, Illinois); Pawnee Davis (Oxon Hill, Maryland); Zalana Toomer (St. Augustine, Florida); four sisters Cleophus Johnson (Stuttgart, Arkansas); Helen Summerville (Little Rock, Arkansas); Gladys Williams and Lynette Bagsby (Los Angeles, California); eleven grandchildren; thirteen great-grandchildren. He is preceded in death by a daughter, Sharon, and a granddaughter, Catherine; brothers Virgil

Davis and Josiah Davis, and a sister, Reesie Humphrey. He also leaves a host of nieces, nephews, and many other relatives and friends that loved him dearly.

Beverly Divers-White
Father Joseph H. Biltz Award, 2010

As a girl, Beverly Divers-White dreamed of being a psychiatrist, analyzing the behavior of individuals. Instead she became a social and educational systems analyst, working to improve things for all of us.

Beverly was raised mostly in East Little Rock, and she never realized that her family was low-wealth because of the nurturing and completeness of her community. She still attends her childhood church, First Baptist in East Little Rock. Although her parents divorced when she was young, they both lavished love and attention on Beverly and held high expectations for her.

Beverly attended the then brand-new Carver Elementary School and graduated from Horace Mann. In the early '60s, she was one of seventy African-American students who filed a lawsuit to be able to attend Central High, but only five of those students were admitted to Central at that time. Therefore, Beverly's K–12 education was completed at segregated schools. Following her high school graduation, Beverly graduated from Little Rock University (now UALR) with a degree in English and history. At that time there were only three African-American students in her class, and only thirty African-American students on the entire campus. She subsequently earned her master's degree in counseling/psychology from State College of Arkansas (now UCA) and her EdD in educational administration from Fayetteville. She has also been privileged to study at Yale, Hebrew University, and Michigan State.

Because of her personal experiences and the experiences of her son, Samuel White Jr., Beverly knows firsthand the good and the bad of school desegregation. Beverly lost her husband when Samuel Jr. was nine years old, so she had the demands of a career to balance with raising a very bright youngster who started his first business when he was in elementary school. Following her son's experiences in the public school system, Beverly insisted that Samuel attend Tuskegee University, which, they both agree, changed his life. Samuel now lives in Cummings, Georgia, with his family and has developed several successful businesses. Beverly and her son own BSW Consulting and Technology and BSW Development, LLC. In addition, her son works as a network consulting engineer for Cisco in Lawrenceville, Georgia.

Just out of college, Beverly worked as a community organizer working with low-income preschool children and seniors in four neighborhood centers in Pulaski County. In 1969, she began her teaching career in a "cross-over" program as one of only thirteen African-American teachers at Central High School, and she credits Dr. Morris Holmes, who was her principal at Central, for supporting her move from the classroom into school administration. She also remembers fondly that many of her colleagues at Central, black and white, made a concentrated effort to work and play together as a model for the students, but also because they wanted to personally reach across the racial divide of the past. She quickly moved into the central office of the Little Rock School District where she worked through some of the most challenging years of desegregation efforts within the district. In 1989, she left Little Rock to become the superintendent of the Lee County School District in Marianna, Arkansas.

In Marianna, Beverly made a difference. Through her myriad statewide and national contacts, she was able to bring amazing resources to the small, rural, economically impoverished, Lower Mississippi Delta School District, often hosting people like Governor Bill Clinton, Rob Walton, national educational leaders, and international guests as they visited the district and community. Because of her core beliefs, she focused on parent and community involvement, and increased student achievement as statewide student academic requirements increased.

Her achievements in Marianna did not go unnoticed, and she was hired as senior program manager for education and workforce development at the Foundation for the Mid South. She worked in Arkansas, Mississippi, and Louisiana, and became a vice president for programs and institutional vice president of the Foundation before returning to Arkansas to open a private consulting business in 2007. A trip to Washington DC for a Children's Defense Fund Conference in 2007 led Beverly to take on another challenge: Arkansas's statewide response to "America's Cradle to Prison Pipeline." Too many of America's children (especially at the crossroads of race and poverty) head down the path to prison rather than to success.

Beverly led a team of volunteers that raised over $100,000 to gather 500 adults and 600 youth for a two-day conference last year. Diverse leaders from government, health, education, business, the non-profit and faith community, and the judicial system participated. A study has been completed to identify the issues that perpetuate the cradle-to-prison pipeline in Arkansas, and a coalition has been formed to address these problems. As these teams begin their work, Beverly has been persuaded to chair the process at least through 2011. One interesting way that Beverly and team members are continuing to learn is through visits with adult prisoners in Arkansas. She's asking them, "What did you need that we didn't provide?"

Through Beverly's leadership, Arkansas has done more than any other state to define the problems and prepare to address them. If she has her way, Arkansas will dismantle the cradle-to-prison pipeline. When you are with Beverly for any length of time, you realize she just might get her way because she has the persistence and dedication, not to mention the energy, to work for changing social and educational systems.

Since September of 2010, Beverly has served as the school improvement officer for the Clarksdale Municipal School District in Clarksdale, Mississippi. This contract allows her to work across the district, with a concentrated effort on W. A. Higgins Academy of Arts and International Studies (Grades 6–8) and Clarksdale High School (Grades 9–12). Higgins received a $3.75 million school improvement grant in

2010, and Clarksdale High received a $4.0 million school improvement grant in 2011. Every school in the district is a magnet school, and tremendous strides are being made in the academic achievement of the district's students.

In 2011, Higgins Academy opened a state-of-the-art performance arts center that includes courses in strings, keyboarding, dance, choir, and band. The school has its own dance studio and recording studio. The students are in demand all over the state of Mississippi.

Clarksdale High School is one of three high schools selected by the Mississippi Department of Education to pilot the Excellence for All educational model. The model uses a different, more rigorous curriculum and assessment process. Excellence for All gives students more than one path to graduation, and in some cases allows students to begin college level courses at two-year institutions so that they can get a head start on their level of education.

Beverly Divers-White is still making a difference!

Colonel Dutch Dorsch (Ret.)
Father Joseph H. Biltz Award, 2003

Colonel Dutch Dorsch spent almost thirty-two years in service to our country, and he retired in Arkansas. During the first week of his retirement, Father Joseph Biltz called Dutch to ask him if he would help with the Refugee Resettlement Program of the Diocese of Little Rock. Thinking he would work a few hours a week for a short time, Dutch said, "Okay." That short-term, part-time commitment turned into a full-time job of fifty to sixty hours a week for more than twenty years as Dutch directed the resettlement program.

In talking about his work, Dutch is hesitant to take any personal credit and mentions a long list of people and groups who worked with him to help settle more than 18,000 men, women, and children in Arkansas. Families came from more than eighty nations and every continent except Antarctica.

Here's what we learned about Dutch by visiting with others who work in the resettlement program:

Dutch treated every refugee with respect, no matter what their race or religion. He was on call seven days a week for anyone who needed him.

He met every plane...which sometimes meant waiting for hours at the airport.

He gave his home phone number to new arrivals.

He helped recruit sponsors who were responsible for finding the newcomers a place to live, food to eat, and such things as transportation for a job or for English classes.

Dutch's primary goal was to help the new residents become self-supporting, which meant finding them jobs right away—and he had a great track record there.

At the same time, Dutch took a personal interest in every individual or family that came here; he also worked on some system changes such as getting an Immigration and Naturalization Service testing station in Little Rock and later in Fayetteville, so that newcomers wouldn't have to travel to Memphis to begin their application for American citizenship.

It is for his compassion and his sense of personal investment in the lives of so many newcomers to our country and our state that we honor the work of Colonel Dutch Dorsch, a worthy recipient of The Father Joseph H. Biltz Award.

Mimi Dortch
Father Joseph Biltz Award, 1995
(*August 25, 1930–February 26, 2011*)

Driven by faith, zest for culture
By Andy Davis, March 1, 2011
Reprinted with permission from the Arkansas Democrat-Gazette

Whether it was helping start a professional theater company or a shelter for homeless women and children, Mimi Dortch had a knack for bringing people together to accomplish a goal.

But the Reverend Stephen Copley said he will also remember the way Dortch tried to brighten people's lives in less-visible ways. Every April, on the day Copley's mother died in 2002, Dortch would give him a phone call, Copley said. "She would call me and say 'I know this is the day your mother died, and I'll be thinking about you and praying for you,'" said Copley, a United Methodist pastor. "For her, prayer was very, very central to her life."

Dortch, eighty, of Scott died Saturday of lung cancer, her daughter, Madalyn Dortch said.

She was director for twenty years of the Arkansas Interfaith Conference, formerly known as the Arkansas Conference of Churches and Synagogues. She also helped open the Our House shelter in Little Rock in 1987 and the Arkansas Repertory Theatre in 1976. "She just absolutely committed herself for the first twelve years of the theater to helping bring that organization into existence and having it reach as many people as it could," said Cliff Baker, the theater's founding director.

In an interview with the *Arkansas Democrat* in 1986, Dortch said she developed an interest in theater while attending Mount Vernon College in Washington DC. The college later merged with George Washington University and became known as its Mount Vernon campus.

"I love Little Rock and Arkansas, and I wanted those wonderful things to happen here," Dortch said. She was also inspired by the example of her father, Fred Breitzke, who helped start the North Little Rock Boys and Girls Club and the Little Rock YMCA. Dortch believed that the arts "added a certain layer of civility in society, and she wanted to see that celebrated," Baker said. "She represents a generation of patronage that has not been replaced."

A graduate of Little Rock High School, now known as Central High, Dortch also attended the University of Arkansas at Fayetteville. She was married for thirty years to William P. Dortch until their divorce about thirty years ago, Madalyn Dortch said. She had two children and three grandchildren. "She was the most truly Southern belle lady," Madalyn Dortch said. "If you walked in her house, she was handing you an iced tea with mint."

As director of the Interfaith Conference, Dortch helped expand the coalition to include representatives from Muslim and Baha'i faiths, said Copley, interim director of the conference. She also started a tradition of members of the churches meeting with their legislators at the Capitol during every session, Copley said.

Dortch's projects were often inspired by events close to her heart, her daughter said. For instance, during a rough period in her life, Madalyn Dortch and her then four-year-old son came to live with Mimi Dortch, arriving at 3 a.m. on Christmas Eve. "She said, think of all the young mothers that don't have a place to go," Madalyn Dortch said. Shortly afterward, Dortch said, her mother persuaded the Catholic Diocese of Little Rock to lease the Interfaith Conference a building for the Our House shelter for $1 a year.

Similarly, Madalyn Dortch said, when the Trinity Cathedral dropped its sponsorship of an interfaith choir camp, Mimi Dortch, as director of the Interfaith Conference, had the conference take over sponsorship of the camp. Dortch's grandson attended the camp, and she didn't want him to miss it, Madalyn Dortch said.

"She saw a need and she did it," Madalyn Dortch said. "That's just the way she was."

Early NCCJ dinners were well attended, reportedly attracting up to 1,000 guests, and the programs were telecast by a local television station.

The Most Reverend Albert Fletcher, Mrs. David D. (Adolphine Fletcher) Terry, and Dr. Ira Sanders, all former Humanitarian honorees, at dinner, circa 1972. (Used with permission from the Arkansas Democrat-Gazette.)

NCCJ leaders Bill Pharr, B. Finley Vinson, Henry Spitzberg, Dave Grundfest Sr., James E.
Penick, and John A. Healey surround 1967 Humanitarian Award honorees Jeannette and
Governor Winthrop Rockefeller.

NCCJ Executive Director Dr. Bill Pharr, Alan Patteson Jr., and Dr. William R. Carmack
confer at the Annual Meeting of the board, December 5, 1972.

Dr. Joe Bates at the podium, flanked by Phil Kaplan, honorees Katherine (Kackie) Hardie and Richard B. (Preacher Dick) Hardie Jr., and Robert L. Brown Sr. Seated are dinner chair Sheffield Nelson, and dinner speaker Senator Dale Bumpers at the 1978 dinner.

E. Charles Eichenbaum presents a plaque to 1971 Humanitarian honoree J. N. Heiskell. Mrs. David D. (Adolphine Fletcher) Terry was also honored.

Senator Dale Bumpers, dinner speaker, and Sheffield Nelson, dinner chair, in 1978.

Senator Edward Kennedy was dinner speaker in 1972. (Photo by Jordan Davie)

Senator Hubert H. Humphrey (Democrat, Minnesota) was the dinner speaker in 1977 when Margaret Kolb received the Humanitarian award. (Photo by Jordan Davie)

Representative Wilbur Mills, 1972 honoree, and William L. "Sonny" Walker, dinner chair, share a laugh.

Dinner chair Sid McMath, honoree Dr. Lawrence Davis, and board chair Phillip Carroll at the 1970 dinner held in Robinson Auditorium. The speaker was Mrs. Lenore Romney, mother of Mitt Romney, 2012 candidate for United States president.

At the second annual dinner, in 1965, E. Grainger Williams was event chair, Dave Grundfest Sr. was honored, and Senator John Pastore (Democrat, Rhode Island) was the speaker. The dinner was cut short by a bomb threat.

For years, the dais guests would march into the banquet hall just before dinner was served. Leading this group in 1970 are William L. "Sonny" Walker and James Binder, NCCJ board chair.

Henry E. Spitzberg accepted the Humanitarian Award in 1976.

Elizabeth Eckford

Father Joseph H. Biltz Award, 1997
(*Interview conducted July 23, 2012*)

Most Arkansans know a lot *about* Elizabeth Eckford; few really know Elizabeth. Those of us who think about her as the lonely girl sitting on a bus bench outside Central High School or being taunted as she made her way to school in September of 1957 know only a small part of her story.

Elizabeth was brought up in Little Rock and describes her community as protective, safe, and nurturing. She said everyone knew her parents, and everyone felt as if they could correct a child who misbehaved—and then tell the parents, too! She says, "I was raised by the community."

Her mother read to her, building the foundation for a lifelong love of literature. One of Elizabeth's favorite stories was *The Legend of Sleepy Hollow*, by Washington Irving, which recounts the adventures of Ichabod Crane and the Headless Horseman. There were nursery rhymes etched into the linoleum of one of the rooms of their home.

Elizabeth had five siblings, but the ones she mentioned by name in this interview were her older sister, Anna, and a younger brother, Oscar III. She grins when she says her mother often called her brother "Three I." (Elizabeth and Anna mostly called him Baby Brother.) As a child, Oscar III rarely spoke. He was labeled as mentally retarded and mute and attended the Arkansas School for the Deaf and Blind Negro. It was only when Oscar III was an adult that he was correctly diagnosed with autism.

Elizabeth's mother, Birdie, worked in the laundry room at the Veteran's Home, but she was not re-hired for the 1958-59 school year after Elizabeth had tried to attend Central High School. Her dad, Oscar Jr., worked for the railroad, but he also had a pickup truck that he used for hauling things to make extra money. Both of her parents had attended Dunbar High School (now Dunbar Middle School). Elizabeth attended Stephens Elementary School, named for Charlotte Stephens, the first Negro teacher in the Little Rock School District. Elizabeth's favorite teacher was her ninth grade civics teacher, Mr. Friday. After all, she recalls, he was the one who taught her to say "*sam*-mon" instead of "*sal*-mon."

In 1958, when all of the Little Rock high schools were closed, all but four of the Little Rock Nine went off to school in other states. Elizabeth remained in Little Rock taking correspondence courses. She explains that had all of them left the state, the NAACP's lawsuit could not have gone forward. Elizabeth had a lot of time on her hands, so she often spent her days at her grandfather's grocery store at 1200 Wright Avenue.

Her grandfather was an "overwhelming presence," much more interested in dispensing advice to his customers than in selling them something. Elizabeth mimics him using an "old-man" voice, "Ms. Betty (his wife), bring me a soda," and giggles at the memory. She recalls that when someone came in, her granddad would ask them, "Now who are your people?" No one got out of that store without a healthy dose of good advice from him. Elizabeth's family had lived next door to her grandparents until she was eight years old, so they were very close. Elizabeth must have been special to her grandfather, because he never gave her chores at the store, although he expected her brothers to help out.

Most people also don't know that Elizabeth spent almost five years serving in the U.S. Army. One of her postings was at Fort Benjamin Harrison, a training post in Lawrence, Indiana. Neither she nor her fellow soldiers found the post exciting, commonly referring to it as "Uncle Ben's Rest Home." Another posting took her to Fort Lewis, in Washington State. There she was a pay clerk, a job she found boring. Recently discharged Vietnam veterans on their way back to civilian life stopped first at Fort Lewis. She remembers that they often seemed dazed, and she felt they needed more transition time before returning to their stateside homes.

Elizabeth took a short discharge to attend journalism school so that she could become a military journalist. She re-enlisted to write for the military paper in Fort Benjamin Harrison and in Fort McClellan, Alabama, mostly covering retirements, transfers, promotions, and the like. She was incredibly frustrated with her editor over a story about a visiting Brazilian general. The editor insisted that she call Brazil "a free world ally" in the story. But Elizabeth argued, "Brazil is a military dictatorship, and that is an intellectual lie!" Elizabeth lost that argument. However, what she really enjoyed was feature writing. She says, "I like to create my own stories." One favorite assignment was her opportunity to profile a young woman who was part of the Women's Army Corps marching band there at the post.

Elizabeth returned to Little Rock in 1974. As one of the Little Rock Nine, she is often recognized, especially when important anniversaries arise. Over the years, she has been amazingly gracious in telling her story, and she continues today to speak to school groups. She wants students to know that they *can* make a difference. Another thing she stresses with students is the importance of language. Elizabeth thinks any person of color who uses the N-word, no matter how they pronounce it, is expressing self-hatred, and she doesn't approve. She shows students how important it is to support someone who is being harassed, rather than to be a silent witness. That support can make all the difference to someone who is hurting.

Now retired, she has returned to live in the house she moved into with her family when she was eight years old. When I visited, the front garden was in bloom despite the characteristically sweltering Arkansas summer weather, and she welcomed me into her small, beautifully appointed living room. As we talked, the family's two dogs, Black and Brownie, kept wandering in to see if we would play fetch with them. Elizabeth would send them out with a gentle, "Not now," but they would persistently return a while later. She's still an avid reader, consuming history, literature, and what she calls "fast food reading," including romance and mysteries.

I asked her, "If you had it all to do over, would you choose to attend Central High School?" Her answer was no.

She says that at fifteen years old, she was aware of meanness and violence in other places, but she naively thought that couldn't be true about her home town. And she never would have thought that adults might hurt children. As she has learned more over the years, she has realized that the hostile attacks toward her and the others were often coordinated and actually led by adults from outside the school. And she never felt truly protected by the adults in the school, with few exceptions. She agrees with her good friend, Minnie Jean Brown Trickey, that what they experienced that year at Central was *American terrorism*.

Elizabeth seems to be at peace now about her experiences in 1957. She even laughs heartily when she describes some of the ways the nine students devised to protect themselves from the constant mistreatment. For example, Carlotta Walls LaNier, who was an athlete, moved so quickly from room to room that she wore out her personal body guard and got a new one practically every week.

Elizabeth also remembers some of the good things. She says three of the nine had secret telephone friends who would warn them of planned attacks. One male student called Jefferson Thomas and asked, "Would you accept a coward as a friend?" And she remembers her speech class at the end of the day as a respite where no one called her names, and where two white students, Ken Reinhardt and Ann Williams Wedaman, reached out to her in friendship.

Americans will be forever indebted to Elizabeth and the other members of the Little Rock Nine for bravely helping us to change our world. But as important a figure as she is in the history of the Civil Rights Movement in this country, there is so much more to Elizabeth Eckford. I am grateful to her for sharing more of her life with all of us.

E. Charles Eichenbaum

Humanitarian Award, 1992
(May 30, 1907–June 28, 1993)

Eulogy for E. Charles Eichenbaum, delivered by Rabbi Eugene Levy on June 30, 1993, Temple B'Nai Israel. Reprinted with permission from Temple B'Nai Israel and Rabbi Eugene Levy

I suppose that if one hears something enough times, repeated by friends and family alike—it *must* be true. So it was yesterday when I basked in the rays of the wonderful family of E. Charles Eichenbaum. And to a person, each told me how great a man Charlie was, especially when it came to helping so many people, nationwide, to become what they are today.

A man for all seasons
Master of all
Passionate for life, enthusiastic about everything
Good, intelligent, believed in himself
Tremendous memory and a great sense of humor
One who made others feel better

Phrases all repeated over and over.

I'll bet that many of you who are here this afternoon could easily be saying right now:

I would not be where I am today if it were not for the goodness and the good works of E. Charles Eichenbaum—the personification of Mitzvah—the doing of deeds, both because these deeds were commanded of us by God, and also because Charles just enjoyed helping others, with no fanfare and with no expectations in return.

My first real encounter with Charles was that cold rainy Monday morning, October 19, 1987, the day the stock market fell over 500 points. Between the radio and phone calls, and the "several pagers" Charles kept on his desk and the many other desks in his room, we really could not find the time to find out much about each other. We did talk about religion: reform Judaism, the way it used to be. Charles, then, and Charles, recently, did not hesitate to tell me which parts of temple life he most enjoyed and which, shall we say, could use a little change, to his way. Our last meeting together, other than my three hospital visits and calls, was at the Univeristy of Arkansas at Little Rock for a monumental library project that was to be supported by the Ottenheimer Foundation.

When it came to the type and placement of French history reference books, Charles made it clear, in his own philosophical and thoughtful style, just how he wanted it, where and why, almost as though he were in the courtroom.

E. Charles Eichenbaum, attorney extraordinaire, husband, brother, father, grandfather, great grandfather, hunter, fisher, golfer, philosopher—friend.

E. Charles Eichenbaum died Tuesday morning, and we gather here today not only to mourn his loss, but also to remember what he was and who he was.

Using some of the materials printed about him in the last five years, let me briefly relate to you just a few of the many highlights of Charles's life.

Born in Little Rock, Arkansas, in 1907, Charles was a graduate of the Little Rock public schools and Washington University in St. Louis, Missouri, where he received his doctorate of Jurisprudence in 1928. In June of that year, he opened his own law firm in the Bathurst Building at 216 West Second Street in Little Rock.

Expansion and growth marked the firm into the '30s and '40s, as he and his partners developed their practice, particularly in the areas of bankruptcy and federal income tax.

The business prospered and the offices moved a few times more to gain added space. It is said that Charles was really Arkansas's first true tax lawyer and worked closely with Arkansas's elected officials on Capitol Hill.

In the late '60s and early '70s, the Eichenbaum Law Firm added retail stores, malls and shopping centers to its clientele, further expanding its commercial to business practice—and further expanding its need for space.

A member of his own firm for sixty-five years, Charles had served the Pulaski County, Arkansas and American Bar Associations on a multitude of committees.

He was for twenty years a Fellow of the American Bar Foundation, having served as Chairman of the Arkansas Fellows from 1973 to 1988. That year Charles was the only attorney in the country to be honored at the American Bar Foundation's annual meeting with the presentation of the Foundation's prestigious Fifty-Year Distinguished Service Award.

E. Charles Eichenbaum's life and career are filled with honors and citations. But perhaps the greatest honor is the E. Charles Eichenbaum Scholarship Fund, established by his clients and his firm in his name. It was the largest single scholarship endowment of the Arkansas Bar Association.

That was the business side of Charles.

On the personal side—Charles leaves us a most precious family: His dear wife, Helen, to whom he was married ten days short of sixty years, so accomplished and fine in her own right; his sister, Betty Werner, of Shreveport; daughter, Peggy Tabnak, of Memphis, and her husband; four grandchildren, Laurie, Terri, Jan, and E. Charles and their families; and two great-grandchildren.

Family, look around and you'll see faces of those your Charles touched.

In describing himself in an *Arkansas Democrat* profile, Charles said, "I am a scribe, analyst, research scholar, and, above all, an even-handed presenter of the law and facts so that my many clients may fare well in the Halls of Justice."

Above all, Charles, in our description of him, was a cut way above the average—though he felt comfortable with prince and pauper alike.

He gloried in his family and they rallied to him as philosopher-king. With a wink and a smile—he was firm but loving. He was their guiding light and their inspiration and they were and are so proud to have called him theirs. When confronted with new and difficult situations or tasks, the family members would often say—What would Charles have done in that situation?—and then do it.

Charles believed in what religion is all about. He loved his temple and his Judaism and the demands of Ethical Monotheism—the one God commands you to do good—And he did and he was.

I guess Charles's words to those of us who are here today would be what guided his own life—

Work hard and play hard
Love life and all that it holds
Do good and be a blessing.

Charles will indeed be missed—by his family, his temple, his friends, and his clients and associates. But as he would want us to be a blessing, we thank him for being that special blessing, that special man to each of us.

The memory of the righteous will be a blessing.

Dr. M. Joycelyn Elders
Humanitarian Award, 2007

Joycelyn Elders's deputy director at the Arkansas Department of Health once said about her, "Our director walks on the edge, so we have to make sure she's got all the support and tools she needs." Joycelyn has been walking on the edge her entire life.

Joycelyn was born, one of eight children, in Schaal, Arkansas, in Howard County. Her parents, Haller and Curtis Jones, were poor sharecroppers in a town of only ninety-nine people. She and her siblings attended segregated schools and sometimes missed school to help with picking cotton, harvesting corn, and picking "the best-tasting peaches" in Arkansas. Joycelyn was admitted to Philander Smith College as the valedictorian of her high school class, and the United Methodist Women gave her a tuition scholarship to attend. However, her siblings had to pick cotton to pay her bus fare of $3.43 to get her to Little Rock. She said she was scared to death to go and thought about dropping out more than once. An aunt who worked as a maid in Detroit had sent her hand-me-down clothes, but when she arrived with saddle oxfords and bobby socks, she learned that Philander women were required to wear stockings. She cleaned the dorm to earn the money for those stockings, and for materials and books not covered by the small scholarship. After graduation from Philander, she joined the Women's Medical Specialist Corps of the U.S. Army so that she could use the GI Bill to attend medical school.

Entering the Univeristy of Arkansas for Medical Sciences in 1956, Joycelyn went on to be the only woman and one of only three blacks in her class to graduate, and although she attended during the Little Rock schools crisis of 1957, she said that she and her classmates were so concerned with passing that they were hardly aware of the controversy in the community. After a University of Minnesota internship, she returned to UAMS for a residency in pediatrics, where she was named chief resident. Early in her career at UAMS, she received the prestigious National Institutes of Health Career Development Award, which provided for five years of training and support for research. She earned a master's in biochemistry and conducted groundbreaking research on growth in children. During her tenure at UAMS and Arkansas Children's Hospital, she also served as president of the Southern Society of Pediatric Research and worked with Planned Parenthood with an emphasis on improving the health of pregnant teenagers. It's no wonder that Governor Bill Clinton tapped her to serve as the director of the Arkansas Health Department in 1987.

Joycelyn credits a wonderful staff and supportive boss at the Arkansas Department of Health for helping her accomplish some remarkable things during her six years there, such as establishing ten school-based clinics, mostly in the Delta where the need was great; improving the immunization rates across the state; and establishing in-home health services for Arkansans. A prominent legislator once remarked about Joycelyn, "Don't even let her talk or we'll end up giving her the whole damn state!"

When President Clinton asked her to become Surgeon General, she originally turned him down because she already had a great job in Arkansas. At her mother's urging, she accepted the appointment, which resulted in a grueling confirmation process and a stormy sixteen-month tenure as the nation's chief medical officer.

It turned out that she loved the new job, too, primarily because she met and worked with so many wonderful people from all across the nation. Her brave public statements, particularly on matters of sexual health for adolescents, resulted in her short stay in Washington DC; her only regret is that her outspokenness gave conservative thinkers a reason to become more organized and more focused in fighting progressive policies.

After returning to Arkansas Children's Hospital for three years, Joycelyn retired in 1998 and has since traveled the country as a speaker. If Joycelyn could effect one change, she would provide early childhood education for all children. "If you get things right for kids when they are three years old, you don't have to worry about them when they are thirteen."

Coach Oliver Elders
Humanitarian Award, 2007

Oliver Elders was always a talented athlete, but he was surprised when he learned
that his father had been a tremendous baseball pitcher. That's because Coach Elders
never saw his dad wear anything except a
blue serge suit, always with a necktie.

Coach was born in DeWitt, in
Arkansas County. His parents, Leona and
Oliver B. Elders Sr., had more than 100
years of teaching between them, his mother as a third and fourth grade
teacher, his dad as a history teacher and an administrator. But his parents
also had other jobs. His dad kept books for the owner of one of the
largest rice farms in the community and helped others prepare their
taxes, and his mother sold insurance burial policies to make sure that
everyone in Arkansas County had a proper burial. To better provide for
their children, Oliver, Sr. moved with his son to Pine Bluff, where he
became the veteran's coordinator at AM&N College. Ultimately, Coach,
his two sisters, and his mom all graduated from AM&N, now the
University of Arkansas at Pine Bluff. Coach Elders eventually earned a
master's degree in 1963 and a specialist degree in 1965, both from
Indiana University.

Coach never wavered in what he wanted to do with his life, and
that was basketball. But after one year playing with the Harlem
Magicians, an offshoot of the Harlem Globetrotters, he was drafted into
the army. He enjoyed the army immensely, and as a soldier, he was able
to play basketball, run track, swim, and teach English. He was tempted
to stay in the army, but with his mother's urging, he returned to his
Arkansas hometown, Almyra, to teach high school physical education
and physical science at his alma mater, Immanuel High School.

Immanuel had no gym, so they practiced outside on the dirt until he persuaded the principal to let them set up a goal in the auditorium. Coach said most of his players were actually his cousins, big, strong country farm boys who had never played ball before. The mothers made the uniforms, they got a schedule, and it turned out they were pretty good. One cousin, Hubert Clemmons, urged Coach to bring his team to a tournament in North Little Rock at Scipio Jones High School. They borrowed socks and shoes and won three games in one day to qualify for the championship game. They lost to Jones High, the home team, by only two points. Sure enough, they were pretty good.

Again urged by his cousin Hubert, Coach applied at the brand new Horace Mann High School in Little Rock. As coach at Mann, he called the University of Arkansas medical school to send a physician over to give the players their physicals. To everyone's surprise, the physician who showed up was a woman, Joycelyn Jones. Two months later Coach and Joycelyn were married.

Elders spent thirty-six years coaching, most of that time at Hall High School, to which he transferred from Mann as one of the first African-American teachers at the formerly all-white high school. When he retired in 1993, he was the most successful high-school basketball coach in Arkansas history, with 656 wins and 305 losses. But he is most proud of his wins with the hundreds of players whom he taught that discipline, respect, and hard work were the keys to success. Eighty-five of his players received college scholarships, and fifty had received college degrees by 1993.

Upon transferring to Hall, Coach found there were no black officials in the formerly all-white school leagues. Through his determined pressure and with the support of the Hall principal, Weldon Faulk, that was changed, and Coach said that ultimately when the teams and the officials became truly integrated, it became a non-issue. He characterizes that challenge as excruciatingly painful, but worth it.

Coach retired in 1993 to accompany his wife, Dr. Joycelyn Elders, to Washington DC, where she would serve as Surgeon General for

President Bill Clinton. Coach took the position of director of the intern program at the U.S. Department of Education and worked to develop special programs for minority males. Back in Little Rock, Coach runs a rental management business. Still today, he and his wife sponsor students by helping them with jobs and scholarships.

Joycelyn and Oliver Elders have two sons, Eric, a vice principal at Jack Robey Junior High in Pine Bluff, and Kevin, a real estate investor in Jackson, Mississippi.

Honorable Joyce Elliott
Humanitarian Award, 2006

Early on it was clear that Joyce Elliott would enter politics. At the age of ten, she was sent out of math class because all she wanted to do was talk about the Kennedy/Nixon debates of the night before. But she had a lot of schooling to complete and teaching to do before she would be elected to the Arkansas House of Representatives in 2001.

Joyce never set out to be the "first black woman...," but she often was. Joyce, one of seven children, was born and raised in Willisville, in Nevada County, Arkansas. She attended segregated schools until the tenth grade, when, through a "freedom of choice" plan, four black families were able to send their children to a formerly all-white high school. Joyce found the students in her new school, with some exceptions, mostly indifferent and sometimes outwardly bigoted.

After graduating, Joyce had an opportunity to attend college fully paid by an uncle, but only if she would leave Arkansas to attend school in Michigan. Joyce decided that she needed to stay at home and work for change here. So she used loans and part-time work to get through Southern Arkansas University in Magnolia. Despite instances of blatant racism, Joyce loved college. Joyce described herself as a news junkie even then, and she loved her classes more than the card games that occupied many students. She entertained the idea of becoming a news reporter, but ultimately decided that we needed teachers who treated kids right, and she felt that through teaching she could really make a contribution.

So again, she was the "first black woman" when she accepted a job as a high school English teacher, first in Texas and then in Minnesota. After returning to Arkansas, Joyce continued to teach English and became a union activist for education. When her son, Elliott Barnes, graduated from high school in 2000, she decided it was time to run for office.

That first race was very tough, even more so because right in the middle of it, Joyce became a kidney donor for one of her sisters. After taking office, Joyce said her first concern was to try to "be a voice" for those who have never been listened to before. But right away, she realized that another priority was to do everything she could to defeat proposed bad legislation. Her first appointment was to the Judiciary Committee, where she felt she had a lot to learn, and which she hated leaving when she chose to move to the Education Committee. Whatever committee Joyce serves on, she clearly makes a difference.

Some of the legislation for which she is most proud includes the Colorectal Cancer Act, which promotes education and screenings throughout the state; an act that enables Arkansas to do a better job of engaging minority business owners for state contracts; and an act making trafficking of persons a Class A felony. She is still working on other issues, and is very proud to have "begun the conversation" on hate crimes legislation, emergency contraception for rape survivors, and access to post-secondary education for youngsters of immigrant families (the DREAM Act). Joyce left the Arkansas House at the end of 2007 because of term limits.

Along with her service in the legislature, in 2004, Joyce left the classroom to accept a position with the Southwestern Region of the College Board to create access and equity for under-represented groups of students in high school advanced placement courses.

Since being honored with the Humanitarian Award in 2006, Joyce Elliott has twice been elected to a seat in the Arkansas Senate, where she has provided leadership, including as Majority Leader and Majority Whip, and continued to speak up for those whose voices are often not heard.

LaVerne D. Feaster
Father Joseph H. Biltz Award, 2002

LaVerne D. Feaster, where do we begin? Perhaps we should talk about the 4-H model, which is "Learn By Doing." LaVerne has always done, and continues to do, a lot.

Born and raised in the Arkansas Delta, in Cotton Plant, LaVerne was one of four children. Her mother was a teacher, and her father managed the store, the cotton gin, the post office, and the farm.

LaVerne says of her parents and upbringing: "Daddy took care of the store and farm. Momma was in charge of the school and community. And Momma and Daddy were both in charge of the home and church." She says that even though discrimination and prejudice toward blacks were evident everywhere, she and her siblings were instilled with the belief that they were as good as anyone and probably twice as smart. LaVerne has proved that to be true over and over.

LaVerne graduated from Tennessee State University. She later earned a master's degree from the University of Arkansas. She began her career as a home economics teacher at Swift Junior College in Rogersville, Tennessee.

In 1961, LaVerne went to work for the Arkansas Cooperative Extension Service, in Clark County. She rose through the ranks and was appointed state leader of 4-H in 1986. In that position, she directed 4-H programs in all sevety-five Arkansas Counties, interacting with over 50,000 youth ages nine to nineteen and 6,000 volunteers each year.

LaVerne was nurtured by her family, her community, and her church. So she has spent her life nurturing others. In addition to her work with the Cooperative Extension Service, where she helped thousands of Arkansas youngsters become all that they could be, she has served in many volunteer roles.

LaVerne retired from her "full-time" job in 1990, just in time to take leading roles with Arkansas Repertory Theatre, the NCCJ, the Keep Arkansas Beautiful Commission, the Commision for Arkansas's Future, Arkansas Rice Depot, Delta Sigma Theta, Links Inc., Southern Development Bancorporation, and several other groups. She is also an ordained elder of Allison Presbyterian Church.

LaVerne is married to William D. Feaster. LaVerne explains that since they were never blessed with children of their own, she adopted children through her teaching, her 4-H work, her church, and her other volunteer commitments. She calls all of the young people in her life her "blessings," and it is clear that she means that.

Lots of people and organizations have lined up to give LaVerne well-deserved awards and recognition over her years of service.

If you want a creative, tireless, and enthusiastic leader, you can do no better than LaVerne Feaster.

Most Reverend Albert L. Fletcher
Humanitarian Award, 1966
(October 28, 1896–December 6, 1979)

First Bishop Born in Arkansas,
Reprinted with permission from Arkansas Catholic

As the fourth bishop of Little Rock, Albert L. Fletcher guided the diocese through a period of profound social, racial ,and theological conflict and change. His twenty-five-year episcopacy spanned the Cold War, the Civil Rights Movement, Vatican II, and the Vietnam War. Bishop Fletcher's calm, courtly manner stood in stark contrast to the upheaval around him. He was the first Arkansan raised to the Roman Catholic hierarchy and remains the only native son to serve as Little Rock's bishop.

As a young man, he attended Little Rock College and St. John Home Missions Seminary, leading to his ordination June 4, 1920. Father Fletcher taught chemistry and biology at Little Rock College, which he served as president in 1923. The tall, scholarly priest also earned a master of science degree from the University of Chicago. Later, he was a professor of theology and canon law at St. John seminary, where his students labeled him a "born professor."

His installation as auxiliary bishop on April 24, 1940, marked the first episcopal consecration to take place in Arkansas. He was installed as bishop on February 11, 1947. After several years of relative calm, the U.S. Supreme Court outlawed segregation in 1954, prompting Bishop Fletcher to issue a pastoral letter stating that the Catholic Church never made distinctions based on race but had provided separate churches and schools for blacks owing to laws and customs. He rebuked the Arkansas governor for acting to block the desegregation of Central High School in 1957.

The bishop and his diocesan newspaper, *The Guardian*, advocated peaceful integration and racial brotherhood. By 1959, all Catholic hospitals in Arkansas had been integrated and black students were attending Subiaco Academy. Catholic High School and Mount St. Mary Academy began accepting blacks in 1962, but few were willing to attend the predominantly white high schools. Over the next decade, several black churches and schools in the state closed.

Bishop Fletcher participated in the four fall sessions of the Second Vatican Council (1962–65) and announced the change in language of the liturgy from Latin to English (in America), effective with the first Sunday of Advent in 1964. The bishop declined to establish a role for permanent deacons as Vatican II suggested. He also found himself at odds with the younger priests teaching at St. John seminary—a group more liberal on social and theological questions. After the state's largest newspaper in the spring of 1967 printed a series of articles by seminary priests that differed with the Catholic Church views on birth control and questioned papal infallibility, Bishop Fletcher announced that the seminary would close.

In 1971, Bishop Fletcher declined to vote for a resolution by the American Catholic Bishops calling for an end to the Vietnam War. Fervently anti-communist, the bishop didn't support amnesty for war resisters and draft dodgers. He turned seventy-five (retirement age for bishops) on October 28, 1971, and eventually stepped down in July 1972. He died December 6, 1979, in Little Rock after attending a funeral Mass for a friend.

Jean Gordon
Father Joseph H. Biltz Award, 2007

One of the many pieces of advice that Jean Gordon's father gave her was, "It's okay to get out front on a controversial issue, but don't get so far out front that no one will be with you." Most of the time, Jean has taken that advice.

Jean came to her activism and for-ward-thinking attitudes from the example of her dad, Herbert Thomas, who was a close friend of Senator Bill Fulbright and, among other things, was the chair of the board of trustees at the University of Arkansas at Fayetteville in 1948 when Silas Hunt was the first African American admitted to the law school there. When we recall that the school put a fence around Hunt in the classroom, we have to thank people like Herbert Thomas and Jean Gordon for helping us to learn better ways to interact over the past five decades. And we can be proud that the dean of that same law school in 2007 was Cyndi Nance, an African-American woman.

Jean graduated with a degree in philosophy from Wellesley College, got married, and had three children. She's now married to Walter Clancy, and she has three grandchildren and a great-grandson. She began her community work early by joining the Women's Emergency Committee, working to get Little Rock schools re-opened in 1959.

Jean has always worked on huge issues (civil rights and world peace) in a very personal way. An important moment occurred for Jean in 1959 when she was going door-to-door to gather signatures for the Stop This Outrageous Purge (STOP) campaign when the Little Rock School District had fired forty-four teachers and principals. She knocked on the door of Joe and Evelyn Bernhardt, Orthodox Jews and the owners of Joe's Hobby Shop. The Bernhardts embraced Jean and her mission and confessed that they wondered if someone "would be coming for them next."

Another highlight of her work came when as a member of the Panel of American Women she and the other panelists were refused service in the only café in the small town because one of their members was "colored." They declined the offer to eat in the kitchen, left the restaurant without any supper, then went to the high school and made their presentation. When the students questioned them and learned they were refused service, the students decided to do something about it. As a result, the panel members were invited back two weeks later to be seated and served in that restaurant.

Jean has also served with the Arkansas Council on Human Relations, the Political Action Committee of Church Women United, the Little Rock School Board, Arkansas Peace Links, Arkansas Peace Center, and Arkansas Council of International Visitors, very often in leadership roles. Actually, we could make a shorter list of the civil rights or world peace groups that Jean has not been involved with than of the ones she has. Her commitment and leadership have been important to our human family and particularly to our Little Rock family.

Much of Jean's focus is on working for peace. She is a founding member of Arkansas WAND (Women's Actions for New Directions), and a board member of the national WAND organization. If you want a provocative program about our government's spending priorities and the effect of our military budget, just invite Jean with her WAND posters and brochures.

Reverend Wendell Griffen
Father Joseph H. Biltz Award, 2009

For Wendell Griffen, there are three important pillars in his life: his private practice as
an attorney, his public service, and his Faith
in God and in humankind. But if you ask
him what the most important thing he's
ever done is, he gets a gleam in his eye and
talks about his sons Martyn and Elliott.

Wendell was the oldest of three children born to Bennie and Josephine Griffen.
His father was a laborer in the timber industry, and his mother worked
in poultry processing. This rural Southwest Arkansas couple were devout
Christians and taught their children the importance of helping others
and community involvement by their example. His mother valued the
skill of oratory, and Wendell remembers the family watching the *Huntley-
Brinkley Report* each night partly to learn diction and good grammar. His
parents also valued education, and all three children attended the
University of Arkansas at Fayetteville.

Wendell was encouraged to work hard—to be a contributor, not a
consumer. Once when he was proudly showing off his report card with
all As and Bs, his uncle asked, "Why so many Bs?" Wendell first attended
an integrated school in the tenth grade, and he remembers fondly the
students and their parents who went out of their way to make him feel
welcome. Because he was skipped along in grades, he learned early to get
along with peers a few years older. One thing he learned was how to control his temper, since he was the youngest and the smallest in his class.

When Wendell graduated from Law School in 1979, he was hired
to join the Wright, Lindsey & Jennings firm and became the first
lawyer of color in any major firm in Arkansas. He immediately felt included, and learned from his mentors there to "work hard and fair;

treat opposing lawyers with civility; and treat clients with compassion."
He was made partner in 1984, which made his decision to go into public service more difficult.

However, after his appointment to the Workers' Compensation
Commission by Governor Bill Clinton, and his subsequent appointment
to a newly expanded Court of Appeals by Governor Jim Guy Tucker,
Wendell, as they say, never looked back. He said working with the
Workers' Compensation Commission taught him how judges make fac-
tual determinations by reading transcripts and making decisions based
on law. In his thirteen years on the Court of Appeals, he treasured the
opportunity to argue, negotiate, and collaborate with the eleven other
members of the most diverse court in the state.

Even those who don't know anything else about Wendell
Griffen probably remember that he has gotten into hot water more
than once because of his outspokenness on issues of equity surrounding race and class. Many have asked, "Why did you speak out?"
Wendell answers, "When the Supreme Court ruled in 2002 that
judges were protected in their right to comment off the bench on matters not before their court, I felt ethically and politically compelled to
speak up when I witnessed injustice." Chances are, Wendell Griffen
will continue to speak up.

Finally, Wendell's faith is a cornerstone of his life. Ordained as
a minister in the Baptist Church, he cites his relationships across de-
nominational and ecumenical lines as informing how he attempts to
live out his faith today. Wendell says, "If God is who we claim God
to be, then we must transcend our histories, our patterns, folkways
and prejudices, if we are to live fully in God's authority. There is no
concrete road for us. We must risk rejection and allow ourselves to
be vulnerable if we want to realize and make manifest God's love for
every human being."

Wendell believes our biggest challenges are our seeming lack of
faith and confidence in God, in ourselves, and in each other, and our

inability to imagine that all things can change for the better. If we follow Wendell Griffen's lead, we will have an abundance of confidence that we can do and be better.

Back to those sons, Martyn and Elliott. Wendell and his wife, Patricia, wanted to have children but were unsuccessful for the first ten years of their marriage. In the mid-'80s when Martyn and Elliott were born, Wendell says it changed him, challenged him, and expanded his life in a way he hadn't expected. Both boys are multi-talented, were Eagle Scouts and were good students. Martyn works and lives in the Washington DC area, while Elliott studies music and history at Henderson State University in Arkadelphia. At the 2009 inauguration of President Obama, the young Griffens were the tour guides as opposed to when Bill Clinton was inaugurated and the boys made their first trip to Washington DC with their parents as guides.

Dave Grundfest Sr.

Humanitarian Award, 1965
(1901–1974)

Printed with permission from Arkansas Business Hall of Fame

In 1922, Dave Grundfest, along with his brother Sam, founded Sterling Stores Company Inc., an organization of retail variety stores and the forerunner of today's retail phenomenon. Over the next fifty years, he built 100 stores in six states and brought merchandise from around the world to rural communities. In 1965, he founded Magic Mart Discount Department Stores, building it into a fifty-store operation. Known as "Mr. Dave" by his employees, Grundfest led more than 6,000 people at the apex of his operations.

Ingrained in Retailing

The Grundfest brothers were among eight children born to a Russian immigrant who had settled in Cary, Mississippi. Their father Morris peddled sundry items to Delta farmers until he had enough money to open a general store. Retailing became ingrained in the brothers while they were raised in the store.

Dave was one of two people in his senior class, graduating "magna cum second," as he joked. His mother wanted him to get an education so he attended Mississippi State University for two semesters, but his education did not end there.

Following a stint in the U.S. Army during World War I, Sam and Dave founded Cash Wholesale Company, a wholesale business for general stores in Little Rock. In 1921, one of their customers fell deeply in debt to them, and the owner, F. S. Rasco, offered his store as payment.

Evolving the Variety Store Concept

Sam sent Dave—at the age of twenty-one—to El Dorado to run the store. Dave said, "I was looking for an opportunity to do something." Thus, the concept of the variety store for rural communities began to evolve. Around the time there was a successful chain of variety stores called Silver Stores, so Sam suggested the name Sterling Stores.

In 1927, a Sterling Store opened in downtown Little Rock, and the headquarters moved there. The secret of the Grundfest brothers' success was to buy high quality goods on a volume basis from major markets to supply their stores. Dave bragged, "As I've said many times, with Sam's brain and my brawn, we made a pretty good team." Prior to Sterling Stores, small Arkansas towns had to rely on under-stocked general stores. Soon the brothers branched out to Camden, Conway, and Russellville. They opened the sixth store in North Little Rock and moved their headquarters to the second floor.

Dave met and married Maureen Frauenthal of Little Rock in 1926. They had two children, Dave Grundfest Jr., who married Julianne Dante of Dumas, and Barbara "Bobby" Bauman, who married Stanley Bauman Jr. of Little Rock.

There were almost seventy Sterling Stores in 1931 when the "panic" struck. In debt afterwards, the Grundfests reorganized and began again with twenty-seven stores. In 1941, Sam fell ill and moved to New York, and Dave took over. With the help of an excellent management team, he made the '40s and '50s the heyday of Sterling Stores, which had become essential to the way of life of the residents in small rural towns. Highly sought-after goods like stylish apparel, cosmetics, home appliances, radios, and sundry items were available for the first time. Dave Grundfest Jr. said, "His theory was that the only way to make Sterling Stores grow was to make Arkansas grow."

Dave and his buyers roamed the market places of New York, Hong Kong, London, and Paris in search of new items. Hundreds of salesmen called on the executive offices in Little Rock to sell American products.

In many towns, the modern Sterling Store fronts encouraged other merchants to update their establishments.

Grundfest opened his 100th store in August 1967. With the '60s also came the dawn of the discount store. Joining the future, he opened the Famous Discount Department Store in Pine Bluff in 1960. In 1965, he opened a 30,000-square-foot unit called Magic Mart in Little Rock, followed by stores in Pine Bluff and Searcy.

With revenue of more than $110 million and approximately 150 stores in 1983, the company was sold.

Speaking on America

Warmhearted and gregarious, Grundfest was noted for his speaking skills on the civic club circuit, which he considered his patriotic duty. His first speech for the Rotary Club in Benton in 1944 was entitled "Sterling Stories." Living for America became his theme. He lent an ear to the personal problems of his employees and friends who often lined up outside his office. When his burdens grew heavy, and he couldn't go fishing to escape, he wrote poetry.

When interviewing a potential secretary for the position, Grundfest said, "If you come to work as my secretary, I will ask you [to do] three things: Put your family first, your church second, and your job with me third."

Serving the Community

A committed community servant, he took a special interest in the Arkansas Chamber of Commerce, serving as president for many years. In 1957 and 1959, Grundfest was involved in several trade missions to Europe for the State Department. He was also president of the Little Rock YMCA and the Rotary Club of Little Rock. He co-founded the Arkansas chapter of the National Conference of Christians and Jews, and was honored as the second recipient of its National Humanitarian Award. In addition, he served on numerous boards of other businesses in the community.

Grundfest's one dream was to see that every deserving young person should have a college education, so he and Sam established the Grundfest Foundation in memory of their father to fund college scholarships.

Among Grundfest's many other community involvements were serving as president of the Leo N. Levi Memorial Hospital in Hot Springs; member of the board of directors of the Arkansas Crippled Children's Home; vice president of the Arkansas Economic Council of the State Chamber of Commerce; and vice president of the Arkansas Live Stock Show Association. During World War II, he served on the Ration Board and as war fund chairman of the American National Red Cross. In addition, Grundfest made land and facilities available so that the Little Rock YMCA could start Camp Grundy, a day-camp experience for children.

Grundfest said, "Out of gratitude for the blessings which I enjoy, comes a responsibility to share material things and give myself to those who have not been so fortunate. My religion teaches me that I am my brother's keeper." Grundfest was a member of Congregation B'nai Israel.

When he died in 1974, he had earned a sterling reputation as a bona fide retailing pioneer and the forerunner of the state's other retail legacies, Sam Walton and William T. Dillard.

Willie D. "Bill" Hamilton
Father Joseph H. Biltz Award, 2002
(1938–2003)

Willie D. "Bill" Hamilton has been a leader
for justice in Arkansas for several decades.

Bill was born in Hope—one of thirteen
children. His mother was a homemaker and
his father did whatever work he could find,
sometimes having to travel out of state to
work for the railroad.

The primary thing Bill says about his
family is that he was surrounded by love.
Having been born into poverty, but being able to get an education and
escape the cycle of poverty, Bill has always been about giving back to a
community that nurtured him.

Bill made his way to Little Rock and Philander Smith College,
where he received a degree in mathematics. He also studied at Iowa State
University, Rutgers University, and the University of Arkansas at Little
Rock and at Fayetteville. He was later awarded an honorary doctorate
from Philander Smith College.

Bill began as a public-school math teacher but moved into public service in 1966 when he became the administrative director of the Family
Planning Program of the Economic Opportunity Agency of Pulaski County.
He soon assumed the executive director's position there and served as the
executive director of the Arkansas Family Planning Council for almost two
decades. From 1988 until he retired in 2001, Bill was director of the Division
of Reproductive Health for the Arkansas Department of Health.

Throughout his career, Bill has been responsible for promoting the
health and well-being of all Arkansans through programs, community
action, establishment of health clinics, and establishment of policies that
promote dignity and empowerment.

In addition to his illustrious career, Bill also has served in many, many volunteer positions ... most notably, perhaps, on the Little Rock School Board, for ten years. In that role, Bill made many friends and was a friend himself to all the staff and students in the Little Rock district.

Bill has been married to Wanda for more than forty years, and they have three grown children, Scott, Tracy, and Carmen. They are also proud grandparents of Kennedy and Olivia Parks.

If you want a soft-spoken, compassionate, LEADER on your team, you ask Bill Hamilton to serve.

Bill Hamilton died in 2003, and the Little Rock School District named the Hamilton High School Learning Academy to honor his service in 2007. I was invited to speak. Here are my remarks on that day:

I am so honored to be part of this dedication today. I heard recently that those we meet sometimes leave "handprints" on our heart. Bill Hamilton certainly left a handprint on my heart.

I knew that others would talk about Bill's many accomplishments today, so I thought I would talk about Bill Hamilton, my friend.

I first met Bill when I was elected in 1984 to serve on the Little Rock School Board. I vividly remember my first board meeting because I was so nervous I could barely speak to say "present" when the roll was called. But from the very beginning, Bill Hamilton welcomed me with a smile.

He not only made me feel comfortable; he made me feel like I belonged, like I had something important to offer to our group. He asked for my opinion, and he listened to what I had to say.

But beyond serving on the school board together, Bill and Wanda Hamilton welcomed Steve and me to be a part of their lives. We were entertained in their beautiful garden, we attended their twenty-fifthth anniversary party, and we met their beautiful children, Scott, Tracy and Carmen.

Over the years (after our school board time together), I learned a lot more about Bill. I learned that he came from a family of thirteen children in Hope, Arkansas. I learned that his mother only agreed to marry his father upon the condition that he build a house for her, which he did, and one member of the Hamilton family still lives in that house today. Their family never had a lot of material possessions, but they had a lot of love and the good values that created the Bill Hamilton that we knew and respected.

I learned that Bill would never quit working for justice through his days with the Family Planning Council and the State Health Department....promoting the health and well-being of ALL Arkansans through programs, community action, establishment of health clinics, and establishment of policies that promote dignity and empowerment.

And one of the last times I spent visiting with Bill, we both knew that his death was imminent....and what I remember about that day was his concern about Wanda and if she was going to be okay after he was gone.

With this dedication today of the Hamilton High School Learning Academy, we are honoring a man who made a difference for so many, and now this school will continue to make a difference in his name.

I remember Bill as a soft-spoken and compassionate man. I also remember that Bill was a big man, and he had big hands; he did, indeed, leave a big handprint on my heart.

Ruth D. Shepherd

Reverend Dr. Logan Hampton

Father Joseph H. Biltz Award, 2012

When talking with a new student at the University of Arkansas at Little Rock, Dean of Students Dr. Logan Hampton might say, "Expect us to be all up in your business." That's because to ensure the success of even the most at-risk student, Logan and team follow the three I's: identify the needs; intervene with the right supportive services; and be intrusive, in other words, "be all up in the students' business" to make sure they are on track. With this method, they are demonstrating the adage, "A student doesn't care what you know until they know that you care."

It all started when Vice Chancellor Dr. Charles Donaldson took a look in 2007 at the graduation rates of UALR's African-American male students and concluded that that group was too often failing to graduate because somehow the university was failing those students. Dr. Donaldson called a meeting with Logan and another colleague, Darryl McGee, and said, "We've got to fix this. Now! We don't have time to study the issues or convene a committee; we've got to do something, now." Thus UALR's African-American Male Initiative was born. The results were immediate and astounding. Within their target group, the fall 2009 average GPA was 2.695 compared to 1.812 (which is "on probation") for non-participants.

One of the most interesting interventions has been the Peer Success Advisors—upper classmen who are trained to work directly with the incoming students. Turns out the advisors seem to benefit almost as much as the students they are serving. During the four years of the program, Logan has seen a "culture of success" develop among the incoming and continuing African-American male students.

So, when Logan was tapped to oversee the Chancellor's Leadership Corps, which are students who have demonstrated outstanding grades, service, and leadership in high school, he was delighted with this opportunity. However, the first year, those outstanding students didn't necessarily continue to perform at an outstanding level—only forty-eight percent retained their Chancellor's scholarship. Thinking they just hadn't selected the right students, Logan added a face-to-face interview. But they still didn't perform up to expectations. Hmm? Logan thought, why don't we treat these scholars as if they are at risk? So, using the same "I's," they brought the CLC students to campus one week early to teach them "how to be a college student" and required them to live on campus. They got "all up in their business," too. The results were again staggering: they doubled their retention rate to eighty-eight percent. Logan and team are now planning similar programs for African-American females and for Hispanic students.

With all that, you might forget that Dr. Logan Hampton is also *Reverend* Logan Hampton, pastor of Bullock Temple CME and current president of the Christian Ministerial Alliance. Through his church, he has supported Unity in the Community, a neighborhood effort to celebrate racial progress since the 1957 desegregation crisis at Central High School, which is just across the street from Bullock Temple. At the fiftieth Anniversary of the crisis, in 2007, a time capsule was constructed to hold items that reflect our memories, ideals, and hopes about life in Little Rock. The time capsule will be opened again in 2057.

Logan Hampton says the most challenging leadership experience he has ever had was serving for three years as the chair of the State of Arkansas Daisy Gatson Bates Holiday Committee at the invitation of then-governor Mike Huckabee. Why so challenging? Logan explains that every person in our state claims the legacy of Daisy Bates in a very personal way, so there are many differing opinions about what is right and proper as we celebrate her impact. During his tenure, the task force held a Humanitarian Awards banquet and events across the state. Logan feels extremely grateful to those members of the Christian Ministerial Alliance who began the restoration of the Bates home, and at the same time he feels a great responsibility to continue their work of preserving the home and legacy for the future.

Like so many of us, Logan feels personally connected to Mrs. Bates in that he benefitted directly from her leadership for racial equality. He says, "I never attended a segregated school with inferior books or supplies. I personally owe Mrs. Bates."

Logan explains that his parents, Lena and Logan Sr., both taught at segregated schools in Parkin, Arkansas. When he and his sister were ready for first grade, however, their parents chose to send them to the integrated school because they felt it would give them better opportunities. The family soon moved to Pine Bluff, where Logan was a good student and outstanding in track and field. When it came time for college, Logan and his buddy Greg Sargent chose Arkansas Tech, a primarily white school in Russellville, mainly because the Track Coach Tim Rutledge just wouldn't take no for an answer. Logan says he had always had a sense of being black, but never did he embrace that racial and cultural heritage as much as he did in college where he pledged a fraternity and held campus-wide leadership positions. Since graduation, Logan has earned additional degrees and has worked with students at universities in Louisiana, Texas, and Arkansas. He has been a pastor since 1982.

Logan has a clear sense of his personal mission today. As a Christian minister and educator, he believes that it is our responsibility to be intentional about leading the conversation that begins with, "God loves you, and I love you. Now how can we best celebrate, appreciate, and embrace each other, particularly those who are not just like us?" Maybe we can start by more intentionally connecting with one another— getting a little more "up in each other's business."

Dr. Sybil Jordan Hampton
Humanitarian Award, 2002

Sybil Jordan Hampton is quick to credit her family and her high school minister, Reverend Rufus K. Young Sr., with building her self-confidence and nurturing the determination that was required for her to be a trailblazer as one of the first African-American students to attend Central High School. She was, in fact, the first black Central graduate to have attended tenth, eleventh, and twelfth grades. She recalls, "I never had a (white) student talk to me in three years. It was very, very hard." In high school, she chose to be calm so that she wouldn't reinforce negative stereotypes. In 2002, that aura of calmness still surrounds Sybil Hampton as she leads one of the premier philanthropic institutions of our state and nation, the Winthrop Rockefeller Foundation.

Sybil earned her bachelor's degree in English literature from Earlham College in Indiana, a master's degree in elementary education at the University of Chicago, and a master's degree and her doctorate from the Teachers College, Columbia University in New York City.

Sybil has had a distinguished career in education, serving in leadership roles at Southwestern University in Georgetown, Texas; at the University of Wisconsin-Madison; and at the School of Arts and Science at Iona College in New Rochelle, New York. In addition, she served as Contributions Manager-Education and Culture at GTE in Stamford, Connecticut.

Sybil was named in Arkansas Business Top 100 Women in Arkansas 1997, 1998, and 1999; she won the Earlham College Outstanding Alumni Award in 1998; she was named Woman of Achievement at Iona College in 1986; and she was included in *Who's*

Who Among Black Americans in 1980–81 and 1985–86. These are just some of her many honors.

Sybil has made a long journey and has proven that "You CAN come home again" with honor and prestige to begin making a remarkable contribution to the lives and welfare of many Arkansans and others through her leadership of the Winthrop Rockefeller Foundation.

Sybil is married to Alfred Hampton and has one brother, Leslie W. Jordan, Jr.

Mrs. Richard B. Hardie
Humanitarian Award, 1978
(1926–1983)

UALR Professor, Wife of Pastor, Dies at Age 57
Reprinted with permission from the Arkansas Democrat-Gazette

Mrs. Katherine Johnson (Kackie) Hardie, aged fifty-seven of 208 Schoolwood Lane, assistant professor at the University of Arkansas at Little Rock, died Friday. She was the wife of Reverend Richard B. Hardie Jr., pastor of Westover Hills Presbyterian Church.

Mrs. Hardie joined the faculty of UALR, then Little Rock University, in 1964 and was instrumental in establishing its anthropology program. She was the first instructor at the school to be named an associate of the Danforth Foundation, in 1970-71, and received a stipend for research to improve student-teacher relationships on a commuter college campus. She later served on the Danforth Advisory Board.

She also received two Donaghey Foundation grants for anthropology and archeology, as well as a grant from the National Science Foundation to do graduate work in anthropology at the University of Colorado.

Shared Award

In 1978, she and her husband received the Brotherhood Award of the Arkansas chapter of the National Conference of Christians and Jews. The award recognized the Hardies' "total community contributions," which included a long association with the Civil Rights Movement. In

1957, the Hardies, as well as the Westover Hills Presbyterian Church governing body, had stood publicly for peaceful school desegregation.

In the early days of statewide school desegregation, Mrs. Hardie was a consultant for the desegregation institutes that were sponsored by the federal Health, Education and Welfare Department for public school teachers.

Mrs. Hardie received her bachelor's degree from Centenary College at Shreveport and a master's degree in Bible studies from Presbyterian School of Christian Education at Richmond, Virginia. She did postgraduate studies in comparative African cultures with the University of California.

Before becoming a college teacher, she had worked as an educational consultant for the Presbyterian Church, leading training sessions for the teachers of children's classes and writing educational materials. At Westover Hills Church, she had once served as church secretary and led Bible study groups.

She also had served on the Common Cause advisory board.

Mrs. Hardie was born in Little Rock, daughter of Mrs. Kitty Sneed Johnson and the late William Johnson. Her mother now lives in Shreveport. Other survivors are a son, Richard B. Hardie III of San Jose, Costa Rica; two daughters, Kathleen Hardie-Stenger of Redding, California, and Elizabeth Hardie James of Yosemite National Park, California; a sister, Arline J. Taylor of Charlotte, North Carolina; and a grandson.

Reverend Richard B. Hardie Jr.

Humanitarian Award, 1978
(1922–2011)
Reprinted with permission from Reubel Funeral Home

Richard Bladworth Hardie Jr., Pastor
Emeritus, Westover Hills Presbyterian
Church and prominent civil rights leader in
the 1960s, died Tuesday, November 29 at
Presbyterian Village in Little Rock, AR at
the age of eighty-nine. "Preacher Dick," as
he was called with affection by three generations of parishioners, was born in Dallas,
Texas, in 1922 to Mr. and Mrs. Richard
Bladworth Hardie Sr. After graduating from Austin College, Sherman,
Texas, he served as an officer in the U.S. Navy during World War II. He
attended Union Seminary in Richmond, Virginia, where he obtained
his theology degree and met his first wife, Mary Katherine "Kackie"
Johnson. They moved to Little Rock in 1949 when Dr. Hardie became
the first minister of Westover Hills Presbyterian Church. He served as
pastor there for thirty-six years, during which time it became Little Rock's
second largest Presbyterian congregation. He received an honorary doctor of divinity degree from Arkansas College (now Lyon College) at
Batesville in 1962.

One of Dr. Hardie's proudest moments came in 1957 when his
congregation's deacons bought the back page of the *Arkansas Gazette* in
order to call the city to orderly compliance with the order of the federal
government to integrate Little Rock Schools and to oppose the closing
of the schools by then-governor Faubus. *Life* magazine ran a picture of
his entreaty to his congregation to support desegregation of the schools.

In 1964, Dr. Hardie marched for civil rights with Dr. Martin
Luther King Jr. in Montgomery, Alabama. That same year, he and his

wife hosted a breakfast meeting of black and white leaders in their home, which led to the formation of the Little Rock Council on Human Relations. Also in 1964, the British Broadcasting Corporation produced a television program on Dr. Hardie and his family as part of a series that profiled the lives of individual Americans, in which his stance on civil rights figured prominently.

In 1978, Dr. and Mrs. Hardie received the Brotherhood Award of the Arkansas chapter of the National Conference of Christians and Jews. The award recognized the Hardies' "total community contributions," which included a long association with the Civil Rights Movement. In 1981, Dr. Hardie was one of the plaintiffs in the case against a law passed in Arkansas that mandated the teaching of creationism in public schools whenever the theory of evolution was discussed. The law was struck down in a 1982 ruling as a violation of the constitutional doctrine of separation of church and state.

Throughout his long life of service, Dr. Hardie served as moderator of the Synod of Arkansas, a trustee of Montreat Association and Montreat College, and a member of the denomination's General Assembly Committee on Evangelism. He was a past chairman of the Arkansas Tuberculosis Association and was a member of the board of numerous community agencies, including the Arthritis Foundation, Arkansas Mental Health Association, American Red Cross, Urban League of Arkansas, Salvation Army, Pulaski County Council on Aging, National Conference of Christians and Jews (now Just Communities of Arkansas), Arkansas Council of Churches (now Arkansas Conferences of Churches and Synagogues), Stewpot, Regional Aids Interfaith Network, and the Arkansas Alcoholic Council.

In addition to his commitment to civil rights and community service, Dr. Hardie was known and respected as a devoted scholar. A program that he established during his tenure as minister at Westover Hills arranged for national and international biblical scholars and theologians to lead the annual Cotham Lectures at Westover Hills and to speak at public schools. During his active years in the ministry he continued his own studies at St. Andrews Institute, St. Andrews, Scotland; Divinity School of The Pacific, Berkley, California; and Vancouver School of Theology, Vancouver, British Columbia.

In 1984, after the death of his first wife, Dr. Hardie married Carolyn Cole McEwen. In 1985, Preacher Dick retired from Westover Hills and completed his term as elected moderator of his denomination's Presbytery of Arkansas. The following six years, Dr. Hardie served as Director of Church Relations for Austin College, Sherman Texas.

In 1991, the Hardies fulfilled a life-long dream of his and traveled to Scotland for six months where he served as a volunteer Associate Minister at St. Mary's Parish Church in Dumfries, Scotland. On their return home, Dr. Hardie served as an interim pastor at First Presbyterian Church, Little Rock; Park Hill Presbyterian Church, North Little Rock; St. Andrews Presbyterian Church, Little Rock; and various other Presbyterian churches throughout the state.

In 2004, the Little Rock Board of Directors approved a resolution to rename a portion of Kavanaugh Blvd. in honor of Dr. Hardie. In their letter to the city, church members noted, "As a leader in building community relations, he sought to create an environment in which people of faith, who were white or African-American, Christian or Jew could live in peace and harmony. His goal at all times has been to bring people together in mutual respect and understanding, but he has never lost sight of what is fair and just." That renamed portion of Kavanaugh Boulevard is now Richard B. Hardie Drive.

Dr. Hardie is survived by his wife of twenty-seven years, Carolyn; his children, Richard B. Hardie III and Celeste White; Kathleen Hardie and Joseph Stenger, their children Bret and Patrick, and his wife, Becky, and daughter Arabel; Elizabeth and Ted James, their children Will and Katherine. He is also survived by Ellen McEwen, her children Josh Minter, Jesse Minter and wife, Rachelle; Debbie Cooper; Melissa and Tim Stillings and children Haley and Gregory; Matthew and Mandy

McEwen, their children Peyton and Sydney; his sister Mary Frances Martin and her husband, Bill; his sister-in-law Annette Watson and her husband, Terry; his brother-in-law Jerry Cole and his wife, Beverly; his sister-in-laws Arline Taylor and Margery Johnson, as well as many beloved nieces and nephews.

Joyce Hardy
Father Joseph H. Biltz Award, 2011

Ask Joyce Hardy's friends to describe her in one word, and you will hear this list: consistent, loyal, dedicated, caring, faithful, passionate, and creative.

It all started when Joyce was raised in that bastion of political liberalism during the 1950s and '60s, Pryor, Oklahoma. (Who knew?) Joyce thought all were like her family, attending political rallies every weekend where she and her sister would sing candidate jingles, or discussing issues around the dinner table with her parents, Reba and Dale Hardy. She is also grateful to her aunt Rosemary Hardy, an English teacher who recommended that she read books such as *Catcher in the Rye* and *A Separate Peace*. Joyce doesn't remember any African Americans in Pryor, or any Republicans for that matter. Questions of race in Pryor centered around whether you were three-quarters or full-blood Cherokee, because everyone was "part" Cherokee.

But somehow, Joyce knew that the Lion's Club annual minstrel show was inappropriate, particularly the year that Dr. Martin Luther King was killed. She remembers rushing to the rehearsal hall to tell them why they must not portray Dr. King in one of the skits. They listened and complied even though Joyce was only a high school student at the time. She was further sensitized to racial issues in college at the University of Arkansas when John Richardson became the first African American to join the Razorback football team, and there was a racially motivated shooting on campus. The anger of the black girls in her dorm was frightening, so Joyce asked if they could talk about it, building bridges even then.

She also witnessed firsthand the struggle for women's equal rights when her mother, Reba, a recent graduate of nursing school, couldn't get a bank loan without her husband as a co-signer. Dale Hardy visited the bank and mentioned that he might have to move his account, prompting them to change their policy and grant the loan to Reba.

Joyce was raised in the Methodist Church, but was drawn to a new church family in college by the Episcopal Chaplain, David Johnson, who led discussions regarding the war in Vietnam, and the fight for civil rights for blacks and women's equality. Together, they were trying to discover "Where is God in all these things?" She also joined the Associated Women Students and became an activist working particularly hard for passage of the Equal Rights Amendment for Women. There's a resigned smile on her face when she notes that we are still holding rallies to pass the ERA.

Like many women her age, Joyce's first career was teaching, which she loved. However, she found her real calling when she studied for and became a deacon in the Episcopal Church in 1985. She describes a deacon's role as "bringing the good news of Christ to the Community, and getting members out of the church and into the community." We see her doing just that with consistency, loyalty, dedication, caring, faithfulness, passion, and creativity. The list of her commitments is inspiring:

She has directed Summer Celebration, a program of arts and crafts, swimming, drama, sports, field trips, and cooking, to prevent drug use and gang involvement with at-risk youngsters.

She has served in various church roles, particularly youth and outreach ministry in Oklahoma and Arkansas, most recently at Christ Church here as coordinator of outreach. She also serves as archdeacon for the Episcopal Diocese of Arkansas and on the National Executive Committee for the Episcopal Peace Fellowship.

She has worked on passage of hate crimes legislation in Arkansas.

She has worked on equal rights for gays and lesbians, including opposition to ACT I, which prohibited adoption or foster parenting by GLBT individuals.

She has worked with the Arkansas Interfaith Alliance with the aim of reclaiming "what it means to be a person of faith."

She has lobbied to raise the minimum wage.

She helped establish the Harmony Health Clinic and has served as the volunteer coordinator there.

She has campaigned for the Employee Free Choice Act.

She has worked on behalf of the West Memphis Three.

She has served as director of the Arkansas No Kid Hungry Campaign with the Hunger Relief Alliance.

Oh too, she was at the Little Rock ERA Rally on May 7, 2011.

If Father Joseph Biltz were still around, we know he would be looking for Joyce Hardy to help him with whatever injustice he was fighting today. Former colleague and retired bishop Larry Maze says, "If I were poor, marginalized, or just out of luck, I would want Joyce Hardy on my side!"

If she could fix "just one thing," Joyce would create a place where all parties (on any side of any issue) could come together to talk and listen; not necessarily to agree; but to hear and respect each other. In the meantime, she celebrates every small victory.

Imam Johnny Aleem Hasan
Father Joseph H. Biltz Award, 2000

Imam means "leader," and that certainly describes Johnny Hasan.

Johnny presently serves as president of the Central Little Rock CDC—Community Development Corporation. Their current project is the hoped-for renovation of Westside Junior High into a community building of some sort. Westside has been vacant since 1984, and they see it as pivotal in revitalizing the neighborhood, possibly providing jobs, rental space, and space for social service organizations. They treasure Westside School as a significant historical landmark in the Central High neighborhood. (*In 2003, The Arc of Arkansas, an organization that provides services to individuals with developmental and physical disabilities, completed the renovation, and the building now contains forty-three loft apartments for people with and without disabilities. The auditorium/cafeteria part of the building has been converted into a children's medical clinic and office space for the University of Arkansas for Medical Sciences (UAMS). Westside is listed on the National Register of Historic Places.*)

The City of Little Rock has also formed a partnership with the CDC to build twelve new houses in the neighborhood to be sold to low-to-middle income families.

As a leader in the Islamic community, Johnny helped establish a prison ministry in 1978. Originally they established a proper Jumah Prayer Service every Friday in five prison units; by 2000, there are now Jumah Prayer Services in ten units, all led by volunteers under the leadership of prison coordinator Johnny Hasan.

One of the things that Johnny is most proud about it the establishment of DIGNITY—Doing in God's Name Incredible Things

Yourself. DIGNITY grew out of a request from Representative Bill Walker, whose mother lives in the neighborhood of the Islamic Center at 1717 Wright Avenue. She, along with other neighbors, was troubled by the drug activity there.

Members of DIGNITY formed a nightly patrol, and after only a few weeks, the drug activity was no longer a problem. They were not confrontational. Their theory was, "Our presence and our signs would run off the customers, and then the drug dealers would leave." That's exactly what happened. Young Muslim men were the first patrol members, and they were later joined by Christians and other groups.

One evening, their DIGNITY patrol was joined by then-governor Bill Clinton and his wife, Hillary. On another occasion, comedian Dick Gregory joined the group. The news media began to pay attention, and the DIGNITY program has since been replicated across the nation. As part of their efforts, they persuaded local grocery and variety-store chains to discontinue selling drug paraphernalia such as cigarette papers without tobacco.

Johnny was formerly the resident Imam at the Wright Avenue Mosque and currently serves on a National Mutual Consultation Body. And he has had many firsts.

For example, Johnny was the first faith leader to open the Arkansas State Senate with a prayer in a language other than English. He gave the opening prayer of the Qur'an in Arabic and then in English.

As a member of the NCCJ board of directors, he helped organize the first Christian-Muslim-Jewish dialogues in Central Arkansas.

Johnny was the first Muslim to participate in a presidential inauguration ceremony, when President Bill Clinton first took office in 1993.

And Johnny was the author of a letter that led to the Arkansas Conference of Churches and Synagogues changing its name to the Interfaith Conference.

Johnny's work and witness has indeed helped all Arkansans to understand the meaning and value of interfaith leadership.

Assalaam alaykum—Peace be upon you, Johnny Hasan.

Dr. Charles E. Hathaway III
Humanitarian Award, 2003

Since assuming the position of chancellor of the University of Arkansas at Little Rock in 1993, Charles Hathaway has made a remarkable impact on the university and the larger community.

Believing that a university must serve society in a direct and meaningful manner, Hathaway led a strategic planning effort, UALR 2000, designed to inform the university what the region expected of the institution in the future. The university continues to address the needs expressed in UALR 2000. In his tenure as chancellor, Hathaway eliminated more than $7 million in debt, steered UALR into a major technological presence in central Arkansas, and began numerous community-based programs.

Hathaway has also provided leadership as vice president for education on the board of the Arkansas Symphony and as the chair of the Arkansas Science and Technology Authority. He serves on the board of CARTI and previously chaired the board of the United Way of Pulaski County. This year, 2003, he has been recognized by the Office of Women in Higher Education for his efforts to advance women in the higher-education profession, and he received the Diamond Award from the Arkansas Public Relations Society for his use of the principles of public relations to enhance the image of our state.

Hathaway is proud of the advances that UALR has made in recent years, both on and off the campus. Notably, UALR today has a student body that is approximately one-third African-American, and minorities are routinely elected and chosen for positions of authority without notice, a sign of successful integration. The UALR Home Work Center, supported by Children International America, reaches out to children in need throughout Little Rock, while the American Humanics Program prepares undergraduates for careers in not-for-profit organizations. The Cyber College, with its information technology minor, is preparing a workforce that will serve Arkansas well into the twenty-first century.

Betty and Charles Hathaway have three grown children, Sarah, Steve, and Eric.

Honorable Brooks Hays

Humanitarian Award, 1964
(August 9, 1898–October 12, 1981)

Brooks Hays: A Baptist Treasure,
A testimonial by his "spiritual son"
by Warren I. Cikins, March 2006
Reprinted with permission from Mr. Cikins*

As one who had the great privilege of being associated with the Honorable Brooks Hays of Arkansas, congressman from 1943-1959 and Southern Baptist Convention president from 1957-1959, I am eager that the memory of this great man's contributions to American religious life and national public life not be forgotten. He often said that there was no limit to the good one could do in this world if one did not care who got the credit. I am afraid that people have too often taken him at his word and not given him credit for many of his great achievements. Some—through ignorance, prejudice, or just plain jealousy—have attempted to play down or even negate the significance of his achievements. Their judgment must not stand. I feel a deep moral obligation to try to the best of my ability to make sure that the record of past events, especially ones that I personally witnessed, is chronicled in an honest and forthright manner.

The philosopher John Dewey once said that history is man's recollection of what he would like to think happened in the past. That makes it all the more important that we challenge revisionist historians whose writings are designed to fit their pre-determined perspectives on the events they have chosen to write about. In setting the record straight, I hope to emulate Brooks Hays, who often quoted Paul as saying "one should speak the truth in love" (Ephesians 4:15), however difficult that may be in certain circumstances.

When I first met Hays as a twenty-five-year-old Jewish Harvard graduate from Boston, he had hired me for six months to be his legislative assistant to research many important national matters. It was immediately obvious that he was a profoundly religious Southern Baptist who, while deeply grounded in his faith, recognized the need to keep church and state very much separated. That did not mean that he believed one in public life should not be concerned about the welfare of all citizens of whatever walk of life or status in life they occupied. This commitment was demonstrated in a book he wrote in 1958 while he was president of the Southern Baptist Convention, published by Broadman Press, titled *This World: A Christian's Workshop*. In this book he demonstrates how an elected official can apply his deep religious convictions in helping solve national problems without violations of the separation of church and state.

I came to observe in Brooks Hays a personality and a style of living that made all those around him take notice of his presence and his innate humanity and modesty. His wife, Marion, said that "Brooks loves everybody; he even loves some of my relatives that I can't stand." It was obvious that all his colleagues in the Congress—Democrats and Republicans, liberals and conservatives alike—had the greatest respect and affection for him. It was because of this respect for him that the Congress voted to support his recommendation to create a prayer room in the U.S. Capitol for members of Congress of all faiths to use to seek spiritual guidance. He was the essence of kindness and gentility, of civility and moderation. Here again he often quoted Paul, who called on all of us to "let thy moderation be known to all persons" (Philippians 4:5).

The extent of Brooks Hays's depth of knowledge and understanding of the chapter and verse of the Bible, both Old and New Testaments, was awesome indeed (as I could tell from my earlier rabbinical training on the Old Testament). Consistent with his general demeanor, he reflected this scholarship in such a low-key way that all persons, of whatever class or educational status, felt quite comfortable in listening to the many sermons he delivered.

The Lord granted him outstanding oratorical skills that he used to remarkable effect, mixing theology with gentle humor that had significant relevance. He used these talents to co-author a book in 1963 titled *The Baptist Way of Life*, which he inscribed to me as "my spiritual son on all non-Baptist matters." He recognized that he had no monopoly on righteousness and that others who disagreed with him might have more than a little validity to their viewpoints. As he saw it, it was the combined perspectives of all religious persons that would lead us to divine truths. As both a political leader and a religious leader, he felt an obligation to lead his brethren to help find those truths. Nonetheless, he often cited Edmund Burke, a British philosopher, who said that a leader must exercise his conscience and his judgment, but he must not get so far ahead of the views of those he is attempting to lead that he breaks the bond that ties him to them. I treasure a theological discussion I had with him when we could not agree, and I said I would ask the Messiah when He comes which of us is right. He agreed to that procedure but requested that I ask Him first, "Haven't you been here before?"

Brooks Hays once quoted one of the greatest Baptists, Roger Williams (1604–83), who founded the First Baptist Church in America in 1638, and commented on one of his trips back to England (as paraphrased by Hays), "On this boat returning to England, there are men and women of diverse views; we have Protestants and Catholics and Jewish adherents and a small number of Moslems, and the composite should give us assurance, since each has captured an important truth and I feel safer with the cross-section of religious devotion."

The city of Little Rock became a center of racial strife in the mid-1950s, and Congressman Hays felt he must try to find middle ground so that blacks and whites could live in peace and harmony. Attempting to bring the two sides together in a manner that both could be comfortable with turned out to be a formidable task. No other public official in

Arkansas was willing to be a peacemaker between Governor Orval E. Faubus and President Dwight D. Eisenhower, and people asked Hays why he was willing to undertake such a dangerous task. Hays answered simply, "I can do no other." When Governor Faubus decided to fan the flames of racial hatred, he distanced himself from Hays and later engineered Hays's defeat in the next election. President Eisenhower admired Hays, even though Hays had supported Adlai Stevenson, and offered him any job in his administration he wanted. When Hays said he wanted to stay in his beloved South, Eisenhower named him to the board of the Tennessee Valley Authority. Later when John Kennedy was elected president, he brought Hays to the White House, and said to him, "If I write a sequel to *Profiles in Courage*, you will be Chapter One." At this time Bill Moyers, who had first met Hays when he was ordained a Baptist minister and accepted Hays's advice to work for Lyndon Johnson as a "ministry of public service," said of Hays, "Brooks's courageous stand during the 1958 school desegregation crisis cost him his seat as congressman from Little Rock, but it won for him a place in legions of hearts."

After Hays's political career had ended, he spent his remaining years lecturing at several universities and preaching at many churches, with no diminution of his spiritual fervor. His proudest achievement was the establishment of the Ecumenical Institute at Wake Forest University in Winston-Salem, North Carolina. President Ralph Scales asked him to undertake this venture, and he threw himself into it with great energy and dedication. Building bridges between different faiths was a mission he was destined to do. Back in 1963, he visited the remarkable Pope John XXIII, who greeted him as a brother in Christ, the first Catholic-Baptist exchange in many years. Until he died in 1981, he organized many ecumenical conferences not only at Wake Forest but also in many places throughout the country. As I say in my memoirs titled *In Search of Middle Ground*, published in 2005, "Brooks Hays became referred to as an 'ecumaniac,' dedicated to a course of religious outreach consistent with his profound Baptist roots." I call on the many people of all faiths whose lives were touched by Brooks Hays to join with me in ensuring that his memory is given proper reverence, even though he himself never sought such recognition.

*During his fifty-year career in Washington, Warren I. Cikins has served three members of Congress, two presidents and two Supreme Court justices and was a senior staff member of the Brookings Institution. He recently published In Search of Middle Ground: Memoirs of a Washington Insider (Devora Pub., Jerusalem/N.Y. 2005).

J. N. Heiskell
Humanitarian Award, 1971
(1872–1972)

J. N. Heiskell's Heritage
Editorial, December 29, 1972
Reprinted with permission from the Arkansas Democrat-Gazette

The *Arkansas Gazette* traces its history back over 153 years and through a long succession of editors but from the turn of the century there was one man more than any other who left the stamp of his life and personality upon this newspaper. He was John Netherland Heiskell, editor since 1902, who died yesterday eight weeks after observing his 100th birthday.

Mr. Heiskell's life spanned a century, but his very editorship of the *Gazette* spanned seven decades. In a real sense, then, the *Gazette* of the twentieth century has been J. N. Heiskell's. Upon this newspaper he lavished his energies, his gifts, his principles—even his love—and so it is that his death brings sorrow to all of us who have worked with him on the *Gazette*, and who must now bid him hail and farewell.

The sense of loss we feel in the *Gazette* family is shared widely across the state, we know, because of the legend that J. N. Heiskell built in Arkansas. Yet his intimate identification with the state that he adopted in 1902 might possibly obscure, for Arkansans, the larger identification that he had in the South and nationally.

It is only in perspective that we would observe that J. N. Heiskell was one of the great figures in Southern journalism. The recent outpouring of expression on the occasion of his 100th birthday celebration was, in itself, reminder of the recognition that he had earned in his region and his country. Mr. Heiskell made his imprint on his time and place in much the same way that Henry Watterson, Ralph McGill, and Hodding Carter, among others, had made theirs. He was, for one thing, one of the last of the breed of those who fashioned the era of personal journalism.

Certainly he was not a "personal journalist" in the style of a Bertie McCromick, or even of Watterson's famous ego. Indeed, J. N. Heiskell was a man of restraint, and in certain ways he was even self effacing. Nevertheless, he fashioned the *Gazette*'s image. Its style and typography, its principles, its goals, after his own image. He sought to achieve in the *Gazette* a dignity of manner, an elegance of style in writing, a courage of purpose, a relentless concern with accuracy—which is to say with truth. In this way he sought to build the *Gazette* after his own personality and convictions.

Clearly the honors bestowed upon him testified to the success of his work and his ambition. The *Gazette* won two Pulitzer prizes in the school crisis of 1957, when Mr. Heiskell put his newspaper on the line in support of the rule of law. He received personally the Elijah Lovejoy and John Peter Zenger awards, among others; he also won special recognition from Sigma Delta Chi, the journalism fraternity (which designated the *Gazette* as a historical site), and from the University of Missouri's School of Journalism.

Certainly the passing of J. N. Heiskell is a milestone in the history of Arkansas. The state bears enduring imprint deriving from his pen (especially his editorials on public affairs), from his guidance of news and editorial policy; and from his tutelage of other Arkansas newspapermen (as well as the *Gazette* "alumni" who work everywhere in the country). From his editorial office in the *Gazette* building in Little Rock, his personality reached out through his newspaper into every corner of the state.

It is doubtful if any of his Southern contemporaries brought up and trained so many editors and reporters; certainly none trained so many under such rigorous reputation in the newspaper business for his defense of the English language against the ungrammatical and the trite;

he was a deadly foe of the cliché, and heaven's own protection was needed by the editorial writer who resorted to journalese or other venerable popular expression when his own words failed him.

His own style of writing was spare, even lean, and he was ever engaged in combat with his editors to pare the dimensions of their imperishable prose. His sense of humor was legendary, both in the editorial paragraphs which he wrote long after they were out of fashion in the newspaper business and in his celebrated irreverent remarks to associates and employees. He had a tremendous sense of history, which expressed itself both editorially and in his endowments for state historical purposes. He was, on occasion, prescient; early on, he recognized the Vietnam War as a historical blunder of such proportion that it would bar Lyndon Johnson, he once remarked, from re-election to another full term. J. N. Heiskell was an aristocrat, in his quiet way; a man of proud and distinguished ancestry, he was ever mindful that the continuity of a great family and a great institution depends on rededication in every generation.

Mr. Heiskell's success and recognition derived from his deep understanding of the newspaper's dual responsibility, which is to present a comprehensive, well-written news report, with background in depth, and to offer as well its own views separately in a stout editorial voice. He was dedicated to exacting, indispensable standards of excellence in the publication of his newspaper but he was equally dedicated to the responsibility of the newspaper to take its stand on great issues. He had the inner resources of courage and principle that were needed so desperately in the crisis of 1957, when historic forces of unreason unleashed themselves upon Little Rock. It was Mr. Heiskell's greatest trial as an editor and it was his finest hour, one which has been related in many forums.

In summing up the life of John Netherland Heiskell, certainly it may be said that he lived it in the full measure. He won a broad sweep of national honors in his editorship; he reached his 100th birthday and presided over the occasion in the midst of his family and amid a great outpouring of well wishes and congratulation. But what was worth most was his work over seven decades building a private institution for public services, under tight standards of performance and principle. It is a heritage of worth to his state and country, and a heritage for which, more than incidentally, all of us who work for the *Arkansas Gazette* may be proud.

Bishop Kenneth W. Hicks
Father Joseph H. Biltz Award, 2004

In his work for social justice, retired Bishop Kenneth W. Hicks has shared the podium with the likes of Senator Edward Kennedy, Senator Paul Simon, and the Reverend Jesse Jackson.

In his own words, Ken has said, "I've realized we're not going to change the world, but if we can change ourselves, we will make a positive difference. To foster peace and justice, we must keep the vocabulary of peace alive. We must continue to say the words that help lift up peace both here and around the world."

Ken was born in Iola, Kansas, and after farming, working in an airplane factory, and being turned down for the army because of flat feet, he felt a calling to the ministry. He served United Methodist churches in Colorado and Nebraska and was elected Bishop in 1976. He served as Bishop of Arkansas for eight years, and for Kansas for eight years until his retirement back to Arkansas in 1992.

Throughout his ministry, he was a social activist concerned not only with the plight of Americans but also with injustice around the globe. His leadership and service have been recognized many times, and in 1987, when he received the Distinguished Alumnus Award from Iliff School of Theology, it was said, "Bishop Hicks has distinguished himself as a pastor, as an advocate of peace and justice, as an intellectual, as a champion of the church's missions and as an administrator of competence and compassion."

One of the most striking things about Ken is his humility. If you were just chatting with him, you'd probably never dream that he has visited Third World countries to fight for justice in dangerous circumstances and walked with some of the most powerful leaders in the United States.

When asked what he considers special in his life of service, Ken remembers his involvement in the Arkansas creation science trial in 1981. As the executive of the Methodist Denomination, he was the lead witness in the trial. One of his lessons learned was the importance of responsible citizens being vigilant.

Since his retirement, Ken has continued to be vigilant and to serve with organizations such as Arkansas Advocates for Children and Families (AACF), Arkansas Friends for Better Schools, Governor's Partnership Council for Children and Families, among several others. He continues to be a voice that urges, coaxes, and inspires us to care about each other.

Ken is married to Elaine; they have two daughters and two grandchildren. His teenage granddaughter Kiley recently received a Volunteer of the Year award from the Capra Foundation in Topeka, Kansas, for her work with children with disabilities. Caring is obviously a Hicks family value.

Dr. Fitz Hill
Humanitarian Award, 2012

Fitz Hill believes in destiny, faith, and justice. His life proves that. In 2006, when Dr.
Hill came to Arkansas Baptist College, it is
believed that there were between 150 and
175 students. No one knows for sure exactly
how many students were attending because
the records were poorly kept. In the fall of
2011, there were exactly 1,193 students enrolled. That's the difference that Fitz Hill
has made at ABC.

Fitz's faith in God led him to serve at Arkansas Baptist College,
and Fitz is quick to share the credit for his success with others, such as
Little Rock Mayor Mark Stodola and City Manager Bruce Moore, the
Neighborhood Association leaders and the neighbors themselves, the
Cooperative Baptist Fellowship, the Nehemiah Network, the New Life
Church, ABC's Board of Trustees, as well as other churches in Arkansas
and across the U.S., particularly congregations affiliated with the
Consolidated Missionary Baptist Convention of Arkansas. Under Fitz's
leadership, Arkansas Baptist is truly living out its mission to "prepare
students for a life of service grounded in academic scholarship, the liberal arts tradition, social responsibility, Christian development, and
preparation for employment in a global community."

Arkansas Baptist was founded in 1884, primarily to educate former
slaves and to train ministers. When Fitz first saw the campus in 2006,
its oldest building was boarded up and considered by most to be hopelessly beyond repair. In 2010, Old Main was reopened with busy classrooms, offices, and chapel services. Today, Old Main stands as a symbol
of ABC's dedication to serve those who are traditionally left out of the
educational process.

Fitz was a successful recruiter in his former sports career, and now he applies his talent for recruiting to students. He routinely visits communities where most colleges wouldn't bother to look, seeking students with potential. Fitz brings them to Arkansas Baptist, where he leads a faculty and staff committed to nurturing these mostly first-generation college students until they can earn their degrees. The secret of student success at ABC? Caring faculty with high expectations, an academically and professionally integrated curriculum, and a safety net of student services, along with opportunities for students to serve their greater community. Fitz says that new buildings or sports programs might get the students to ABC, but the caring faculty keeps them there.

It was destiny rather than intention that led Fitz to become president of Arkansas Baptist College. He helped develop the Delta Classic, where two HBCU (historically black college or university) teams play a football game to raise money for literacy programs. The Delta Classic has been wildly successful in its mission. As Fitz says, 30,000 people don't attend a chemistry lecture, but a football game is something else. When he called on the ABC trustees in 2006 to ask for their support of the Delta Classic, they turned the tables by asking him to become the thirteenth president of Arkansas Baptist. He was reluctant to accept their offer; he had never even seen the campus. When he drove by the dilapidated buildings the next day, he was even more reluctant. But in the end, he felt God was calling him to this position, and his family was ready to move home to Arkansas from San Jose, California, where Fitz was head coach of the San Jose State University Spartans for four years, from 2001 to 2004.

Now, not only has Arkansas Baptist College begun to thrive, the entire neighborhood has a new look and a new vibrancy. For example, the car wash near the campus, which had thirty-six police calls in 2006, was bought by the college and re-named "Auto Baptism," and students learn business skills there. In addition, the college purchased and renovated a nearby produce market, remodeled Yancey's Cafeteria, and is developing aquaculture to increase the availability of nutritious food in what was once labeled a "food desert." Childcare is available on campus, and a Kids First primary healthcare facility is planned.

ABC students have a chance to give back to the community in programs such as OK (Our Kids), where college students work with police officers to mentor middle and high school students. Starting at Central and Dunbar, officers and Arkansas Baptist students now also work with Hall, Forest Heights, and Jacksonville High Schools.

Fitz says that you can't break the cycle of poverty or low achievement overnight, but surely Fitz Hill is doing his part. We are fortunate that Fitz and his wife, Cynthia, along with their children, Destiny, Faith, and Justice, have come back to Arkansas.

Ted Holder
Father Joseph H. Biltz Award, 2009

Ted Holder is an attorney with the Arkansas Securities Department; a historic preservationist who has rehabilitated three homes in Little Rock's Quapaw Quarter; a tree-hugger and the current president of Tree Streets, an organization that plants trees in the oldest part of Little Rock; a faithful Episcopalian; a collector of fine art; and he's gay. His work for equal rights for gays and lesbians highlights one of the biggest risks for gay persons—that they, themselves, and others, tend to define them based solely on their sexuality rather than any other attribute. That's just one of the things Ted has struggled to change.

When Ted first began to come to terms with his own sexuality in his early thirties, he found an underground gay culture that was anonymous in most every way. Unsatisfied with a dual existence, Ted decided to work to change things. His first step was to work at accepting himself, systematically coming out to family, friends, and colleagues, telling others who he really was. He knew he couldn't feel good about himself until he quit hiding from others. He did not want to lead two lives, a secret gay one and a public heterosexual one.

As he began his "coming-out" journey in 1990, he worried that he would lose his ten-year position with the Attorney General's office. With great nervousness and even fear, Ted came out to his boss, then Attorney General Steve Clark. Clark was accepting, and Ted didn't lose his job. Not every gay, lesbian, bi-sexual, or transgender person is so lucky, because, shamefully, in Arkansas, a person can be fired simply for being homosexual.

Ted was one of the founders of the Arkansas Gay & Lesbian Task Force in the mid-'80s. At that time, many members were still afraid to have their full names printed in light of possible repercussions. Despite the fear, the Task Force accomplished some amazing things. Ted was editor of their newsletter, *Triangle Rising*, and served as president in the early '90s.

Two of the significant Task Force accomplishments include: organizing witnesses for three sessions of the Arkansas legislature to testify in support of then State Senator Vic Snyder's bills to repeal the sodomy law, and leading 200 Arkansans in April of 1993 to the March on Washington for gay rights, where they also met with staff members of Bumpers, Pryor, and Thornton.

The Task Force established four important programs: the newsletter, which was distributed to over 1,500 people a month; a youth support program that still operates today as PALS, supporting teens who are gay, lesbian, bi-sexual, transgender, or questioning; a gay and lesbian switchboard that took calls for information and help; and a radio show on KABF. These outreach communications were vital in the pre-Internet days, when youth and adults alike had little access to good information, particularly about sexuality. Through his work with the Gay & Lesbian Task Force, Ted became known by some of the local and national media and often was their source for comments when a gay news story was being written or reported. He and his partner, Joe van den Heuvel, even broke onto the international scene when they were interviewed and filmed in their home by a Japanese television crew during Bill Clinton's first run for the White House.

In 1994, Ted helped found Integrity/Arkansas, a chapter of the long-standing Episcopalian organization seeking full inclusion of gays and lesbians within the denomination. Often the convener, in 1997, Ted helped bring Gene Robinson, who went on to become the first openly gay Episcopal bishop, to Little Rock for a diocesan-wide conference on gay and lesbian issues. In 1998, he helped arrange the visit of the celebrated Bishop and author John Shelby Spong to Little Rock for an integrity conference. Although Bishop Spong was unable to attend due to illness, his wife took his place, and it was a great success.

Ted was involved with NCCJ at Camp Anytown the year that homophobia was first addressed along with the other prejudices. Today, Ted is a panelist for JCA's Straight Talk program in which gays, lesbians, family members, and friends tell their story about what it means to be gay in Arkansas. Panel members answer questions with "straight information" from their own experience to promote understanding about gay issues and concerns.

What has been most important for Ted? The blessing of his eighteen-year partnership with Joe in a ceremony at St. Michael's Episcopal Church on September 6, 2006. Ted and Joe appreciate the unwavering support of the Reverend Ed Wills and the congregation of St. Michael's Episcopal Church and the then bishop, the Right Reverend Larry E. Maze. Ted and Joe were subsequently married in City Hall in San Francisco, California, on August 27, 2008. Their framed marriage license hangs among their important works of art in their Quapaw Quarter home.

Over the past two decades, there have been some successes but many disappointments for those who have sought full inclusion of gays and lesbians in the fabric of society. Ted explains that although he knows that things are better now, it has not been a steady rise in acceptance of gays and lesbians. However, Ted has come to the conclusion that the most important thing he can do to further his cause is to live his life as though the change he seeks has already happened, to live openly, as a gay man, to be a witness for all, gay and straight. There is no doubt that Ted has been a witness to each of us about what one person, living with integrity, can mean to all of us.

Colette Honorable
Humanitarian Award, 2013

Colette Honorable takes her work as chair of the Arkansas Public Service Commission very seriously. After all, each decision the PSC makes ultimately affects every Arkansan through the utility rates, safety, and reliability of our public services such as electricity, telephone, and natural gas. Even before her appointment to the PSC, in 2007, Colette used each of her jobs to help others.

Colette and her twin sister, Coleen, were the youngest of five children born to Wallace and Joyce Dodson. The family lived in Los Angeles until her parents divorced, at which point Joyce Dodson moved with the children back to Arkansas, where Colette and Coleen entered second grade at Levy Elementary School. Joyce Dodson had dropped out of cosmetology school to marry, so things for their family changed radically when she became a single mother supporting five children. Joyce found a job in maintenance at the Federal Building. Years later, Colette would serve as an attorney in the same courtrooms that her mother had once cleaned.

Despite their struggles, Colette says it was a blessing to come back to Arkansas, where she was surrounded by her extended family. Their next-door neighbor, Dr. Margaret Scheer, a professor of biology and zoology at Philander Smith College, became a godmother to Colette and Coleen. Mrs. Scheer was widowed and her children lived out of state, so she had the time to teach Colette how to knit, crochet, and do macramé. The children also attended church with Mrs. Scheer at Trinity Lutheran, where they participated in the choir and served as acolytes. Colette remembers spending hours in Mrs. Scheer's library, helping in her garden, and traveling with her to visit her daughter once. Mrs.

Scheer, who was white, introduced the two of them (with their French-braided hair) as her girls, and they got some puzzled looks.

Colette knew from her mother's experience that it was important for her to do well in school and to get a college degree. She was especially interested in business, and she credits her Central High School business teachers, Eula Willis, Jewell Peyton, and Wanda Baskins, with helping her excel. In addition, then-vice principal Othello Faison took a special interest in her. Colette remembers being called to Mrs. Faison's office more than once, and wondering if she was in trouble each time. She wasn't. Instead, Mrs. Faison would ask such things as, "How are you doing in your classes? Have you chosen a college yet? Have you applied for any scholarships?" Colette lived up to the high expectations of her teachers, and she even served as president of the Future Business Leaders club and as president of the senior class.

Colette attended Memphis State University (now the University of Memphis) to study business, but an elective course in criminal justice ignited her passion to work for creating justice herself. Following her graduation, she returned to earn her juris doctorate degree from the University of Arkansas at Little Rock School of Law. With that accomplished, Colette married her high-school sweetheart, Rickey Honorable, and went to work.

Her first job after law school was as staff attorney for the Center for Arkansas Legal Services, where she represented indigent clients in a variety of non-criminal matters. There she became even more adamant that every person and every family deserves the best representation. When she moved on to clerk for Arkansas Court of Appeals Judge Wendell Griffen, she appreciated that he shared her social concerns. In Colette's words, "Some judges just call balls and strikes. Judge Griffen was not one of those." Next, Colette served as an assistant public defender in Jefferson County, where she worked on theft, robbery, rape, and murder cases. Even though many of her clients were guilty of serious crimes, Colette still remembered her oath "to defend the defenseless." She loved her job, but, understandably, she also found it very stressful.

One day she ran into Mark Pryor, who was running for the office of Arkansas Attorney General at the time. She boldly said, "I know you are going to win your race, and I want to work for you." After the election, Attorney General Pryor hired Colette to work in consumer affairs, and she continued in her advocacy role there when Mike Beebe became the next attorney general. Ultimately, Beebe tapped her to serve as his chief of staff in the AG's office. After Mike Beebe became governor, Colette spent almost a year as head of the Arkansas Workforce Investment Board, until Governor Beebe appointed her to the PSC in 2007, designating her as chair in January 2011.

Colette has loved each job she has held, and each one has afforded her the chance to create opportunity and justice for others. Colette relishes her role on the PSC for the same reasons. In a constantly changing energy environment, the PSC has a clear mission: to deliver energy to every citizen in the state that is safe, affordable, and reliable. Most of us only worry about whether the lights come on each morning, but Colette worries about a whole lot more. She adds that if the average person is not worried, then the PSC is doing its job.

Colette's expertise has been recognized by others who have elected her as first vice president of the National Association of Regulatory Utility Commissioners. She also serves on several national committees and task forces, including the Bipartisan Policy Center's Energy Project policy board which issued reports and recommendations to congress in January 2013. Some of the important challenges, according to Colette, are conservation, infrastructure investment and how those costs will be passed on, innovation in our delivery systems, and cleaner sources of energy.

Colette also finds time to be an active volunteer, serving as a mentor through her church, St. Mark Baptist, and through the law school. In 2004, she chaired a statewide non-partisan election protection drive, and Arkansas's initiative was recognized nationally as a "Best Effort" in making sure that no eligible voter was disenfranchised. Colette takes every opportunity to read to children in schools or to visit classes to talk about career possibilities. When Colette had just finished college, someone said to her, "Come back home to Arkansas; we need you." And she often says that to other young people today. Her community board service has included the graduate chapter of Alpha Kappa Alpha, Arkansas Advocates for Children and Families, Positive Atmosphere Reaches Kids (P.A.R.K.), the Women's Foundation of Arkansas, and Just Communities of Arkansas.

Colette clearly makes a difference for Arkansans through her work. However, if you ask her what her most important job is or has been, she replies without hesitation, "It's being a mother to my eleven-year-old daughter, Sydney." She has many important roles, and she fulfills them all with skill, diplomacy, and friendliness.

Keith Jackson
Humanitarian Award, 2005

Keith Jackson graduated from Little Rock Parkview, where he was a three-sport letterman and Parade All American in football. He also played the cello with the Parkview orchestra. Keith attended the University of Oklahoma, graduating with honors and a BA in communications in three-and-a-half years. During college, he was selected three times to the All Big Eight team and named two-time Athletic All-American.

In 1988, the Philadelphia Eagles made Keith the thirteenth pick of the first round in the National Football League draft, where he made an immediate impact during his rookie season. He was the offensive rookie of the year and the only first-year player to be selected by the NFL for the Pro Bowl. He played in the NFL with the Philadelphia Eagles and the Miami Dolphins, before finishing his career with a Super Bowl championship with the Green Bay Packers. Keith's playing honors include six Pro Bowls and three All-Pro selections. He is considered one of the greatest tight ends ever.

Keith spent his time off-field promoting the vision God entrusted to him of developing an academic center that would give the youth in his hometown of Little Rock hope, strong values, and academic confidence. In 1992, this vision became a reality with the incorporation of P.A.R.K. (Positive Atmosphere Reaches Kids). Keith serves as president of the P.A.R.K. board, giving his name, personal money, and countless hours to the youth of this program.

P.A.R.K. serves junior and senior high school students who appear to be at risk of dropping out of school or succumbing to the pressure of drugs, alcohol, sex, or gangs. P.A.R.K. provides after-school tutoring, recreation, summer programs, and community service. Keith strongly believes that an atmosphere of love, nurturing, and discipline can put children on the path toward a positive future.

Keith has also combined his college degree in communications and his professional playing experience to become a broadcast analyst with TNT television for one year, the Oklahoma Sooner football radio network in 1998, Fox Sports Network in 1999, and the Arkansas Razorback Sports Network in 2000. He has also become one of the most dynamic and inspirational speakers in the country. His speaking engagements include churches, civic groups, corporations, and schools.

Keith Jackson is a family man of Christian values. His wife is Melanie, and they have three children, Keith Jr., Kenyon, and Koilan.

Keith has been recognized with numerous awards: Honorary Doctor of Humanities degree from Ouachita Baptist University, Boys Club Man of the Year, Channel 4 Community Service Award, Jaycee's Young Arkansas Award, Arkansas Black Hall of Fame, Mayor's Town Spirit Award, Arkansas Sports Hall of Fame, College Hall of Fame, High School Hall of Fame, NFL top 85 players, and Oklahoma University Offensive Player of the Century, and has been appointed to the Help America Vote Commission by President George W. Bush.

Judge Henry L. Jones Jr.
Humanitarian Award, 2010

When Henry Jones was still in high school, he dreamed of going somewhere outside Arkansas. In fact, his plan included graduating from the Air Force Academy, being a test pilot and astronaut, and being the first man on the moon! That didn't work out because in 1963, neither Senator Fulbright nor Senator McClellan was willing to nominate a young man of color to one of the service academies.

However, Henry was encouraged by school counselors and other adults, so he applied to fifteen schools across the country and was admitted to all but one. His choice was Yale, where he majored in history and literature. Henry was one of only thirteen black students in the freshman class of 1,000, and Henry felt that the leadership of Yale really didn't have high expectations that students like him would succeed, as much because he was from the segregated South as because of his race. With the encouragement of a freshman counselor, Henry was successful. Upon graduation, Henry was tempted to accept a Time-Life internship, and he was admitted to divinity school. But the promise of the leadership of Governor Winthrop Rockefeller brought Henry back to Arkansas. He says that Rockefeller was amazingly progressive, making decisions that were non-political but good for all Arkansans, so that Henry felt like it was the beginning of a new era. He returned to work as a research assistant for the governor. Henry was right about Governor Winthrop Rockefeller, who clearly changed the course of history for our state.

Judge G. Thomas Eisele, at that time a legal advisor to Governor Rockefeller, urged Henry to attend law school. After graduating from the University of Michigan Law School, Henry clerked for Eisele and for Judge Gerald W. Heaney. He also practiced civil rights law with the firms of Walker, Kaplan & Mays and Walker, Hollingsworth & Jones before he was appointed as a U.S. magistrate judge in 1978. During his time on the federal bench, Henry has watched the face of our state change: African Americans and women began to get a share of the economic pie. Businesses changed the way they hired, promoted, and fired. School desegregation created unprecedented opportunity for all students. Federal law and programs such as Medicare and Social Security gave new stability to families and individuals. His biggest frustration in serving as a judge: Things don't always change fast enough. "Even though our legal system is the best in the world, lots of people are still left behind and could have had better lives if we had recognized and confronted injustice sooner."

Henry also served many causes in his home town. In addition to his legal associations, he has, among a long list of commitments, been a teacher and deacon of Mt. Zion Baptist Church and a board member of Arkansas Repertory Theatre, the Arts and Humanities Promotion Commission for the City of Little Rock, the Winthrop Rockefeller Foundation, and the Afrocentric Development Committee of RAIN. Henry has also been a long-time board member of Just Communities of Arkansas (formerly NCCJ). Henry says he stayed with JCA because he sees no better place or way to accomplish the unity and equity we are all seeking within our community.

Following his retirement in 2010, Henry looks forward to "letting things come together" in this continuing adventure with Pat, his wife of thirty years. They have three children, eleven grandchildren, and one great-grandchild, who will surely keep them busy. One of his continuing projects is compiling a history of his family in photos and videos that he made before the death of his mother.

What were the things that most shaped Henry's hope-filled view of our world?

- His parents. His mother was a school teacher who worked every
  night on something for her students but also made time to answer
  his every question and to read to him every evening. His father
  worked two jobs, but took Henry to movies and cooked dinner for
  the family while his mother completed her education.
- The Residential College at Yale where 250 students lived, ate, and
  studied together. Henry remembers those late-night conversations
  with people from many backgrounds, and many of those Yale classmates are still close friends today.
- His choice to graduate from Horace Mann. Henry could have been
  one of the few black students who attended Central High School
  in the early 1960s but he chose to remain at Horace Mann for a
  very important reason: Central didn't have a baseball team.
- His mentors and role models, too many to mention, who had faith
  in Henry.

On the bench, and through his community service, Henry L.
Jones Jr., in his quiet and unassuming way, has advanced the cause of
justice and helped create opportunities for countless Arkansans.

Father Joseph H. Biltz worked with Sunny Vongsaravane and retired Colonel Dutch Dorsch (2003 Biltz Award winner) in the refugee resettlement program of the Arkansas Catholic Diocese up to his untimely death in 1986.

Herschel H. Friday served as dinner co-chair in 1989.

Skip Rutherford, 1988 dinner chair, compares notes with Ron Lanoue, who served as NCCJ executive director from 1985 to 2000.

Atlanta Mayor Andrew Young was the dinner speaker in 1984 and 1988.

Governor Bill Clinton and Arkansas First Lady Hillary Clinton were honored in 1988.

Vice President Walter Mondale, 1987 dinner speaker, with Louise and Hugh Patterson.

Louise (Weetsey) and Hugh Patterson proudly show off their plaque at the 1987 banquet. Joyce Williams Warren and Bill Clinton are also on the dais.

Mayor Lottie Shackelford, 1989 dinner co-chair, with Coretta Scott King and Daisy Bates.

Humanitarian Award winner Jerry Maulden and his wife, Sue, invited Coretta Scott King to be the featured dinner speaker in 1989.

Honorable Jim Keet

Humanitarian Award, 1995
(Interview conducted July 12, 2012)

If Jim Keet is anything, he is an entrepreneur. After all, since his graduation from college in 1971, he's started more than fifteen businesses. He laughs when he admits that not all of those projects were successful, but he says he learned just as much from endeavors that didn't work out as from those that did. Jim has mostly developed restaurants and hotels, but his businesses have also included construction, land development, and even an environmental corporation.

Jim was born in 1949 in Springfield, Missouri. His dad, James Holland Keet Jr., was an attorney and Circuit Judge. His mother, Sis Keet (no one knew her first name was Ethel) was a school teacher and later a real estate agent. Jim excelled at Greenwood High School, where he played football, basketball, and golf and was president of the Student Council. He recalls two of the faculty in particular: Dr. Grace Gardner, who taught history and sponsored the Student Council, and his football coach, Paul Mullins. Both always expected the best from Jim and got nothing less—or he had to run the bleachers after practice.

For his post-secondary education, Jim chose Southern Methodist University (SMU) in Dallas thinking that he wanted to practice law or go into business. SMU was an expensive private school, and Jim worked his way through, often logging more than fifty hours a week. Jim says he had learned from his parents that you had to work hard for what you wanted. That tenacity was rewarded at SMU when Jim received the "M" Award, an honor bestowed upon ten or fewer outstanding graduating seniors each year. Jim also served as the president of the Business School student body at SMU.

Jim feels privileged to have worked at the original Steak & Ale Restaurant in Dallas, the forerunner of theme restaurants across the United States, where he started as a dish washer. The owner and his boss, Norman Brinker, subsequently built an empire of theme restaurants including, among others, Chili's and Macaroni Grill. From Norman Brinker, Jim learned the value of hard work and the determination to be the best. (As I had lunch with Jim at his Taziki's restaurant in West Little Rock, I saw firsthand his attention to detail and commitment to making everything just right.) At Steak & Ale, he learned every facet of the restaurant business by working his way from dish washer to prep cook, to bus boy, to waiter, to bartender and finally to bar manager.

Jim met Doody, his soon-to-be wife, at SMU, and they were married after his graduation but before hers. Jim beams as he recounts that Doody took several years to get her undergraduate degree, and she also got a law degree and had their first two children while in law school.

After graduating in 1971 with a business degree and working for Winegardner Hammons operations, where he became the youngest innkeeper in the Holiday Inn system, Jim was fortunate to meet another remarkable man, Gerald F. Hamra in 1975. Along with Hamra, Jim eventually opened twenty-seven Wendy's and Sisters Restaurants across Arkansas and Texas. Jim says that he and Doody sold practically everything (including two cars, a motorcycle, and camera equipment) except the bed they were sleeping on to buy into the deal. Jim loved working with Hamra, who was well known for his civic engagement and generosity toward charitable causes. Jim definitely viewed Jerry Hamra as a role model. Jerry, who had contracted polio as a child, served as a board member of March of Dimes. Jim, following in the footsteps of Hamra, began as a volunteer for the Easter Seals annual telethon, and served as a board member for twenty years and eventually board president.

Jim also served on more than twenty other civic and charitable boards, including Arkansas Children's Hospital, and he was appointed to the state Literacy Commission by Governor Bill Clinton. He was also appointed to the first Martin Luther King Jr. Commission by Governor Jim Guy Tucker.

Jim Keet was elected to the Arkansas House of Representatives in 1988. He was later elected to the Arkansas Senate in 1992. He also made a couple of unsuccessful runs for office, including a race against Governor Mike Beebe in 2010. As a legislator, Jim worked on solving the vexing illegal drug abuse problem in Arkansas and promoting literacy. He later put his concern about illegal drugs to use by chairing the Arkansas Red Ribbon Campaign, for which he was recognized with the FBI Director's Community Leadership Award, for demonstrating outstanding contributions to his community.

Jim has gotten some recognition along the way, which he appreciates, but he says the real reward is watching a disabled child take his first unassisted steps, or hearing a child talk by using an augmentative communication device.

Jim and Doody have four children. Sons Jake and Tommy work with Jim building and operating Taziki's Mediterranean Café restaurants. Daughter Chase is an attorney; daughter Cassie is a writer and actress. They also have three grandchildren. Jim describes them all as "smart, considerate, and vibrant." Sounds like they take after their dad.

Margaret Kolb

Humanitarian Award, 1977
(November 27, 1920–January 5, 2009)

Worked to reopen schools during crisis
By Evin Demirel, January 8, 2009
Reprinted with permission from the Arkansas Democrat-Gazette

Margaret Kolb, who in the fall of 1958 turned part of her home into a makeshift headquarters for a group of women supporting the reopening of Little Rock's four public high schools, died Monday from complications of a stroke at Arkansas Hospice in St. Vincent Doctors Hospital.

She was eighty-eight.

Born Margaret Sparks on November 27, 1920, in Newport, Tennessee, Kolb, the eldest of three children, grew up in Asheville, North Carolina. She intended to be a teacher, like her mother, and after graduating from Furman University in Greenville, South Carolina, in 1941, entered a Baptist seminary in Louisville, Kentucky, relatives said. There she began dating a medical student, Payton Kolb.

"He proposed to her under a pear tree. She [later] planted a pear tree in our backyard because of it," her daughter Salli Kolb said. "The squirrels get them all ...," she said laughing. The couple married in 1946. Of their four children, only Salli Kolb survives.

While her husband served abroad, Margaret Kolb served as the director of religious education for the First Baptist Church in Asheville, her younger sister, Marie Clay, said. In 1947, the family moved to Little Rock, where Payton's father lived. Kolb taught at a private kindergarten, served on a state race-relations committee, and met with local black Baptist ministers to discuss race relations, relatives said.

"Mother was a very devout Christian and believed deeply in the formation of the United States—that all men were created equal. And it flows both ways, the Christianity into the patriotism," Salli Kolb said.

In 1957, nine black students entered Little Rock Central High School under the Little Rock School District's plan for complying with the 1954 U.S. Supreme Court decision that declared unconstitutional the laws mandating racial segregation of schools. Opposition to desegregation prompted a referendum leading to the closure of Little Rock's public high schools in 1958-59, affecting about 3,600 students, according to the Little Rock Central High School National Historic Site.

In 1958, Kolb joined the Women's Emergency Committee to Open Our Schools, "the first organization to publicly condemn the school-closing action and to support the reopening of the schools ...," which eventually included about 1,322 women, according to the site.

Kolb and her husband put a mimeograph machine, two typewriters, a desk, and a separate telephone line into an eight-by-thirteen-foot room behind their Hillcrest home's garage, their daughter said. Day or night, three to five women called lists of hundreds of people to seek support for the schools' reopening. "One would be typing, one would be on the phone, and one would be chatting with somebody else," Salli Kolb said.

"There were threatening notes left under the door and sent through the mail every day," Salli Kolb said, recalling a recurring letter upon which a rifle sight had been drawn. Kolb said her "even-keeled" mother and father "kind of ignored" the constant threats "and tried to make it like it wasn't that big of deal so that we wouldn't be scared."

In 1959, Little Rock's public high schools reopened on an integrated basis.

Nina Krupitsky
Father Joseph H. Biltz Award, 2004

Nina Krupitsky was probably considered a child of privilege in her home country of Rumania. The daughter of a lawyer and French teacher, she spoke German from birth and graduated from high school while taking evening courses in French. In June of 1941, Hitler's army entered the city where she lived, and immediately it was clear to all that it was no longer safe to remain there. Nina's mother sat her down and said, "This won't be easy. I don't think we will see each other again. But I will be okay because you will be alive." The next morning, Nina, at seventeen years old with only a backpack, left with a group of college students, escaping to Russia with the German army always just behind.

The story of Nina's almost two-year ordeal could make a movie. She remembers many details, such as watching a father lose his child off the side of a bridge. She remembers being able to see the gloating faces of pilots as they shot at the fleeing crowd. She remembers being housed with a family where there was little food and dirty children that she cleaned with soap made of ashes. She remembers frostbite that made her hands purple. She remembers many kindnesses, too.

In 1943, Nina was drafted into the Soviet army, where she served primarily as an interpreter in Berlin and Vienna. In Vienna she met and married her husband, Emmanuel, and they returned to the Soviet Union to live and raise their children. She said she could have deserted from the army, but she was always frightened for her brother. He, in fact, had safely immigrated earlier.

Years later in 1980, after her immigration to America, it was while watching the movie *Schindler's List* that Nina realized how she wanted to finally face her own memories and help others to understand and therefore never repeat the inhumanity of the Holocaust. Thus the Knowing Our Past Foundation was born.

Nina explains that most Holocaust survivors lost their families and feel guilty to have survived themselves. Therefore, they often try to "put a lock on their memories and feelings." The Knowing Our Past Foundation helps both survivors and others to unlock this part of our common history.

Nina began the foundation in 1997 with nothing but her will and a credit card. She is quick to recognize the contributions of others for the accomplishments of the foundation since then, but it is clearly an example of what one person can achieve when they have a dream and determination. Marvin Schwartz, one of the foundation supporters, explained that it was easy to be motivated by Nina's passion for using Holocaust education to help all of us understand how we can resist the negative forces in society, how each of us can be called to a higher ethical and moral purpose in our lives.

Since its creation, the Knowing Our Past Foundation has reached thousands of students across Arkansas with its lessons.

Nina and her husband, Emmanuel, have two children and four grandchildren. In 2010, her life and her experiences during World War II were the basis for a novel entitled *The Broken Vase* by Phillip H. McMath and Emily Matson Lewis.

Dr. Dean Kumpuris
Humanitarian Award, 2006

In 1991, what many considered a great idea called The Diamond Center, which among other things would have replaced Barton Coliseum on the State Fairgrounds with a downtown multi-use sports arena, went to Little Rock voters, but all ten proposals were defeated. With not much more to lose, city leaders decided that we needed to listen more closely to our citizens from all sectors, so Future Little Rock, a goal-setting process was begun. Gastroenterologist Dean Kumpuris started his public service by participating in the Future Little Rock planning group, which was televised on the Little Rock public access station. Dean called it "drama on television." Dean also characterizes this as a pivotal time for the city, as citizens, some of whom had previously never had a voice, began to come together, find middle ground, and work toward the future. When there was an opening on the City Board, Dean was appointed and has since been elected to that position three times.

Dean is still proud of the work of Future Little Rock, where a diverse group of residents set priorities, sent their ideas to voters, and got a sales tax increase to do such things as hire 135 policemen; establish the Prevention, Intervention, and Treatment Initiative for youth; support the Museum of Discovery; and establish a rental inspection program, among other things.

Considered by many as one of the most important builders of Little Rock, particularly the downtown redevelopment, Dean seems always willing to take on a challenging new assignment as a city board member or as a private citizen volunteer. Some of the organizations that Dean has served include the Advertising and Promotion Commission,

Downtown Partnership, Fifty for the Future, Riverfest, and the River Market. Dean has also served in a leadership role with the Little Rock Boys and Girls Club, Regions Bank Board, St. Vincent Infirmary Board, and the UALR Board of Visitors.

If you really want to hear Dean talk passionately, ask him about Arkansas Commitment, which he founded and serves as president. As an early graduate of NCCJ's Ourtown program, Dean kept looking for ways that he could reach across the racial divide and make a difference. The aim of Arkansas Commitment is to recognize promising minority students, nurture and assist them to do well in school, and provide opportunities for meaningful business internships. Finally, the program helps the students get admitted to and earn scholarships for a good college that is right for them.

Arkansas Commitment not only helps the students and their families, but it gives the multiple participating businesses a chance to work with and get to know some of our brightest young people. The program is rigorous for the students, so the "commitment" goes both ways. One of Dean's profound hopes is that these students will want to return to or remain in Arkansas following their education because they have been able to build a network of support here through the Arkansas Commitment program. There are more than forty seniors in the program in 2006 from a start with six students in 1999.

Beginning as a volunteer with Future Little Rock, Dean continues to ensure a bright future for our city.

Marian G. Lacey
Humanitarian Award, 1998
(*Interview conducted June 26, 2012*)

Education was always important to Marian Lacey. After all, her dad always said about an education, "No one can take that away from you." Maybe that's what motivated Marian to provide a good education to so many children during her career. In 1997, Marian was recognized as a Milken Educator by the Milken Family Foundation with an unrestricted $25,000 award "to celebrate, elevate, and activate exemplary K–12 educators." That just proved what everyone who ever met Marian Lacey already knew. She had always been in the business of loving students into learning, maybe even into greatness.

Marian Glover, the oldest of six children, was born in 1940 in Dermott, Arkansas, to a farming family. Her parents were strict, and they lived in a completely segregated world. Their lives were circumscribed by the farm, the church, and their school, Chicot County Training School. Some of Marian's favorite teachers were Odessa Talley (English), LaVerne Feaster (home economics), and Maude Wood (math). They taught not only the academic subjects, but diction and deportment, because they were interested in the whole child. Marian said her parents came straight from the field to support their children any time there was a spelling bee, a play, or a sports event. And her parents believed everything the teachers said, so Marian knew that she had to behave, especially at school.

Marian made her way to Arkansas AM&N, where her dad had studied for two years before returning to Dermott to help his mother at the farm. There she prepared to be an English teacher, and she met her future husband, Jesse Lacey, who was also studying to be a teacher. When she wanted to go to visit his family in Vicksburg, Mississippi, it took several weeks of exchanging letters among her, her mother, Jesse's mother, and the neighbor with whom Marian would stay before that trip was approved by her parents. It all finally worked out, and Marian and Jesse courted throughout college and got married following their graduation. They subsequently had three children, Cynthia, Jeffrey Jay, and Julian, and two grandchildren.

During the summers of her college years, Marian was fortunate to land an internship opportunity with the Southern Baptist Convention. Her responsibilities included helping plan and conduct Vacation Bible Schools in several churches: first in Tulsa, then in New Orleans, and back in Tulsa for the third summer. It was her first time to live outside Arkansas, and it certainly broadened her perspective.

In 1960, Marian and Jesse got teaching jobs in Helena-West Helena, and they became very involved in the community. Jesse was soon hired in Eudora, Arkansas, as principal, and later moved to Clarendon as principal. Marian remembers each of those communities with fondness. She says that in the early '60s everything was still segregated, but they were good days, and as teachers, they knew they were making a difference just as their teachers had with them.

A former student in Clarendon, Rush Harding III, remembers that classes were integrated while Jesse Lacey was the principal and Mrs. Lacey was the English teacher. He says their community handled integration a lot better than some, partially because of the Laceys. "Mrs. Lacey modeled the right attitude. She taught me by caring about me. She helped us understand our new black classmates, and she helped them understand their new white classmates. She invested in me as a young person. Four decades later, I still feel the impact of her caring."

In 1971, Marian and Jesse left Arkansas for Indiana University in Bloomington. There Jesse earned his doctorate degree and Marian worked on her master's. They both reveled in the campus community, which abounded in stimulating friends and mentors and cultural opportunities. While there, in one of her few forays outside the field of education, Marian interviewed families and individuals to determine their eligibility for federal assistance, her only experience as a social worker.

In 1973 they returned to Arkansas, this time to Little Rock, when Jesse was offered a job at UALR. Marian applied to teach English at Dunbar Junior High School and was hired on the spot when she volunteered to teach the basic-level classes. One day, one of her students, who was going to be away for two years, asked her, "*Mrs. Lacey, where are you going to be when I get back?*" That chance question started her thinking about her own future. Ultimately Marian enrolled in UALR's evening program, and with the friendship and support of Dr. Angela Sewall and Dr. Charles Donaldson, she, too, earned a doctorate.

In the Little Rock School District, Marian served as a teacher, a department chair, an assistant principal, a principal, and finally assistant superintendent for secondary education. Marian left her mark in every place that she served, probably because everyone knew that Marian really cared—about the students, about their parents, and about the teachers and staff. When she retired, in 2005, the district instituted the Marian G. Lacey Teacher of the Year Award, which is presented every year to an outstanding Little Rock teacher.

Even after her retirement from the LRSD, Marian continued as a teacher by working with the Arkansas Department of Education to mentor principals throughout Arkansas. In addition, she has served on several community boards including Just Communities of Arkansas, World Services for the Blind, Public Education Foundation, and the Central Arkansas Library System. Marian also serves youth in the community as a member of Beta Pi Omega Chapter of Alpha Kappa Alpha Sorority.

One of Marian's first students in Helena-West Helena was Zernon S. Evans, who is now a reading specialist in ninth through twelfth grade in the Helena-West Helena schools. Zernon says that Mrs. Lacey is still her role model because she taught more than just English and never played favorites. "Mrs. Lacey insisted that we speak grammatically correct English to be prepared for our professional careers." And Zernon remembers bringing her cousin's copy of *True Romance* magazine to school one day. Mrs. Lacey gently suggested that she needed to be reading something that took more than one day to read. "Whatever you put into your head becomes a part of you," she remembers her teacher saying. "Choose carefully to prepare for your future role in the world." Zernon shares that same advice with her students today.

Marian is modest and soft-spoken, but her loving interactions with others scream, "You can do it—and I'm here to help in any way I can!" Countless students have benefitted from knowing this lovely woman whom we call teacher.

Roland W. Lanoue
Humanitarian Award, 2000
(Interview conducted July 2, 2012)

When Arkansans think about the NCCJ, many think of Ron Lanoue, who served as director of NCCJ in Arkansas from 1985 to 2000. During that time, Ron was the face and voice of diversity education, prejudice reduction, and interfaith dialogue through his tireless efforts.

Ron laughs when he says he was born to work with an organization like NCCJ: his mother was a Protestant, his dad was a Catholic, and the doctor was Jewish. He was raised in rural Rhode Island, and only when he went to Rhode Island College did he realize that there were no Blacks or Jews in his hometown of Cumberland. But coming of age in the turbulent 1960s left its mark on Ron. After completing his degree, he got his draft notice and was accepted for Officer Candidate School in the air force. After four years in the military, he entered graduate school at the University of Wisconsin at Madison. With an undergraduate degree in history, he earned a master's in urban planning, and he landed a job as a staff member for the chair of the Wisconsin House Municipalities Committee. They organized hearings around the state, and he interviewed power brokers in the savings and loan and insurance industries, which led to the creation of the Wisconsin Housing Finance and Development Corporation. He called it "heady stuff" to be involved in those major decisions.

By the time he earned his graduate degree, he was married to Joyce Smoler, and they had a daughter, Elise, and another child on the way. They both wanted their children to grow up in a more diverse community than Madison was at that time, so when a job was offered in Little Rock, they packed their bags and moved south. Ron said he realized that it was easy to be a liberal in Rhode Island or Madison. And although they had no idea what Little Rock was like, other than what they'd learned about the crisis at Central High School, they thought it would be a good place for their family. Their son Joel was born in 1973 at St. Vincent's Hospital.

When Elise entered a Jewish pre-school here, Ron began a Judaism class with Rabbi Zeke Palnick. Ron had long been estranged from the Catholic Church of his childhood. He says that when he began the study of Judaism, he felt as if he had come home, and he was graciously accepted by the Jewish community here. Rabbi Palnick was one of the outstanding progressive voices in Arkansas and was recognized with the NCCJ Humanitarian Award in 1982.

When he first moved to Little Rock, Ron honed his leadership, planning, mediation, and facilitation skills working with Virgil Gettis, director of manpower planning for Metroplan. From there he was hired by Dr. Howard Barnhard at UAMS, where he managed the capital budget for more than eleven years. He is still proud of the work they did to build new labs and a new medical library and to upgrade patient facilities. But it was at NCCJ where Ron really made his mark.

Because of Ron's abiding interest in history, he always viewed the work of NCCJ as a way to influence individuals who in turn make our history. He said that when he came to work each day, he felt like he was doing his favorite kind of volunteer work, and he loved the freedom and creativity of creating new opportunities for program participants to grow. He especially appreciated the willingness of the NCCJ board to debate controversial issues in the community. He never remembers the board "taking a vote" on any issue. Instead they lived into the mission of NCCJ by coming to a consensus even on the most difficult topics.

Ron took an innovative approach to growing new programs at NCCJ. One such endeavor was a High School National/State Issues Congress, in which 200 students from across the state spent two days working on important political, economic, and social issues. Board member Jim Guy Tucker helped him get that program started. This was before computers were ubiquitous; staff members spent hours into the night typing up the student resolutions and taking them to the copy shop to be ready for the early sessions the next day.

It was through Ron's vision that JCA's longest-running program came into being. Ron taped a *Today Show* segment about the Anytown Program at NCCJ in Phoenix and showed it to board members at their next meeting. Inspired by what they had seen, board members Arnold Mayersohn and Jerry Maulden wrote checks right then to start Anytown here in Arkansas. Begun in 1987, Anytown (now Ourtown for Teens) is preparing for its twenty-sixth year.

Ron created the Ourtown Institute for Adults following a request from Chamber of Commerce leaders to offer some way for community leaders to better understand, confront, and ameliorate tough local racial issues together. More than 500 leaders attended Ourtown retreats between 1990–1999. Probably the most important residual effect of Ourtown was the trust that black and white leaders developed through the intensive program. Most graduates can tell you how they have a different perspective and how they have made different choices because of their Ourtown experience. More than once during that decade, Ron called together Ourtown graduates to work through a tough local issue together.

There were many other programs to follow, two of which Ron is particularly proud. The first of these is the 1987 Memorial Service honoring those who served in Vietnam. The other is the National Leadership Summit: Race Relations and America's Public Education System, September, 1997, held in conjunction with the fortieth anniversary of the Central High Crisis. In both cases, Ron felt that we were recognizing our history appropriately, and seeking to inform our shared future for the better of all of us. He still speaks about both these events with emotion.

Upon leaving NCCJ of Arkansas, Ron served as executive director of the NCCJ in San Diego for five years, later returning to Little Rock to work as director of Arkansas Legal Services Partnership. He also served as secretary to the Access to Justice Commission, a role that he relished. Retired now, Ron enjoys traveling and getting to visit his four grandchildren in Chicago more often.

Ron's favorite quote is the one Reverend Martin Luther King Jr. immortalized, "We shall overcome because the arc of a moral universe is long, but it bends toward justice." Ron has doubtlessly helped to bend that arc toward justice in countless ways.

Brownie Ledbetter

Father Joseph Biltz Award, 1991
(April 28, 1932–March 21, 2010)
Reprinted with permission from Cal Ledbetter and Ruebel Funeral Home

Mary Brown "Brownie" Williams Ledbetter is a lifelong political activist who worked in many controversial and crucial campaigns in Arkansas, as well as nationally and internationally. A catalyst in many local grassroots organizations, she has exhibited a dedication to fair education and equality across racial, religious, and cultural lines.

Born on April 28, 1932, in Little Rock, Mary Brown Williams was the first of four children born to William H. Williams, a businessman and dairy farmer, and Helon Brown Williams. Born with brown eyes, she was nicknamed "Brownie" by her family. After her mother's death in 1947 and her father's death in 1950, Brownie and her siblings were raised by relatives Grainger and Frances Williams, who moved into the Tall Timber Jersey Farm (the Williams family farm) with their own two children.

Brownie graduated from Little Rock High School (later named Central High School). She went on to attend Agnes Scott College in Decatur, Georgia, from 1950 to 1953, but felt she did not fit the image of Southern womanhood the school projected and did not finish her degree. On July 26, 1953, she married Calvin Reville Ledbetter, an attorney and political science professor. The pair relocated to Germany, where Ledbetter was stationed with the U.S. Army for three years before returning to the United States, residing first in Illinois and later in Arkansas. The couple had three children. Her middle son, Jeffrey Ledbetter, died unexpectedly in 1986.

While in Germany, Brownie first learned about the growing crisis surrounding the desegregation of Central High School. Her aunt signed her up for the Women's Emergency Committee to Save Our Schools (WEC), which supported the reopening of public schools in Little Rock. When Brownie returned to Little Rock, she immediately began volunteering with the group. After the dissolution of WEC in 1963, Ledbetter worked with the Panel of American Women, a nonpartisan forum focused on religious and racial diversity in which women discussed their experiences in an effort to bridge the gap between people of different races and cultures. In 1981, the panel became the Arkansas Public Policy Panel and expanded its mission to include organizing and assisting grassroots groups. Brownie served as volunteer executive director before retiring in 1999 and oversaw the creation of the Arkansas Citizen's First Congress, a progressive political force in Arkansas legislative and political affairs.

In 1983, Brownie founded the Arkansas Fairness Council, a coalition of twenty-three organizations representing labor, African Americans, teachers, and environmental and church organizations, serving as president and lobbyist for fifteen years. Other organizations on Brownie's résumé include the Arkansas Women's Political Caucus (founding member), the ERA/Arkansas Coalition (organizing member, 1973 to 1978), Arkansas Career Resources, Inc. (founder and executive director from 1985 to 1990), the Southern Coalition for Educational Equity (state director from 1982 to 1985), the Arkansas State Advisory Committee to the U.S. Commission on Civil Rights, the State Federation of Business and Professional Women (legislative director), and the Women's Environment and Development Organization (co-founder with Bella Abzug).

In addition to her grassroots activities, Brownie worked with many state and national political campaigns. In 1967, she served as campaign manager for her husband's successful bid for the Arkansas General Assembly. Brownie served as organizer and consultant in Dale Bumpers's run for governor in 1970. She ran the Arkansas McGovern for President campaign and was a senior consultant to the Fulbright

senatorial campaign in 1974. Brownie served as the first political action
chair of the National Women's Political Caucus in 1973 and was part
of the successful statewide effort to support the appointment of the
first African-American federal judge from Arkansas. Her work with the
Democratic Party also includes a place on the State Democratic Central
Committee, from 1968 to 1974, and the position of Affirmative Action
Committee coordinator for the State Democratic Party in 1973 and
1974. She was the organizer of the first Planned Parenthood affiliate
and clinic in Arkansas in 1984 and spearheaded the defeat of the first
statewide ballot initiative to restrict private and legal forms of birth control and abortion.

Through her service on the Women's Environmental and
Development Organization (WEDO) and the Brooklyn-based National
Congress of Neighborhood Women, she had the opportunity to work
with women and minorities from many countries. Brownie has participated as a nongovernmental delegate in UN preparatory and commission meetings in New York; at the UN Conference on Environmental
and Developmental in Rio; the UN Conference on Population and
Development in Cario; the Fourth World Conference on Women in
Beijing; the UN Conference on Racism in Durban, South Africa; and
the World Summit on Sustainable Development in Johannesburg.

Brownie has received countless awards and recognitions, including
the American Civil Liberties Union Civil Libertarian of the Year, the
Mary Hatwood Futrell Award from the National Education Association,
the Father Joe Biltz Award from the Just Communities of Arkansas, and
the National Women's History Month Award. She was the inspiration
for the Brownie Ledbetter Dragonslayer Award given each year by the
Arkansas Public Policy Panel and the Arkansas Citizen's Congress for
outstanding achievement in the field of social justice.

Since her retirement, she has worked on public school issues involving the achievement gap among low-income and minority students
and served on the national board of the Center for the Advancement

of Women in New York City. Brownie was a founding member of the Women's Foundation of Arkansas. An ordained elder in the Presbyterian Church, she was active in church affairs.

Brownie is survived by her husband, Cal Ledbetter; son Grainger and wife, Sherry Curry; daughter, Snow, and husband, Chris Moen; siblings, Grainger "Bish" Williams, Quendy Veatch, June Williams, Ann Wedaman, and Alfred Williams; Uncle Grainger Williams; and Aunt Frances. She leaves five grandchildren, Gwyneth, Lily, Mary, Jeffrey and Campbell, and numerous nephews and nieces.

Rabbi Eugene Levy
Humanitarian Award, 2010

Gene Levy came from a Reform Jewish home, but there was no expectation that he would become a rabbi one day. In fact, his father was an accountant, his mother helped run the family business, and Gene was good at math. No one would have been surprised had Gene become an accountant, too, and worked in the family business. As a youth, Gene was wholly involved in Scouting, attaining his Eagle Scout Badge, and held leadership positions in the local and regional youth groups. While on a high school youth group exchange, Gene asked to be excused from the Friday night program to find a quiet place on the lake for some private time to observe Shabbat. That night at Methodist Youth Camp, Gene felt the call to become a rabbi.

As a resident of San Antonio, Gene chose San Antonio College and then the University of Texas for his undergraduate studies in history, philosophy, and Hebrew literature. As a junior on his very first day at UT, Gene went to the Hillel Jewish Youth Center and met Bobbye Waltzer. When he proposed to her on Valentine's Day two years later, she responded, "Does this mean I have to break my date for Saturday night?" It's not difficult to understand what a good pair they've been ever since.

Gene completed his theology and rabbinic training at Hebrew Union College in Cincinnati and was ordained in 1972. His first position after ordination was as director of B'nai B'rith Hillel at the University of Oklahoma. There, as the only rabbi, he learned to work with Jews who were Reform, Conservative, and Orthodox. Good experience, no doubt, for his continuing commitment to building community with Jews and non-Jews wherever he serves.

Gene's next position was for twelve years as rabbi with Congregation Beth El in Tyler, Texas. The Levys enjoyed their time in Tyler, but eventually Gene wanted to find a larger community and began to look around. In 1987, Gene became the rabbi at Congregation B'nai Israel in Little Rock. Gene was chosen to give the challenge at President Clinton's Interfaith Inaugural Service in 1993, and later spent the night at the White House during Clinton's tenure. One interesting note is that each time they moved, they also had a baby. They are the proud parents of Ari, Jeremy, and Shayna, and will soon welcome Anne Smith as a daughter-in-law.

Gene is well known as an irrepressible punster—something he probably inherited from his dad, who had cartoons taped on his office walls. Members of Rotary Club 99 would describe Gene as a tireless worker on building literacy and student scholarships. Temple B'nai Israel members would definitely think of Gene as their counselor and teacher/rabbi, titles he is quick to claim proudly. To most members of the Arkansas community, he might also be known as "The Guy Who Shows Up!" And this is nothing new for Gene Levy.

Besides leadership positions in Jewish organizations, Gene Levy has been an active Rotary member, a Pastoral Care Board chair for UAMS, an officer of Arkansas Interfaith Conference, and co-founder of Arkansas Interfaith Alliance. He has served on the boards of Regional AIDS Interfaith Network, the Shepherd Center—now LifeQuest, Little Rock's Racial & Cultural Diversity Commission, and Just Communities of Arkansas. When you want someone to give wisdom and work, call on Gene Levy. He truly is the guy who shows up.

In Tyler, Texas, one program he developed was "How We Celebrate," bringing together members of disparate faith groups for six weeks to share their religious practices with each other. In Arkansas, we've learned to count on Gene Levy showing up when the issue is: equal inclusion and rights for gays and lesbians; fair wages; separation of church and state, for the benefit of all faith groups; passage of a hate crimes law; or interfaith issues, helping to bring people together to promote understanding and acceptance particularly when our faith perspectives differ.

Rabbi Gene Levy is proud to proclaim his own Reform Jewish heritage, and when Gene describes some of what "Reform Tradition" means, we can see why he so often "shows up" when and where he is needed.

- Reform is inclusive, engenders and fosters equality and fairness, and specializes in outreach.
- Reform stresses compassion and justice, and is willing to admit mistakes.
- Reform appreciates tradition and modernity at the same time.
- Reform stresses interfaith co-operation and understanding.

Surely, we could find no better example than Gene Levy of someone who lives his faith out loud, in public, and as an example for us all.

Pat Lile
Father Joseph H. Biltz Award, 2010

Pat Lile insists she's not a hero. So maybe she's a hurricane, disguised as a butterfly. You've probably heard of the butterfly effect: "That small difference in the initial condition of a dynamic system may produce large variations in the long term behavior of the system....or, put simply, that a hurricane is started by the flap of a butterfly's wings." Pat has certainly been known to cause a flap or two.

Pat's parents were divorced when she was still an infant, and her mom moved several times trying to find a way to support herself and her daughter. Pat moved into her grandparents' home in Hope, Arkansas, for her fifth-grade school year and there found stability and security, something she longed for as a child. She describes her grandparents as good people but not progressive in their view of racial "place." Pat found mentors in her school and church. She remembers fondly Miss Kathleen, who was a stern but constant presence with the youth in the church. Pat still treasures the Bible that Miss Kathleen gave to her with the admonition, "Let this book be your guide."

Because she was a woman of her time—the fifties—and perhaps because of her family background, Pat had one overarching goal: to be married and have children. She accomplished that, but so much more.

As a good student in high school, she earned a scholarship to Hendrix College, where she met John Lile just three weeks into her first semester. Folks from Hope called Hendrix "that Communist School" at the time. She was a very good student in college as well, but left before her senior year to marry John and accompany him to Duke University for his law schooling. To help make ends meet, she worked as a secretary on campus, and they had their first child, a boy who died just three days after his birth. Pat and John were subsequently blessed with four healthy children, Gar, Gretchen, Jennifer, and Sue, and they now have five grandchildren and two step-grandchildren. In 2009, Pat and John celebrated their fiftieth wedding anniversary with their entire family.

Pat supported John in his career and supported her children in their many activities and endeavors. At an organizational meeting for potential Girl Scout troop leaders, Pat created one of her early "flaps." When she agreed to serve and was presented with the list of eligible Brownie Scouts, she noted that only white girls were on the list. She explained to the Scouting organization that she would not be a Scout leader unless the African-American girls were allowed to join her troop. She thinks the Scouting leaders only agreed so that there wouldn't be a public fuss.

The Lile family lived in Pine Bluff until 1990. For twenty-eight years, they all thrived in a community that they love. Pat and John worked together to develop the Chamber of Commerce Leadership Program in 1981. After twenty years of volunteer leadership, Pat went to work full-time for the Pine Bluff Chamber as a vice president for community development. She believes she was hired there because the Chamber executive at the time wanted to keep a watch on her activities after she had created a "flap" by insisting that the "civic organization" database include and track the African-American groups that had never been included before. Another time, she realized that the elementary-age African-American boys were only allowed to watch the football team practicing on the public school grounds. The teams were sponsored by the local Boys Club, which was "for whites only." When she suggested that that should be changed, it made the local paper, and her nine-year-old son Gar said, "Mom, I know what you are doing is right, but did you have to put it in the paper?"

Most of us know Pat, who retired in 2008, as the intrepid and effective leader of Arkansas Community Foundation, which grew from assets of $15 million to $130 million during her eleven-year tenure. It is one of the five largest grantmaking foundations in the state, making grants of more than $7 million annually. Between her Chamber job in Pine Bluff and Arkansas Community Foundation, Pat also served as the head of the Commission on Arkansas's Future, an appointment of Governor Bill Clinton, and as an interim director of the Family Service Agency.

Pat's mother's innate sense of fairness and her faith community's teachings gave her the drive to work for equality. With that drive, she learned one of her most important life lessons: "When you genuinely care about others and want them to succeed, they will 'get in the same yoke with you' and incredible things can be accomplished."

Pat believes without doubt that: "A community is strongest when the fabric of the community is woven with all of the possible threads!" She has learned that all persons can contribute and has made it her personal responsibility to make opportunities available to all.

Everywhere that Pat Lile has been, she has definitely made a difference in the fabric of her community...of our community, and we are the better for her (and her flaps). Aren't we lucky that she wasn't just a social butterfly?

Dr. Betty Lowe
Father Joseph H. Biltz Award, 2005

What everyone seems to like best about
Betty Lowe is that she is just Betty Lowe:
constant, true, honest, and forthright, as
one colleague describes her.

Betty was born in Grapevine, Texas,
and raised mostly in Fourche Valley,
Arkansas. Her parents were educators, serving as an English teacher, librarian, principal, and superintendent in small rural
school districts. Although their combined salary was never more than
$10,000 a year, they never told Betty or her three siblings that they were
poor. Instead they taught them that they could do whatever they wanted
as long as they got an education.

For example, Betty's dad agreed that she could play basketball in
high school as long as she made good grades, so she made all As. Later,
one of the reasons she decided to go to medical school was because she
wasn't tall enough to play college basketball.

In college, Betty liked science, and a couple of women physicians visited Fayetteville and invited all undergraduate women interested in medicine to a meeting—only seven attended. One of the visitors, Dr. Pearl
Waddle, a pediatrician from Fort Smith, invited Betty down to spend the
day with her. Betty caught a bus from Fayetteville to Fort Smith and loved
her day with Dr. Waddle. Subsequently, at the urging of her sister Mary,
Betty applied to the only two medical schools that she could afford,
Arkansas and Tennessee. She was accepted at both schools but she needed
$50 to attend....money she didn't have at the time. That very week, she
won an award as the "Outstanding Junior Woman" and the prize was $50.

Betty graduated first in her class from UAMS in 1956. She began
as one of six women in a class of ninety; only three of the women grad-

uated. Actually, her timing was bad all around. Before her time, in the 1880s, women had dominated the fields of obstetrics and pediatrics. As all medical disciplines became more valid and prestigious, medical schools began to exclude women. Betty felt and experienced both overt and subtle discrimination in the male-dominated medical community, particularly in school and as a young resident physician. She had one professor who explained that only members of the class choir got As in his class—an all-male choir, by the way. Today, after Betty has retired, medical schools have classes that are fifty percent female with sixty percent of the students in pediatrics being women. Role models like Betty Lowe probably have something to do with those numbers.

Betty said her biggest challenge was actually learning how to serve her patients. She had learned a lot of facts in medical school, but she needed to learn how to apply that knowledge in real-life situations. Clearly, she figured it out, and she became a teacher to many others. One of her proudest honors was receiving the Golden Apple award for outstanding teacher in the UAMS School of Medicine, which is voted on by the class members.

Betty came back to Arkansas Children's Hospital in 1975 as director of education. Within a year, she was tapped as medical director. This was a time of phenomenal growth and change for ACH. During Betty's first decade at Children's, the number of pediatric doctors grew from 15 to 100. One of the most important things for Betty at Children's was that the board agreed that they would serve everyone regardless of their ability to pay.

Betty is quick to credit her colleagues for the remarkable growth of Arkansas Children's Hospital, which is now recognized as one of the largest and best Children's Hospitals in the country. No doubt Betty had a lot to do with that recognition.

One of her greatest concerns is that we often put child health care issues at the bottom of our list of concerns rather than at the top. She cites gaps in mental-health services and poverty as two of the biggest challenges facing us today in child health.

Betty was a founding member of Arkansas Advocates for Children and Families, is past president of the American Academy of Pediatrics, has authored and co-authored numerous papers, and served on a huge number of medical society and state committees to advance care and treatment of Arkansas's children.

Jo Luck

Humanitarian Award, 1997
(Interview conducted August 16, 2012)

At four years old, Jo Luck traveled on a ship with her twenty-four-year-old mother, Annette, from Arkansas to Yokohama, Japan, along with 800 other military dependents. There, they would join Jo Luck's father, one of the military servicemen remaining in occupied Japan for one year following the end of World War II. That trip, and its aftermath, was full of lessons for Jo Luck, and she has used those lessons wisely to make a remarkable difference throughout our world.

Inexplicably, the homes of Japanese citizens were confiscated to provide housing for American military families. Realizing this, Jo Luck's mother invited Hatona, the actual owner of their assigned home, to pose as Jo Luck's governess so that Hatona and her ten-year-old daughter could remain in their home. Jo Luck learned to speak Japanese, even though she wasn't allowed to play with Japanese children. Hatona made kimonos for them, and Jo Luck was allowed to share chocolate with the other children. They broke their chocolate bars into small pieces, placed them on a tray, walked to the end of their lane, and the neighborhood children politely took one bite apiece and backed away slowly bowing and saying thank you. Jo Luck remembers that as "so beautiful, so special." Frustrated at being separated from the other children, Jo Luck one day stomped her foot and told her mother, "When I grow up, children in every country will be able to play together!"

Back home in the states, Jo Luck entered school and proudly took her most prized possessions for sharing day in first grade: a kimono, a Japanese doll, and shoes. The reaction from her teacher was fierce disapproval, as the war remained a bitter memory for many. Jo Luck never shared those treasures again on sharing day, but neither did she did learn the lesson that she should do what others expected in order to fit in. In high school, while attending a four-state student council workshop, she chose the best dancer in the room, an African-American boy, to dance with when it was the girls' turn to select a partner at the sock hop. She was called ugly names afterwards.

Jo Luck's parents divorced when she was only five years old, and both remarried shortly thereafter. Jo Luck spent the school year with her mother and stepfather, and her summers with her father and step-mother. Because of this arrangement, she lived all over and attended six different schools in her first seven years of school. She had four living parents for fifty-nine years of her life, and all made a difference for her. For example, her stepmother, Merle, insisted that she learn how to catch, kill, pluck, clean, and cook a chicken, and her mother told her to get a degree in education in case her husband died and she had to support herself. It's easy to imagine the value of the "chicken lesson" for Jo Luck, as she has since dined with families from all over the world through her Heifer International travels. If that might entail killing the main dish, Jo Luck knew that she could help out.

Jo Luck also got that education, mostly at Hendrix, and then she graduated from David Lipscomb College in Nashville, following her mar-riage to Bill Wilson. They had two children, Elizabeth Ann in 1967 and Mark in 1970. Today, Jo Luck is known as Granny Duck (or Gan Duck) to her grandchildren and great-grandchildren.

As a young mother, Jo Luck began her career by writing a Community and Economic Development Associates grant to offer pre-school parenting education through the San Diego Public Schools while Bill Wilson was serving in the military there. When the schools were closed in the summer, she earned another grant to organize field trips for children and their parents. That experience prepared her to become the first executive director of Arkansas Advocates of Children and

Families (AACF) in 1978. Following that, Jo Luck was the first appointment of Governor Bill Clinton, who tapped her to serve as the executive director of the Arkansas Department of Parks and Tourism. She served for more than a decade, during which time she was re-appointed by Governor Frank White and then again by the re-elected Clinton. Someone once asked Jo Luck how she had been so successful at working with the legislature during her Parks and Tourism days, and she said with a wink, "I was a mother and had been a first-grade school teacher, so I was well prepared."

In 1989, Jo Luck joined Heifer International, and her success there is legendary. During her tenure, mostly as president and chief executive officer, Heifer grew from a $7 million organization annually to $130 million. The number of supporters of Heifer grew from 20,000 in 1992 to more than 500,000 by 2009. Since its founding in 1944, Heifer has assisted, directly or indirectly, 62 million people, or 12 million families, in more than 125 countries through its mission to work with communities to end hunger and poverty while caring for the earth. Heifer gives livestock and training to help families improve their nutrition and generate income in sustainable ways. They call the gift animals "living loans" and expect the recipient to "pass on the gift," of the animal's female offspring, to create an ever-expanding network of hope and peace.

In 2010, Jo Luck was recognized as a World Food Prize laureate. In 2011, she retired from Heifer and was appointed by President Barack Obama to the Board for International Food and Agricultural Development (BIFAD). As a recognized international expert, she serves on several other boards that address the issues of hunger, poverty, sustainability, and agriculture. She is frequently invited as a speaker for meetings and commencements, which she loves to do, and she is working on her memoir. Today, Jo Luck is particularly concerned with gender equity and global food security. She seeks to empower women because she has seen across our globe what a positive difference women can make when they have resources and choices. She also reminds us that by 2050 we will have nine billion residents in this village we all share called earth. Therefore, global food security should be important to all of us.

When giving commencement speeches, she often tells stories to remind the graduates that there is beauty and dignity in the midst of poverty...that there is great generosity in the midst of need. She then asks the graduates to do two things on their graduation day: write down your core values, and make a list of the most important things you want in your life. Then when you make major decisions, ask yourself, "Am I compromising my core values?" and "Is this moving me toward what is truly important?"

As the first director of AACF, Jo Luck had worked closely with one of the founders, Hillary Clinton. One day Jo Luck had admired a small necklace that featured a globe. Later Hillary gave that necklace to Jo Luck and said, "The world is your oyster. You can do anything you set your mind to." Jo Luck says, "I didn't believe it then, but Hillary did. And that's made a world of difference for me." Clearly, Hillary Clinton was right.

Frank Lyon Sr.

Humanitarian Award, 1975
(1910–1998)

Frank Lyon, a true titan, dead at 88
Arkansan contributed mightily to his state

By Linda S. Caillouet, September 19, 1998
Reprinted with permission from the Arkansas Democrat-Gazette

Frank Lyon Sr., one of Little Rock's and Arkansas's most powerful and prominent businessmen throughout the second half of this century, died Friday of heart failure. He was eighty-eight.

Through the years Lyon, for whom Lyon College in Batesville is named, has been referred to as a "born salesman" and a "shrewd investor" as well as a "masterful leader and motivator of people." In recent years, his family holdings have been listed in *Forbes* magazine's Top 400 wealthiest Americans. Lyon maintained a low profile throughout his life. Lyon built his fortune from the most humble of rural Arkansas beginnings.

He was born February 5, 1910, in Camden to Bessie Lancaster and James Leonard Lyon, who had a 100-acre farm. James Lyon was also in the livery business.

Lyon began working early and later prided himself on never having been out of work since age ten, when he began delivering milk. Other childhood jobs included riding a pony to throw newspapers on his route and selling ten-cent buckets of homegrown turnip greens and black-eyed peas. Lyon and his sister shared their home with five adopted brothers and sisters, distant cousins his parents took in after two families' parents died. By the time Lyon was fourteen, his father had died and his mother, unable to find work in Camden, moved the family to Little Rock, where she became the second welfare worker in Arkansas.

In Little Rock, Lyon attended public schools and soon got a job as a collector for the old Hollenberg Music Co. to help support his family. He attended the Branham and Hughes Military Academy in Springhill, Tennessee, and then the University of Alabama. While going to college in the late '20s, he collected delinquent accounts for Ford Motor Co. and later sold $29 tailor-made suits—the height of fashion at that time— for a Chicago company at the campus's fraternity houses.

He graduated from college about the same time the Depression set in, and even Lyon's drive to succeed couldn't overcome the lean years. During the '30s, he was a traveling salesman for General Foods Corp. and later became a sales manager with Gunn Distributing Co., an appliance wholesaler in Little Rock, where he soon worked his way up to sales manager. In 1932, he married his high school sweetheart, Marion Bradley, whom he often lovingly referred to as "my Marion." The couple had a son, J. Frank Lyon Jr. In 1940, still a new father, he faced health problems.

He was diagnosed with tuberculosis after his six-foot frame had dropped to 128 pounds. For five years, he traveled weekly to Booneville for treatment but kept working even though he had to rest each day for two hours. He was eventually cured, but before it was all over, one of his lungs had collapsed. During his time at the tuberculosis sanitarium, he had come to know other patients. While he didn't have a lot more money than they did, he began to send many a little money each month to help them get by. Later he gave jobs to recovered tubercular patients. He also helped young people find jobs, gave others college scholarships and provided loans and gifts of money to still others.

As other men were sent off to fight in World War II, Lyon—unable to go because of his health—in 1942 used his savings of $14,085 to found his own business at 1020 Main St. in Little Rock. The wholesale business became the exclusive distributor for RCA products in Arkansas. But when RCA had trouble keeping Lyon supplied with the appliances demanded by the Little Rock market, he began selling furniture on the side. Eventually becoming the exclusive distributor of RCA Victor, RCA, Whirlpool, and furniture, he supplied more than 600 RCA and Whirlpool dealers in five states.

Through the next four decades, he continued increasing his holdings with an array of companies that included soft drink bottling companies, such as the Coca-Cola Bottling Co. of Arkansas, bought from the Bellingrath family in 1969, and 13,000-acre Wingmead Farms Inc. in Prairie County. In 1968 he bought a controlling interest in Twin City Bank in North Little Rock.

His other investments included such downtown Little Rock commercial buildings as the Worthen Bank and the First Federal Savings and Loan buildings. Ten years ago Lyon's financial empire had an estimated worth of at least a half-billion dollars.

In 1985 his son, a Harvard business school graduate who had guided the company for the past twenty years, was diagnosed with cancer. The disease went into remission, but four years later rumors that the Lyon family was selling its holdings surfaced. In 1989 he sold off several of his holdings, including the soft-drink bottling company to Coca-Cola of Atlanta, reportedly for close to $250 million.

While he was succeeding in business, Lyon also spent time with his family at his longtime home at 9 Sunset Drive in Cammack Village, where he resided until his death. He took up duck hunting when his son was about nine so the two could share a hobby.

"It is as bad not to know how to play as it is to play too much," he once said. Asked about the proudest moments in his life while being interviewed for an *Arkansas Democrat* profile thirteen years ago, Lyon cited his wedding and the birth of his son, not his first million.

He was a fast-paced, driven man—the animal he most identified with was a horse—but he was humble, saying once that the one word to sum him up would be fortunate.

He was also active in his church, Second Presbyterian, and community and became a major philanthropist through the foundation he and his wife established. Through the years he gave more than a million dollars to Arkansas College in Batesville, which he took an interest in through his wife, who died in May 1997. The small, Presbyterian-run liberal arts college was named in his honor on July 1, 1994, after Lyon initially said no but finally agreed. Besides money he gave the college to erect buildings and establish scholarships, he contributed his time and business advice. He served on its board for forty-two years, beginning in 1946. During his eleven years as chairman of the board in the '70s and '80s, the college endowment grew from less than $3 million to more than $40 million. Over the years, he served as chairman of the Pulaski County Tuberculosis Association's Christmas Seal drive and as president of the Little Rock Boys Club and the Committee of 100. He also served on the boards of Arkansas Children's Hospital, St. Vincent Infirmary Foundation, Little Rock Chamber of Commerce, Worthen Bank & Trust, Arkansas Arts Center, and Presbyterian Village. "There are certain things you can't delegate, like one's responsibility to your community and church," Lyon once said.

"You can never reach the place where you can say you've done enough."

Sister Catherine Markey, OSB
Father Joseph H. Biltz Award, 2006

Sister Catherine Markey, OSB, probably was destined to join a religious community from the day that her dad went to the Catholic boarding school in Newton, Massachusetts, to ask if his four children could attend as day students with a reduced tuition that their family could afford. Fortunately for all of us, Catherine, her sisters, and brother were accepted. Sister  Catherine said the nuns there never pressured them to enter the church, but that's how it turned out for all three of the girls.

Catherine's sisters were older, and when Catherine was a teenager she had opportunities to visit both of them in their religious communities. At thirteen, Catherine remembers seeing Sisters in Lafayette, Louisiana, throwing snowballs in a rare Christmas Eve snowfall...the first time she remembers seeing Sisters having fun. When she decided to join the community after her high school graduation, it was her father who supported the choice, and he delivered her to the train station in New York to begin her journey to New Orleans. When she became a novice, her name was changed to Sister Mary Thomas, and she was called Sister Thomas. In 1979, she returned to her Baptismal name, Catherine Markey.

Sister Catherine taught elementary and junior high school students and some high school classes in math and science while she studied as a postulant and novice. She also earned her undergraduate degree from the University of Southern Louisiana and was sent to Notre Dame for a master's program. She speculates that her opportunities for education were enhanced because she was a member of a religious community, and she became a teacher of chemistry and physics. Ultimately, she earned a master's degree in library science from Louisiana State University.

In 1977, she applied to the Diocese to work on the archives of the Catholic Church in Mississippi, Alabama, and Louisiana and was accepted for that job. The next year, the Fort Smith Benedictines were celebrating their 100th year anniversary and they tapped Sister Catherine to write their history. In 1979 she came to Mount St. Mary's in Little Rock and really began her work in social justice.

Serving along with Father Joseph Biltz, Sister Catherine became active with Bread for the World, the Arkansas Interfaith Conference, Arkansas Impact, and NCCJ sponsored dialogues, among other things. She vividly remembers Father Biltz's funeral, which Bill Clinton attended and at which a black choir sang, "We Shall Overcome." Also in attendance were many refugees who had been helped by Father Biltz.

After Father Biltz's death in 1987, Sister Catherine was not assigned by the church to work on social justice full-time, so she continued the work on her own time while serving as the diocesan archivist from 1979 to 1996. In 2006, she's still working for social justice.

After meeting Freddie and Vic Nixon through Father Biltz, Sister Catherine became actively involved in the Arkansas Coalition to Abolish the Death Penalty, including writing and visiting prisoners on death row in Cummins. Over the years, she has served on the coalition board and attended many vigils at the State Capitol and at Cummins. In 2006, she continues to monitor execution dates across the country and often writes letters to those with the power to change the death sentences. In 1996, Sister Catherine was named Abolitionist of the Year at the coalition's annual meeting. Sister Catherine continues to write a death row inmate, Raymond C. Sanders Jr., and she visits him approximately three times a year. (*Sanders is still on death row in 2012.*) She said she feels the personal contact is important for the inmate and herself. "As with any exchange...you never give something without receiving." Sister Joan Pytlik, DC, of Little Rock and Sister Mary John Seyler, OSB, of Jonesboro cite Sister Catherine as inspiring them to visit prisoners on a regular basis.

Sister Catherine has also worked with the Arkansas Coalition for Interfaith Worker Justice, and she is still concerned about labor issues and the declining power of labor unions to affect needed reforms for their members. In 2005, Sister Catherine was the recipient of the fifth annual Bishop Andrew J. McDonald Worker Justice Award presented by the Arkansas Interfaith Committee for Worker Justice.

This year, Sister Catherine is busy on many other things, too, including the Community Clearing House Backpack Program and Food Bank, serving as a guardian ad litem, and gathering with others weekly to protest the war in Iraq.

Her dream is that all the elected people, as well as their advisors, would work together to respect the dignity of ALL the peoples in the world. "After all," she adds, "God loves all people without exception."

Sister Catherine is retired and lives at St. Scholastica Monastery in Fort Smith. But being retired certainly doesn't mean that she doesn't work. Clearly, she is still committed to fostering justice in any way she can.

Hazel Bryan Massery
Father Joseph H. Biltz Award, 1997
(*Interview conducted August 28, 2012*)

Hazel Bryan Massery describes herself as a wife, a mother, a grandmother, and a great-grandmother. She is fortunate to have her eleven great-grandchildren living within sixty miles of her home, and she postponed this interview appointment until after the recent birthday party for the youngest, who just turned three, and until school had begun for the older children.

After the photo of fifteen-year-old Hazel Bryan taunting Elizabeth Eckford appeared in the newspaper in September of 1957, Hazel's mother felt that it wasn't going to be safe for Hazel to attend Central High School. Therefore, she quickly made arrangements for Hazel and her younger sister to transfer to Fuller High School, part of the Pulaski County school district, and actually closer to their home. As they were filling out their enrollment forms, some of the senior boys were "checking out the new girls." When Hazel spotted a tall good-looking fellow named Antoine Massery, she said to her sister, "Hands off. That one's mine." Sure enough, after Antoine's graduation in 1958, Hazel married him. They will celebrate their fifty-fourth wedding anniversary in November of 2012.

School rules then dictated that any girl who got married had to drop out of school for six weeks, and within three months Hazel had become pregnant, so then she was barred from returning to school for her senior year. After their first child was born, Hazel tried to study for her GED, but she quickly realized that taking care of a baby and studying were incompatible. Finally, in 1987, after her three children were grown, Hazel went to the GED office to inquire about a course of study. They asked her to take a test. When they saw the results, they gave her another test, and then another test, and finally they gave her "the" test. She easily earned her GED without any course work. (She says math wasn't her strong suit, however.)

Through the years, Hazel has thrown herself wholeheartedly into her role as wife, parent, and church member. For example, her husband just retired after forty years from running a business that they established, Antenna Systems of Arkansas. Hazel explains that Antoine began as a television repairman, and he was good at all things electronic, so the business expanded to cover all sorts of communication systems. She paid the bills, kept all the records, and occasionally climbed onto roofs or into attics, as they built and maintained their business.

As a mother to her three children, Hazel drove carpools, participated in school functions, and later graciously welcomed their spouses, children and step-children. She now enjoys being great grandmother to eleven, ages three to fourteen years old. As church members, Hazel, Antoine, and the children were there every time the doors were opened. Hazel had been a studious Bible student as a child, and she can still recite the books of the Bible in order. However, after much reading and reflection, Hazel became frustrated with the narrowness of perspective that she found within the church, among its leaders particularly. She hasn't been an active church member since the late '70s. Her current quest includes reading Karen Armstrong and other scholars of religion. She is fascinated by the origin and evolution of world religions and of the powerful influence they have had on our culture and personal lives.

She says that when she has had a problem or a question over the years, she went to the library. Her library research paid off when she and Antoine were expecting their third child. She decided that she wanted more information about natural childbirth, so she checked out a bunch of books. She thought the book by Marjorie Karmel, *Thank You, Dr. Lamaze,* made the most sense and asked her obstetrician if he would support her in using the Lamaze method. He said he thought that was the silliest thing he had ever heard of, so she found a new obstetrician and had a Lamaze birth at St. Vincent's Hospital in 1966, almost a decade before any Lamaze classes were taught in the Central Arkansas area, and before any fathers were allowed into the delivery room, both common practices in 2012.

Upon the occasion of the fortieth anniversary of the Central High Crisis in 1997, she again visited the library. Over the years, she had pretty much ignored the incident, but when she was called upon to talk about what had happened, she had to study up on the facts surrounding and following that fateful day, September 23, 1957, when the nine black students had first attempted to enter Central High School. Hazel had actually called Elizabeth Eckford in 1962 and apologized for her behavior, five years after the incident involving both of them. In 1997, when journalist Linda Monk wrote about the apology in a nationally syndicated news story, suddenly the unknown girl from the famous photo was thrust into the limelight.

The public occasion of Hazel and Elizabeth meeting in 1997 was again documented with photos and a front-page story. For the following two years, they made many presentations together talking about what had happened, how it had affected each of them, and what they were trying to do to heal the racial rifts of our community. Together, they took a six-week Healing Racism course offered by the City of Little Rock's Racial and Cultural Diversity Commission. Each clearly had a lot to learn from the other.

At one of their presentations, they were asked to explain how and what they were teaching their children, and whether they thought we had made any progress. Hazel shared the story of her son, whose best friend from elementary school, Larry, was African-American. The boys played together and often visited each other's homes. Hazel's son was fascinated by Larry's grandmother, an accomplished seamstress. "Mom, Larry's grandmother even makes his underwear!" he said one day. Larry's grandmother was amused and gave a pair of those homemade undershorts to Hazel's son. Tragically, Larry drowned the summer before the boys entered junior high. Years later, after Hazel's son married and moved away from home, she was clearing out his things and found those shorts. She cried that day, and as she told this story, there were again tears in her eyes.

Hazel does believe that we have made progress, but she wonders if we will ever be able to completely heal from our mistakes. At seventy years old, she questions whether she has any part yet to play.

When she talks about that September day in 1957, she freely admits that she just didn't "get it," a common charge leveled at white people even in 2012. Hazel says she never wanted or intended to be the "poster child for racism." Over the years, she has worked as a facilitator for parenting classes at the Parent Center (now part of Centers for Youth and Families), and she became a member of Betty Bumpers's organization, Peace Links. She credits those experiences with helping her to realize that her "outrageous behavior" in 1957 had "disgraced myself, my family, my school, my city, and my nation. I will be forever sorry for the harm that I did to Elizabeth and other African Americans." She gets it now, and she has been determined to never be so oblivious again.

As Hazel says, and photographer Will Counts agrees, "Life is more than a moment." And Hazel's life has included so much more than one glaring mistake and her personal atonement. At forty years old, Hazel attended the International Fest in downtown Little Rock and was delighted by the Middle Eastern dance troop's performance. She approached Mirana, the teacher and leader of the group, and inquired about how to get involved. Hazel took lessons, had gorgeous costumes, performed in recitals and at Riverfest and the International Fest, and even delivered "singing bellygrams." The belly dancing must have freed some inner spirit, because she also became Posey the Clown to entertain at children's birthday parties. Her most important gig as Posey was a birthday party for then-governor Bill Clinton. Her most important gig in real life is surely wife, mother, grandmother, and great-grandmother.

Reverend Ed Matthews
Father Joseph H. Biltz Award, 2009

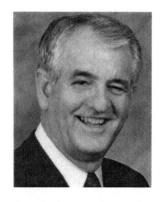

Ed Matthews tells a story about when he and his wife, Pat, served as missionaries in the Congo from 1959 to 1963. One of the other missionaries was the designated hostess when they had visitors. When all were ready to retire for the night, the hostess would say to the guests, "If you awaken and need *anything* in the night, just find me, and I will explain to you why you don't need it."

Ed has an uncanny sense of what we don't need and what we do need... which is relationship. He's been building relationships for his entire life.

It all began with that first call to serve in a tense Belgian Congo that was shedding its colonial past. For one thing, Ed and Pat experienced racial discrimination in reverse and grew in their understanding of why people react as they so often do when they are members of an oppressed group. On their return to the states, they were assigned to travel around the country preaching and sharing with others, beginning to build relationship as, Ed firmly believes, God still calls us to do.

During his pastorate at the Lakeside United Methodist Church in Pine Bluff, Ed had the opportunity to work with other visionary Methodist leaders on the Area Task Force on Hunger. Their first event brought 225 United Methodists from across Arkansas to a consciousness raising event on hunger, held at Hendrix College. As a symbol of their commitment "to live more simply so that others might simply live," most of the attendees slept on the floor of the activities building in the First United Methodist Church of Conway. That weekend culminated in the beginning of the annual Arkansas Ingathering, as a leadership network was established across the state. In-kind gifts of livestock and financial contributions were brought to the Ingathering, and United Methodist congregations from across Arkansas found a way to fight hunger both here at home and around the world. The goal for the first Ingathering was to raise $200,000. More than $500,000 was, in fact, raised. The Ingathering is still an annual event, and well over $20 million has been raised to date.

Always mindful of racial injustice, during Ed's first pastorate in Little Rock St. Andrews United Methodist Church, in the early 1960s, he participated in a sit-in at the Capitol to protest its racial segregation policy. He says, "An overwhelming majority of the congregation stood with us and even those in opposition tolerated us."

Ed talks fondly of his next appointment, in Fordyce, where he and Pat *lived* the Civil Rights Movement, with Pat being the first white teacher in the all-black public school and Ed serving as interim minister for the African-American Methodist Church in addition to his pastorate at the white church.

Ed served churches in Arkansas and Texas before he returned to Little Rock in 1990 as Senior Pastor of First United Methodist Church here. He retired from the ministry in 1998. He hasn't retired from working to build healthy relationships.

A couple of his proudest achievements since retirement are worth noting. During 1998, Arkansas experienced three tornadoes that caused devastation across the state. At that time there was no coordinated system of getting help to affected areas. For example, a truck of food from Rice Depot was dispatched to a hard-hit town with instructions to unload the food and return immediately for another load for another town. Instead of returning right away, the truck sat in the small town while local folks argued about how best to distribute the food. Ed sat down with Mayor Jim Dailey, County Judge Buddy Villines, Police Chief Louie Caudell, and others to discuss how we might do better. With help from James Lee Witt, they developed a statewide coordinated system of disaster response. Arkansas now has a disaster coordinator in every county.

In the mid-1990s, Ed overheard a conversation between the super-intendent of schools, Dr. Ruth Steele, and the police chief about the truancy problem in the Little Rock School District—there was no suitable and safe place to take truant students when they were picked up. Again Ed collected a group of concerned residents. Working together, they helped create the Alternative Learning Center in the old Carver School. It was partially staffed by interfaith volunteers who called parents and helped nurture both the students and their families to get the kids back into school. The Alternative Learning Center has been expanded and still operates as part of the LRSD today as the W. D. Hamilton Learning Academy, housed in the former Southwest Middle School.

That's the kind of thing we've come to expect from Ed Matthews. When he sees a need, he begins to gather the people who can get that need met. In his autobiographical piece in *Crisis of Conscience: Arkansas Methodists and the Civil Rights Struggle*, Ed wrote, "...how aware I am that through it all I was entirely too careful and cautious...how guilty I have felt as colleague after colleague took strong, prophetic stands while I stood by as a 'reconciler.'" Though he may feel as though he "played it safe," through his reconciling spirit, Ed has continued to work tirelessly for equal opportunities and rights for all races, for gays and lesbians, and for women.

Jerry Maulden

Humanitarian Award, 1989
(Interview conducted June 22, 2012)

Jerry Maulden was born during the Great Depression. He remembers being terrified when his dad once left in the back of a pickup truck to find work out of town. He didn't know if his dad would come back. From the insecurity surrounding this early experience to his life's many successes, it would be perfectly understandable, even appropriate, to hold Jerry's life up as an example of what it means to "live the American Dream."

But that dream did not come without challenges. Jerry met and married his wife, Sue, when they were both still teenagers. By the time Jerry began night school to earn his BS degree and later his CPA certificate, they had two children, Karen and Mike. They were blessed with two more children, Kris and Kelly, but they lost Kelly at the age of eight to a degenerative disease that had required Sue's constant attention for many years.

Jerry discovered early that he had a talent for management. In fact, he actually began honing those management skills at the age of ten, when he organized a baseball team, recruited and signed up his players, and got local businesses to sponsor their t-shirts.

Jerry began his career at Missouri Pacific Railroad (MOPAC), completing an apprenticeship followed by various accounting positions before becoming controller working for Dillards when they opened their first store in Austin, Texas. Jerry joined Arkansas Power & Light Co. in 1965. He was elected president and CEO of AP&L in 1979. Later he became the president and chief operating officer of Entergy Corporation, a U.S.-based global energy company.

He credits his rise through the ranks at Entergy to his ability to recognize talent and potential in others. He's incredibly proud that eight of his executive staff members later became CEO's of other companies. Jerry says he was never the smartest one in the room, but he had a talent for selecting and managing others—and he has used those same skills to become not only successful in business, but a champion of many important causes.

One of his favorite causes has been the Watershed Family Resource Center, founded and directed by Jerry's good friend Reverend Hezekiah Stewart (another Humanitarian Award honoree). Watershed provides a wide range of services, including assistance with basic needs, substance-abuse help, child care, and disability services. Jerry calls Stewart "a man of God." He was delighted when his church, First Baptist in Little Rock, also became a supporter of the programs at Watershed.

Jerry has also given long service to the Boys and Girls Club's Southwest region and national board. That was a direct payback for Jerry, who says that from age eight to eighteen he spent more hours than any other kid in history at the Boys Club in North Little Rock. They even gave him a key to the building so that he could play basketball on Sundays when the club was closed. As a local Boys Club board member, Jerry was delighted when it became the "Boys and Girls" club. Subsequently, the North Little Rock Boys and Girls Club made Jerry the first recipient of their Hall of Fame recognition.

Jerry also spent twelve years on the National Board of the NAACP, including a stint on the three-person executive committee as treasurer and chief financial officer. He served during a time when the NAACP had to re-invent and re-invigorate itself following the advances gained through the civil rights movement. He names Benjamin Hooks, executive director from 1977 to 1992, as the best thing that happened for the NAACP during that time because Hooks always respected the contributions of the elders who had been leaders during the turmoil of the 1960s while successfully engaging young people in the work of the organization.

Back home in Little Rock, Jerry served Arkansas Repertory Theatre as a board chair and developed The Rep's first ever corporate fund-raising campaign. He tapped his good friend, attorney Herschel Friday, to head that first campaign, and the theatre has enjoyed remarkable corporate support ever since.

Jerry also served on the St. Vincent Infirmary board during the time that Sister Margaret Blandford was the CEO. His friendship with Sister Margaret was an incredibly important one—it was she who listened and supported him when he realized that he was suffering from acute depression during the height of his professional career. Sister Margaret referred him to the right doctors, who in turn helped him get the proper medication. Jerry is not reluctant to share his experience with others in order to further remove the stigma of this very treatable disease. He calls Tipper Gore, who publicly shared her own story of depression, one of his role models for her work to de-stigmatize mental illness and encourage others to seek treatment.

Jerry Maulden has received many honors and served many causes, but he is quick to add, "None of my accomplishments would have been possible without my lifelong partnership with Sue, and the backing of Entergy." Jerry is retired now, and he and Sue love spending more time with their family, which now includes seven grandchildren and two great-grandchildren.

Looking back over a long career of making a difference, there is one more thing that he would do if he could: provide meaningful jobs to those who need them. Jerry says, "A man should be able to work to provide food, shelter, and clothing for those he loves." Jerry has been blessed to do that and so much more for others he's never even met. Guess that is the American Dream after all—to rise to a level of personal and professional success, and then to turn around and give back with joy.

Susan May
Father Joseph H. Biltz Award, 2012

Susan May grew up in Little Rock and
never had to think about injustice beyond
whether high school fraternities and soror-
ities would be allowed on campus with full
privileges. She said she was raised like a
princess with everything she needed or
wanted. Her first time away from home was
to attend junior college at Mt. Vernon, a
women's college in Washington DC. After
two years away, she wasn't ready to come home, so she entered the
University of North Carolina as a junior. She majored in political science and began to hone her leadership skills. She was one of only two
students from west of the Mississippi River, but was elected president
of her sorority.

Like all good girls her age, Susan got married after graduating from
college; she then spent two years in England while her husband served
in the Air Force. It was on the air base there that Susan first seriously
confronted the question of race. The wives had planned a huge party
celebrating the Old South, with Mint Juleps, of course. The day before
the party, they learned that their first black officer was to arrive with his
wife the next day. After some soul-searching, they decided to proceed
with the party as planned. The new black officer disarmed and charmed
them all by taking the microphone to thank them (with a wink of his
eye) for the lovely event in his honor, and then he proceeded to dance
with every woman at the party. Susan says it was the first time in her life
she had ever met a black person as a social equal.

Upon returning to Little Rock, Susan had her first baby, and
began to help with the Women's Emergency Committee. One of the
founders of the WEC, Margaret Kolb, lived up the street from Susan,

and she decided she wanted to be like Margaret and the other leaders of that group. They were using their time, talent, and influence to make a difference.

When she was invited to join the Junior League of Little Rock, she had to ask what it was, but it soon became a focal point of her life, giving her the opportunity to give back to her community while learning leadership skills. She held several offices and was a delegate to a regional conference in Jackson, Mississippi, all with great enthusiasm. However, she was troubled by one thing. One of her best friends, Sally Rosen Phillips, who was Jewish, had never been invited to join the Junior League. The admissions system was confidential then, but Susan and several others worked for three years, proposing Sally each year for membership. Working behind the scenes, Susan felt sure that Sally would be invited for membership that third year, but the committee vote was one short. Devastated by the outcome, Susan and ten other League members resigned.

She calls her decision to resign from the Junior League a turning point that changed her life dramatically. She turned her attention to other community causes and served on boards from the Museum of Natural History to Youth Home which her parents had helped to found. She also served with her friends on the Panel of American Women. By the early '70s, she was divorced with three children, so she entered the workforce beginning in ad sales for radio. In 1975, she married Ron May, and continued to raise the children, work part-time, and volunteer for many causes.

Another turning point occurred for Susan in 1990. Her son Jimmy, thirty-two years old at the time, a law school graduate and working in Washington DC, told her that he was gay. As she tells it, she responded calmly if a bit mystified, put Jimmy on his plane to fly home, and then fell apart. This had not been anything she had ever considered and didn't fit her "plan" for her son's life. She recalls a favorite *Peanuts* joke where Charlie Brown asks, "Do you want to make God laugh? Then tell him your plans."

She began to learn everything that she could, but was again caught off-guard a few months later when her daughter Suzy shared the same story. "Mom, I'm gay, too." As Susan tells it, "My children came out of the closet, and I went into the closet." Hesitantly, she began to reach out to other parents of gay children, but often found them unwilling to even talk about their children. As she saw the shame in another mother's eyes, she realized that she was living with shame, too. She got very angry and decided no one was going to make her ashamed of her bright, beautiful, and successful children. Susan May came roaring out of that closet in her trademark style and has since worked tirelessly to build understanding regarding what it means to be gay, lesbian, bi-sexual, or transgender.

Susan has worked with Parents and Friends of Lesbians and Gays (PFLAG) and with churches to promote understanding. She has supported others, individuals, parents, and friends, to "come out of the closet." Susan is also a frequent member of Just Communities of Arkansas's Straight Talk Panels, where her story has touched the hearts and minds of many. In her own journey, she has confronted hatefulness but also incredible caring.

Susan sites three significant events in her advocacy for GLBT rights and inclusion. In 1994, she lobbied the Arkansas congressional delegation in Washington DC with a group of PFLAG members from all over the United States, in favor of the Employment Non-discrimination Act. In 2000, she walked with her children, Jimmy and Suzy, in the Millennial March for gay rights in Washington DC. And in 2004, she and her husband, Ron, joined the ACLU of Arkansas as plaintiffs in a case filed before the Arkansas Supreme Court that challenged the so-called "Amendment Concerning Marriage."

Susan may never have planned this part of her life, but our community couldn't ask for a more passionate advocate for understanding and acceptance.

Bishop Larry Maze
Father Joseph H. Biltz Award, 2005

During college, Larry Maze was having a beer with one of his favorite professors, Bill Lisenby, when Bill said, "Do you realize how much you complain about what the church is not doing right? Why don't you just get ordained and change things yourself?" It took only a few years for Larry to decide that that was good advice.

Larry was born in Montana into what he describes as a non-churched family, but from an early age he would visit churches on his own. When Larry was in the navy, President John F. Kennedy inspired him to think we could be better as a nation. When he returned from the navy to college, Larry began to try to get more politically active and wanted to work through the church. He was extremely frustrated one time when he gathered a group of Episcopalian students to hear a local priest discuss some of the challenging issues of the time, which was the '60s, and the priest chose to speak on the meaning of the synoptic gospels. Larry found the church to be avoiding the real issues, not doing or saying much, in Montana at least. You could never say that about Larry Maze, as he has lived his vocation in the church.

In the late '70s, as a very young Vicar of St. James' Episcopal Church in Port Gibson, Mississippi, Larry partnered with a black preacher from down the street to plan an Easter sunrise service for their combined congregations. The first hurdle was finding a place that would allow them to meet. Finally they called an armory, which as a federal institution couldn't deny them. They began to publicize the service, and optimistically set up eighty chairs in the parking lot. They had the black choir and pianist with a piano brought in on a truck. When the morning came, they actually had to get more chairs, and those two congregations still have their combined Easter service to this day. What Larry learned later is that his congregation was okay with the combined service, but they were aghast when Larry arranged for all in attendance to eat together. His church members explained later that they only went along with the highly unusual plan of black folks and white folks eating together because they didn't want to embarrass their young minister.

Larry has continued to ask his church and its members to step beyond their comfort zones and to live out their faith principles.

Larry understood the dynamics of bias from his boyhood because of the downtrodden situation of the Native Americans in his community. He remembers the neighborhood store that had a sign: "No Beer Sold to Indians." He saw the parallels in the racial divide in the South. Later he saw the same dynamic as his and other churches excluded gays and lesbians from full participation.

Larry won't tell you this, but others will attest that he has been an unfailing leader in the Episcopal Church's inclusion of all persons. As a member of the House of Bishops, Larry Maze has consistently championed the rights of gays and lesbians. And he was the first bishop from the South and Southwest to vote consistently for inclusion. Therefore, to put it mildly, he has lived through some tense times within his church, and today the Episcopal Church is one of the most welcoming Christian churches in the United States. According to those who have worked with Larry, he is one of the most profound yet least pretentious bishops in the church today. They call him an enabler, seldom taking the credit but always willing to do the work.

Within Arkansas Larry has been a convener for interfaith groups to work on issues of gay rights, hate crime legislation, racial and religious bias, and misunderstanding, among others.

Ask Larry what he's most proud of and he immediately mentions his four children. "Somehow they've all managed to grow up without the deep-seated prejudices so common in folks who are older."

When asked about the future, Larry thinks our greatest need is to continue to work with our young people—to help them overcome the fear that is often preached from our highest offices and biggest pulpits. "Only when we overcome our fear of those who are different," according to Larry, "will we be able to ensure that no one is suffering from our injustice."

Cora Duffy McHenry

Humanitarian Award, 1996
(*Interview conducted June 27, 2012*)

Cora Duffy McHenry still can't get a license to teach in Louisiana, and she's proud of that. The irony? Cora McHenry led the Arkansas Education Association, the largest organization of education and support professionals in Arkansas, for fifteen years.

Cora was the third-oldest of thirteen children. Her parents were cotton farmers, and her most detested job on the farm was cleaning slaughtered hogs. Her best job was delivering water in a pail to her father. She always tried to walk fast to deliver the water while it was still cool. To this day, she moves at a clip.

She credits her teachers—Mrs. Thelma Smith, who taught English; Mrs. Carolyn Gaylord, who taught home economics; Mr. Curtis Sykes, who taught social studies; and an elementary teacher, Mrs. Earlene Brown—with developing her love of learning and academics. Mrs. Smith told her one day, "I think you would make an excellent English teacher." So that's what she set out to become.

Her older brother took off for college with nothing but a tin suitcase containing all his clothes. Three years later, she packed her own tin suitcase and made her way by bus to Pine Bluff to attend Arkansas AM&N. When she arrived without notice at the beginning of the summer, the first person she encountered sent her to the registrar's office, which sent her to the business office, which sent her to the President's office. No one knew quite what to do with this tiny, poor child from Augusta, Arkansas. She waited for what seemed like a very long time for the opportunity to meet AM&N President Dr. Lawrence A. Davis Sr. It was a meeting that would change her life.

Dr. Davis said, "If you want it this badly, I'm going to make sure you get it." He gave Cora a job cleaning his personal residence, which led to a job in the snack bar, then to a job as a residence assistant, and later, to work in the library. There she memorized the Dewey Decimal system, catalogued new books, and even learned to bind books. Cora says she didn't know that trip to Pine Bluff was courageous at the time. All of the Duffy children must have shared her courage, because every one of them went to college, got a job, and then helped the next one in line to go to school. All of them graduated.

Cora majored in English and excelled in her classes, just as Mrs. Smith expected. Her only setback was her first encounter with an IQ test, on which she scored badly. She remembers one of the questions that asked, "Which one is NOT like the others?" One of the choices was a picture of a bowling pin. Never having been to a bowling alley, Cora mistook the object for a milk bottle. The bias against poor or minority children in those early IQ tests was later well-documented.

After Dr. Lawrence Davis took a year's sabbatical in Africa, Cora followed another mentor to complete her education at Southern University in Baton Rouge, Louisiana. Cora notes that to keep from integrating their schools, Louisiana had poured many resources into Southern, including building a lab school on campus, where Cora did her student teaching. There she was also re-tested, rectifying the inaccuracy of the early IQ test.

Right in the middle of her student teaching, and during the early civil rights struggles across the United States, two African-American law students at Southern were arrested for a minor infraction. The bail set for them was disproportionately high. The students gathered in the stadium, passed a hat, and paid the bail within three hours. Plans were made to boycott classes. The president, fearful for his job, said that any student who didn't attend class would be immediately dropped. Instead, the students lined up and withdrew themselves. Since the students had already paid their fees, they remained on campus.

Ultimately, the president lost his job, and two weeks later, the students went back to classes to finish the year. However, Governor Earl Kemp Long issued a ruling that no student who had participated in the disobedience could be granted a license for anything in the state. That included teachers, lawyers, engineers—*anyone* requiring licensure to practice his or her chosen profession.

After graduation, Cora secured a teaching job in Camden, Arkansas, where she met fellow teacher Henry McHenry. They were married in 1962. They have one daughter, Stephanie, who is now the CFO and VP for Business and Advancement at Cleveland State University.

Better jobs brought Cora and Henry to Little Rock, and she was named by the Arkansas Teachers Association, the black professional education association, as a leader of the Merger Committee. When the ATA and the Arkansas Education Association, the white teachers group, were merged in 1969, executive secretary Forrest Rozzell hired Cora to provide in-service education across Arkansas for teachers in newly desegregated schools. As a result of that project, Cora wrote the publication "Together We Can, A Guide to School-Community Relations," which was published by the U.S. Department of Education.

Later, as director of the AEA, Cora presided over many significant accomplishments. They decentralized their services by opening offices across the state, resulting in a dramatic increase in membership among teachers. They passed the Educational Excellence Act, which requires education funds to come off the top of our state budget allocations. They filed the Lake View case, which ultimately established mandatory curriculum standards, better teacher pay, and pre-kindergarten for low income children, among other things. With legislation sponsored by Representative Grover Richardson in 1972, they removed all the vestiges of Jim Crow education laws still on the books in Arkansas. And Cora was appointed by the governor to serve on a fifteen-member Education Standards Commission, chaired by Hillary Clinton, that set standards for accreditation of Arkansas public schools.

Helping her siblings attain a college education was only the first of many ways Cora has been "paying it forward" during her long years of service. Following her retirement from the AEA, she began volunteering to raise money for Shorter College and ultimately served as its president for nine years, until she retired on July 1, 2010. She's still moving at a clip, serving on boards and commissions such as Arkansas State's Daisy Bates Birthday Celebration Committee and the Little Rock Residential Facility Housing Board, and as Director of Christian Education for Bethel AME Church in Little Rock.

Freeman McKindra Sr.
Father Joseph H. Biltz Award, 2011

How does the eleventh of fourteen children uphold the high standards expected in his family? For Freeman McKindra, the answer to this question has not been found by seeking to stand out; rather, Freeman has distinguished himself through a lifetime of service to community and humanity.

In his poem "If," Rudyard Kipling wrote:

If you can talk with crowds and keep your virtue,
Or walk with kings—nor lose the common touch...

Freeman seems to have an innate ability to work with crowds and kings alike, bringing out the best in them. His father was a successful farmer and community leader in the Union Chapel Community in Conway County, Arkansas, but curious Freeman pursued a love of science, ultimately earning his degree from AM&N (now the University of Arkansas at Pine Bluff) after a three-year break for military service in the Marine Corps. Freeman, who found college classes easy, majored in biology with a minor in chemistry. He even took night courses during his military service, not surprisingly preferring his classes to guard duty.

After his graduation from college, Freeman entered the Peace Corps and served in West Pakistan for two years as a zoology teacher for junior college and pre-med students. As he got to know his students, they accepted him and often invited him to their home villages to visit with their families. He was impressed, even charmed by their knowledge of the culture, especially their renowned regard for the elders of their families.

Upon returning to the United States, Freeman accepted a position in Washington DC as a high school science teacher in the Cardozo

Project in Urban Teaching. Freeman and one of his colleagues repeatedly visited in students' homes despite the students saying, "Don't you come to my house!" Freeman witnessed firsthand the difference engaged parents can make in a child's school performance and classroom decorum. His next two years were spent teaching chemistry and biology and testing an ecology curriculum in Kwara State, Nigeria, West Africa.

By this time, with both of his parents gone and most of his siblings moved on, there was nothing to pull Freeman back to Arkansas, so he worked in various roles for Volunteers in Service to America (VISTA) in the Southwest Region of the United States and had a short stay in graduate school in Illinois before returning to Arkansas in 1976 as a program officer for the Federal Domestic Volunteer Agency–ACTION. These experiences fostered in Freeman interest and expertise in managing initiatives using community volunteers, so it was natural for him to join the staff of the Winthrop Rockefeller Foundation in 1984 as a senior program officer for community and economic development. After meeting Wilma Jean Kelley of Texarkana, he assumed another important job in 1978, that of husband. Wilma and Freeman have three grown children: Fatima Jo'wan, Freeman II, and Frederick.

As a program officer with the Winthrop Rockefeller Foundation, Freeman worked throughout the state developing and managing grant programs in economic development, leadership development, community organizing, and community development. He designed and managed the initiative that promoted rural community development corporations as tools for local communities. If residents named buildings after one of the persons who truly changed their community, there would be Freeman McKindra Centers all across Arkansas. Freeman is quick to point out that he doesn't tell others what they need. In his role, he helps them to identify what they need for a healthier community, and then helps them to plan how to deliver services to strengthen all the members of their community.

Lured back to work by Dr. Tom Bruce, Freeman continues to serve as a community liaison for the College of Public Health at UAMS. What every non-profit executive lucky enough to work with Freeman knows is that he has knowledge of and friends in every county in our state. And Freeman has shared his knowledge freely, serving on many boards and advisory councils, including The Governor's Advisory Committee on Volunteerism, The Neighborhood Funders Group, Rural Community Assistance Program, The Little Rock School District Foundation, and Just Communities of Arkansas, among many others.

Freeman's work has been recognized by many: the Arkansas Rural Development Commission with the Rural Advocate of the Year Award; the Martin Luther King Salute to Greatness banquet with their Community Service Award; Reed Memorial CME Church with the Evanda Evans Faith Based Community Service Award; and the Office of the Governor, DHS Division of Volunteerism, and KARK-4 with the Distinguished Citizen of the Year Award in 2010.

What Freeman says he's loved most about his work is the opportunity to help create learning spaces for people, so that they can make the best use of their own talents and resources.

Donna McLarty

Humanitarian Award, 1991
(Interview conducted August 30, 2012)

Donna Kay Cochran McLarty is an advocate for the arts and has always had a heart for women, children, and families. Her influence is now felt worldwide, and it all began in Arkansas.

Donna was born in 1946 in Texarkana, the only child of Lucille and Virgil Cochran. She attended the University of Arkansas at Fayetteville, and she smiles when she says, "Studying paid off for me." At the end of her first year as a business major, she was invited to attend the Beta Gamma Sigma banquet for outstanding business students. There she met Thomas F. "Mack" McLarty III, also an outstanding business student. They dated throughout their college years, married following their graduation in 1968, and moved to Little Rock, where Donna had a job with the Arkansas Legislative Council and Mack was the reading clerk for the House of Representatives. The McLarty family automobile business took them back to Mack's hometown of Hope, Arkansas, for five years, and then brought them back to Little Rock in the mid-'70s when Mack took over management of a truck leasing division of McLarty Companies.

As a young mother of two boys, Mark and Franklin, Donna was delighted to join the Junior League of Little Rock in 1975. Donna calls her membership in the Junior League a "point of entry" for understanding the opportunities for service and for getting the training to be an effective volunteer. She still recalls and lives by lessons learned during her provisional year. And she appreciates one Junior League practice in particular: giving ownership of any project or program to the people who are being served. For example, over its ninety-year history in Little Rock, the League has helped establish programs that have grown into the Arkansas Arts Center, the Centers for Youth and Families, and Riverfest, among many others.

When Donna was appointed the community vice president of the Junior League, she became the League's representative on the Riverfest board and the Arkansas Arts Center board. She later served a full term on the AAC board and appreciated the education programs that helped teachers in the public schools to incorporate art projects into teaching core subjects such as math, history, and reading.

Growing out of a Junior League conference, Parenting is Primary, The Parent Center was established by the Junior League in 1984 to provide parenting education. As The Parent Center board chair, Donna provided leadership in 1987 when The Parent Center, The Elizabeth Mitchell Children's Center, and Stepping Stone merged to become the Centers for Youth and Families. In describing the wisdom of the merger, Donna says, "Together, we were able to provide education and support for parents, social services, crisis intervention, psychological counseling, and even foster care, as needed." Donna is incredibly proud of the growth of the Centers, and in 2000, Centers was named nonprofit of the year by *Arkansas Business*. In November of 2012, Centers celebrated its twenty-fifth year, and Donna helped to plan the activities.

Donna also joined Hillary Clinton and Amy Rossi to address problems in the Arkansas juvenile justice system during these same years, and she was active in the public schools, particularly through the Arts in Education program. In thinking about her broad involvement, Donna cites a great appreciation for the shared experiences and generational relationships of her Arkansas home.

Even though she had served in many leadership positions in the non-profit sector of Central Arkansas, Donna McLarty was a bit at sea when she moved to Washington DC in January of 1993 with her husband, who had accepted the job as President Bill Clinton's first White House chief of staff. She knew that Mack would be consumed by his responsibilities and that she would need to find her own place in their new community, so she called her friend Tipper Gore to ask for advice. Tipper, wife of Al Gore, the new Democratic Vice President, invited Donna to have lunch with her and another "Washington wife," Susan Baker, whose husband, Republican Jim Baker, had previously served as White House chief of staff and as Secretary of State. Their non-partisan advice to Donna was, "Just say yes."

Saying yes when she was called has led Donna to serve as a trustee of the Kennedy Center for the Performing Arts, on the Blair House board, with the World Conference of Religions for Peace, on the board of Wesley Theological Seminary, and as a member of the Women's Foreign Policy Group. Following that lunch, Donna and Tipper worked together to establish two groups: Cabinet Spouses and White House Spouses. Donna explains, "Spouses come to Washington as strangers, and through these groups, they are able to form lifetime friendships."

When they moved to Washington DC, Donna and Mack kept their home in Little Rock and have divided their time between the two cities. Donna actually beams when she describes her current board service with Vital Voices Global Partnership. This nonprofit grew out of work begun in 1997 by then-first lady Hillary Clinton and former secretary of state Madeleine Albright to promote the advancement of women as a U.S. foreign policy goal. The initial response from women was so much greater than expected that the Vital Voices Global Partnership was organized in 2000 as a public/private endeavor. To continue the work, Vital Voices identifies and invests in women around the world to advance women's economic, political and social status, by providing skills, networking and other support. Vital Voices' international staff and team of over 1,000 partners have trained and mentored more than 12,000 emerging women leaders from more than 144 countries in Africa, Asia, Eurasia, Latin America and the Caribbean, and the Middle East. Those women have returned home to train and mentor more than 500,000 additional women and girls. In sum, Vital Voices is advancing women's economic, political, and social status around the world. And as Donna would point out, "We have learned by examples worldwide that when we elevate the status of women, the family and entire community prospers."

Donna and Mack have created a McLarty Global Fellowship Program to connect University of Arkansas students and faculty—from the Clinton School of Public Service, the Walton College of Business, and the Fulbright College of Arts and Sciences—with Vital Voices women around the world. The scholars and faculty are providing technical assistance for women who run small businesses and who need additional skills to grow their organizations successfully. Research of leadership skills is being conducted as well. This group has worked in Ghana for the past two years, and they are learning about the different perspectives and challenges that exist in other cultures.

The McLartys also support two Study Abroad Scholarships annually and a Presidential Fellows Program that allows students to participate in the Center for the Study of the Presidency in Washington. The goal is to develop a new generation of national leaders committed to public service.

Donna McLarty is living proof of the incredible things that can happen when one smart and motivated woman has the vision to just say "yes." Fortunately, Donna has been saying "yes" for a lot of causes, for a long time, to the benefit of countless women, children, and families in Arkansas and around the world.

Thomas F. "Mack" McLarty III

Humanitarian Award, 1991
(*Interview conducted August 30, 2012*)

Soon after winning election, President-elect Bill Clinton asked his longtime friend Thomas F. "Mack" McLarty III to serve as his chief of staff. After careful consideration and discussion with his family, Mack accepted the responsibility—grateful for the honor to serve his president and his country and mindful of the reality, as his friend Howard Baker had put it, that when the president calls, it's difficult to say no.

The transition team's first task, even before they went to Washington, was to put together the president's Cabinet. Knowing that Cabinet appointments had to be confirmed by Congress, the members of the team were understandably nervous. They didn't want a big fight during their first weeks in Washington, and they also needed to be ready to go to work. To facilitate the process, Mack suggested that he call his longtime friend, Republican Minority Leader Trent Lott, with whom he had worked while serving as CEO of the natural gas company Arkla. The team's seasoned advisors were aghast. "You can't just call the other party's leader!"

But Mack has always understood the power of personal relationships—for building trust, for reaching compromise, and for getting things done. He prevailed and made the phone call to the Lott home in Pascagoula, Mississippi. He had a pleasant chat with Lott's wife, Tricia, and then he told the senator what was on his mind: "We need to get our team in place." Senator Lott said that he understood, but added that they would likely give the nominee for Commerce, Ron Brown, a good going-over. Still, Clinton's entire Cabinet (including Ron Brown) was confirmed within a week. Mack recounts that this was one of the fastest confirmation processes ever.

Mack was born in Hope, Arkansas, to Thomas F. McLarty Jr. and Helen Hesterly McLarty. Mack's father was the second generation of McLartys to own an automobile dealership, and his mother was active in the community, while also helping with the family business. Her private-sector knowledge, civic involvement, and friendship with Governor David Pryor helped lead to her appointment as the first woman to serve on the Arkansas Industrial Development Commission (now the Arkansas Economic Development Commission)—a McLarty family honor made all the more special years later when Mack's son Franklin served as AEDC chairman under Governor Mike Beebe.

In addition to the positive influence and example of his parents, Mack recalls the impact of his English and Spanish teacher, Mrs. Anna E. Williams. Mrs. Williams was the Hope High School student council sponsor, and she taught Mack how to make and prioritize a "to do" list, among other skills. She was "exacting," rather than "strict," says Mack, and she certainly didn't suffer fools. Thanks to her tutelage, Mack was chosen for the Hearst Fellowship program, which sent him to Washington DC. During his month in the nation's capital, Mack met President Lyndon Johnson, Secretary of State Dean Rusk, and Arkansas leaders such as Senator William Fulbright.

Mrs. Williams retired from teaching to live in Mississippi. Years later, when Mack was giving a speech in Jackson, Mississippi, he invited Mrs. Williams to attend. There, in front of a thousand people, he talked about the influence she had been in his life. The crowd gave her a standing ovation. As Mack put it, "I got the sense they were applauding not just for Mrs. Williams, but for all the special teachers who had made a difference in their lives."

Mack attended the University of Arkansas at Fayetteville, where he earned a degree in business administration with honors and met his future wife, Donna Kay Cochran. While at Fayetteville, Mack served as student body president and began the first mass-transit system for the campus.

At age twenty-three, Mack was elected to the Arkansas House of Representatives. After serving one term, he chose to return to Hope to help expand the family business. In 1973, he and Donna moved to Little Rock with McLarty Companies. Later, from 1983 to 1992, he served as chief executive officer of Arkla, Inc., an integrated natural gas company listed on the New York Stock Exchange.

Mack says his most gratifying community involvements include serving on the Hempstead County Industrial Commission and as president of the Greater Little Rock Chamber of Commerce. He firmly believes that there are many ways to contribute to one's community; his advice to someone who wants to make a difference is, "Just get involved. Tutor a child; support a charity event; volunteer at your church. There is no shortage of opportunities or needs, and you will feel the thread that binds us together when you do your part to help and support others."

As President Clinton's first White House chief of staff, Mack championed the 1993 deficit reduction package, which moved the federal budget from a deficit to a surplus for the first time since 1969. He also played important roles in the passage of the North American Free Trade Agreement, the Family and Medical Leave Act, and welfare reform legislation.

After nearly two years on the job, Mack stepped down as chief of staff. The President named him Counselor to the President and Special Envoy to the Americas. Mack described one of his assignments in that latter role as a "mission impossible"—yet, once again, the value of personal relationships came to the fore.

The assignment concerned the inaugural Summit of the Americas, to be held in Miami in December 1994. At the time, Itamar Franco was the lame duck president of Brazil, and Mack was sent to ask him if he would invite the newly elected Brazilian president, Fernando Henrique Cardoso, to attend the gathering as well. It was, understandably, a sensitive topic.

As Mack visited with President Franco, he learned that the Brazilian leader had been educated at a Methodist school. Mack shared that as a teenager, his son Mark had lived in the Brazilian city of Belo Horizonte, where he had worked with the Methodist Church. Franco recalled his school days with great fondness, and a bond between the two men formed. When Mack asked his difficult question, Franco said yes, and Cardoso was included in the 1994 Summit. Mission impossible—accomplished.

For all of Mack's achievements, his greatest pride is his family and the fact that his and Donna's two sons, Mark and Franklin, are the fourth generation to work with McLarty Companies. Arkansas also remains close to Mack's heart. The McLartys have kept their family home in Hope, and Mack considers Arkansas his "Temple of the Familiar." Northwest Arkansas also holds special significance for Mack: "I received a wonderful education at the university, and I met Donna there, after all."

Jane Mendel

Father Joseph Biltz Award, 1993

(1925–2006)

That was Jane

By Paul Greenberg, Wednesday, January 25, 2006

Reprinted with permission from the Arkansas Democrat-Gazette

I'd bet that every person in the throng that filled the spacious sanctuary of Congregation B'nai Israel for Jane Mendel's memorial service Sunday afternoon felt they shared a deep, personal, unique bond with her—the kind of special bond no one else could. Even more remarkable, each did.

That was Jane. She connected with people. Personally. One by one. Now, one by one, the members of the legendary Women's Emergency Committee that saved Little Rock's schools when the men couldn't during the Crisis of '57 recede into history and even myth. The Great Faubusfear may have intimidated just about everybody else in Arkansas, but not Jane and Friends.

Jane Billstein Mendel, who was eighty-one years young when she died Friday, was one of the brightest stars in that constellation of ladies. You might even say she was the key to it, since she was the head of the telephone chain that sent the word out to everybody else whenever anything was needed—a good turnout at the polls, a show of support at a school board meeting, baked goods, you name it.

Miss Jane had the perfect personality for the job—friendly, engaging, charming ... and tireless.

Hillel—the talmudic sage who asked, "If not now, when?"—would have liked Jane B. Mendel. She saw no point in putting off anything good, and that included having a good time.

Despite the light air with which she went through life (what a joy she was to be with!) and the way she rose above all of her own difficulties, including the recurring back and neck pain that plagued her the last decade of her life, Jane Mendel was utterly serious—even urgent—about some things. Like justice. Like stewardship. Like treating people as people.

The French might call hers a sense of noblesse oblige. The Jews call it being a mensch—a decent person in all respects. Southerners just call it being a lady.

Her two favorite words, whether reacting to a witticism or coloring with her great-grandchild, were Delicious! and Adorable! She was as sharp as a whole box of tacks, and as kind as she was sharp. The lady may have been utterly serious about seeing that wrongs were righted and justice done in this world, but she was never solemn about it. It didn't surprise me to learn that, like many a political operative, she was adept at poker. And knew her Scotches.

Jane also knew that a soft word not only turneth away wrath but could get things done. Before you knew it, she had you on her side. Or if she didn't, you wished you were. Her side always seemed to be having more fun.

How a woman born and reared in Toledo, Ohio, would become the perfect Southern lady, as in Iron Magnolia, I have no idea, but, as I said, she was sharp. It didn't take her any time at all to adjust to any social setting, including a move south of Mason-Dixon's when she married a Southern boy.

Another thing about Jane Mendel: She made no short-term commitments. After the Women's Emergency Committee had dealt with the emergency in Little Rock's schools, and after she and her friends in STOP (Stop This Outrageous Purge!) had stopped a purge of school-teachers in the local schools, she went on to found Volunteers in Public Schools. She wasn't out just to save the public schools; she wanted to improve them. Jane didn't believe in doing things halfway.

VIPS still gives out an annual Jane Mendel Award in her honor. So does the Jewish Federation of Arkansas. And if I don't mention all the other awards that she earned or that have been named for her, forgive me. There are so many. I got the impression she was embarrassed by all the attention.

It wasn't so much the things she did that came to mind when folks thought about Jane, but how she did them—with a twinkle in her eye and, behind it, an intelligence that saw right through you, for good or ill. Her B.S. detector must have been on automatic; it was never turned off. But she tactfully didn't say everything she thought, thank God, and for that we lesser beings will always be grateful.

This was Jane Mendel: The only text in the program handed out at her memorial service, besides the traditional prayers and the dates of her birth and death, were the simple words on the cover: May the work I've done speak for me. And it does—eloquently. Just as, lest we forget, the work we do here will speak for all of us.

At the end of the service, the crowd milled around for the longest time, as if loath to leave the memory of Jane. Then, as each of the mourners left, they were handed a small bottle of champagne in accordance with her last wishes. In her friendly but firm manner, Jane had left only two instructions for the service—"Tell the rabbi to keep the eulogy under twenty minutes, and get everyone a glass of champagne."

That was Jane—bubbly, hospitable, generous, life-enhancing. She was a champagne kind of girl long after she was no longer a girl.

They say the light we see from distant stars may come to us long after the star itself has gone. That was Jane, too. She still shines.

Clarice P. Miller
Humanitarian Award, 2004

Clarice Pettigrew Miller grew up in Pine
Bluff, Arkansas, the daughter of a grocer
and a beautician. She remembers her childhood as almost idyllic, surrounded by extended family and friends. Clarice describes
her segregated high school as a nurturing
environment where she had skilled and dedicated teachers who always expected (and
got) the best from their students. She also
fondly remembers her "Girl's Club" where she learned the social graces
from Miss Hortense. She and a cousin were two of the first black Girl
Scouts in Arkansas.

She attended AM&N College, now the University of Arkansas at
Pine Bluff, where she met and married Raymond Miller the summer before her senior year. While Raymond completed his medical internship
and residency, Clarice was a teacher of social studies for the Little Rock
School District, one of two African-American teachers at Pulaski Heights
Junior High. Following the birth of their second child, Clarice decided
to take a few years off from teaching, at Raymond's urging. Subsequently
Clarice became a "full-time" volunteer in our community as she reared
their two children, Phillip and Terri.

Clarice's volunteer résumé is long and varied, with service ranging
from the United Methodist Church, the Arkansas Symphony Orchestra,
and NCCJ Ourtown, to the Coalition for a Healthier Arkansas. Two of
her current commitments are St. Vincent Health System Board of Directors
and program coordinator of the Little Rock Chapter of The Links, Inc.
Many good causes have benefitted from Clarice's time and talent.

But Clarice's most dedicated work has been in support of children
and families. Beginning with the PTA, Clarice has served with many

youth and family support agencies. One of her strongest commitments was the Parenting From Prison project. Every week for five years, Clarice and other volunteers drove from Little Rock to the women's prison in Pine Bluff, where they taught parenting skills to the women there. Other volunteers in the program say that Clarice was truly a friend to the women she met, never judging them, and always able to make a real connection with them because she was a mother, too.

Dr. Raymond P. Miller Sr.

Humanitarian Award, 2004
(November 26, 1936–August 23, 2005)

To understand how outstanding Raymond Miller is, one could just list his awards, among them the Distinguished Trustee Award from the Association of Governing Boards of American Colleges and Universities, the Distinguished Service Award from the University of Arkansas College of Medicine, the Distinguished Service Award from the Razorback Foundation, and the Robert Shields Abernathy Award for Excellence in Medicine from the American College of Physicians–American Society of Internal Medicine. But that wouldn't be the whole story.

Raymond Miller grew up in Cotton Plant, Arkansas, a town of fewer than 2,000, where his dad was originally a share cropper, and later a farmer who owned 160 acres, which he cleared himself to grow cotton and corn. Raymond was one of fourteen children, the oldest boy in the family. He attended the segregated Vocational High School, and he was elected president of the also segregated "New Farmers of America." His opportunity to travel to their national meeting in Atlanta and the encouragement of his high school teachers gave Raymond the ability to imagine a life beyond Cotton Plant. He originally majored in agriculture at AM&N. During his freshman year, Raymond realized that his dad could teach him more about agriculture than his professors, so he gave up a scholarship to change his major to pre-med.

He doesn't dwell on it, but others attest to the fact that Raymond faced enormous prejudice as one of only two black students in his medical-school class. However, Raymond excelled and graduated from the University of Arkansas Medical School in 1963. After his formal medical training, he served on the staff at Walter Reed Army General Hospital as a major, where he assisted with the care of Dwight D. Eisenhower. With opportunities to move elsewhere, Raymond chose to return to Little Rock following his military service to open a practice with Hoyte Pyle, Jack Wagoner, and Bob Moore, the first integrated medical clinic in Arkansas. Raymond is quick to credit his many supporters, teachers, and mentors who helped him along the way.

Raymond has served on many prestigious boards and received many honors for his work as a physician and his civic service. But his most important legacy is surely the example he set for other medical students and the loving care that he has provided to his thousands of patients throughout his medical career.

Raymond Miller fell ill shortly before the 2004 annual dinner where he was honored along with his wife, Clarice Pettigrew Miller. Their children Terri Miller and Raymond Miller Jr. made the presentations to their parents. Raymond died in August, 2005.

Honorable Wilbur D. Mills
Humanitarian Award, 1972
(May 24, 1909–May 2, 1992)

Ex-Congressman Mills dies at 82
By John Haman, May 3, 1992
Excerpted with permission from the Arkansas Democrat-Gazette

Wilbur D. Mills, the legendary thirty-eight-year Arkansas congressman who became the most powerful man on Capitol Hill, died Saturday at age eighty-two.

Mills, first elected to congress in 1939, served as chairman of the powerful House Ways and Means Committee for seventeen years. His influence in Congress crossed party lines, carrying weight with both Democratic and Republican presidents.

Praise for Mills came Saturday from leaders of both political parties.

President George H. W. Bush expressed sorrow for the loss of a friend and colleague.

"Barbara and I are deeply saddened by the death of Congressman Wilbur Mills," Bush said in a statement to the *Arkansas Democrat-Gazette.*

"Congressman Mills served with great distinction in the House of Representatives, and I had great respect for his ability. As chairman, he provided me with a solid education on this nation's tax laws when we served together on the House Ways and Means Committee.

Wilbur Daigh Mills was born May 24, 1909, in Kensett, the son of Ardra Pickens Mills and Abie Lois Mills.

He attended Searcy High School and received a degree from Hendrix College in 1930. He attended three years at Harvard Law School but did not receive a degree.

Shortly thereafter, Mills became active in Democratic politics. He was elected county and probate judge for White County, defeating Lieutenant Governor Jim Guy Tucker's grandfather.

Mills married his high school sweetheart, Clarine "Polly" Billingsley. The couple had two daughters.

Mills was first elected Arkansas's Second District congressman in 1939.

He was chairman of the House Ways and Means Committee from 1958 to 1976. Mills wrote legislation and made important decisions on taxes, Social Security, health insurance, revenue-sharing and welfare reform.

During his legendary congressional dynasty, Mills served during the administrations of—and frequently influenced—seven presidents: Roosevelt, Truman, Eisenhower, Kennedy, Johnson, Nixon, and Ford.

A 1968 feature article in *The New York Times Magazine* heralded Mills as "the most important man on Capitol Hill today."

(Mills was at the peak of his power in 1974 when, intoxicated and accompanied by stripper Fanne Foxe, he was stopped by Washington police. The resulting fallout, known as the "Tidal Basin scandal," would have ended most political careers. However, Mills survived the uproar to win re-election, and he retired in 1976.)

Won re-election

Despite the national attention from the Tidal Basin scandal, Mills won election to his nineteenth consecutive term a month after the accident. But he also checked into a Florida hospital for extensive treatment of alcoholism.

Mills retired from Congress on December 31, 1976, and his seat was won by Jim Guy Tucker. Tucker said Mills served as his mentor for years after he left Congress.

Kennedy his favorite

Mills played poker with Truman, but he said Kennedy was his favorite president "because he would listen to me." He said Roosevelt was the president he knew the least and Nixon had "the most brains of them all."

Mills was greatly admired by colleagues for his expertise on the complex subject of taxation. He reportedly could cite sections of the immense tax laws from memory and recall the history of Social Security changes since its inception.

He was also a leading expert on foreign trade.

U.S. Senator Dale Bumpers of Arkansas is one of Mills's many admirers.

"Wilbur Mills was the personification of a concerned man," Bumpers said. "He held unprecedented power but was only concerned with how he could us it for the betterment of his people."

'An awesome respect'

U.S. Senator David Pryor called Mills a "most unique man, who in the peak of his career possessed an awesome respect. He had tremendous power which he never abused. I was honored to have had the opportunity of serving with him."

Many observers said Mills guided the Ways and Means Committee by building consensus, rather than ruling by intimidation.

Ways and Means bills under his guidance, almost always went to the House floor with the proviso that they could not be amended. The house almost always passed them.

But others said that Mills was better at following than leading. He was gifted with excellent timing, and he knew exactly when to jump on the bandwagon of an issue.

Mills voted against the Civil Rights Act of 1964, but he recently explained that "it was the thing to do at the time. I was for it at heart. I really was."

Helping alcoholics

When he left the limelight at age sixty-six, Mills worked diligently to help others who had suffered from alcoholism. And it was this effort that earned Mills the highest praise.

"I thought it was a failure on my part," Mills told the Senate Finance Subcommittee on Health in July 1982. "It's a disease from which you can recover and gain back your position in life."

On Saturday, Governor Bill Clinton called Mills "one of the most powerful and brilliant members of the House of Representatives in this century."

"But his most enduring legacy, at least for me, as his friend, would be that he had the courage and character to start his life over again at sixty-six." Clinton said.

"He was a genius," explained Gene Goss who served as Mills' administrative assistant in Congress from 1963 to 1977.

Both Gene Goss and Tucker said Mills' greatest asset was the attention he paid to individuals, before and after his congressional tenure.

"He always believed that government needed to protect those who couldn't help themselves," Tucker said. "He kept the secretary of the Treasury waiting in his lobby while he finished talking with people from his district."

Fought for Medicare

Mills spearheaded the battle to enact the Medicare system—a struggle that finally succeeded in 1965 after spanning portions of the Eisenhower, Kennedy, and Johnson administrations.

Mills had no known business interest during his congressional career and accepted no financial honoraria. He never itemized tax deductions—although it could have saved him money.

"I don't want anybody to be able to say that I took advantage of some provision I have put in the law," he explained.

Mills's popularity at home is reflected by the number of structures and establishments that carry his name. They include a high school in Little Rock, a substance abuse treatment center in Searcy, an education cooperative in Beebe, a dam in Desha County, a social sciences building at Hendrix College, and an expressway in Little Rock, later renamed Interstate 630.

Leadership donors to NCCJ in 1990 were Tom Steves, Buddy Sutton, Margaret Preston, Charles Stewart, Jo Luck, Jim Shelley, and Steve Bauman.

Sidney Moncrief visits with Daisy Bates (Humanitarian, 1991) when he was honored in 1997.

A social conscience honored

United Methodist lay-woman Freddie Nixon of Little Rock accepts the Father Joseph Biltz Award presented by the National Conference of Christians and Jews in Arkansas at the group's 32nd annual awards program and dinner April 6. Nixon, a member of Pulaski Heights UMC and the wife of senior pastor Victor Nixon, was honored for her social activism, especially as it relates to her work with prison ministries and the Arkansas Coalition to Abolish the Death Penalty. State Sen. Jim Keet and the Rev. Hezekiah

Freddie Nixon, who received the Biltz award in 1994 for her work to abolish the death penalty, was featured in the Arkansas United Methodist newspaper.

All former honorees are invited each year, asked to wear their Humanitarian medals, and seated on the dais—a tradition that continues in 2013. Former honorees that were recognized in 1991 are, from left: Dr. Ben Saltzman, Sister Margaret Blandford, Honorable Ray Thornton, Hugh Patterson, Governor Bill Clinton, and Louis L. Ramsay Jr.

Donna and Mack McLarty were honored in 1991, along with Daisy Bates.

Ernest Green, Jerry Maulden, Charles Stewart, and Bill Bowen at the 1990 dinner. Green, the first African-American graduate of Central High School, was dinner speaker. Bill Bowen was dinner chair, and Charles Stewart was NCCJ board chair.

Skip Rutherford, Cora McHenry, and H. Maurice Mitchell accepted the Humanitarian award in 1996.

The National Conference of Christians & Jews
in Arkansas
cordially invites you to

The 33rd Annual
National Humanitarian Award Dinner

Wednesday, April 10, 1996
Arkansas' Excelsior Hotel - Clinton Ballroom
6:30 p.m.
Reception 6:00 p.m. - Ballroom Foyer

$125 per person   *Black Tie Optional*

1996 Dinner Invitation

Governor Bill Clinton congratulates his good friend Mack McLarty who, with his wife Donna, was honored in 1991. When Clinton became president in 1993, Mack served as his Chief of Staff.

In 1997, White House Correspondent Deborah Mathis was dinner speaker.

Katherine Mitchell, Judge Joyce Williams Warren, Hazel Massery, and Elizabeth Eckford attended the 70th Anniversary of NCCJ's founding in 1997.

Sidney Moncrief and Jo Luck, 1997 Humanitarian Award honorees, greet friends following the dinner presentations.

H. Maurice Mitchell

Humanitarian Award, 1996
(October 23, 1925–April 2, 2011)
Reprinted with permission from Mitchell, Williams, Selig, Gates &
Woodyard., P.L.L.C.

On April 2, 2011, Mitchell Williams sadly
announced the passing of our counselor,
mentor, and cherished friend, H. Maurice
Mitchell at the age of eighty-five. The firm
founder and distinguished attorney left a
legacy of philanthropy and civic service that
continues as part of the core fabric of our
culture today.

Mitchell was instrumental in establish-
ing the firm's statewide and regional reputation in the field of banking
and finance law, having handled the first conversion of an Arkansas fed-
erally chartered savings and loan association into a national bank.

He also spent many years representing Arkansas nationally on the
political front, including having served as chairman of U.S. Senator Dale
Bumpers's campaign finance committee in 1992 while also serving as a
member of the William J. Clinton presidential campaign's national finance committee, and delegate to the Democratic National Convention
the same year. Additionally, he served on the Clinton-Gore national finance committee in 1996 and was legal counsel to the Democratic Party
of Arkansas from 1993 to 1998.

As a graduate of the Little Rock school system, Mitchell had an in-
tense personal interest in the polarizing 1957 desegregation crisis at Little
Rock Central High School. He worked behind the scenes in an unsuccessful attempt to prevent the closing of the area's public schools in 1958,
and then aided a successful effort to recall segregationist school board
members in 1959 (known as the STOP campaign). Mitchell's lifelong

commitment to the city's public school system was further evidenced by his service as chairman of numerous campaigns to secure additional funding for the public schools.

Mitchell's progressive views and civic-mindedness were never confined to education. He was an active member and leader of numerous organizations, including the Little Rock Junior Chamber of Commerce, Arkansas State Junior Chamber of Commerce, Fifty for the Future, Baptist Health Foundation, Pulaski Heights UMC Foundation, and the University of Arkansas at Little Rock Foundation Fund Board.

Among Mitchell's many accolades and awards, the 1992 dedication and naming of the H. Maurice Mitchell Courtroom at the University of Arkansas at Little Rock Bowen School of Law was one of the most significant. His efforts were recognized often by a varied and distinguished group of organizations, including the National Humanitarian Award from the National Conference of Christians and Jews in Arkansas, the Vincent Foster Jr. Outstanding Lawyer Award from the Pulaski County Bar Association, the Edwin Hanlon Memorial Award for Outstanding Individual Contributions to the Arts from the Little Rock Arts and Humanities Association, the Outstanding Service Award from the Arkansas Bar Foundation, the William F. Rector Memorial Award for Distinguished Civic Achievement from Fifty for the Future, the Citizen of the Year Award from the Arkansas Chapter of the March of Dimes, and the Winthrop Rockefeller Memorial Award from the Arkansas Arts Center.

Sidney Moncrief

Humanitarian Award, 1997
(*Interview conducted August 31, 2012*)

About Sidney Moncrief, former Milwaukee Bucks head coach Don Nelson said that he was "the greatest player, the greatest human being I ever coached."

Sidney was born in Little Rock, the next-to-youngest of seven children. They lived in the John Barrow addition in a house with only two bedrooms and no bathroom or running water. His parents divorced when Sidney was five, but he still saw his dad once every week or two. He remembers helping with the chores when he spent the day with his dad. His mother remarried when Sidney was fourteen, but in the meantime, she struggled to support her family with a job cleaning rooms at Howard Johnson's, where she made less than fifty dollars a week. "Since that had to take care of her and seven kids, she never had the money—or the time—to take us to stores, or movies, or parks. I never experienced those kinds of things. We only left the house to go to school and to church."

Sidney was exposed to petty crime and drugs throughout his youth, and he credits several things with making it possible for him to rise above his circumstances. First was his mother, Bernice Perkins, whom he describes as "a strong and determined person. She set a great example by owning up to her responsibilities.... If she caught us doing wrong, she punished us; if we did right—that's what we were expected to do." He also credits his strong Christian faith and the influence of his childhood sweetheart, Debra, who later became his wife. Sidney joined the Cub Scouts when the Salvation Army sponsored a troop, and that provided two things: his first time to be involved in any organized activity that offered a learning atmosphere, and his first interaction with a white person, a volunteer Scout leader from Boston, Dave Shaeffer. And, of course, there were his coaches.

Sidney wasn't a star basketball player from the beginning. He was skinny and weak, but in junior high school he decided he wanted to play even though he was on the C Team. He recounts that he was more frustrated with the fact that he couldn't get his hair to grow into a big Afro, which was stylish at the time, than he was with not being on the A Team. But he practiced, alone and with the team, and finally made the main team in the ninth grade. Sidney cites Coach John Kelly from junior high, and Coaches Oliver Elders and Charles Ripley from high school, as not only teaching him how to play ball, but how to handle himself, how to present himself, how to be a man, and how to be part of a team. Under their tutelage, Sidney realized he wanted to get an education, and ultimately to become a coach himself. He became a stand-out player, and as a high school senior he was recruited by lots of schools, but he narrowed his choices to Louisiana State University, Arkansas State University, and the University of Arkansas. He ultimately chose U of A because of their new coach, Eddie Sutton.

For Sidney, it was the perfect choice. "After Debra and my mother, Eddie Sutton has probably had more influence on me than anyone. He was a hard coach—very demanding, very firm, but he was also very fair. He was a perfect motivator not only from an athletic standpoint, but from an academic and public relations standpoint as well. He wanted each of us to be the best basketball player we could be, but he also wanted us to be prepared for life." Many Arkansans would count 1975 to 1979 as a highlight of basketball in Arkansas. Coach Eddie Sutton, with his team, including Sidney Moncrief, Marvin Delph, and Ron Brewer (dubbed "the Triplets" by the media), won the Southwest Conference title in 1977 and 1979, and in 1979, the Arkansas team competed in the final four of the NCAA tournament, losing to Indiana State (and Larry Bird) by one point.

Upon graduation from the University of Arkansas, Sidney was drafted by the Milwaukee Bucks. Sidney says, "When Milwaukee drafted me in the first round, my main thoughts were, *I'm going to get a chance very few people get, and I'm going to freeze to death.*" He further said, "When I first arrived in Milwaukee I was afraid—not intimidated, just plain afraid." He was unsure about playing professional ball, about his new teammates, about the travel, and Milwaukee "seemed so big to me," he said. Veteran Bucks teammates took Sidney under their wing, and again he excelled, not just at basketball.

Beginning in high school, when Coach Oliver Elders stressed more than just basketball fundamentals, Sidney was preparing himself to be a role model, and he has continued to speak with students and even developed his own basketball camp for youngsters. After his ten years with the Milwaukee Bucks, he has been a professional and college basketball coach, a business owner, and a television sports broadcaster. He has developed and leads workshops to teach team-building and leadership skills for youth and adults and for corporate teams. He has written three books: *Moncrief: My Journey to the NBA*; *Your Passport to Reinventing You: The Travel Guide to a High Performance Lifestyle at Home and in Your Career*; and *Your Passport to Becoming a Valuable Team Player: The Travel Guide for Peak Performance at Work and at Home*. In 2012, "Sir Sid," as they call him in Milwaukee, returned there to became an assistant coach of the Milwaukee Bucks, serving with head coach Scott Skiles.

When you ask Sidney what he is most proud about now, he immediately talks about his four sons: Brett, John, Jeffery, and Jason. And next he talks about his leadership training workshops. At fifty-three years old, he no longer resembles that skinny kid who showed up for the C Team in junior high school. But he remembers his values, like taking responsibility and being willing to change, and he lives them every day.

Bruce Moore
Humanitarian Award, 2008

If you want to know why Bruce Moore is passionate about building a vibrant city, it can be summed up in two words: "Luke Thomas," the name of Bruce's eighteen-month-old son. Bruce's vision for Little Rock is a city that is healthy and responsive for all its citizens, both young and old.

Bruce's dad, Vernell, was an Army dentist and his mom, Sarah, a registered nurse. He was raised in El Dorado where his family was active in church and community affairs. His mother remains one of the most important influences in his life.

Bruce was a standout in high school, serving as the editor of the student newspaper and involved in many activities. His life plan then was to become a basketball coach. The summer before his senior year, he needed a job, so he joined the Army Reserves at seventeen years old. At Fort Dix, New Jersey, for basic training, he was one of the youngest recruits. He returned to graduate from El Dorado High School before he completed his advanced training at Fort Lee, Virginia, again one of the youngest in the program. He characterizes his army training as a "growing experience."

He wanted to remain in Arkansas for college and applied to Henderson State in Arkadelphia. As a social work major, he enjoyed the campus, the teachers, and the students. After serving an internship as a family services case worker in Clark County, where he helped clients who had multiple problems, he felt prepared to do almost anything. However, as he considered attending graduate school, he was called up by the Reserves for service in Operation Desert Storm. After the operation was concluded, he returned home, and a chance conversation gave him a new direction.

On campus he had become acquainted with one of the security guards, mainly, Bruce says, because he was always trying to talk his way out of a parking ticket. That guard, Joshua Ware, learned that Bruce was interested in the management of cities. Ware said, "You need to meet my son," who was at that time an assistant city manager of Austin, Texas. Bruce agreed and what he thought would be a short, polite visit turned into a two-hour mentorship session that still resonates with Bruce today.

Bruce chose Arkansas State for graduate school, and he was named the Masters of Public Administration Student of the Year by the Arkansas City Managers Association. That led to his receiving a very competitive appointment as an intern in the Little Rock City Manager's office, then headed by Charles Nickerson. In his journey from intern to City Manager, he credits Nickerson, Brenda Donald, Cy Carney, and especially former mayor Jim Dailey, who each took a chance by giving him ever-increasing responsibilities. In December of 2002, Bruce was appointed City Manager after a nationwide search. By all accounts, he clinched the job when, as Interim City Manager, he successfully helped the mayor and city board in the onerous task of trimming $10 million from the city budget.

As assistant to the mayor, Bruce was the key city staff person in the William J. Clinton Presidential Library site selection, working in conjunction with City Director Dean Kumpuris. After successfully guiding the city's efforts to be selected as the site for the library, Bruce played a key role in the development and subsequent grand opening of the Clinton Presidential Library and Park. Another project in which his leadership and vision played a key role was the fiftieth anniversary commemoration of the 1957 desegregation of Little Rock Central High School.

When asked about the biggest challenge facing Little Rock, Bruce immediately cites resources. Therefore, he is especially proud of the renewal of the millage in the 2004 bond issue election. That successful campaign brought citizens from across the city into the process, kept everyone informed, and projects throughout the city were completed within the three-year schedule. Just one of the results of that bond issue was the 311 call system for citizens to report non-emergency needs. Bruce says he uses the 311 system, just as any other city resident does, and he has been proud of the way city employees respond to all 311 calls. The citizen involvement in that successful 2004 bond issue also began to restore trust and faith in Little Rock's city government. Bruce's calm leadership has continued to build that trust, and he is committed to making Little Rock the finest, most vibrant capital city in the Southern U.S.

Bruce has big dreams. His dreams for the future of Little Rock include improved quality of life in all our neighborhoods; thriving public schools and resources for children so that all begin school ready to learn; safe, secure, and flourishing neighborhoods; cutting-edge opportunities for professional development; training for adults; and economic growth in all sectors.

Dr. Estella Morris

Father Joseph H. Biltz Award, 2013

Estella Morris got her job with the Veteran's Administration by having the right experience and being in the right place at the right time. Following the landslide election of Ronald Reagan in 1980, VA officials knew that there would soon be a hiring freeze on federal jobs. Estella had worked as a VISTA member since 1977, and because of that, she could be hired quickly without a competitive process. The VA had only one open position, and they knew they wanted Estella, who began her work with veterans in their independent-living program in Little Rock. Thirty-three years later, Dr. Estella Morris serves as program manager at the Comprehensive Homeless Center, for the Central Arkansas Veteran's Healthcare System, Department of Veteran's Affairs.

Estella was born in Dermott, Arkansas, and graduated from high school there in 1966. At that time, in the heart of the Delta, everything was still segregated, despite the changing landscape in other areas of the state. Estella won 4-H contests in sewing, cooking, and public speaking, which gave her the opportunity to attend a national 4-H meeting in Chevy Chase, Maryland. She particularly credits her godmother, Evangeline Brown, who was also her English teacher, with preparing her for a life beyond the small town of Dermott. Estella says that in English class she learned literature *and* American history. She knew what the Thirteenth, Fourteenth, and Fifteenth Amendments to the constitution meant to her people and to her personally. (Those were the amendments that outlawed slavery, made African Americans full U.S. citizens, and gave all men, regardless of race, the right to vote. Women were not given the right to vote until the Nineteenth

Amendment was ratified.) For college, Estella attended the University of Arkansas at Fayetteville, and she lived in the first integrated women's dorm in 1966.

By the time Estella earned her undergraduate degree in 1976, she was married to Sherry Caleb and had two young children. She joined VISTA the following year. The VISTA program had grown out of President Lyndon Johnson's War on Poverty and the Economic Opportunity Act of 1964. It was considered by some to be the most radical of all the anti-poverty programs of that era. Through her VISTA work, Estella particularly learned the value of collaboration. She explains that the national volunteers were often young and a bit starry-eyed, thinking they were going to eradicate poverty. Therefore, they were most effective when they were matched with local volunteers who had a "sense of realism and an understanding of the dynamics (of the) community." She also learned to work with a diverse group of people, with unique gifts and viewpoints, who came from all over the United States. She's been using those lessons about collaboration and appreciating diversity ever since in her work with veterans.

Estella describes her current work as "No Wrong Door." In short, the Comprehensive Homeless Center is prepared to accept and assist homeless veterans, no matter how they enter the system or what their specific needs might be. About Estella's work, Dr. Greer Sullivan, who is director of the South Central VA Mental Illness Research Education and Clinical Center and a professor in the Department of Psychiatry at the University of Arkansas for Medical Sciences, says, "Dr. Morris has been a leader in the VA, locally, regionally, and nationally, in the movement to end homelessness among military veterans. She is recognized within and outside of the VA as a national expert and advocate in the area, and she has brought national attention to Little Rock because of her advocacy."

When Estella first entered the VA system, there was a culture of letting the veterans remain in a hospital or nursing home without much emphasis on rehabilitation. By 1987, there was more focus on residential shelters, but they had limited space and the concern of the VA was still primarily the medical needs of the veterans. Over time, Estella has broadened the scope of concerns and available services to include housing, employment, and successful re-integration into the community and re-unification with their families. They have, for example, instituted quarterly events for vets and their families, such as a fishing derby and a fall festival. The local staff has grown from one, Estella herself, to thirty-five in 2012. Her leadership has resulted in the Central Arkansas office being designated, in 1994, as a Comprehensive Homeless Center, one of only seven such designations at that time. In addition, the Little Rock office was named a "Center of Excellence" by the Department of Veterans Affairs in 1997, 1999, and 2002, the only facility in the nation to receive this distinction all three years that is was given.

Over the years, the office has collaborated with local groups such as Salvation Army, St. Francis House, and the Arkansas Department of Human Services, and with national agencies such as VISTA, Housing and Urban Development (HUD), and the Department of Labor. For example, in 1988 Estella applied for and received two VISTA members who provided AIDS education, two VISTA members who worked on housing issues, and two VISTA members who specialized in job placement. In 1992, the Central Arkansas office also became one of the first eighteen in the nation to offer the HUD–VASH (Veterans Affairs Supportive Housing) services to eligible vets and their families.

The VA currently serves veterans of wars ranging from WW II to Afghanistan. Estella explains that following each war, our veterans return with problems unique to their service. And it takes the VA some time to appropriately respond to or care for those returning service members. For example, the first diagnosis approved for post-traumatic stress disorder (PTSD) didn't occur until 1980. Fortunately, Estella has been an advocate for the homeless since before it became "popular" and at a time when there was a great deal of public disdain for homeless people. According to Greer, "Estella tirelessly built and staffed our center to make it what it is today. She has established wide-ranging outreach across Arkansas and fought to bring more resources to improve the lives of homeless veterans."

Along the way, Estella returned to Jackson State University to earn her PhD in social work. She has also served on many boards and committees, including chairing the Community Advisory Board (CAB) for the Mental Illness Research Education and Clinical Center at the VA. The CAB actively brings the real concerns of veterans and family members to the table to assure that those concerns are appreciated by leadership. She served as the regional homeless coordinator for fourteen years and served for ten years as a board member of the Women's Project helping develop a prison project for incarcerated women and working on such difficult issues as homophobia, hate crimes, and domestic violence. She also served on the board of the Arkansas AIDS Foundation and is a current board member of the Central Arkansas Team Care for the Homeless (CATCH) Coalition. In 2012, she chaired a program at Mosaic Templars Cultural Center that looked at the first African-American teachers to desegregate schools in the Little Rock School District following the signing of the 1964 Civil Rights Bill.

Obviously, Estella Morris is not afraid to tackle anything. Greer notes about her, "What I especially value about Dr. Morris is that she has never been afraid to speak the truth, even when the truth was not popular. She has spoken openly about racism, poverty, and discrimination in situations when it made many in the room uncomfortable. This kind of advocacy is greatly needed in Arkansas and requires great courage. I can count on Dr. Morris to tell me what I need to hear!"

Estella's children are grown now, and on Election Day 2012 she attended a play performed by her grandson's fourth-grade class. She was delighted that he and other students were learning all about the constitutional amendments...the same ones she learned about back in Dermott, Arkansas, in her segregated school. Things have changed for the better in the years since Estella was in high school. And many of the better things that have happened for our veterans have been because of her.

Sheffield Nelson

Humanitarian Award, 1983
(*Interview conducted July 17, 2012*)

Sheffield Nelson might be called a "man on the move." When he was a boy, his parents moved from town to town in the Arkansas Delta so that his dad could find work. As a teen, he was completing high school in Brinkley, serving as student body president, and playing sports. As a young adult he graduated from Arkansas State Teacher's College (now the University of Central Arkansas), where he also served as student-body president. He earned his law degree in 1969 from the William H. Bowen School of Law. And then he really got to work.

Just out of law school, Sheffield entered the one-year management training program with Arkansas Louisiana Gas Company—Arkla (now CenterPoint Energy) in Shreveport, Louisiana. After holding the positions of sales manager and vice president, at the age of thirty-three, Sheffield became president of Arkla, which he continued to lead, eventually becoming chairman and then CEO, until December 31, 1984. His mentors at Arkla, Witt Stephens and Lindsey Hatchett, taught him all about natural gas, including drilling and gas acquisition, pipeline operations and regulations, and about business in general. During his time at Arkla, the country weathered an economic recession, oil embargoes, and energy shortages. The company also had to adjust to constantly fluctuating regulation—first there was more regulation, then there was less. Sheffield is proud of his work with the Arkansas Public Service Commission (PSC), one of the utility regulators, which resulted in a new state gas-pricing formula called "Replacement Cost Pricing." Arkla was allowed to charge higher prices in return for delivering better supplies to its major corporate customers, resulting in significantly lower prices for residential customers. The stock price went from $20 to over $100 per share, and excess income was spent on drilling. He is especially proud that during his tenure, the company raised salaries, promoted from within, replaced worn-out equipment, and appointed the first African American (Sidney Moncrief, Humanitarian Award 1997) and the first woman (Myra Jones) to the utility's board.

During that time, Sheffield also worked on many boards and commissions in the community. He was appointed to the State Board of Higher Education, where he worked to assure that all public colleges in the state were treated fairly. He also served on the University of Arkansas at Little Rock Board of Visitors and the Philander Smith College Board. He served as president of the Little Rock Chamber of Commerce, and on the board of Arkansas Children's Hospital. In addition, Sheffield has raised funds for many organizations, including United Way of Pulaski County (now Heart of Arkansas United Way), Arkansas Heart Association, Arkansas Game and Fish Foundation, Advocates for Battered Women, Arkansas Opera Theatre, and the Arkansas Chapter of the American Lung Association. He founded Junior Achievement in Arkansas.

Sheffield served as vice chair and chair of the Arkansas Industrial Development Commission, chair of the Economic Expansion Study Commission, as a member of the Arkansas Game and Fish Commission, and chair of the Committee for a Better Arkansas. On the national level, he served on the U.S. Commission on Civil Rights.

Like any "man on the move," Sheffield has hit a few speed bumps along the way. One was choosing to run for governor of Arkansas against two of the most popular Arkansas governors. Sheffield lost to Bill Clinton in 1990 after beating then-Second District congressman Tommy Robinson for the Republican nomination. He then was defeated by Jim Guy Tucker in 1994. He calls those races "bad timing." However, during the same time he teamed up with Asa Hutchinson to build the

Republican Party in Arkansas by serving as co-chair of the party in Arkansas from 1991 to 1992, and as Republican National Committeeman from Arkansas from 1993 to 2000.

Arkansans should never count Sheffield Nelson out of any race. During 2011, he was practically a one-man band in seeking to raise the natural gas severance tax to pay for road improvements. He explains that a seven percent rate would put Arkansas in the middle of natural gas-producing states. He's had formidable opponents, including the State Chamber of Commerce and several large energy companies. Sheffield is undeterred by the opposition, but the proposed ballot initiative failed to get enough signatures to be placed on the ballot for the November 2012 election. Chances are good that Sheffield will continue to work on this and other issues that he believes will benefit our state.

Sheffield married Mary Lynn McCastlain, an artist, when he was a junior in college. They have two adult daughters and thirteen grandchildren. Sheffield and Mary Lynn have often been partners in their community work. Sheffield says with a big smile, "Mary Lynn helps develop the program, and I raise the money to support it." Their current commitment is to Easter Seals, where severely disabled children and adults are able to create works of art through a special program. Sheffield is also currently a partner in the Jack Nelson Jones & Bryant Law Firm, specializing in corporate and commercial law.

Sheffield is still on the move. But he knows where he's headed: working to improve Arkansas through his commitment to public and private service.

Dale Nicholson

Humanitarian Award, 2000
(*Interview conducted July 6, 2012*)

When Dale Nicholson answers his phone, he sounds like a radio announcer, and that's exactly where he got started in the media business. As a fourteen-year-old, he got a gig as the "sign-off" guy at a small radio station in Warren, Arkansas, owned by the late State Senator Lee Reeves. When he was late for his job one night, the Senator fired him. Dale protested, "But you can't fire me. I'm not being paid!" Reeves responded, "You're still fired." Reeves actually hired him back a couple days later (with an actual paycheck), once he felt that Dale had learned his lesson. Dale has probably never been late again, and he has certainly been in the right place at the right time to have led a fascinating life, coming of age along with unimagined changes in the electronic media that he loves.

In Warren, Dale's dad worked for Bradley Lumber Company, and the Nicholsons lived in a company house and shopped at the company store. As an only child, Dale was pampered by his mother, and grandmother and great grandmother. He said he couldn't wait to get out of Warren to enter Henderson State Teachers College (now Henderson State University). At Henderson, he worked as a disk jockey at the local radio station and found that he could often get a date when a coed called in with a record request. He remembers his first date with his future wife, Pat Outlaw, vividly. They saw *Teacher's Pet*, starring Doris Day, at the drive-in movie theater, where he had a reputation for taking all his first dates.

After graduation and marriage, they moved to El Dorado, where Dale began his television career as a booth announcer. In those days, an on-air guy did everything—including kiddie shows. After a brief sojourn

in Memphis at WMPS, Dale and Pat made their way to Atlanta, but nei-
ther liked it there. Anxious to return home, they came back to El
Dorado, and on March 12, 1961, Dale got an on-air job with KATV—
Channel 7 in Little Rock.

Channel 7 was bought by the Allbritton family from Houston in
1961, and Dale remembers being nervous about whether they would be
happy with their new station. For the grand opening, they booked the
Excelsior Hotel, hired the Arkansas Symphony String Quartet and figu-
ratively "put on the dog—Arkansas Style." The Allbrittons were charmed.
So much so that they later asked Dale, who was by then general manager,
to train their only son, Robert, in the television business. Dale and Robert
have remained good friends, and they even traveled together with their
wives over the years. Dale says the travel was one of the biggest perks of
working for a television station owned by Allbritton. Dale and Pat made
six European trips, two Hong Kong trips, and even visited Africa. All of
the trips were "first-class," and among them was a Concorde flight from
JFK to Paris. Dale was able to turn the tables and impress his Allbritton
friends when they invited him to sit on the front row across from the
White House for the 1992 Presidential Inauguration. When President
Bill Clinton got out of the limousine before the swearing-in ceremony,
he gave Dale a wave and called him by name. That was certainly a highlight in what Dale describes as a "magical life."

Dale's mentor at Channel 7, Bob Doubleday, had pegged him as
a future general manager, so he insisted that Dale learn the sales part of
the business, too. Dale said he hated sales, so he tried to quit every
Monday morning for at least six months. He even opened his own advertising agency, but that was short-lived. Doubleday persuaded him to
come back to KATV as vice president and general manager. Ultimately
he served as general manager for fifty years during the heyday of network
television, and he now holds the title of chairman.

As general manager of the highest-rated station in our market, Dale
was able to make a real difference for Arkansas through the years. He

pulled his weight on several nonprofit boards including Goodwill Industries, The American Heath Association, Arkansas Repertory Theatre, and the NCCJ, which he chaired for three years. He helped Dr. Trudie Kibbe Reed raise money for capital projects at Philander Smith College. And most important, he had the backing of his station owners to editorialize on community projects. Two that came about were the Clinton Presidential Library and Verizon Arena, both of which have had a remarkable impact on life in Central Arkansas. He's very proud that Channel 7 has a studio in the River Market area.

Pat, Dale's wife of fifty-two years, died in 2010, and he still misses his favorite traveling companion every day. Together they raised two children, Nick and Kelli. Dale says that their lives revolved around their children, and their Little Rock home became the off-campus Sigma Alpha Epsilon house while Nick was in school at the University of Arkansas at Fayetteville. Today, Dale talks proudly about their five grandchildren and two great-grandchildren.

As the interview ends, Dale pulls out his cell phone to show me the Channel 7 weather app and their news app. Together, they had more than four million hits last month, he says. He's still fascinated by media and still loves his work.

Frances "Freddie" Nixon
Father Joseph H. Biltz Award, 1995
(*Interview conducted June 21, 2012*)

Everyone who knows anything at all about Freddie Nixon knows this: If she could, Freddie would abolish the death penalty, first in Arkansas and then everywhere else. This is not an intellectual cause for her. It's personal.

Freddie grew up in a progressive family in McGehee, Arkansas, and several early experiences helped her to value diversity. Her father's best friend from the military was a Native American from Sallisaw, Oklahoma, and as a high school student, she worked alongside a well-respected African-American man who was the assistant to the owner-pharmacist of the local drug store. There was also a thriving Jewish community and a Temple in McGehee where she met for Girl Scouts each week. She was about as cosmopolitan as a girl from small-town Arkansas could have been. And she was fortunate to attend Hendrix College, where she met her future husband, Vic Nixon.

At Hendrix, Freddie had a course in ethics with Dr. Matt Allis. When he explained his opposition to the death penalty, Freddie got it, but it was still an intellectual understanding at that time. It was later that she would take a real stand—by sitting down and writing a letter.

Freddie and Vic were married following graduation, and after two years as a church youth minister, Vic entered the Perkins School of Theology at Southern Methodist University (SMU) in Dallas. There they lived in a dormitory-style setting for families. Freddie says they treasured their three years there, living alongside folks from many different backgrounds. They talked about all kinds of issues, and those conversations continued to broaden Freddie's perspective.

Freddie's defining moment came later, when she was a staff member for Arkansas Attorney General Bill Clinton. The AG's staff had many spirited discussions regarding the death penalty. On one occasion, a co-worker came into Freddie's office, threw down horrific photos of a death row inmate, and asked with disdain, "You think this *animal* should be allowed to live?"

About the same time, the *Arkansas Gazette*, then under editor James Powell, had run an editorial against use of the death penalty, and Freddie was moved to write a letter voicing her support of their stance. This letter was only the precursor to the most important letter Freddie would write.

After her letter was printed, Freddie got a call from Pat Bailey Page of the Arkansas Coalition Against the Death Penalty asking her if she would like to join their group. Pat explained that they advocated for getting rid of the death penalty, but even more significantly, they befriended the inmates themselves, writing them letters. Would Freddie be willing to help with that? One inmate in particular was totally without family. The guards didn't like him; even the other prisoners didn't like him. When Freddie heard his name, she gulped, recognizing the name instantly as that of the very man who had been held up as an example by her co-worker. Freddie did join the Coalition board and has continued to serve since the late 1970s.

She wrote her first letter to John Swindler in 1978. John was uneducated but got others to help him correspond with Freddie. At one point he asked her to send him a dictionary, which he then used to continue their correspondence. Freddie, sensing that John was afraid to ask, offered to visit him. That actually gave her the opportunity to get to know all the death row inmates. When John was executed in 1990, he became the first person executed in the state of Arkansas in more than twenty years. Following his execution, more people began to join the Arkansas Coalition Against the Death Penalty, which subsequently changed its name to the Arkansas Coalition to *Abolish* the Death Penalty. To Freddie, this distinction is very important. She has always felt that we would eventually do away with the death penalty, simply *because it is wrong*. She is hopeful that she will witness an end to the practice during her lifetime—and she won't stop working to make that happen.

Another cause close to Freddie's heart was her work on a Regional AIDS Interfaith Network (RAIN) Care team. What began in Russellville, Arkansas, as a support group for AIDS patients and their families and friends, blossomed when Vic Nixon became senior pastor at Pulaski Heights United Methodist Church in 1992. The church, with the leadership of Trudy James and Dr. Tyler Thompson, sponsored training for Care Team members and provided a place for RAIN board meetings. At the time, Freddie saw one striking parallel between working with people with AIDS and working with death row inmates: both had received a death sentence. Fortunately that is no longer true for those with HIV and AIDS.

Two other commitments have had Freddie's long-time attention. One is the United Methodist Women (UMW), which she has served in many ways, including as Arkansas Conference President. And growing out of the UMW, Freddie helped found "MIWATCH," a ministry for incarcerated women and their children. MIWATCH provides transportation for children to visit their mothers in prison. For more than twenty years, Freddie served as the volunteer transportation coordinator, only retiring when Vic retired from his pastorate at Pulaski Heights. And in the interim, Freddie has served on the boards of Philander Smith College, the Women's Project, the Central Arkansas Library System, United Methodist Children's Home, and Arkansas Advocates for Children and Families.

In 2012, Freddie and Vic continue to serve on several boards and are active in the Methodist Church, but they are also traveling more, enjoying the lake house they jointly own with their daughter Aubrey, and catching up on their reading.

If you ask Freddie what inspired her many good works, she will talk about the remarkable people with whom she has been privileged to work. But she might also mention that her seventh grade Sunday School teacher introduced her to the life of Albert Schweitzer, who said, "A man can do only what he can do. But if he does that each day he can sleep at night and do it again the next day."

Sounds like Dr. Schweitzer might have met Freddie Nixon somewhere along the way.

Monsignor James O'Connell

Humanitarian Award, 1975

(1909–2005)

Reprinted with permission from Arkansas Catholic

Monsignor James E. O'Connell, the last rector of St. John Seminary in Little Rock and the oldest diocesan priest in Arkansas, died February 17 at age ninety-six.

Msgr. O'Connell spent his active years as a priest teaching men in high school and college and helping them prepare for the priesthood. He celebrated seventy-two years as a priest on February 5.

Called "the most outstanding Catholic preacher in the diocese," Msgr. O'Connell also made a name for himself as a humanitarian, ecumenical leader and promoter of the Little Air Force Base in Jacksonville.

The Brockton, Massachusetts, native came to St. John Seminary at age seventeen to study and was ordained for the Arkansas diocese in 1933 by Bishop John B. Morris. "It was quite an adventure for me and my friends," he said in 1988 of his decision to study here. "We wondered what the wilds of Arkansas might have in store."

From 1934 to 1944 he was a math teacher and later rector at Catholic High School in Little Rock. From 1944 to 1967 he served as a professor and rector of his alma mater. When the seminary closed, he was the director of seminarians for the diocese. He also managed the seminary burse fund, which was named in his honor in 1995. Even until his death he was considered the treasurer of the burse fund even though a board oversaw the fund.

In 1942 he was named papal chamberlain, and in 1944 he was appointed domestic prelate. On his fiftieth anniversary as a priest in 1983, he was given the title protonotary apostolic, which is the highest honorary title awarded to a priest by the pope. In 1947 he was elected president of the Catholic Theological Society of America and in 1952 he became president of the Major Seminary Department of the Catholic Educational Association.

Through his position at the seminary, Msgr. O'Connell was well known in the community. He was elected Little Rock Man of the Year in 1954, was president of the Urban League of Greater Little Rock and chairman for the Committee on Prevention for the National Association of Mental Health, and served as chapter chairman of the American Red Cross. In May 1975 he was awarded the annual Brotherhood Award by the National Council of Christians and Jews.

Msgr. O'Connell was also a skilled pilot. He earned his commercial pilot's license with flight instructor rating in 1942 and taught navigation and meteorology in war-training services at Adams Field in Little Rock. He joined the Civil Air Patrol in 1952 and instructed pilots in the CAP. He was instrumental in bringing the Strategic Air Command base to Jacksonville. It was at the Little Rock Air Force Base that he met Col. Stan and Anna Lucich. The couple invited the priest to recuperate after hernia surgery in the late 1960s in their Little Rock home, and he was invited to stay permanently. Bishop J. Peter Sartain has expressed hisgratitude to Anna (Stan died in 2002) for taking care of the priest, especially over the past fifteen years when his health had slowed him down. It was only seven years ago that Msgr. O'Connell had to stop celebrating Mass because his memory failed. Over the past few years, Msgr. O'Connell struggled with hearing and remembering facts and details. The Luciches would take Msgr. O'Connell to Saturday evening Mass at Christ the King Church in Little Rock and sit with him on the front row.

Msgr. David LeSieur, pastor of Our Lady of the Holy Souls Church in Little Rock and former vocations director, attended high school at St. John Seminary when Msgr. O'Connell was rector. After the seminary closed, Msgr. LeSieur transferred to the University of Dallas for college and Msgr. O'Connell was the director of seminarians. "He always took us out to dinner and made us feel that the Diocese of Little Rock was interested in our welfare and progress in our vocations," he said. "Years later it was an honor to be his fellow priest, and while we may have been equals in that sense, I always admired his giftedness in preaching, his theological knowledge, his urbanity and his faithfulness to the priesthood and to the training of future priests."

Abbot Jerome Kodell, OSB, remembers Msgr. O'Connell leading the annual community retreat at Subiaco Abbey. "He was very impressive both in what he said and the way he said it, with his Boston accent and his stentorian voice," he said. "You didn't nod off for long. "After that, through sharing ministry in the diocese, we began a long-term friendship, which grew stronger especially in these later years when he was being cared for so beautifully by Stan and Anna Lucich."

Msgr. O'Connell also set an example for the younger generation of priests who never heard him preach or teach. The current vocations director, Father John Antony, never knew Msgr. O'Connell when he was active but was inspired by his example. "I always admired him for living his priesthood 24/7," he said. "His dedication to being a priest is an inspiration to me."

Father Greg Luyet, pastor of St. Michael Church in West Memphis, recalled hearing Msgr. O'Connell talk when Father Luyet was a seminarian. "I recall Monsignor telling me to always remember that the most important thing a priest could do was to pray and to trust God," he said. "In his later years, he showed me that he lived what he believed. Over the last few years, Msgr. O'Connell taught me that the greatest gift a priest can give is to show up. Over the past few years as his health has declined he has shown me a lesson of how to live ones' senior years with dignity and grace.... It does not matter what we do, it's who we are that counts. Msgr. O'Connell was a priest's priest."

Dr. Eddie Ochoa
Humanitarian Award, 2012

If Eddie Ochoa could fix just one thing, it would be immigration. He thinks President Ronald Reagan had it right when he extended amnesty to undocumented immigrants in 1986. Today, for many immigrant families the only choice is to go back to their home country and risk never returning to the United States. In the meantime, those families live in the shadows—often without a driver's license or car insurance, without job security or adequate health care, without having a voice when their rights or their families are threatened. All that despite the fact that they may have lived in the United States for years, held jobs, paid taxes, attended church, bought homes, and made a life for their families here.

Eddie was born in El Paso, Texas, where two of his grandparents were born and where two had emigrated from Mexico near the end of the Mexican Revolution. His granddad from Mexico opened a print shop in El Paso in 1929 and called it American Printing Company. Eddie was the oldest of five children, and he grew up speaking Spanish at home. Being bilingual today is a key asset in his chosen life work.

Eddie remembers his pediatrician, Dr. Irving J. Golfarb, and Golfarb's associate, Dr. Carlos Gutierrez, as two of his role models. Gutierrez, a Latino physician, was also the high school team doctor, who was, in Eddie's words, "warm, approachable, caring." It probably helped when they built a hospital right behind his boyhood home. He could "climb over the rock wall and poke around over there" any time he wanted.

All of these fortunate circumstances, and other medical school mentors along the way, eventually led to Eddie finding the perfect match in Arkansas Children's Hospital. He says, "ACH's mission aligns with everything I want to do. No child and their family is turned away at Children's. There are NO constraints on serving children." That freedom to serve has led Eddie, with the help of a supportive network of equally committed people, to help create a system of care for children of Spanish-speaking parents who have special needs such as syndromes, chronic disease, or development disabilities. They currently serve almost 150 families. That's just one of the things that Eddie does with his time.

When Eddie was in his residency at Children's in 1999, Dr. Gary Wheeler suggested that he apply for a Soros Advocacy Fellowship sponsored by The Open Society Institute in New York. Eddie teamed up with Amy Rossi at Arkansas Advocates for Children and Families (AAFC) and became the youngest fellow and the only one west of Pittsburgh to earn the appointment that year. The purpose of the fellowship was to build capacity for both the non-profit partner and the advocate. The OSI got a real return on their investment. Eddie explains that because of that experience, he's not intimidated by the legislative process. And sure enough, we often find Eddie at the Capitol testifying about immigration, health, children, or the medical profession. His voice has made a difference in the laws of our state.

Another proud moment for Eddie was the opening of Ventamilla de Salud (Health Window) inside the Mexican Consulate in Little Rock in January, 2010. Families can find health information, networking, help in making appointments, assistance with forms, explanations of rules and rights, and even flu immunizations. An initial grant from Blue & You Foundation got this project off the ground. And then there are the ongoing statewide health disparities studies, implemented by Eddie and fellow UAMS faculty member Dr. Creshelle Nash, which are informing policies and procedures in the Arkansas State Health Department, the Minority Health Commission, and countless other academic and non-profit institutions. One very tangible result: There are twenty-four interpreters on staff at Children's Hospital.

Eddie has left his mark on professional organizations like the Arkansas Chapter of the American Academy of Pediatrics, and many community organizations such as League of United Latin American Citizens, AAFC, JCA, and La Casa, whose mission was to advance the education, health and well-being of the Hispanic population through advocacy and partnership. Through his work as a founder of La Casa, Eddie says he learned a lot: how to work with partners, employees, and within the system—all things not taught in medical school.

Eddie's wife, Kelly, is a marathon competitor, and every morning she and their daughters Rosemarie (age thirteen) and Amelia (age ten) run together before the girls go to school. Eddie is running a different race: providing the most effective and culturally sensitive care to children and their families and at the same time working to change the systems that sometimes prevent that. If anyone can win that race, it will be Eddie Ochoa.

Dr. Elijah E. Palnick

Humanitarian Award, 1982
(January 23, 1935–March 4, 2005)
Reprinted with permission from Irene Palnick

Rabbi Elijah Ezekiel Zeke Palnick, a leading figure of the civil rights era in Little Rock, Arkansas, died March 4. He was seventy. Rabbi Palnick, spiritual leader of Temple B'nai Israel for twenty-three years, helped integrate the city's civic clubs in the 1960s and welcomed blacks to attend services at the temple. He was president of the Arkansas Council on Human Relations, and a member of the board of the Pulaski County United Fund, the state Arts and Humanities Council, and the Governor's Council on Human Relations. In 1982, he was awarded the Humanitarian Award by the Arkansas unit of the National Conference of Christians and Jews. He was a leader in the formation of the Arkansas Conferences of Churches and Synagogues and was a member of its predecessor organization, the Religious Roundtable, and the Advisory Council of the Arkansas Conference of Churches and Synagogues. Rabbi Palnick's involvement with the Civil Rights Movement is highlighted in *The Quiet Voices: Southern Rabbis and Black Civil Rights, 1880s to 1990s,* edited by Mark Bauman and Berkley Kalin.

Rabbi Palnick was born in 1935 in Montreal, Canada, to Lazar Isar Palnick and Chaya Marie Rosenfeld Palnick. He attended McGill University in Montreal, graduated from Mount Allison University, New Brunswick, Nova Scotia, and was ordained from the Hebrew Union College in Cincinnati, Ohio, in 1959. He received a doctorate of theology degree from Burton Seminary and a doctor of philosophy degree from the Hebrew Union College. He served congregations in Miami

Beach and Tuscaloosa, Alabama, before moving to Little Rock in 1963. He moved to Albany, Georgia, in 1986, where he served at Temple B'nai Israel as Rabbi until 1999 and as Rabbi Emeritus until the time of his death. Rabbi Palnick revitalized the Jewish community in Albany and led the congregation through a time of transition, which included the construction of a new synagogue. He was also very active in civil rights affairs in Southwest Georgia. Rabbi Palnick served on many committees and associations and was highly respected by congregants of all faiths. He also served as president of the Association of Ministers in Albany.

After retiring in 1999, Rabbi Palnick and his wife, Irene, moved to Iowa City, Iowa. He was an active grandparent, attending events at Longfellow Elementary School and Southeast Junior High School. He enjoyed attending and actively participating in discussions at the Iowa City Foreign Relations Council Luncheon. Rabbi Palnick also enjoyed serving as chaplain for the Philmount Scout Ranch in New Mexico, which he did continuously since 1964.

He is survived by his loving wife, Irene Melton Palnick; son Lazar M. Palnick and daughter-in-law Susanne Gollin; daughter Rachelle Palnick Tsachor and son-in-law Uriel Tsachor; grandchildren, Oren Tsachor, Jacob Palnick, and Doron Tsachor; sister Ena Palnick and numerous uncles, aunts, cousins, nieces, and nephews.

Hugh B. Patterson
Humanitarian Award, 1987
(February 8, 1915–May 31, 2006)

H. B. Patterson, 91, Arkansas Publisher, Dies
by Roy Reed

Hugh B. Patterson Jr., who was the publisher of the *Arkansas Gazette* in 1957 when that newspaper was thrust into national prominence for its stand against segregated schools during a federal-state confrontation, died Monday (May 29, 2006) in Little Rock, Arkansas, where he lived. He was ninety-one.

His son Ralph B. Patterson announced the death.

By supporting desegregation, the *Gazette* suffered severe losses in advertising and circulation. It also won two Pulitzer Prizes for its coverage.

The Little Rock confrontation was instigated by Governor Orval E. Faubus, who called out the Arkansas National Guard to block nine blacks from enrolling at Central High School. The school board was under a federal court order to desegregate the school.

President Dwight D. Eisenhower eventually sent in troops to enforce the court order and escort the students past a crowd of angry whites.

The *Gazette*'s decision to oppose Mr. Faubus and support desegregation was made largely by Mr. Patterson and Harry S. Ashmore, the executive editor. Its senior owner and editor, J. N. Heiskell, the son of a Confederate colonel under General James Longstreet, was reluctant to go against the South's tradition of racial segregation, even though he disdained the white mobs and segregationist leaders.

Mr. Heiskell, the editor from 1902 until his death in 1972, was also Mr. Patterson's father-in-law. Mr. Patterson once told an interviewer that Mr. Heiskell's reluctance was overcome at a family dinner when Mr. Patterson and his wife, Louise, persuaded him that his grandchildren should not have to grow up in a racially unjust society. For its coverage of the confrontation, the *Gazette* was awarded a Pulitzer Prize for public service and another for editorials written by Mr. Ashmore, who died in 1998.

The paper also received a Freedom House award. But thousands of readers canceled their subscriptions, and a segregationist group, the Citizens Council, pressed for an advertising boycott. The boycott failed because large advertisers, especially department store owners, refused to honor it.

Mr. Patterson once recalled the day a *Gazette* delivery truck was blocked by a large group of white men in a town in eastern Arkansas.

The driver, he said, told the men: "I don't have anything to do with the content of the paper. I'm in the business of distributing these, and that's my business. And what I'm going to do is to back up about 500 yards, and when I get here again, I'm going to be going about fifty miles an hour, and I'm not going to stop." The crowd parted.

Unlike most other Southern publishers, who either actively opposed the Civil Rights Movement and the Supreme Court's desegregation efforts or simply kept quiet, Mr. Patterson was part of a small but influential minority who bucked generations of history to work for an end to legal segregation.

All suffered varying degrees of opprobrium from the region's white majority, but Mr. Patterson's paper, among the larger dailies, was hardest hit. Its losses amounted to $1 million or more, a serious setback for a family-owned newspaper at that time, Ralph Patterson said. The *Gazette* under Hugh Patterson's financial leadership not only recovered its losses but also went on to set Arkansas records in circulation and advertising. In addition, it became a magnet for bright young journalists.

Mr. Patterson was the *Gazette*'s publisher for forty of the forty-two years he worked there. He modernized the paper's equipment and financial structure and created an accounting system that many other papers emulated. Hugh Baskin Patterson Jr. was born Feb. 8, 1915, in Cotton Plant, Mississippi, to Hugh B. and Martha Rebecca Wilson Patterson. The family moved to Arkansas when Hugh was a boy. He grew up in Pine Bluff, went to work for a Little Rock printing company in 1936, then spent two years in New York as a salesman for the Art Metal Construction Company.

Mr. Patterson was hired by Mr. Heiskell in 1946 after leaving the Army Air Corps. He served as a supply officer during World War II and was discharged as a major.

Mr. Patterson's college career at Henderson State Teachers College in Arkadelphia, Arkansas, was cut short because of financial pressures.

He married Louise Heiskell in 1943. They had two sons and were divorced in 1988. In 1992, he married Olivia Owen Nisbet, who survives him.

In addition to his wife and son Ralph, of Little Rock and Blowing Rock, North Carolina, Mr. Patterson is survived by another son, Carrick H., of Little Rock; a stepson, A. Wyckliff Nisbet, and a stepdaughter, Olivia Wyatt; nine grandchildren and one great-grandchild.

Mr. Patterson left the *Gazette* shortly after he and the Heiskell family sold it to the Gannett Company in 1986. He became bitterly critical of Gannett's ownership.

Founded in 1819, the *Gazette* was closed in 1991 and merged with its politically conservative rival, the *Arkansas Democrat*, after years of fierce competition.

Louise Patterson

Humanitarian Award, 1987
(1921–1990)

Funeral Wednesday for Louise Patterson
Former Gazette board member honored
for her role in 1957 Central High crisis
By Leroy Donald, September 18, 1990
Reprinted with permission from the Arkansas Democrat-Gazette

Funeral for Mrs. Louise Caroline Heiskell
Patterson, sixty-nine, of Little Rock, a former
member of the board of the Arkansas Gazette
Co. who died Sunday, will be at 2 p.m.
Wednesday at Trinity Episcopal Cathedral.

The Very Reverend Joel W. Pugh will
conduct the service. Burial will be in Mount
Holly Cemetery.

As the daughter of J. N. Heiskell who
was president and editor of the *Arkansas Gazette* for seventy years, and
the former wife of Hugh B. Patterson, who was publisher for decades,
she played an important behind-the-scenes role at the *Gazette*.

She considered herself a representative of the Heiskell newspaper
legacy, and her philosophy influenced the newspaper.

For this, and particularly her role in the newspaper's stand for law
and order in 1957 Central High desegregation crisis, she and Hugh
Patterson were named co-recipients in 1987 of the Humanitarian Award
of the Arkansas Council on Brotherhood of the National Conference
of Christians and Jews.

Mrs. Patterson was active in civic and cultural affairs. In her position, she often entertained the famous in arts and politics when they visited Little Rock, but her role as hostess was not limited to famous visitors.

She was vitally interested not only in what went into her newspaper, but the people behind those words. When the staff was much smaller, she knew most of them and their families.

Pat Carithers, the *Gazette*'s longtime telegraph editor, remembered that when his daughter, Kelly, was critically injured in a car accident at age nine, Mrs. Patterson brought books to the hospital for her to read. And years later, when Kelly was married, Mrs. Patterson was at the wedding.

Staff members frequently were visitors to the Patterson home. Although in ill health, Mrs. Patterson made certain she would be at the *Gazette* last January when Harriett Aldridge, the newspaper's longtime food columnist retired.

Betty Fulkerson was not only a friend as society editor of the *Gazette*, she was a friend of Mrs. Patterson as they grew up in the Trinity Cathedral neighborhood. It was about this time that Mrs. Patterson acquired the nickname "Weetsey" from her family because she was the smallest of the children playing in the neighborhood, Mrs. Fulkerson said.

"She was always deeply interested in the paper and I think always wished that she could be a part of it herself. Mrs. Fulkerson said.

The editorial staff of the *Gazette* knew that Mrs. Patterson read the paper closely every day, paying particular attention to the editorial page. But, they recalled, she never sent notes or visited their offices, only to appear once a year for the annual board meeting.

James O. Powell and his wife, Ruth, came to Little Rock thirty-one years ago, when Powell was named editor of the editorial page. Through the paper, the Powells and Pattersons became fast friends. They traveled frequently, much of the time on newspaper business but often on personal trips.

Mrs. Patterson particularly liked South America, southern France, and London and New York, Ruth Powell recalled.

"New York was one of her favorite places to go, especially at Christmas, because she was able to see the crèche at the museum," Mrs. Powell said, referring to Mrs. Patterson's interest in Christmas.

She made Christmas-tree decorations and Christmas packages for family and friends, contributing her original decorations to the Trinity Episcopal Cathedral Christmas Bazaar.

"She was a perfectionist," Mrs. Fulkerson said of these efforts.

"She was creative and smart," Mrs. Powell said.

Mrs. Patterson is survived by two sons, Carrick H. and Ralph B. Patterson of Little Rock; three grandsons, John Netherland Heiskell Patterson, Hugh Andrew Patterson, and Nicholas Gilbert Patterson, all of Little Rock; and a step granddaughter, Julie Cotherine Jones of Little Rock.

Funeral arrangements are by Griffin Leggett Healey & Roth.

Memorials may be made to Friends of KLRE, the fund-raising arm of the public radio station. Mrs. Patterson was chairwoman of Friends of KLRE in 1986.

Alan Patteson Jr.

Humanitarian Award, 1981
(*Interview conducted August 1, 2012*)

You might describe Alan Patteson differently depending on when and where you first met him. That's because he's been a speculator in bean futures, a cotton-gin owner, a radio station owner, a community activist, a caretaker, a business manager for a convent, and a tutor for English-language learners. And it's very clear that Alan has relished each and every opportunity that he has been afforded.

Alan was the oldest son and one of five children. His parents, Alan G. and Katherine Carter Patteson survived the Great Depression and the loss of a cotton gin by fire. Luckily, his dad had bought some land during the Depression. Most people thought his dad a fool, but following the floods of 1937, levees were built, and the land became very valuable. As kids, Alan and his friends pretty much had permission to ride their bicycles anywhere in Jonesboro, Arkansas, which had around 12,000 residents at the time. One of their favorite trips was out to a gravel pit where they could swim and picnic.

Alan's first job was on his dad's farm, but he says he would have starved had he had to pick cotton for a living. He was, in fact, grateful when he was hired to do manual labor at Barton Lumber Company for thirty-five cents an hour. Alan graduated from high school at New Mexico Military Institute, and then he attended the University of Missouri because they had a good program in agriculture. College was transformative for him.

One of Alan's fraternity brothers was studying to be a Presbyterian minister. Rather than trying to convert Alan, this fraternity brother urged him to learn more about his own Catholic faith and introduced him to magazines such as *Commonweal* and *America*, a Jesuit publication. And then there was the debate: "Should or should not Negroes be admitted to the University of Missouri?" Alan describes it this way:

The room was packed, and all the pros and cons had been presented. Following, there was a time for audience response. Alan was ashamed when a white student stood up and said with a cocky air about him, "I've never met an educated Negro...." In response, a tall handsome woman, probably from the NAACP, said, "They tell me that now is not the time. My father, who is ninety years old, was told, 'Now is not the time.' I cannot help but wonder when it will be the right time. Young man, you tell me that you have never met an educated Negro. May I assure you that they exist in all walks, and I further assure you that the fact that you have not met them is your loss, not theirs."

At the end of the meeting, Alan went up to the woman, introduced himself, and told her, "I was embarrassed by the comments here tonight, but truthfully, I have never met an educated Negro either." The woman asked him where he was from and said kindly, "But how could it be otherwise?" That experience certainly got Alan ready for his summer training in ROTC, where he had his first opportunity to interact with a peer group of black ROTC students from South Carolina.

After college graduation, Alan went into business with his dad and younger brother Carter, and he met and married Carol Busch. Alan explains that he and Carter learned the cotton gin business from their father, inherited it after his death, and then expanded it. In 1958, he and Carter also purchased an AM/FM radio station, where Alan became the general manager. When they sold the station after 35 years, he expected to do some traveling, but a friend persuaded him to serve as the business manager for Holy Angels Convent, owned by the Olivetan Benedictine Sisters. After talking with Henrietta, the Mother Superior, who was a friend from grammar school, he agreed to serve for one year—on a part-time basis. That one year turned into eleven years, and in 2005 he retired again.

While running those businesses, Alan was an active member of
the Jonesboro community. He served on the board of St. Bernard's
Regional Medical Center for thirty years, was a commissioner of the
Jonesboro City Water and Light Board for twenty years, and served on
the local library board for fourteen years. But he didn't limit his commitments to Jonesboro, serving on the State Library Commission which
helped develop public libraries across the state. He also served on the
Arkansas Council for Human Relations, chairing it during 1970 and
1971. He loved the fact that he could pick up the phone and find both
black and white leaders in every corner of our state who were willing to
work on issues such as fair housing, integration of public schools, greater
employment opportunities for blacks, and prison reform. At the request
of Irene Samuels, he initiated the formation of a Human Relations
Council in Jonesboro, too. At its height, the Jonesboro council brought
together a bi-racial group of approximately ninety leaders. Alan credits
such Central Arkansas leaders as Winthrop Rockefeller and Frank Lyon
Sr. for making it easier for folks in small towns to speak up. But it didn't
hurt the cause that Alan had already served as president of both the
Jonesboro Rotary Club and the Chamber of Commerce. In recognition
of his service and stature in our state, Alan was appointed by President
George H. W. Bush to serve on the U.S. Civil Rights Advisory
Committee for Arkansas. He enjoyed that, but found it a bit frustrating
when his trip to the White House Rose Garden was more ceremonial
than substantive.

On their fiftieth wedding anniversary, Alan first realized that something was not right with his wife, Carol. She had almost died after being
hit by a drunk driver a few years earlier, and like many people who suffer
severe head trauma, she was beginning to show signs of dementia. For
the next decade, Alan cared for Carol as she progressed through the
stages of Alzheimer's disease in what he calls a textbook fashion. There
were very difficult times, and some very good times. For example, just
three days before her death, Carol recognized every family member in

some home movies they watched. Alan says their five children were incredibly helpful, and he joined a support group where he found strength. Carol died in early 2012, a few months before they would have celebrated their sixtieth wedding anniversary. Alan still attends those support group meetings, offering to others what was so important to him. And he's very grateful that he had the ability and the means to care for the woman he loved in their own home during the final decade of her life.

At the urging of his children, Alan went back to Arkansas State University to earn a second degree in Spanish in 2010, exactly sixty years after earning his first degree. Following Carol's death, he also completed an immersion course in Spanish by living in Costa Rica for seven weeks. Back home again, he attends the Spanish Language Mass at his Catholic Church, has a "conversation partner" to help him, and plans to continue what he began last year: tutoring at two high schools. One of his pupils was a young man who had been expelled; the other was a young man who could read the words but didn't understand their meaning.

Oh, and about that foray into bean futures. That happened when Alan was just out of college, and he actually made some money, but he said he learned that betting his future on bean prices was not what he wanted to do with his life. He chose instead to bet on hard work and building relationships. That clearly paid handsomely, too.

James H. Penick Sr.

Humanitarian Award, 1973
(July 14, 1897–December 4, 1975)

Banker Dies at Age 78

Reprinted with permission from the Arkansas Democrat-Gazette

Community Leader Was Business Titan

James H. Penick, aged seventy-eight, senior board chairman of Worthen Bank and Trust Company and one of the authentic titans of business and civic affairs of Little Rock and the state, died Thursday of heart failure.

Mr. Penick had served his profession at virtually every level, starting out in it as a bookkeeper and general utility man and rising to become president and then board chairman of the state's largest financial institution, one he himself largely built.

In virtually every civic cause of merit, Mr. Penick's name recurred again and again; he distinguished himself as a soilder in two wars and was recognized for his humanitarianism in 1973 with a National Brotherhood Citation of the National Conference of Christians and Jews for, among other things, having worked quietly to open the facility of the city to all races.

Mr. Penick, even though deeply occupied in business affairs, devoted countless and often unsung hours to such organizations as the Little Rock Boys Club and the Boys Clubs of America; to the Little Rock Chamber of Commerce; the United Way and its predecessors; and dozens of others.

Was Devoted to Education

He contributed to the city's artistic life as well, serving seven years in the 1950s as president of the Little Rock Community Concert Association. He was devoted to the cause of education and was instrumental in Little Rock Junior College's achieving the status it now enjoys as a part of the University of Arkansas System. He served his profession in a variety of state and national offices.

Mr. Penick was born at West Plains, Missouri, July 14, 1897, but moved with his family as an infant to Hot Springs, and then to Little Rock in 1904. Educated in the city's public schools, he attended Washington and Lee University at Lexington, Virginia, interrupting his college education to join the army in World War I. He spent part of his two years of military service in that war in France and returned home a first lieutenant. He returned to the army in War World II and spent much of his second tour at Rome as chief of the Allied Financial Agency, helping to rebuild the banking systems of Africa and Italy. Italy awarded the Order of the Crown of Italy to him for his service, and the U.S. Army recognized his work with a Legion of Merit. He left the army a lieutenant colonial.

Was Married During War

In 1918, while still in the army in World War I, Lieutenant Penick and Miss Mary Worthen, daughter of the late W. B. Worthen, founder of Worthen Bank, and Mollie Peay Worthen were married. They had three children, Mrs. W. N. Brandon Jr., Edward M. Penick, and James H. Penick Jr.

Both sons are officers of the bank, Edward M. now serving as Board chairman and chief executive officer and James Jr. as president.

Mrs. Penick died in January 1950, and a year later Mr. Penick and Miss Virginia Ivey were married. They had two children, Virginia Ivey Penick and James Carroll Penick.

Mr. Penick joined the staff of what was then called the W. B. Worthen Co., Bankers, on February 15, 1919, as one of about twenty employees of an institution with deposits of $1,214,840. The bank occupied space in the Boyle Building.

He rose through the ranks to teller, cashier, executive vice president, president, and board chairman, retiring from active bank management in the mid-1960s but retaining his seat on the bank's board and continuing to serve the institution in an advisory and consulting capacity.

Held Law Degree, Honorary Doctorate

Mr. Penick earned a law degree from the Arkansas Law School, and an honorary doctor of laws degree was awarded him by the University of Arkansas. He was admitted to the Arkansas Bar in 1918.

Mr. Penick had served as president of the Little Rock Clearing House, as chairman of the Bank Management Committee of the Arkansas Bankers Association, as president of the ABA, as a director of the Federal Reserve Bank of St. Louis, as a member of the Federal Advisory Council of the Federal Reserve System, and as president of the State Bank Association. He also had served as chairman of the Executive Committee of the State Bank Division of the American Bankers Association, as a member of the Executive Council of the ABA, and as chairman of the Advisory Council of the National Association of Supervisors of State Banks. For three years he was a member of the state Bank Board.

In nonbanking fields, Mr. Penick had served as president of the Community Chest, the predecessor of the United Way of Pulaski County; as president of the Little Rock Chamber of Commerce and the Pulaski County Citizens Council (later called the Committee of 100); and as chairman of the Little Rock Civic Committee. He served many years on the Board of the Little Rock Boys Club and as its president, and as a director of the Boys Clubs of America.

In 1946, Mr. Penick and other lenders formed a small group to raise funds that he hoped would be the basis of growth of Little Rock Junior College into Little Rock University. The group engineered the move of LRJC from its old quarters on West Thirteenth Street to a new 80-acre campus at West Thirty-second Street and University Avenue, since greatly expanded. From that, Mr. Penick became president of the Little Rock University Foundation. He later served as a trustee and chairman of the Board of Trustees of LRU.

He was a former president of the First Arkansas Development Finance Corporation and served on its executive committee.

Mr. Penick had served as a vestryman and senior warden of the parish of Trinity Episcopal Cathedral and had been chairman of the Standing Committee of the Episcopal Diocese of Arkansas and a member of the Diocesan Board of Trustees.

He was a Mason, a member of Scimitar Shrine Temple, a past grand commander of the Knights Templar and a former secretary of the Arkansas Division of Knights Templar Educational Foundation.

Was a Founder of Arkansas NCCJ

Mr. Penick was a founder and the first Protestant co-chairman of the Arkansas Region of the National Conference of Christians and Jews and the recipient of its 1973 Brotherhood Award. At that time, then-governor (now Senator) Dale Bumpers praised Mr. Penick for the work behind the scenes to quiet the racial turmoil that accompanied the Little Rock school desegregation crisis, and William J. (Sonny) Walker, head of the Southeastern Region of the office of Economic Opportunity in Atlanta, called Mr. Penick "A man whose whole life has become dedicated to the concept of brotherhood and human rights espoused by the NCCJ."

Mr. Penick was instrumental in the construction of the two most recent homes of Worthen Bank and Trust, at East Fourteenth and Main Streets, a four-story building occupied by the bank in 1929, and the

twenty-four-story structure at Capitol Avenue and Louisiana Street, occupied in November 1969. The institution now employs more than 750
employees and has assets exceeding $425 million.

Survivors, in addition to his wife, three sons, and two daughters,
are two sisters, Mrs. H. Fay Jones and Mrs. M. J. Kilbury Sr. both of Little
Rock; eight grandchildren; and four great-grandchildren.

Jim Pickens
Humanitarian Award, 2004

In 2003, Jim Pickens was listed as one of "10 People Who Have Made A Difference" in *Southern Business and Development* in its feature about the South's best places for business and development. That's just confirming all that Arkansans already knew. Specifically, Jim was recognized for his work as director of Arkansas Department of Economic Development (ADED) from February 2001 to December 2003, but Jim started making a difference long before he accepted the ADED position.

Jim is a native of Jonesboro and earned his degree in business administration from Arkansas State University. He later studied at Rice University and Louisiana State University, and he served in the U.S. Army as a Company Commander.

Jim began his business career in Pine Bluff as a customer service representative for Arkansas Power & Light Company, now Entergy. He rose through the ranks at Entergy to assume the position of vice president of public affairs before his retirement. Always a key leader in the business world, Jim also found time to serve many other institutions that are important to Arkansans.

Jim's record of community service is extensive with groups ranging from Pathfinders, CARTI, Arkansas State University, P.A.R.K., United Way, Arthritis Foundation, YMCA, Chamber of Commerce, Arkansas Arts Center and Boy Scouts of America. There is almost no area of civic life that has not benefitted from his hard work.

Jim had been described as "the most politically savvy non-politician" in the state of Arkansas. That's probably because he is not afraid to face hard truths and not afraid to try to solve difficult problems. And he is a master at getting people to work together for the benefit of all. Jim truly has walked with kings, but never lost the common touch.

When asked what accomplishment he is most proud of, Jim immediately starts talking about creating jobs. Whether it was as head of ADED, through his long career at Entergy, or by working with non-profits, Jim has always been about lifting others up. For example, he helped build the Pathfinders Skills Training Center in Jacksonville, Arkansas, which provides jobs to disabled adults. In 2001, the Pathfinder Skills Center was renamed the Jim Pickens Skills Center.

Jim and his wife, Sue, have two children, Mike Pickens, Arkansas Insurance Commissioner, and Sandy Noble, kindergarten teacher in McKinney, Texas.

Albert J. Porter
Father Joseph H. Biltz Award, 2006

If you want to spend some time with Albert J. Porter, you will have to fit it in between his delivery of gingerbread houses for Treatment Homes and his Meals on Wheels calls. And most likely, when you do catch Al, he will be accompanied by his sidekick Allan Ward.

Al Porter is a native of Mississippi and spent his first ten years in McComb. From the very beginning, he had an insatiable curiosity about the world beyond the confines of his segregated community. In describing his childhood home, Al says, "Everything was separate." You were born, schooled, you attended church, went out to eat, socialized, died, and were buried without crossing that line of segregation. At that time, anyone, whether white or black, who dared to do differently risked personal and family punishment. His parents helped him to understand those unwritten rules by explaining that when he couldn't do something it was because he must obey the "law." Therefore, Al decided early on that he wanted to work to change the law.

Al's dad died when Al was only six months old, and his mother moved from McComb to Jackson, Mississippi, to work. Al stayed with his grandparents and considered his mother's thirteen siblings to be his own brothers and sisters. Al's childhood was more privileged than some in that his Grandfather was a farmer landowner and therefore able to vote, and they had a car which was true of very few black families there. When Al was ten years old, his mother brought him to Jackson so that he could have better opportunities for schooling.

Because he wasn't allowed to attend college in Mississippi, he studied at the Universities of Michigan, Oregon, and Washington. In 1956, Al married Fannye Ranger, and their careers took them to jobs at Lane

College, a black school supported by the Christian Methodist Episcopal Church in Jackson, Tennessee. Students at Lane asked Al to be their sponsor when they planned to desegregate the city bus system. Al, who had studied with Martin Luther King Jr., helped teach the students the principles of non-violence, and he is proud to this day that once the picketing began, the students had desegregated the bus system within forty-eight hours. It was also at Lane that Al met his lifelong friend Allan Ward, who had purposely chosen to cross the color line to teach at the all-black school so that he could also work for civil rights.

Al and Allan will always remember a turning point in their work, when Al was invited to meet with a group of white Methodist women from Lambeth College. Allan went along, and they had to arrive after dark to make sure no one else knew of the "interracial" visit, which was, in fact, against the law, just as Al's parents had always told him. They were served tea, and Allan remembers that the tension was so great that the tea cups rattled on their saucers. The women very kindly asked Al, "Why are you black folks doing this?" He answered, "For equal rights." Just then the phone rang with a call from someone's babysitter. The conversation turned to children and suddenly the tension was gone. Everyone understood. The civil rights activists were working for what is best for the children...all the children.

One of the results of this early work was the founding of the Human Relations Council, which held discussion groups in that community. They also continued to desegregate public facilities and won employment opportunities for blacks, especially in the factories. Al and Allan made many trips to other communities, and to this day they consider themselves a team in working to build understanding.

Al and his wife, Fannye, moved to Little Rock in 1966, and our community has been the better for it ever since. Al retired from Armstrong Rubber in 1974, but has never retired from public service. He is a valued member of many boards and committees and has been recognized with many awards and honors. Consider these numbers: He constructs more than 1,000 gingerbread houses each year, he arranges visits for an average of 150 international visitors in our community each year, and he delivers fourteen meals on wheels each week. That's not even mentioning his many committee meetings and weekly tutoring sessions for VIPS.

Oh, and lest we forget, he's very proud that he has frequently been the "Nanny" for his daughter Portia's sons: Cameron, now a senior at Virginia Tech, and Jordan, a high school senior. Portia is a consultant on aging issues and lives in Washington DC. Al's son Albert lives in Los Angeles and is an electrical engineer.

To satisfy his insatiable curiosity, Al joined the World Communication Association, which made it possible for him to travel all over the world. He has visited twenty-five countries in Europe, Asia, Africa, and Central and South America. His travel has intensified his desire to help make the world a better place. And in 2006, Al is very hopeful about our future because of the remarkable progress he's already witnessed.

Honorable David Pryor

Humanitarian Award, 1984
(Interview conducted in October 2012)

When David Pryor ended his final term in the U.S. Senate in 1996, we might say he retired to be "of counsel" to all Arkansans. Since then, he has been: a professor at the University of Arkansas; director of the Institute of Politics at Harvard University's John F. Kennedy School of Government; inaugural dean of the University of Arkansas Clinton School of Public Service; and interim chair of the state Democratic Party after Bill Gwatney's death. Before that, David Pryor had already served as a member of the Arkansas House of Representatives and the U.S. House of Representatives, as governor of Arkansas, and as a U.S. senator.

David was born in 1934 in Camden, Arkansas, the third of four children of Susan Newton Pryor and Edgar Pryor. He describes his childhood as "comfortable and secure by any standards." Although he lived through the aftermath of the Great Depression and World War II, his parents provided all that the children needed and mostly shielded them from the larger troubles of those times. Camden was a small town, and if they went shopping or to the movies, it was in nearby El Dorado, where there was even a Dairy Queen by 1950.

David's father put everything he had into buying a Chevrolet dealership, which became "a gathering spot for business, local politics, and friendly commerce." Drafted by friends, Edgar also ran for and served as Sheriff for four years. He gladly retired to become a full-time Chevy dealer again. He once told David, "You might live long enough to see Chevrolets sell for as much as $2,000!" At age fifty-two, Edgar was diagnosed with acute leukemia, and he died a within a week.

Susie Pryor, David's mother, came from a well-respected Camden family of "long-time public servants, pillars in the Presbyterian Church." Susie was multi-talented, involved in the community's life, and "the first Arkansas female to seek public office after women earned the vote." She lost her first race, which was for circuit clerk, in 1926. However, she was elected to the Camden School Board in 1947. Five years following Edgar's untimely death, Susie spent several months as a missionary in British Guinea, "tutoring children in English and helping construct new family quarters in the jungle." She wrote in her Christmas letter in 1950 that she thought politics might be too disillusioning for David. He was destined to prove her wrong.

David remembers several teachers who made an impression on him. One was Mrs. Harry Clerget, who taught him Robert's Rules of Order so that he could properly preside as president of his fifth-grade class. Another was Mary Lou Parker, who taught art and drama and instilled in David a respect and love for the stage and for artists. Through the years as a legislator, he was grateful for those parliamentary lessons, and in 2012, he serves as a trustee for the Corporation for Public Broadcasting, where an appreciation for the arts is surely an asset.

David began post-secondary studies at Henderson State Teachers College in Arkadelphia, and the next year he transferred to the University of Arkansas at Fayetteville. He held several leadership roles on campus and graduated with a degree in government in 1957. During his senior year, he met Barbara Jean Lunsford. One can't help but think that when David Pryor fell in love with Barbara, he was likely using his mother, Susie, as a role model for the ideal wife, because Barbara has proved equally talented and adaptable throughout their life together. Following their 1957 Thanksgiving morning wedding and a brief honeymoon in New Orleans, they moved back to Camden to start a weekly newspaper, *The Ouachita Citizen*, which served as a progressive voice for southeastern Arkansas until it closed in 1962.

David Pryor was elected to the Arkansas House of Representatives in 1960 when he was only twenty-six years old. There he joined several other reformist members (called the Young Turks) who were often in opposition to Governor Orval Faubus. Shortly David returned to the University of Arkansas at Fayetteville, and earned his law degree in 1964. He practiced law for only two years before he was elected to the U.S. Congress, in 1966, where he served for three terms. He left the House to run against Arkansas Senator John L. McClellan, who handed David his only political defeat, in 1972.

Instead of then serving in the U.S. Senate, David Pryor was elected the thirty-ninth Governor of Arkansas in 1975, and he served for two terms. Dale Bumpers had preceded him as Arkansas Governor, and Bill Clinton came after. These three progressive governors have since been considered something of an anomaly in what was becoming a more conservative, more Republican South. Governor Pryor continued some of the significant reforms enacted during Bumpers's term. He also called a constitutional convention to reform the 1874 constitution (adoption of the proposed constitution was narrowly defeated by voters), and he created a natural and cultural heritage department for the state. He was unable to pass his "Arkansas Plan," which would have given enhanced power to local communities over taxes and spending.

In 1989, David Pryor was elected for the first of three six-year terms in the U.S. Senate, where he served alongside Dale Bumpers. Pryor's significant work on the issues of taxpayer fairness and aging are well known. And he was elected by fellow Democratic senators as secretary of the Democratic Caucus. When Bill Clinton became president in 1993, Pryor was often called upon as a liaison between the President and the senate.

It's difficult to calculate the impact that David Pryor has had upon our state and our nation. One significant example would be his work on the Taxpayer Bill of Rights, which was first passed in 1988 and extended in 1996 and 1998. Because of this law, we are protected from over-reaching by the IRS even when an audit is being conducted. And through Pryor's leadership of the Senate Aging Committee, there are improved standards for nursing homes and fair pricing practices for prescription drugs. Currently, in addition to serving on the board of the Corporation for Public Broadcasting, he is also a board member of Heifer International and the University of Arkansas Board of Trustees.

In his book, A *Pryor Commitment*, David tells about the early years in Camden, running a money-losing paper, having the first of their three sons, making his first run for political office, and ultimately deciding to return to law school in Fayetteville, where Barbara supported them with a job at a drugstore. About those difficult times, he said, "Over and over, the critic inside me warned of life's greatest burden: an impressive potential." Clearly, David Pryor needn't have worried: he lived up to that potential, and far beyond.

Louis L. Ramsay Jr.

Humanitarian Award, 1990

(October 11, 1918–January 7, 2004)

Reprinted with permission from Arkansas Business Hall of Fame;
published in 2003, the year before Mr. Ramsay's death

Louis L. Ramsay Jr.'s name is synonymous with service and leadership in Arkansas. He is the only person in the state's history to serve as president of both the Arkansas State Bankers Association and the Arkansas Bar Association. As a war hero, lawyer, banker, and trendsetter in the education and health fields, he has had a significant impact on the growth and development of the state of Arkansas. He learned a long time ago that a person does not have to be a public officer to make a difference to his community, state and nation. Former Governor Bill Clinton once described Ramsay as representing "everything that is good about our state."

Ramsay was born in Fordyce, Arkansas, in 1918. He attended public schools in Fordyce. While in junior high, he witnessed the fight between his fellow "Redbug" Paul "Bear" Bryant and a bear. Through a twist of fate, he attended the University of Arkansas—not Alabama where Bryant had tried to recruit him—on an athletic scholarship. Nicknamed "Ramrod," he played quarterback on the Razorback football team, lettering in 1940–41. He further developed his leadership skills on campus as president of Blue Key, president of the Interfraternity Council, president of the "A" Club, Razorback Annual 1942 "Who's Who," Kappa Sigma, and Delta Theta Phi law fraternity.

His academic life was interrupted by World War II where, as a young Army Air Corps captain, he piloted a paratroop carrier in Europe.

He participated in all air drops, including Bastogne and Arnhem, and received combat air medals with four Oak Leaf Clusters.

He returned to school to gain a juris doctorate degree from the University's School of Law in 1947. He then joined the law firm of Coleman & Gantt in Pine Bluff where, in only one year, he became a partner. He continues today to serve as "Of Counsel" for the firm, which is now Ramsay, Bridgforth, Harrelson & Starling.

He had met Joy Bond at the university, and the couple was married in 1945. Joy had graduated from the College of Business Administration in 1943 with a BSBA. Following in the footsteps of their parents, the couple's children, Joy R. Blankenship, BA '78, and Richard L. Ramsay, BA '74, JD '77, graduated from the University of Arkansas. Ramsay's grandchildren include Drew Blankenship, BA '99; Ben Blankenship; Kate Blankenship; Jimbo Ramsay, BSBA '82; Liz Ramsay; Alex Graham; and Clancy Graham.

Ramsay was elected president of Simmons First National Bank in 1970 and was chairman and CEO from 1973 to 1983. He currently serves as chairman of the executive committee for the board of directors. Today, through his leadership, the bank has sixty-three offices in thirty-three communities in Arkansas. In recognition of fifty years of service to Simmons First National Bank, it was announced at the April 23, 2002, shareholders' meeting that the bank's board room would be named the Louis L. Ramsay Jr. Board Room.

He joined the board of directors of Arkansas Blue Cross and Blue Shield in 1985 and served as chairman until 1997. He remains chairman of the executive committee. Founded in 1948, Arkansas Blue Cross is the largest health insurer in the state, serving more than 860,000 Arkansans.

Ramsay began his leadership in the law profession as president of the Jefferson County Bar Association in 1958. In addition to serving as president of the Arkansas Bar Association in 1963-1964, he received its outstanding lawyer award in 1966 and its outstanding lawyer-citizen award in 1987. He served as commissioner to the National Conference

of Commissioners on Uniform State Laws from 1961 to 1969. He was a
member of the American Bar Association's House of Delegates from
1968 to 1972. Ramsay is a fellow in the American Bar Foundation,
Arkansas Bar Foundation, American College of Trial Lawyers and
American College of Trust and Estate Counsel. He was listed in *Best
Lawyers in America* for 1989-1990, 1991-1992, and 1993-1994.

In addition to his banking and legal endeavors, Ramsay is a champion of higher education, trying to ensure that the state's sons and
daughters remain in Arkansas and become leaders in their communities
and businesses. He served as member of the board of trustees of AM&N
(University of Arkansas at Pine Bluff) and on the board of visitors at the
University of Arkansas at Little Rock. He served on the board of trustees
for the University of Arkansas at Fayetteville from 1971 to 1981 and as
chairman from 1978 to 1981. He brought his banking skills to his position as chairman of the University of Arkansas Foundation from 1981
to 1988 and as president of the U of A Endowment Trust Fund. As a
tribute to his work and vision, he received an honorary degree from the
University of Arkansas at Fayetteville in 1988 and the University of
Arkansas at Pine Bluff in 1992. In addition, he was president of the
Arkansas Alumni Association and cited as a distinguished alumnus.

Ramsay served as chairman of the Arkansas Science and
Technology Authority where he encouraged the state to be more selective
about industrial development. Governor Bill Clinton appointed him to
lead the Arkansas Sesquicentennial Celebration in 1986. He traveled
throughout the state that year promoting a positive image of the state,
using the occasion as a "springboard for a new image for Arkansas."

In 1989, Louis L. Ramsay received the Public Relations Society of
America-Arkansas Chapter's first Diamond Award, to recognize someone from outside the profession who has made outstanding contributions in the field.

Ramsay is literally "Mr. Southeast Arkansas." His leadership has
made a significant economic impact on the Pine Bluff community and

Southeast Arkansas. In 1986 poll conducted by the *Pine Bluff Commercial*, Pine Bluff residents elected Ramsay as the "City's Most Influential Citizen." He was honored at a $100 a plate dinner attended by more than 600 people including the "Who's Who in Arkansas." As a permanent tribute, Simmons First National Bank; the Ramsay, Cox Law Firm; and Arkansas Blue Cross and Blue Shield jointly contributed $25,000 to establish the Louis L. Ramsay Education Fund. The proceeds of the endowment sponsor an annual educational project for youth at the Arts and Science Center.

Ramsay served as president of Pine Bluff Chamber of Commerce, president of Pine Bluff Rotary Club, president of Fifty for the Future of Pine Bluff Inc., a member of the board of directors of Jefferson County Industrial Foundation, and a board member of Arkansas Oak Flooring Company.

Among Ramsay's national recognitions are the "Distinguished American Award" from Arkansas Chapter of National Football Hall of Fame in 1987 and listings in *Who's Who in America*, *Who's Who in the World*, and *Oxford's Who's Who*. He received the National Conference of Christian and Jews Humanitarian Award in 1990.

Ramsay's friend, Bradley D. Jesson, of Hardin, Jesson & Terry, Fort Smith, said, "Ramsay's accomplishments and personality have gained him entry and respect in the highest counsels of law, banking and business. While he is a friend of presidents, senators, governors, and CEOs, he remains the same warm, caring person he was when he left Fordyce High School for the University of Arkansas, more than sixty years ago."

Raymond Rebsamen

Humanitarian Award, 1976

(1898–1975)

Reprinted with permission from Arkansas Business Hall of Fame

Raymond Rebsamen's business acumen enabled him not only to establish one of the nation's top fifty insurance brokers, but also to create multiple successful and far reaching companies. Although he passed away in 1975, his civic and philanthropic contributions still impact Arkansas today.

Rebsamen was born in Lancaster, Texas, on April 8, 1898, to William Frederick and Edna Mae Rebsamen. They moved to Fort Smith, Arkansas, where he attended public schools. As a ten-year-old, he delivered groceries to the back doors of the town's finer homes; the experience made him determined to one day be invited in the front doors.

He served as a private in World War I, interrupting his education at the University of Arkansas, where he had joined Sigma Alpha Epsilon. He studied accounting and became a field auditor for the U.S. Treasury after the war. He later served as Lt. Colonel in World War II.

An Amazing Grasp of Numbers

After earning the certified public accountant designation, Rebsamen created his first business, Rebsamen, Brown and Co. In 1927, he discovered that the *Arkansas Gazette* had overpaid its federal taxes and successfully negotiated his fee for one-third of the $96,000 refund. The money accelerated his business career and illustrated how his grasp of numbers would lead to success.

He married Elizabeth Purcell in 1923 and moved to Little Rock. They had two children, Ruth Elizabeth and Frederick Raymond, who also attended the University of Arkansas. He had four grandchildren, eight great-grandchildren, and six great-great-grandchildren.

In 1928, he established Rebsamen & East Insurance Agency and bought Arkansas Printing and Lithography. Rebsamen was a genius at seeing the benefits of synergies and, over the next forty years, he would establish many businesses, including Rebsamen International Inc.; Rebsamen & Associates Inc.; International Graphics Inc.; Manhattan Credit Co.; Riverside Insurance Company of America; Riverside Life Insurance Co.; Rebsamen Ford (now Landers); American Colonial Insurance Co.; Derco Inc.; General Utilities Co.; and Arkansas Motor Coaches. He also invested in other business operations, including Jacksonville State Bank, now First Arkansas Bancshares Inc. In 2001, Rebsamen Insurance was purchased by Regions Financial Corporation. It became Regions Insurance Group in 2008.

Rebsamen said, "The single greatest factor in my business life has been the work ethic. I never remember being inactive. I have always encouraged ... associate executives to accept full responsibility, allowing me time for planning and outside activities." He kept on top of all operations with the aid of ledger sheets where he watched for bad spots and ordered them to be eliminated. He knew at a glance how much money he made or lost on each automobile part, insurance policy, and printing order.

His personal mantra was that you should always abide by the letter of the law and never step over the line, but you should know exactly where the line is so you can get right up to it.

Highly sought for his business expertise, Rebsamen served on the boards of almost twenty companies, ranging from Dillard's Inc. and Arkansas Louisiana Gas Company to American Power & Light and Lithium Corporation of American—to name a few. In addition, he was chairman of the board of the Federal Reserve Bank of St. Louis from 1963 to 1966. In the late 1960s, he began publishing a full-color magazine named *Arkansas State*. In 1966, Rebsamen ran unsuccessfully for governor of Arkansas in the Democratic primary. Winthrop Rockefeller was subsequently elected and served the state well, according to Rebsamen. Still, his campaign slogan, "Reach with Rebsamen," was emblematic of his vision for Arkansas.

A Strong Belief in Education

In the 1940s, Rebsamen donated eighty acres of land that hold the University of Arkansas at Little Rock. The site is now named the Raymond Rebsamen campus. A new gate in his honor was dedicated in August 2008.

In 1971, he gave the Walton College $100,000 to establish a stock management class. The Rebsamen Fund is worth almost $1 million today, and many of the class alumni are now working in the nation's top financial services organizations. Also MBA students continue to benefit from the Raymond Rebsamen Memorial Scholarship. The University of Arkansas awarded Rebsamen a distinguished alumnus citation in 1960 and an honorary Doctorate of Laws in 1974. He also served on the University of Arkansas board of trustees.

A Vision for Central Arkansas

Rebsamen always said, "Arkansas has been good to me and I want to be good to it." He provided leadership and resources in ways too numerous to name. For example, he served on the Committee of 100 to raise more than $1 million for the land now occupied by the Little Rock Air Force Base. He donated elephants named Ruth and Ellen and other animals to the Little Rock Zoo. He made contributions for a public golf course and a tennis center. He helped establish Rebsamen Memorial Hospital (North Metro Medical Center) in Jacksonville. In 1967, he gave a bronze statue of Daedelus and Icarus, which now sits in the Central Arkansas Library garden. He donated a collection of fifty-six ceramic bird sculptures by Edward Boehm to the Arkansas Arts Center.

In the 1950s, Rebsamen helped found the Urban Progress Association and became one of the most knowledgeable people in the state on urban renewal. He often said no child should go to school from a slum. His vision and leadership of the Metropolitan Area Commission (now Metroplan) for Central Arkansas resulted—in the long run—in the blossoming of the River Market district today.

An avid traveler, Rebsamen visited Australia, New Zealand, New Guinea, Central and South America, and Mexico and took nine European vacations and one trip around the world. A man of many interests, he was always a lover of horses and owned and rode champion Tennessee walking horses. Rebsamen was also a voracious reader.

In 1963, the same day Rebsamen became a thirty-third degree Mason, he was chosen to chair the Federal Reserve of St. Louis, and he hit a hole in one on the golf course at the Country Club of Little Rock. It was a lucky day in the life of a man who truly believed that from those to whom much is given, much is expected.

Bobby Roberts
Humanitarian Award, 2011

Some people know from an early age exactly what they want to be when they grow up. Bobby Roberts didn't. As a teen, Bobby worked at his father's service station and drove a gravel truck. To say he wasn't a very good student is an understatement: he ranked 103 out of a class of 106. But today, Bobby is passionate about education and the public library's role as an educational institution.

Growing up in the Arkansas Delta, Bobby understood how complicated the question of race can be. His father and Pete Watkins, who was African American, never visited in one another's homes, despite being the best of friends. In Antebellum Helena, whites and blacks lived on intersecting streets. In the later-developed West Helena, housing was strictly segregated, and blacks were not allowed by city ordinance to cross the railroad tracks after sunset unless they were in a car. His dad's service station was built to Mobil Oil standards with separate restrooms. Because the racist culture was the norm, Bobby says he didn't really question things until in college when he was exposed to professors who were writing about and teaching black history. During a stint in the Navy, which he describes as truly "colorblind," his consciousness about the complexities of race in our culture was raised further still.

After the Navy, Bobby returned to school to earn his PhD, and today Bobby views the public library as another "colorblind" institution where class, race, religion, etc. are not important. That belief likely accounts for his visionary leadership of the Central Arkansas Library System for the past twenty-two years.

Bobby took the "interim" job as library director in 1989 primarily because it came with a big pay raise, but he quickly became passionate about making the library the best it could be. The first thing he learned when he got to the library is that the Arkansas Constitution prohibited libraries from raising millage rates and therefore, the public library was woefully under-funded. Through Bobby's hard work and with the support of Governor Bill Clinton and Senator Jay Bradford, a constitutional amendment was passed allowing libraries to raise the money they needed through a millage tax. Since then, Bobby and CALS have spearheaded fourteen millage votes and won eleven of them—an enviable record.

According to Bobby, one of his most important accomplishments at the library is that he has learned not to think of improving the library as a zero-sum game, with, for example, automating the system being done at the expense of buying books for the collection. While CALS has made a big investment in computers, phone lines, and such, they have continued to make the acquisition of books and other media a priority.

Another important milestone, for which Bobby credits the library board, was building the new main library in the River Market of Little Rock. He calls it an important symbol of the library's commitment to the whole community.

A third accomplishment has been taking care of library employees by increasing salaries and benefits, establishing a good retirement program, and offering benefits for domestic partners of employees.

Because he could only pick a few, the final milestone Bobby mentions is the establishment of the Arkansas Studies Institute. He sees the ASI as the best way to preserve our particular and proud history.

In 1978, Bobby attended a political rally (only for the free food, he attests) and met Bill Clinton. It was a fateful meeting. Between his time as archivist at the University of Arkansas and becoming head librarian for Central Arkansas, Bobby went to work for Clinton, helping to craft policy related to public safety and prisons. Bobby thoroughly enjoyed his work on campaigns and later in the public sector, particularly on the Board of Corrections. Through these experiences he learned a number of valuable lessons: "Have patience. You can't change big institutions except incrementally and over time. Celebrate small victories. And just because someone opposes your idea, that doesn't make him or her the enemy." He also gained respect for the members of the Arkansas legislature whom he described as "hard-working, smart people, trying to do the best they could for Arkansas."

Bobby describes the public library as the "People's University" where all Arkansans have access to a limitless world of information and can participate in community meetings and enriching programs. He envisions the planned Children's Library in Mid-Town as much more than an educational institution. His vision is for young people to come to the library and discover something that will inspire them. He hopes that through partnerships with other local educational and cultural resources, the library will be able to multiply and enhance the experiences available to area children.

Bobby believes passionately that education is the key to healthy individuals who can create healthy societies. He has worked to ensure that Arkansans have access to a world-class library and with it, a wealth of information at our disposal. With Bobby Roberts's leadership, we are sure to have a brighter, fairer, and more informed future.

Reverend William H. Robinson Jr.
Father Joseph H. Biltz Award, 2003

Most folks call him Rev or Reverend
Robinson, but many people call him
PawPaw. You'll recognize him: he's the quiet
one who makes you feel safe just being in
his presence.

In 1980, Reverend Robinson founded
Theressa Hoover United Methodist Church
at Twelfth and Cedar Streets, in Little Rock,
because he saw a need for a church in the
Twelfth Street neighborhood. It soon became the fastest-growing African-
American United Methodist Church in Little Rock, and in 2003 has
400 members.

Reverend Robinson wanted the church to connect with the individuals in the community, and as a result, many community programs
have been born at that location and continue to flourish. Early on,
church members did a mapping of the community, and they try to meet
the needs of individuals on many levels: mental, physical, and spiritual.

For example, there is PawPaw's Day Care Center. There is a substance-abuse program and a homeless center. There's an activity center
for youth, a minority AIDS network, and a housing-development agency.
Today, Reverend Robinson is working with the City of Little Rock on
the new Twelfth Street Corridor program to revitalize the neighborhood.

In the early days, there were many times when Reverend Robinson
didn't get a paycheck. But that was okay with him. In fact, associate pastor C. J. Duvall advises people not to give Reverend Robinson a gift of
money because he is likely to give it away to the first person in need that
he sees. In fact, we've heard that he sometimes drives the program staff
members a little crazy when he refuses to follow policies that might result
in someone being turned away. His reasoning: "How do we know that

this isn't the turning point for that individual, when they will really be able to change their life if we provide assistance?"

Another thing that sometimes happens is that Reverend Robinson is late for Sunday services because he is counseling someone who has come to his office. Church members know to just go on with the service; he'll be there later.

All this began with a seed grant of $5,000 from the United Methodist Church. Now Reverend Robinson manages a 1.4 million dollar budget with thirty-four employees.

A word that many people use to describe Revernd Robinson is "wise." Therefore, he is a great mediator. He's also received an honorary doctorate degree from Philander Smith, so we might want to call him Doctor Robinson. Or we might want to just call him PawPaw. He has certainly been the best "PawPaw" many of us could ever hope for.

Honorable Winthrop Rockefeller
Humanitarian Award, 1967
(May 1, 1912–February 22, 1973)

During the week following the death of former Arkansas Governor Winthrop Rockefeller, there were four articles about him printed in the Arkansas Gazette, *including: "Rockefeller Dies; He Altered Course of State Politics, Won 2 Terms As Governor of Arkansas"; "Day of Mourning Declared; Lawmakers Voice Sorrow"; "'Great Arkansan,' Political Foes, Friends Declare"; and "Rockefeller Used His Wealth to Assist Many." Following are excerpts from those articles, reprinted with permission from the* Arkansas Democrat-Gazette.

Winthrop Rockefeller, aged sixty, who over-came a playboy image to twice win the gover-norship of his adopted state of Arkansas, died of cancer (on February 22, 1973) at a hospital at Palm Springs, California.

At sixty, Mr. Rockefeller was the next to youngest of the daughter and five sons of John D. Rockefeller Jr. His sister, Mrs. Jean Mauze, and all of his brothers, John, Nelson, Laurance, and David Rockefeller, all of New York, survive him, as does a son, Winthrop Paul Rockefeller, and a granddaughter.

Mr. Rockefeller served as governor from January 10, 1967, to January 12, 1971, after losing his first race to former governor Orval E. Faubus in 1964. In both the process of losing and winning, he had steadily built the Republican Party in the state, attracting longtime Democrats to his cause along the way.

Indeed, he may be credited with altering the political course of the state, installing the first Republican administration since Reconstruction after twelve years of the administration of Faubus, under whom Arkansas experienced some of its most traumatic events.

Beyond that, Mr. Rockefeller prepared the groundwork for many of the reforms that have been enacted by his successor, Dale Bumpers, who defeated Mr. Rockefeller in his bid for a third term in 1970.

Mr. Rockefeller's impact, however, was far from limited to the political arena. Throughout the nineteen years he made Arkansas his home, he had an enormous effect on the state's economy, not only through his chairmanship of the Arkansas Industrial Development Commission—by appointment of Faubus—but also through his own personal business investments.

And his philanthropy became so vast that it was almost dismissed as commonplace. It was estimated by an associate before his 1966 race to have totaled up to then more than $8 million, with a heavy emphasis on education. He had spent heavily from his personal funds in his rebuilding of the state Republican Party, which he had served as national committeeman from May 1961 to his death, and in his own political activity.

His Altruism Never Questioned

Arkansans eventually came to "adopt" Mr. Rockefeller as equally as he had adopted them. Although he had his political opponents and personal detractors, he came to be regarded with respect and affection by most, and the charge that he sought political power for personal gain or self-aggrandisement has never been raised; his altruism—a feeling that everything he had done politically or in any other area was motivated only by what he felt was in the state's best interest—was not questioned.

Like all of the Rockefeller offspring, Winthrop was taught the sense of responsibility (or stewardship, as he preferred to call it) of great wealth, and often told of being limited to a twenty-five-cent weekly allowance as he was growing up.

His early years were not very promising. He attended a progressive college preparatory school and then for three years compiled an unenviable record at Yale University, finally leaving it from a sense of lack of accomplishment.

He spent three years in the Texas oilfields as a roughneck, living on his earnings, sleeping in boarding houses, and eating at chili stands. He was to cite this period later in his political races as the time when he came to know and learn about the problems of average working people.

(*Rockefeller entered the Army in 1940 as a private. After a six-year stint during the Second World War, he was separated from the service as a lieutenant colonel with a Bronze Star with clusters and a Purple Heart.*

He came to make his home in Arkansas because of an army friend, Frank Newell, of Little Rock. He bought 927 acres of land atop Petit Jean Mountain, where he created a "showplace" and a working ranch, Winrock Farm.

Winthrop Rockefeller was the first chairman of the Arkansas Industrial Development Commission (AIDC) after being appointed by Governor Orval Faubus.)

...Mr. Rockefeller's personal philosophy of racial equality was not altogether in tune with that of the state's electorate. For many years he served on the Board of the National Urban League, long before it was politically expedient to do so, and he never missed an opportunity to speak out for equality—or to practice it. The superintendent of Winrock Farm was a black. Mr. Rockefeller named numerous blacks to state boards and commissions while he was governor.

Mr. Rockefeller...was married June 11, 1956, to Mrs. Jeannette Edris. Mrs. Jeannette Rockefeller moved to Arkansas and she set about becoming as active in civic and cultural affairs as her husband was to become in the political area.

Left AIDC, Filed for Office

In April 1964, Mr. Rockefeller resigned from the AIDC after eight years as chairman, some 600 new industries and 90,000 new jobs. Shortly afterward, he did the expected, and filed as the Republican candidate for governor.

Faubus defeated Mr. Rockefeller—soundly. Immediately, he (Rockefeller) announced to his supporters, "We've already got our campaign fund started for 1966."

Mr. Rockefeller mounted a massive campaign, and won the election (in 1966) by almost the same margin that he had been defeated by two years earlier.

(Mr. Rockefeller served two terms as governor before he was defeated by Dale Bumpers. Following his time in office, he returned to live at Winrock Farm on Petit Jean Mountain, and in 1971, Winthrop and Jeanette Rockefeller were divorced.)

Rockefeller Used His Wealth to Assist Many

Former governor Winthrop Rockefeller used his vast business empire as a tool, designed by him, to solve social and educational problems, but the actual making of money just for the sake of making it bored him and couldn't hold his interest, his associates said.

(Among his charitable causes, he built and/or supported: a model school in Morrilton, Arkansas; a medical clinic in Perry County; Arkansas's public and private schools and colleges; the Arkansas Arts Center; Vanderbilt University, Yale University and Colonial Williamsburg. Following his death, his personal fortune has continued to provide benefit to others through Winrock International, The Winthrop Rockefeller Trust and The Winthrop Rockefeller Foundation.)

Mrs. Mary McCloud, who administered the charitable activities of the Rockwin Fund, said consideration was given to each request that was delivered personally or in written form. She said the questions asked were, "Will it work? Will it succeed? Is there a reasonable chance that the project will work? Will it benefit several people?"

Because he enjoyed helping solve problems, Mr. Rockefeller sometimes would work quietly, without publicity, to see that his contribution to a charity worked.

Editor's note:

These excerpts tell only a bit of the story of Winthrop Rockefeller and his legacy for all Arkansans. For example, Rockefeller was the only known American governor to hold a memorial service following the Reverend Martin Luther King Jr.'s assassination in 1968. An iconic photo of the governor shows him on the steps of the Arkansas State Capitol, holding hands with African-American leaders and singing "We Shall Overcome," to mourn the death of King.

Jeannette Rockefeller

Humanitarian Award, 1967
(1918–1997)

State's former first lady Jeannette Rockefeller dies at 79

By Tracie Dungan, December 10, 1997
Reprinted with permission from the Arkansas Democrat-Gazette

Jeannette Edris Rockefeller was born too late to be a suffragette.

She was two when American women gained the right to vote, and she never ran for office.

But she showed how women, who married into politics, if not elected themselves, could lead.

The former wife of the late Governor Winthrop Rockefeller and stepmother of Arkansas Lieutenant Governor Winthrop Paul Rockefeller has been credited with transforming the role of first lady in Arkansas to a public partnership with the governor.

She died Sunday of heart failure at a hospital in Palm Springs, California. She was seventy-nine.

Jeannette Rockefeller was divorced from the former governor in 1971, the year he left office after serving a pair of two-year terms as the first Republican governor of Arkansas since Reconstruction. The former governor died in 1973.

She had lived at Palm Springs since 1988. Before that, she lived in Seattle after leaving Little Rock.

As the governor's wife, she "was a pioneering first lady of Arkansas, helping her former husband bring the 'New South' to our state, and leading women into the mainstream of political and public life," President Clinton said in a statement issued by the White House. "She spearheaded education and cultural outreach across the state through the Arkansas Arts Center."

Clinton also called her "a strong voice against discrimination, with an uncanny ability to relate to the common man and woman. The people of Arkansas have lost a true and valued friend."

Jeannette Rockefeller was born in Seattle in 1918, the older of two daughters of Frances Skinner and William Edris. Her father owned and operated the Hotel Olympic at Seattle, the Davenport Hotel at Spokane, and the Hotel Robert Treat at Neward, as well as a chain of theaters in Seattle, Portland, and Tacoma. She was four when her mother died and was reared by her father, who called her "Nan."

She grew up in a large Georgian house next door to her maternal grandparents and was known to school friends as "Jay." She attended St. Nicholas School in Seattle and the University of Washington and Finch College in New York. She majored in psychology in college.

Her charitable work began at eighteen, when she participated in fundraising for the Children's Orthopedic Hospital in Seattle and a nurses' home built in memory of her mother. During World War II, she volunteered for about two days a week for a year and a half as a nurses' aid, mostly at the Swedish Hospital in Seattle.

Her first marriage was to Nathan R. Barrangar.

She had two children, Anne Bartley McNeil of San Francisco and Bruce Bartley of Little Rock, by a marriage to Edson Bruce Bartley.

After her divorce from Donald M. McDonnel in 1951, she resumed her maiden name until marrying Rockefeller in June 1956 at Hayden Lake, Idaho.

The two were introduced by a mutual acquaintance while he was in New York and she was volunteering with teenaged drug addicts and mentally ill children. Two years before the couple married, he divorced his wife, Barbara "Bobo" Sears.

"It was definitely a great change to go from living in Manhattan to a mountain 900 feet above sea level where you have to drive twenty-three miles to get your children to school," said her son, Bruce Bartley, Tuesday, of the move to Winrock Farm on Petit Jean Mountain in Morrilton. He was fourteen when the couple married. His sister was twelve.

He said his mother loved to read.

"Everything from Gothic novels to Plato to cookbooks."

His memories of the early years with her revolve around The Studio, a present from the former governor, where she worked in the abstract with enamels—fused particles of glass on copper or steel.

"He gave her a two-story enamel studio with three kilns on the first floor and two bedrooms and a bathroom on the second floor," Bartley recalled. "We'd go there every night after dinner and conversation to work in the studio with her. And many guests did, too. I remember well sharing so much from the wonderful cross section of the steady stream of people always through the house."

Those guests ranged from politicians and industrialists to volunteers for the Cystic Fibrosis Research Foundation and mental health organizations.

The First Lady was involved in numerous charities, but focused on mental health and the arts. She once served as president of the National Mental Health Association and the Arkansas Association for Mental Health. She was a founding member of the advisory board for the U.S. Jaycees National Committee on Mental Health and Mental Retardation.

She was president of the Board of Trustees of the Arkansas Arts Center and was instrumental in the $1.5 million expansion of the old Museum of Fine Arts into Arkansas Arts Center.

She and her husband raised money and spoke on behalf the new museum, which opened in May 1963.

"I got to know her in 1961 when I was living in Memphis and had a one-person art show at the old museum," said Townsend Wolfe, executive director of the Arkansas Arts Center. "She bought some of my enamels and paintings."

Today, an abstract sculpture stands in front of the museum: Tal Streerer's *Standing Red*, dedicated to Jeannette Rockefeller.

In more recent years, she was chairman for the AIDS Assistance Program in Palm Springs. "She was a refreshing example for so many Arkansas women for the time who walked three feet behind and one to the left of their spouses," her son said. "She was up front and on the side."

Honorable Winthrop Paul Rockefeller

Humanitarian Award, 2001

(*September 17, 1948–July 16, 2006*)

Lieutenant Governor Winthrop Paul Rockefeller was the kind of "hands-on" leader that every organization, commission, board, or state is lucky to have. Son of the late Governor Winthrop Rockefeller and grandson of the late John D. Rockefeller Jr., Win Rockefeller epitomizes the adage, "Those to whom much is given, much is expected." And Win Rockefeller delivered.

Long before entering public service, Rockefeller served as president of the Quapaw Area Council of the Boy Scouts of America and on the Scouts' national board. Perhaps more importantly, Rockefeller served as the local Scouts' vice president for membership where he recruited other Scouting volunteers and served as a den and pack leader.

From 1981 to 1995, Rockefeller served on the Arkansas State Police Commission and in 1991, he was appointed by President George Bush to serve on the President's Council on Rural America, which he chaired. He was a board member for The Nature Conservancy, the Arkansas Cancer Research Center, and the Arkansas Arts Center Foundation, and he was the founder and chair of the International Billfish Conservation Foundation.

As Arkansas's lieutenant governor, Rockefeller served as the president of the Arkansas Senate and as a goodwill ambassador for Arkansas across the state and nation. He championed the issues of economic development and education. In 1997, he created Books in the Attic, a program using existing resources and volunteers to ensure access to reading opportunities for all children.

Rockefeller attended the University of Oxford in England and graduated from Texas Christian University.

(Lieutenant Governor Winthrop Paul Rockefeller died in 2006. He was the father of eight children, and his widow, Lisenne, lives in Little Rock.)

Larry Ross
Humanitarian Award, 2000
(*Interview conducted August 7, 2012*)

Larry Ross might not have learned all he really needed to know in kindergarten, but he certainly did during his study of early childhood education. He's used that knowledge, both practical and theoretical, throughout his work as a manager of a Head Start program, as president of many organizations, as a telephone executive, as a pastor, and now as a Presiding Elder of his church.

Larry was the third son of twelve children born to Minnie Cheatham and Junius Ross. They lived near Shorter College in North Little Rock, and today there is a street called "Ross Circle," which was named for Larry's father. The family owned the Community Shoe Shop and the Community Beauty Shop. Larry's father was the businessman who kept up with current events. He taught his children that one of the best investments they could make would be their own home. His mother was a prolific writer who loved to read and work crossword puzzles. Though neither of his parents played a musical instrument, they bought a used upright piano for their children. Several of Larry's sisters are classically trained musicians, and Larry attended college at Philander Smith with a music scholarship after graduating from the all-black Scipio A. Jones High School in 1964. Larry was a percussionist, and Philander Smith had both a symphonic and marching band. Once he demonstrated that he could actually read music, his scholarship was increased from $200 per semester to $750.

Larry chose elementary education as his major not because he wanted to teach, but because he knew there would be great opportunities for a man in that field which was (and is still) dominated by women. He

was fortunate to have one of those women, Dr. Bettye Caldwell, a nationally recognized expert in early childhood development, as one of his
professors at Philander. Along with Caldwell, other professors challenged
Larry to get a graduate degree, which he earned from Arkansas State
Teacher's College (now the University of Central Arkansas) in 1971.
Immediately after completing graduate school, he was hired to direct the
largest Head Start program in Arkansas. Under his purview, there were
700 youngsters enrolled in eighteen centers with 150 employees in
Pulaski County. The Pulaski County program was a flagship for the rest
of the state because it served both urban and rural families and had a
budget of 1.5 million. During his three-year tenure, Larry was also elected
president of the National Head Start Directors' Association.

One day when Larry had gone into the phone company office to
pay his bill, he noticed a sign inviting job applications. He says that on
a whim, and very casually, he walked into the personnel office and filled
out an application. Before he thought much about it, he had fielded
calls from the St. Louis and Houston offices. Soon after, he was offered
a job in Management with Southwestern Bell Telephone Company (now
AT&T). He worked with them for twenty-seven years, until his retirement in 2000. Larry served in a management role in every department
of AT&T except for legal, engineering, and personnel. As a manager,
Larry realized that everything he had learned studying education in college and graduate school was relevant in a corporate setting; adults have
essentially the same needs as children. He says, "Not everyone who is
smiling is happy. So to be a good manager, one has to reach out in love,
create a safe space, be supportive, and meet people where they are."

Larry has worked for many community causes, including serving as
chair for the Philander Smith College Board; the Bank Board Business
Development Committee; the North Little Rock Rotary Club; the
Arkansas Ethics Commission; the Arkansas Educational Television
Network Commission; the North Little Rock Library Commission; and
KUAR Public Radio. He has also served as a board member for many

other groups. He counts his service with the NCCJ as one of the most important. In 1987 he helped NCCJ executive director Ron Lanoue to establish JCA's Anytown, the summer high school program, and in 1990, he supported the first Ourtown Leadership Institute for adults, which he believes is still paying dividends in 2012. He explains that working with NCCJ gave him hope that we can build understanding among disparate groups. "If we can understand why people believe and feel as they do, we can work together to solve our common problems. For every problem, there is a solution." He was also fortunate to work with other NCCJ leaders such as Rabbi Zeke Palnick, Elijah Coleman, T. E. Patterson, and Father Joe Biltz. In fact, it was his relationship with Father Biltz that helped Larry accept his calling to become a pastor in the Christian Methodist Episcopal Church in the mid-1980s. They were together in Houston at a national Urban League meeting when Biltz counseled Larry, "You don't have to be a saint to work for the Lord. Just be a faithful servant."

Larry was probably destined to work for racial justice. His mother had been a good friend of Daisy Bates and a community activist herself. When the schools were first integrated in North Little Rock, Minnie Ross helped save some of the black teachers' jobs. Larry's high-school English and French teacher was Dr. Lois Pattillo, the mother of Melba Pattillo, one of the Little Rock Nine. Larry also arrived at Philander in 1964 at the height of the civil rights movement and joined the Student Nonviolent Coordinating Committee (SNCC) there. About SNCC, Julian Bond said, "A final SNCC legacy is the destruction of the psychological shackles which had kept black southerners in physical and mental peonage; SNCC helped break those chains forever. It demonstrated that ordinary women and men, young and old, could perform extraordinary tasks." Larry clearly took that lesson to heart; he has been excelling in everything in which he's been involved ever since.

Since his ordination in 1993, Larry has served his CME Church, and since 2002 he has been Presiding Elder of the Arkansas Region East District, working with seventy-nine pastors and congregations. He's particularly gratified to see pastors, both experienced and new, grow in their faith and ministry.

Larry married his college sweetheart, Lillian, and they are the parents of three children, Angela, Larry II, and Erica.

Larry has lived his entire life by following the directive of Proverbs 3:27. "Do not withhold good from those to whom it is due, when it is in your power to do it."

Amy Rossi

Humanitarian Award, 2000
(Interview conducted August 1, 2012)

Despite being slight in stature and soft-spoken, Amy Rossi is definitely one of those "uppity women!" For example, she kept her maiden name when she married Joe Bryan; she directed Arkansas Advocates for Children and Families (AACF) for fifteen years; she helped found the Arkansas Women's Foundation; and Amy Rossi truly knows that she can make a difference.

Amy was raised by her extended family in North Little Rock. She says her parents, two grandmothers, and grandfather were her original and long-standing support system who believed there was nothing that she couldn't do. "They never forced me to choose one thing or another nor limited my exposure to things I said I wanted to do. Not that they didn't argue with me—they did!—but when one or the other seemed to be frustrated with my choice, one of the others would boost me up and tell me to move on and offer their help." Her faith life was also strong, and the nuns who educated her instilled in her a strong sense of service. That combination set her on a life path of working on behalf of others.

Amy prepared herself to provide service to others by earning her undergraduate degree in psychology and sociology from the University of Arkansas at Little Rock in 1974, the day before her twenty-first birthday, and then by earning her masters in science and social work in 1977 from the University of Tennessee in Nashville. One professor from UALR who had a big impact on her was Dr. Cal Ledbetter, whom she describes as "wise, funny, and blunt—a great teacher." Another important mentor was a young professor at the University of Tennessee who cajoled her through "systems theory," which she hated. The ironic thing is that her understanding of how systems work turned out to be one of the most important of her assets as she worked for years to change some of those entrenched systems for the benefit of children and their families.

During her college years, and early in her career, Amy learned first-hand the devastating effects of poverty. She worked for Presbyterian Family Services and Youth Home, serving as director of the two Youth Home facilities in Pine Bluff for one year. She saw how deeply rooted and debilitating the cycle of poverty can be. In describing that time in her life, she talks about the oft-told story of someone standing on the bank of a river, throwing life boats to the drowning babies floating by. When she realized that for every child they saved through the services of Youth Home, there was another waiting at the door, she knew that she needed to go up the river to discover why the babies were in the river in the first place, and how she could help prevent them from ending up there. That's when she first began to appreciate that graduate school professor who had insisted that she learn about systems.

When Amy became the third director of AACF (following Jo Luck and Don Crary), she had found her dream job. This was the place where her experience as a social worker and child advocate, her understanding of systems, and her desire to make things better could all come together. She joined Arkansas Advocates in 1980 as director of a juvenile justice project aiming to improve the juvenile court system. At the time, life-changing decisions about protecting children were made by county judges with no legal training and children had no legal representatives to argue their concerns. Children had no rights, per se, and they might be removed from their families, or kept for days in juvenile detention facilities or local jails, without any rehabilitation, for things like skipping school, smoking, or being caught with a beer, and those children with more serious behavior problems might be left in settings without appropriate intervention and treatment as well. Importantly, very little data was kept to document and expose what happened to these children as a result of the actions taken by the county judge. Amy organized volunteer monitors in every Arkansas county to monitor proceedings and record what happened. It was the first time anyone had collected accurate information about how children's rights were being abused. Working with others, like Judges Annabelle Clinton, Tom Glaze, and Judith Rogers; Attorney Grif Stockley; and Senators Mike Beebe, Morril Harriman, Carolyn Pollan, and Wayne Dowd, Arkansas Advocates and Amy helped to win a judgment that found the juvenile justice system in Arkansas unconstitutional. The ultimate result was a revision in the state constitution to better protect all vulnerable children who were abused, neglected, or delinquent.

Amy went on to work diligently for reforms in the child welfare system and to secure funding for early childhood education. Another significant accomplishment for AACF and Amy was the establishment of ARKids First during the tenure of Governor Mike Huckabee. In 1997, more than twenty-five percent of Arkansas's children did not have access to health care because they lacked insurance coverage. In 2012, because of ARKids First, only seven percent of Arkansas children remain without health insurance. The success of ARKids First has led to it being celebrated as a model for other states as they seek to improve their child health systems.

If Amy were an architect who built tall buildings, the equivalent of what she and Arkansas Advocates have accomplished would have altered the skyline of every town in Arkansas.

If you ask her about how she got these monumental things done, Amy says she learned that "power should be shared and not squandered or kept exclusively for yourself. If you are willing to give power away, it will come back to you. No one creates this type of change alone. If you create a diverse table and invite people to work with you, and be willing to share credit when the job is done, change can be accomplished. And importantly, momentum for other big changes can multiply. You have to be willing to put yourself on the line and in front of something when no one else wants to stand with you. Be the leader when it's needed, but always share the credit when the right things happen."

Because of her commitment to fairness and justice, it's not surprising that Amy was a major supporter of the NCCJ including board service and attending the inaugural Ourtown Leadership Institute in 2000. The graduates of the Ourtown Institutes often met for breakfast. Amy said, "Some of the discussions were tough. But we created a safe space. You could say what needed to be said, but you had to listen to what others needed to say." There were strong leaders involved, both black and white, and Little Rock is a better community because of their resolve to work together. Amy was involved in the early Chamber Leadership program and alumni association during those years as well.

In 1998, Amy joined eighty-four other women to found the Women's Foundation of Arkansas, serving on the inaugural board and later as board chair. Its mission is to promote philanthropy among women and to help women and girls achieve their full potential. Programs of the Women's Foundation particularly create opportunities for young girls and women to be exposed to the possibilities of careers in fields such as math, science, and technology.

In the third grade, Amy was elected treasurer of her Girl Scout troop, starting what has been a lifelong pattern of serving in leadership positions. However, as evidenced by her many accomplishments, she knows how to motivate others, too. Her current personal mission is to nurture younger professionals who are also called to serve others, enabling them to do as she has felt so fortunate to do: to blend her work and civic life with being a wife to Joe Bryan and a mother to their sons, Nathan and Nicholas. If anyone can help future leaders to achieve such a rich and rewarding balance, it is Amy Rossi.

Albert J. Porter, 2006 Biltz honoree, is congratulated by First Lady Ginger Beebe. (Photo by Doris Krain)

Sanford Tollette IV, Jean Gordon, and Dr. Sunny Anand received the Biltz award in 2007. (Photo by Doris Krain)

Bishop Kenneth Hicks, Nina Krupitsky, and Annie Abrams were recognized with Biltz awards in 2004. (Photo by Doris Krain)

Biltz awards were presented to Bishop Larry Maze, Dr. Betty Lowe, and attorney John Walker in 2005. (Photo by Doris Krain)

Bob Cabe, former Humanitarian and JCA board member, and his wife, Julie, flank Rev. Betsy Singleton, who gave the invocation at the 2006 annual dinner. (Photo by Doris Krain)

Humanitarian Bobby Roberts, JCA board chair Jay Barth, executive director Ruth Shepherd, and Humanitarian Rep. Kathy Webb following the 2011 dinner. (Photo by Doris Krain)

C. J. Duvall and Joy Secuban joined guests at the 2009 Humanitarian dinner. (Photo by Doris Krain)

Clarice Miller (Humanitarian, 2004), Dr. I. Dodd Wilson, and Ginger Wilson attended the dinner in 2008. (Photo by Doris Krain)

David Mosley, Margaret Preston, Marla Johnson Norris, Mike Maulden, Annette Fry, and Pat Lile were on hand to celebrate NCCJ being named a Finalist for Nonprofit Organization of the Year by Arkansas Business in 2002.

Diane and Rev. Hezekiah Stewart (Humanitarian, 1995) enjoyed the 2008 dinner. (Photo by Doris Krain)

Guests Marion Khan and Senator David Pryor, Annual Dinner, 2006. David Pryor is the only person who has been an honoree (1984), a dinner chair (1988), and the speaker (1983 and 2000) at the dinner. (Photo by David Aston)

Don Munro and Wanda Hamilton at the 2008 dinner. (Photo by Doris Krain)

In 2009, Arkansas Baptist College president Dr. Fitz Hill introduced Governor Mike Beebe, the honoree that year. Fitz Hill was later honored in 2012. (Photo by Doris Krain)

Dr. Sybil Jordan Hampton (Humanitarian, 2002), former board chair Mike Maulden, and Sandra Cherry were in attendance when Governor Mike Beebe accepted the Humanitarian award in 2009.

Gertie Butler was on hand to congratulate Jim Argue when he was recognized with the Biltz award in 2000. In 2007, Argue was named a Humanitarian winner.

First Lady Ginger and Governor Mike Beebe with JCA board chair Sue Weinstein in 2009. (Photo by Doris Krain)

Past honoree Maurice Mitchell (1996) with Dale Nicholson, honoree in 2000.

Special dessert, 2008.

Father Joe Biltz's niece JeJo Mobley, and his sister, Mary Biltz Mobley, with Susie Wiggins at the Gathering of Friends, 2006. (Photo by Doris Krain)

Jerry Maulden, past board chair, with Biltz honorees Jim Argue (2000) and Freddie Nixon (1994).

Judge Wendell and Patricia Griffen with Mexican Consul Andres and Begona Chao at 2011 dinner. (Photo by Doris Krain)

Katya Lyzhina and her mother Jan Scott in 2008. Katya had participated in a JCA youth program and shared her experiences as dinner speaker. (Photo by Doris Krain)

Kerri Sernel volunteered at the dinner in 2009 and served as an advisor at Ourtown for Teens that summer. Since 2010, Kerri has served as development and marketing director of JCA. (Photo by Doris Krain)

LaVerne Feaster (Biltz award in 2002) with board chair Sue Weinstein at the Gathering of Friends in 2009. (Photo by Doris Krain)

Lillian Ross, Sybil Jordan Hampton, and Ann Anderson, Humanitarian dinner 2009

Lisenne and Lt. Governor Winthrop Paul Rockefeller with their son William in 2001, when Rockefeller and Dr. Josetta Wilkins were Humanitarian honorees.

Melanie and Keith Jackson in 2005 when Keith received the Humanitarian Award. (Photo by Doris Krain)

Monsignor John O'Donnell and Father Joseph Biltz were friends when they were both young priests. At the Gathering of Friends in 2006 (and 2013), O'Donnell shared memories of Father Biltz, mostly humorous, about how Biltz kept getting into trouble for his outspoken activism. (Photo by Doris Krain)

Mary Biltz Mobley, Father Joe's sister, with Imam Johnny Hasan, Biltz honoree, and JeJo Mobley, Father Joe's niece at the Gathering in 2000.

Mary Steenburgen, Dr. Dean Kumpuris, and Representative Joyce Elliott accepted the Humanitarian Award in 2006. (Photo by Scott Carter)

Muhammad Abu-Rmaileh, a student at Central High School and youth program delegate, was dinner speaker in 2011. Muhammad, who now attends Duke University, has returned to serve as a counselor for the summer program, Ourtown for Teens. (Photo by Doris Krain)

Fire Chief Rhoda Mae Kerr (then a JCA board member) and County Judge Buddy Villines at 2006 dinner. (Photo by David Aston)

Russ Harrington, past JCA board chair Marla Johnson Norris, and Buddy Sutton at 2008 dinner when JCA recognized Joel Anderson and Bruce Moore with the Humanitarian award. (Photo by Doris Krain)

Executive Director Ruth Shepherd and board chair John Bel make Biltz presentations in 2006 to Rev. Stephen Copley, Sister Catherine Markey, and Albert J. Porter. (Photo by Doris Krain)

Former State Senator Jim Keet (Humanitarian 1995) with his wife Doody at the 2011 dinner. (Photo by Doris Krain)

Senator Joyce Elliott and Representative David Raney were dais guests in 2008. (Photo by Doris Krain)

Shareese Kondo and JCA board member Marian Lacey were in attendance at the 2009 Gathering of Friends when Rev. Wendell Griffen, Ted Holder, and Rev. Ed Matthews received the Biltz award. Someone quipped that JCA was honoring the "three wise men" that year. (Photo by Doris Krain)

Sheila Wright and Nancy Rousseau, guests at 2008 Humanitarian Dinner honoring Joel Anderson and Bruce Moore. (Photo by Doris Krain)

Dinner guests in 2012 included Dr. Sara Tariq, Madeeha Asif and her husband, Dr. Asif Masood, and Dr. Hashim Ghori. (Photo by Doris Krain)

Youth program directors, Elizabeth Akama-Makia and Andrea Gómez, welcome guests at the 2012 Gathering of Friends. (Photo by Doris Krain)

Renie Rule
Father Joseph H. Biltz Award, 2013

For Renie Rule, the Paws in Prison project all began with a loaf of banana bread. And she readily admits she's not much of a baker.

In early August of 1994, Hoyt Clines was scheduled to die by lethal injection at Arkansas's Tucker Maximum Security Prison, in the first triple execution scheduled in the United States in thirty-two years. Clines and two other men had been convicted of murder, and the planned triple execution drew media attention from across the nation. Renie had read in an article about the men that for his last meal, Clines had requested a hamburger, French fries, and banana bread. According to the news story, the prison would not be able to provide the banana bread. For some reason, Renie decided to make some banana bread and take it to Hoyt Clines. That decision set Renie on the path that resulted in the Paws in Prison program, which began twenty years later.

Renie arrived at the gates of Tucker Max in the early morning, and the area was crowded with news people. She found a guard and asked if her gift of banana bread could be delivered to Hoyt Clines. The guard explained that no food could be brought into the prison for "health reasons." Frustrated by the inanity that a condemned man's "health" was of concern, Renie suggested that she might take her case to the members of the media nearby. She also offered to eat some of the bread herself, or cut it up, anything that might make them relent. Because she wouldn't leave, eventually the warden came out to talk with her, again explaining that delivering food to a prisoner was strictly prohibited. She asked him if he could deliver the bread to Clines. He ultimately agreed that if she placed the bread on a nearby picnic table, he would indeed deliver it to

Clines. Renie went home hoping that the bread got through and thinking that that was the end of the story.

Around 9:00 p.m. that night Renie received a collect call from Hoyt Clines. He called to thank her for the banana bread. She explains, still with amazement, that their conversation was not sad. They talked for forty-eight minutes, exactly, according to the charge on her phone bill. They talked about his family, and how he was feeling. He said such things as, "God is waiting for me," and, "I'll get to ride my bike again." She offered to come down to the prison to be with him when he was scheduled for execution the next day, but Hoyt said that wasn't necessary. She asked if there was anything that she could do, and he shyly asked, "Could you build me a chapel here at Tucker Max?"

Along with many others, Renie worked for fifteen years on keeping that commitment to Clines. The little chapel named for Frank King, who did a great deal of work on Death Row, is built to allow all religious groups a neutral place to worship: there is space for Hindus, Muslims, Buddhists, Christians—all faiths. Renie, a devout Christian, fought hard to keep all crosses and symbols of Christianity out of the chapel, and told several stories about how "Christians were sometimes her biggest enemy" in keeping the chapel for "all men." The chapel has a library, a counseling room with sound proof panels so inmates can talk to their counselors without guards hearing what they are saying, and a large worship area with excellent sound equipment. Above the podium reads one sign, "Welcome to all who enter here."

Because of her long association with the leadership of the Arkansas Department of Corrections, they were willing to listen when Renie suggested the Paws in Prison program. That's not to say that they approved everything immediately, but Renie was willing to meet multiple times with director Ray Hobbs, with the board of corrections, and with Governor Mike Beebe, to get the program approved. After overcoming their initial reluctance, Renie traveled with department of corrections personnel to learn more about the program in the Missouri prison system. There they were advised, "Start the program in the maximum se-curity unit. Those inmates have the most to gain from this opportunity."

The model is simple. Professional dog trainers teach inmates (who have earned the privilege with a good record) to train dogs to become good pets. Dogs are chosen from those that are otherwise going to be euthanized, and after being cared for and trained for approximately eight weeks, they must pass a rigorous test to be eligible for adoption. Begun in 2011, Paws in Prison has since placed over 135 dogs in five of Arkansas's prisons. Dogs are saved, and inmates have something to do which gives them pleasure and benefits others. Inmates who have earned the opportunity to train a dog will work with the dog up to eight hours a day. According to prison officials, having dogs, particularly in the max-imum security prison, can change the entire climate, and the relation-ship between prisoners and guards is less adversarial, even friendly. If you want to know how much the department of corrections values the program, go to their website. Paws in Prison is the lead story, and there are photos of more than thirty dogs that are available for adoption.

Renie learned about service and perseverance from her parents, Mary and Tom Prentice. When Renie was little, she, her two brothers, and their parents lived for six years in Brazil where her dad served as a Presbyterian missionary. After her dad contracted typhoid and typhus, the family returned to Malden, Missouri, a town of 5,000 and a great place to grow up, according to Renie. Since the town was small and not steeped in the Southern tradition of segregation, Renie had black and white friends, but there was no religious diversity. She never remembers meeting a Jew in Missouri. Her dad preached at three small churches each Sunday, in Gideon, Campbell, and Malden, and Renie accompanied him to play the piano or organ for the services. Her mother, Mary, had at six-teen years old been one of only six women admitted to Rice University, but she had dropped out after one year to marry. So, when Renie went to college, so did her mother. Mary Prentice earned two master's degrees in five years. It took Renie a while longer to earn her degree.

When Renie was ready to attend college, she chose Trinity University in San Antonio, Texas. By 1978, when she earned her degree in social work from Henderson State University, she had attended seven schools, gotten married, and had two children, Richard Warriner and Prentice Warriner. Renie's first job out of college was as a social worker in Pine Bluff, Arkansas. She says she was the worst possible social worker because she was heartbroken for every person she tried to counsel. Fortunately, she became a member of the Junior League, discovered that she was good at raising money, and she has been doing just that ever since. Her first big project was establishing a soup kitchen for the homeless in Pine Bluff, and the program, Neighbor to Neighbor, is still in business almost three decades later.

After her divorce in 1986, she started a cookbook company, and also served as president of the Junior League in Pine Bluff, the first "working woman" to hold that office. Her marriage to Herb Rule brought her and her children to Little Rock in 1991. Since then, she has raised money for many worthy causes, including Second Presbyterian Church, Arkansas Symphony Orchestra, Wildwood Park, and the Junior League of Little Rock. Today she serves as executive director of development, College of Medicine, University of Arkansas for Medical Sciences.

She unintentionally rocked the social boat shortly after coming to Little Rock, when her daughter Prentice was accepted into Junior Cotillion which, at that time, was a traditionally all-white organization for junior high school students to learn social graces. Renie asked if her daughter's best friend from the Cathedral School could join, too, was told yes, and only when they showed up in the same room, did the adults, including Renie, all realize that the best friend was African-American. Everyone had the grace to pretend nothing was out of the ordinary, and three years later, that best friend was elected queen at the Spring Holly Ball. Renie says that if she had known the race of the best friend, she would have done the same thing on purpose.

Whether she is pushing on purpose, like she did to get the banana bread delivered and the Paws in Prison program started, or pushing by accident, like she did by integrating the Junior Cotillion program, we can count on Renie to be pushing us all to do what's right.

James L. "Skip" Rutherford
Humanitarian Award, 1996
(Interview conducted July 3, 2012)

For the eight years that Arkansas native Bill Clinton served our nation as the President of the United States, Skip Rutherford became widely known as the "go-to" guy, especially for members of the media, for information on "all things Arkansas." But if you ask Skip what makes him proudest, he will cite achievements that will continue to have lasting impact for generations to come, here in Arkansas and far beyond.

Skip was raised in Batesville, Arkansas, the only child of his mother, a surgical nurse, and his dad, a banker. Since both his parents worked, they hired a woman, Jenny McCurn, to help look after Skip and keep the house in order. Jenny worked odd jobs all over Batesville to support her three daughters. She lived in a section of town—ironically named Dry Run—that had no water or sewer lines. One day, Jenny came by with a big metal milk can, which young Skip helped her fill from the water hose. Later Skip asked his dad a simple question: "Why do we have water but Jenny doesn't?" They talked about how expensive it is for a city to run water and sewer lines. Skip asked if the new housing area just being built on the East side of town would have water. Yes, it would, his father answered. Skip said he thought Jenny should be first in line. His dad suggested that he talk with the mayor about it—so Skip did just that. He didn't get water for Jenny's neighborhood, but that experience has informed him for his entire life. He says it shaped his politics, his religion, and his views on the role of government. Fortunately, Jenny lived long enough to see water lines run to her neighborhood. And Skip still thinks about Jenny, whom he calls one of his most important teachers.

Skip attended the University of Arkansas at Fayetteville, where he majored in journalism. He was involved in campus issues, and served as editor of the student newspaper his senior year. Skip was a strong supporter of the young David Pryor when Pryor decided to challenge John McClellan for his Senate seat. That later led Skip to the job of serving as director of Pryor's Arkansas office. While working for Pryor, Skip realized that one of the most important things public officials and their staff members can do is to help citizens understand and gain access to programs that may be available through the federal, state and city government.

In 1991, Skip was summoned to the Governor's Mansion to talk with a small group of friends, including Governor Bill Clinton, Hillary Clinton, Bruce Lindsey, and Craig Smith. The question at hand: "Should Bill Clinton put his hat in the ring for president in 1992?" Skip presented a litany of reasons why that might be a bad idea: "We come from a small state...It will be hard to raise the money...President George Bush's poll numbers are in the nineties..." Before the meeting was concluded, Skip felt pretty sure that Bill Clinton would run for president; he didn't feel at all sure that he could win; and he was *completely* sure that if he did chose to run, it would change all of their lives forever. After Clinton was elected, Skip had the opportunity to follow the Clintons to Washington. He thought about his trips to eat lunch with children at Little Rock's public schools. He realized that kind of family life would be impossible as a member of a presidential administration, so he chose to stay in Little Rock. And as it turns out, Skip has managed to find plenty to do right here at home.

As a member of the Little Rock School Board, Skip was tapped by board president Robin Reynolds to head up the negotiations that led to the historic desegregation settlement among the Little Rock, North Little Rock, and Pulaski County school districts and the state. Skip says that to help write and pass the desegregation settlement was time-consuming, rewarding, frustrating, divisive, and highly politicized. He is proud of the result that acknowledged the fact that the State of Arkansas had contributed to substandard schools for minority children in Pulaski County. Through the settlement, he feels that the children in Central Arkansas have had a better chance at getting an equitable opportunity for a good education.

In 1997, Skip was asked to head up the building of the Clinton Presidential Library in East Little Rock. He naively thought that everyone would immediately be on board for such an exciting project, so he was surprised by the controversy surrounding it. However, the construction of the Clinton Library has proved to be a boon for commercial development and tourism, and Skip is justifiably proud of the library's many contributions to the civic and cultural life of Central Arkansas. His office is in the historic Choctaw Train Station, which is part of the library's campus.

After the library was dedicated and opened, Skip thought he might take time to relax for a while. Instead he received a call in 2006 from Dr. Alan Sugg, president of the University of Arkansas System. Skip assumed that Dr. Sugg wanted to run by him some names that Sugg was considering for serving as dean at the Clinton School, since David Pryor had recently stepped down. Skip was shocked when Sugg offered him the job. Skip demurred, "I've never been the dean of anything." Sugg answered, "You'd never built a library before either."

Actually, Skip seems born for the position of dean of the Clinton School of Public Service. He beams as he shares that as of 2012, Clinton School students have conducted 360 field service projects and given over 110,000 hours of service providing such things as strategic planning, needs assessment, and capacity building for communities in Arkansas and around the world. The Clinton School speaker series has presented more than 650 free speakers and programs that have been attended by over 120,000 people. The programs are also online where additional thousands more can view them.

In what anyone would agree has been an extraordinary life and career, Skip is most proud of his service on the Little Rock School Board, his spearheading the building of the Clinton Library in Little Rock, and his current position as dean of the Clinton School of Public Service. Through these three accomplishments, among many others, Skip has shaped the legacy of our state for generations to come.

Skip is married to Billie Hill, and they have three children, Blake, Martha Luin, and Mary.

Ben Saltzman, MD
Humanitarian Award, 1980
(1914-2003)
Reprinted with permission from the University of Arkansas for Medical Sciences

Ben Saltzman, MD, of Mountain Home, Arkansas, the first professor and chairman of the Department of Family and Community Medicine in the College of Medicine, died July 4, 2003. He was eighty-nine.

Throughout his long career, Dr. Saltzman was dedicated to improving health care and recruiting excellent physicians for the rural populations of his state and country. Friends and colleagues of Dr. Saltzman established an endowed professorship in the Department of Family and Community Medicine, now called the Department of Family and Preventive Medicine, in his honor.

A native of Ansonia, Connecticut, Dr. Saltzman was born in 1914. He is a graduate of the University of Oregon in Eugene, and held the degrees of Bachelor of Arts and Master of Arts in Psychology. He received the Doctor of Medicine Degree from the University of Oregon in Portland in June 1940. On completion of his general internship and residency programs at Gorgas Hospital in Ancon, Canal Zone, he stayed on as an army medical officer until the end World War II.

He married Ruth Elizabeth (Betty) Bohan, a native of the Canal Zone and a registered nurse, whom he met at Gorgas Hospital while completing his residency. Their first child, Sue, was born while they were stationed there. After the war, the Saltzmans came to Mountain Home, then a community of 1,200 people, where Dr. Saltzman began a general practice. Their sons, John and Mark, were born there. Mrs. Saltzman died in 1994.

Dr. Saltzman built the first hospital in Mountain Home and served on the steering committee that brought the Baxter General Hospital into being. A true civic activist, he served the community as city alderman, president of the Chamber of Commerce, commander of the American Legion Post, president of the Rotary Club and Exalted Ruler and Founder of the Elks Lodge. He was founder and president of the Baxter County Association for Retarded Citizens, founder and president of the Ozark Regional Mental Health Center, and the voluntary Baxter County health officer.

When his interests spread to state, national, and international activities, he learned to fly to attend meetings. He served as president of numerous statewide voluntary health organizations, including the Arkansas Lung Association, the Arkansas Association for Retarded Citizens, and the Arkansas Division of the American Cancer Society and the Arkansas Board of Health. He was also president of the Arkansas Brotherhood of the National Conference of Christians and Jews and a past president of the Unitarian Universalist Church of Little Rock.

A diplomat of the American Board of Family Practice, he served as president of the Arkansas Chapter of the American Academy of Family Physicians and was one of its charter members. He was president of the Baxter County Medical Society, and the Arkansas Medical Society.

Nationally, Dr. Saltzman served as chairman of the Council on Rural Health of the American Medical Association, as a member of the U.S. Department of Health, Education and Welfare's Community Health Project Review Committee, and as a member of the National Advisory Health Services Council.

Despite all this, he carried on a very busy practice in Mountain Home and was involved in a successful preceptorship program for the College of Medicine and later served as a clinical associate professor. He still found time to publish numerous articles related to rural health care as it affected the population of his adopted state.

In 1974, Dr. Saltzman joined the faculty of the UAMS College of Medicine as the first professor and chairman of the Department of Family and Community Medicine. During his seven-year tenure, he served as director of Rural Medical Development Programs and director of the Flexible Internship Program in the College of Medicine.

He retired from the university as professor emeritus at sixty-seven and was appointed director of the Arkansas Department of Health by Governor Bill Clinton in 1981. He served in that position with distinction until he retired from that position in 1987.

Dr. Saltzman was a member of the UAMS Society of the Double Helix.

Irene Gaston Samuel
Father Joseph H. Biltz Award, 1998
(March 21, 1915–April 4, 1999)

Irene Gaston Samuel by Jack Schnedler
(*A longer version of this article appeared in the Oct. 4, 1998, edition of the* Arkansas Democrat-Gazette. *Reprinted with permission.*)

Her tongue is tart. Her spirit is strong. She suffers no fools gladly. At eight-three, Irene Samuel still can shimmer with righteous indignation. And she retains razor-sharp recall of her behind-the-scenes impact on Arkansas public life over the past four decades.

In 1958, Samuel signed on as unpaid executive secretary and chief strategist for the Women's Emergency Committee to Open Our Schools. She became a war hawk among the committee's "little bird-like women," as one businessman called them with a whiff of condescension. In fact, WEC's organizing savvy—a great deal of it due to her—played a vital role in a tide-turning civic battle.

The committee's efforts helped bring the desegregated reopening of Little Rock's four public high schools in August 1959, eleven months after voters had elected to close them rather than accept racial integration.

Samuel continued to be a dogged adversary of six-term Governor Orval E. Faubus as he won re-election in 1960, 1962, and 1964.

"I spent twelve years of my life trying to beat Orval Faubus," she says on a recent afternoon in the living room of her Hall High neighborhood home. Victory over Faubus finally came in 1970. She enlisted that summer in the gubernatorial campaign of Charleston attorney Dale Bumpers. Seeking a comeback after four years out of office, Faubus was defeated in a Democratic primary runoff by political fledgling Bumpers, who then beat incumbent Governor Winthrop Rockefeller.

Samuel's scope expanded to the state and federal levels as an administrative assistant to Bumpers during his four years as governor and the first of his four U.S. Senate terms. He remembers her as "one of the most straightforward people I've ever been associated with."

Samuel was reared in Little Rock as the younger daughter of a switchman for the old Rock Island Lines. She set off for Washington to make her own way in life six years after graduating from Little Rock Senior High School (now Central High) in 1931 as the Great Depression engulfed America.

Working in Washington for the federal Public Housing Authority exposed the young Arkansan to "some very liberal bosses. I worked in public housing, a very liberal concept at the time. I gradually moved into management, and I had the occasion to hire black people, and I was very happy to do that."

She moved back to Little Rock in 1939 to marry Dr. John Samuel, a surgeon who'd courted her before she'd gone to Washington. When her husband went to war in 1942 as a field surgeon for the First Armored Division, she returned to a federal job in Washington. There she joined the Urban League before returning to Little Rock after the war.

"There's no question that I believed firmly in racial integration by the 1950s," says Samuel. "So did my husband."

The Little Rock desegregation crisis erupted in 1957. After mob violence that made headlines around the world, nine black students attended Central High in 1957-58 under the protection of federal paratroopers.

In August 1958, the state Legislature passed a package of laws proposed by Faubus, giving him authority to seek a vote on closing public schools to prevent integration. On September 12, the governor ordered such an election in Little Rock—with a ballot worded to give voters the stark choice between full integration and shutting classes.

On September 16, Samuel was one of fifty-eight women who attended a hastily called meeting. Some of those at WEC's organizing session "were definitely liberal on race, and some were not," recalls Samuel. "Some left the meeting when the subject of integration came up."

Like others at the meeting, Samuel agreed to call women she knew: "I was in the doctors' auxiliary, so I tried to call the other members. That was a mistake. Very few of them were glad to hear me talk. People were afraid. Their husbands had told them, 'Be quiet and do not express your opinion.' It was economic fear."

The September 27 vote was a decisive 19,470 to 7,561 for closing the high schools rather than desegregating. With the high schools closed, WEC leaders decided to persevere. They set up a makeshift office in the utility room at the home of Margaret Kolb, a doctor's wife. Samuel volunteered to run the office.

"I said, 'I'll work every day,'" she recalls. "I had no idea what I was volunteering to do, but I had the professional experience in organization and administration. We learned by trial and error."

WEC achieved partial success in the December 6, 1958, school board election, backing the winning campaigns of three members who favored reopening the high schools even if that required desegregation. But the other three members favored keeping the schools shut rather than integrating.

The deadlock persisted through May 5, 1959, when the three school board moderates walked out of a meeting and the three segregationists then fired forty-four teachers and administrators viewed as sympathetic to integration. That night, as Samuel recalls it, lawyer Ed Lester called and invited her along with WEC chairman Vivion Brewer to a May 9 meeting that saw the formation of STOP (Stop This Outrageous Purge). Its aim was to recall the three segregationist school board members.

"This was the first time the men had really gotten together to fight the Faubus forces, and we had the organizational skills they needed," Samuel says. "By then, WEC had well over a thousand members. We knew where our people lived. We knew who would do what. We had an excellent telephone chain that could contact 500 people quickly and get them out to a meeting."

By narrow margins, voters ousted the three board members targeted by STOP and retained the three moderates CROSS had tried to recall. Samuel's perspective is that "we could never have won the recall election without the men, and they could never have won without us."

Little Rock high schools reopened with limited integration in August 1959.

Meanwhile, Samuel started a business, Jetletter Printing & Mailing Co. "Dr. Samuel had lost most of his medical practice during the desegregation crisis," she says. "That was the price of his principles. So it made sense for me to earn some income."

After working for losing candidates against Faubus in 1960, 1962, and 1964, she wound up on the winning side in 1966 backing Republican Winthrop Rockefeller's gubernatorial victory over avowed segregationist Jim Johnson. She helped defeat Johnson again in 1968 when he opposed incumbent U.S. Senator J. William Fulbright.

After the election, Bumpers offered her a staff position handling his official correspondence and minority affairs. She asked her husband's advice, "and he said, 'You've been trying to elect a governor for twelve years. Do what you think is right.' It's the kind of job I would have paid to have had. Dale pretty much let me do what I wanted to do."

Bumpers confirms a Samuel story that she called him "doll" for a number of months. "He grew up with a traditional male background," she recounts. "He was trying not to be sexist, but he'd say to all the women in the office, 'Hello, doll.' To cure him of that, when I saw him each day, I'd say, 'Morning, doll.' It took him a while to catch on, but he finally did."

When Bumpers won election to the U.S. Senate in 1974, Samuel planned to retire. "But then my husband died quite suddenly," she reports. "And Dale called me and said, 'Irene, this is not the time to quit working.' So I worked six years in his Little Rock senatorial office."

Her retirement came at the end of Bumpers's first Senate term in 1981, five years after she was married again, to Wayne Cook, chairman of the state Board of Review. She and Cook traveled widely until his death in 1988.

Rabbi Ira E. Sanders

Humanitarian Award, 1968
(May 6, 1894–April 8, 1985)
Reprinted with permission from the Arkansas Democrat-Gazette

Rabbi Ira E. Sanders, aged ninety, spiritual leader of Temple B'nai Israel from 1926 to 1963 and a leading figure in Arkansas religious life for more than a half-century, died Monday.

In addition to his work with the Little Rock congregation, Rabbi Sanders was a leader in numerous civic activities and an early proponent of interfaith and ecumenical programs. Since retirement in 1963, he had maintained close ties with the Temple B'nai Israel congregation, where he was rabbi emeritus. Rabbi Sanders's thirty-seven-year tenure with the congregation covered the years when the temple, long a Little Rock landmark, was at Broadway and Capitol Avenue.

Missouri native Ira E. Sanders was born May 6, 1894, in Rich Hill, Missouri, the son of Daniel and Pauline Sanders. When he was six, the family moved to Kansas City, where he spent his childhood. He was a graduate of Hebrew Union College in Cincinnati and was ordained to the rabbinate in 1919. He did graduate study in sociology at Columbia University. Before coming to Little Rock, he was associate rabbi for two years at Temple Israel in New York City. Before that he was rabbi of Congregation Keneseth Israel in Allentown, Pennsylvania.

Interest in sociology

Rabbi Sanders's civic activities reflected his life-long interest in sociology. He was founder and first dean of the Little Rock School of Social

Work; the second president of the Little Rock Council of Social Agencies; the organizer and chairman of the Pulaski County Public Welfare Commission, the forerunner of the federal Works Progress Administration; and a founder of the Arkansas Lighthouse for the Blind and the Arkansas Eugenics Association, later called the Planned Parenthood Association. He also was the founder and president of Arkansas Human Betterment League and was one of the founders of the Urban League of Grater Little Rock. He was a member of the board of the Little Rock Public Library for forty-one years and served on the boards of numerous other agencies, including the Arkansas Association for Mental Health and the Arkansas Tuberculosis Association.

Co-founder of Assembly

He had been a member of the national Executive Board of the Union of American Hebrew Congregations and was a co-founder of the Arkansas Jewish Assembly and the Jewish Welfare Fund. He was awarded honorary doctorates by the University of Arkansas and the Hebrew Union College–Jewish Institute of Religion. In 1968, he received the Humanitarian Award from the Arkansas Council on Brotherhood of the National Conference of Christians and Jews.

Rabbi Sanders's wife, the former Selma Loeb, whom he married in 1922, died in 1978. Since then he lived alone, cared for by friends and a housekeeper. Although sightless for the last four and a half years, he maintained an avid interest in current events. Associates knew Rabbi Sanders as a man of great faith in the future. In a 1983 interview with the Gazette, Rabbi Sanders said, "This is a glorious world in which to live. It's a world of challenge and creativity. I can't agree with the prophets of doom. I feel just the opposite. I've been an optimist all my life and I continue to be one."

He is survived by a daughter, Flora Sanders, of New York.

This remembrance of Rabbi Sanders was printed on April 13, 1985.

'We Are the World'
By John S. Workman
Reprinted with permission from the Arkansas Democrat-Gazette

It's strange that such totally different experiences could seem so appropriately related—in this instance a funeral and a popular song. It was early evening and I had just come from the funeral of Rabbi Ira E. Sanders, that eminent spiritual leader whose gentle spirit and prophetic presence blessed Arkansans for more than a half-century. The words of the eulogy, so powerful, so beautiful, so right, lingered as I drove home.

As the traffic moved around me I became conscious of the music from the car radio providing a background for my thoughts. It was that much-heralded popular song "We Are the World," the work of some forty of this country's top music stars who joined hands and voices to appeal for aid to starving children in Africa. The repeated refrain seemed prophetically appropriate to my recollections of Dr. Sanders, a man who witnessed so faithfully to what it means to be human:

> We are the world, we are the children, we are the ones to make a brighter day. So let's start giving.... Send them your heart so they know that someone cares....

The memory of a dear friend and great spiritual leader combined with the power and grace of music and the inspiration of people uniting to respond to human suffering was potent stuff indeed on that lovely spring evening. Yet another thought kept coming to mind, this from John Donne, the seventeenth-century English poet: " Any man's death diminishes me... . So therefore, never send to know for whom the bell tolls. It tolls for thee."

When Ira Sanders died, the bell tolled for us all. But if every person's death diminishes us, every person's life increases us. That was profoundly true in the case of Rabbi Ira Sanders. Dr. Sanders's monuments will continue to be about us: causes worth living for, truth worth standing for, work worth giving one's best for. Rabbi Ira Sanders also knew another truth: God buries the worker but continues the work.

The strains of the popular song, gracing memory at that day's end, confirmed truth spoken long ago and lived among us so beautifully by Ira Sanders: "There comes a time when we heed a certain call, when the world must come together as one. There are people dying and it's time to lend a hand to life—the greatest gift of all. We can't go on pretending day by day that someone, somewhere, will soon make a change. We are all a part of God's great big family and the truth, you know, is love is all we need. We are the world. We are the children."

Stacy Sells
Humanitarian Award, 2012

When Stacy Sells's dad read her the book *The Little Match Girl*, it made a lifelong impact. She then realized there were people in the world, maybe little girls like her, who were cold, hungry and alone. Later her parents, Bob and Georgia Sells, helped her better understand this truth by encouraging volunteer work with abused children, Vietnamese refugees, the hungry, the homeless, and others. Stacy was expected to have a "volunteer plan" for summer breaks, a plan where she would live out the call from John Wesley: "Do all the good you can. By all the means you can. In all the ways you can. In all the places you can. At all the times you can. To all the people you can. As long as ever you can."

Stacy is still living that call.

Born into a "public relations" family, Stacy is often behind the scenes writing press releases, raising money, planning events, developing the "talking points," and helping others prepare to make good things happen. She is firm in her belief that Democracy is not a spectator sport and has devoted countless hours to educating and empowering others to get engaged and to demand more of their governments, schools, and elected leaders.

Because advocacy is her passion, Stacy has been involved with numerous issue campaigns. To be sure, all of her campaigns have made a positive difference for all of us.

A drunk driver killed Stacy's husband when their daughter was only three weeks old. Because of that tragedy, Stacy and her father, along with other community partners, founded the Highway Hero Program. Beginning with an awareness campaign, they soon developed a free taxi service in Central Arkansas for those who'd had too much to drink, then established an alcohol server training program in partnership with the Arkansas Hospitality Association. Next came Project Graduation, where high school graduates celebrate the milestone at an alcohol-free graduation party, a concept that has spread statewide.

When her oldest daughter entered the public school system, Stacy began her "public education" endeavors, which continue today with her service on the Knowledge is Power Program (KIPP) Delta Public School Board and the Philander Smith College Board of Trustees. Her efforts today focus on creating the inspiration and resources for low-income students to aspire to college and meaningful careers. To that end, in 2009 she helped Governor Beebe create and launch ArkansasWorks, an online resource where every Arkansas student can explore and plan for careers and educational training beyond high school. Another element she helped put in place is the College & Career Coaches program, young mentors who work with high-school students in Arkansas's twenty lowest-income counties, encouraging students to better understand their options and opportunities. Stacy rightly says, "You cannot BE what you cannot SEE!," affirming the importance of introducing all students to their many possibilities.

A pinnacle of Stacy's education work came when she was chairman of the State Chamber of Commerce during legislative activity following the Supreme Court's ruling on the Lake View School District case. The Court ruled that Arkansas was neither equitably nor adequately funding public schools, directing the legislature to deliver a constitutional plan. Stacy was appointed co-chair of the state commission charged with advising the legislature on policy actions. In addition, she organized seventy-eight public meetings, one in every Arkansas county and three more for Spanish-speaking families, to educate Arkansans about the issues and receive public feedback to be included in the commission's final report. Ultimately, new laws passed included: mandatory curriculum and Advanced Placement courses in every Arkansas school district, academic and financial accountability standards, increased teacher pay and professional development, and free pre-K for children of low-income families. Stacy credits legislators and education leaders for these courageous steps. Many of them are quick to give her credit for bringing parents and community leaders to the education table.

Besides the policy work, Stacy continues to mentor young students; serves as "foster parent" to homeless dogs; and spends much time with her two daughters: Alyson, public relations manager for the Contemporary Art Museum–St. Louis, and Anna-Lee, a sophomore majoring in social work at the University of Arkansas at Fayetteville. Stacy beams when she talks about her girls.

What would she do if anything were possible? "Every child would be able to read. That would change the entire landscape for improving quality of life." If anyone can make that happen, it would be a Stacy Sells—still doing "all the good she can."

Jim Shelley

Humanitarian Award, 1998
(*Interview conducted July 31, 2012*)

Jim Shelley and his wife, Marcia, make their home in San Antonia now, but they loved their time in Little Rock from 1995 to 1998. And it didn't take Jim long to make his mark on the Central Arkansas community.

Jim Shelley's dad was in the Navy and stationed at Tinker Air Force Base in Midwest City, Oklahoma, when Jim was born. Before Jim was one year old, the family moved to St. Louis where Jim's parents still live. Jim says his childhood there was all about playing sports. The neighborhood kids always had a game going on. They played football in the side yard of someone's house, they went down to the school playground to play baseball, and when the tennis courts were frozen over, they got out their hockey skates and sticks. He says he was never very good, so he didn't play sports at school, but he did become a great fan of the St. Louis Cardinals.

Jim's dad, Bernie, worked for Southwestern Bell (now AT&T) in the accounting department, and his mother, Jean, became a stay-at-home mom to look after Jim and his younger brother and sister. Jean had been among a group of women who were the first females to be admitted as full-time students at the University of Missouri–St. Louis. One of that group of women later became chancellor of the university, and when Jean went back to work many years later, it was her classmate who hired her at the university. From both his parents, Jim learned the value of education, the importance of taking opportunities as they present themselves, and that working hard is a good thing.

Jim's first job was as a caddy at Northwood Hills Country Club when he was only thirteen years old. He said the movie "Caddy Shack" got it about right. It was *not* a glamorous job. One highlight for him was an LPGA Tournament in 1967. The famous women golfers had their own caddies, but the less-than-famous players needed someone like him. Also, he and a buddy went out before the tournament, walked off the course, and put little pink X's on trees that were 250 yards out from the holes. He made $100 for four days work, so he felt it was definitely worth it.

Jim graduated from the University of Missouri–St. Louis with a BS degree in 1976 and earned his MS degree from Washington University in 1988, both in business administration. Jim actually majored in math for his first two years at Missouri. One of his favorite teachers, Sister Karen, had taught him math in the eighth grade. Her confidence in him (even though he never considered himself very good at math) helped him to excel. He counts that as a life lesson about expecting the best from and showing confidence in others.

Jim went to work for Southwestern Bell right out of college, and he's become an expert in regulatory, legislative, and governmental matters. He presently serves as senior vice president–executive operations in the Dallas office of AT&T. In Little Rock, Jim was president–Arkansas for SWBT. Jim felt that his team (including Eddie Drilling, Larry Walther, Frank Taylor, Carol Crosswaite Corley, and Larry Ross) did some very important work. He also appreciated the enlightened leadership of then-senator Mike Beebe and then-governor Mike Huckabee as the changing telephone industry prepared itself to face new competition. Jim notes that it takes a lot of effort and a long time to change laws, but working together, they were able to move the company along in a way that was good for the community, good for the customers, and good for the employees.

According to Jim, his favorite community service in Arkansas was with the United Way. He served on the board and headed its annual campaign. In the late 1990s, the United Way supported more than thirty-five agencies providing countless services in the Central Arkansas community.

Jim was also pleased that Southwestern Bell was a major sponsor of the Fortieth Anniversary Commemoration of the Desegregation of Central High School. Jim had the opportunity to get to know the civil rights icon Daisy Bates, and Southwestern Bell-Arkansas established a scholarship in Bates's name which was given to ten outstanding African-American seniors each year during Jim's tenure. Jim is also very proud of his company's commitment to hiring and promoting a diverse work force. He explains that AT&T believes that having a diverse group of employees broadens their perspective and ultimately makes them more competitive in serving a diverse community. He calls this commitment central to AT&T—a basic tenet of their company identity.

When Jim reminisces about their time in Arkansas, he says he would have been happy to stay in Little Rock for the entirety of his career. He and Marcia found Arkansans to be genuine and caring. They also thought it was a great place to raise their sons, Rob and Ken.

Over the past nine years, Jim has served on the board and raised money for Our Lady of the Lake University–San Antonio. He is proud that OLLU provides opportunities for first-generation college students, which make up seventy percent of the student body. OLLU describes itself as "a school that helps students develop their full potential in an environment that's diverse, encouraging, and stimulating." Sounds like the kind of world that Jim Shelley has been building all along.

Honorable Vic Snyder

Humanitarian Award 1999
(*Interview conducted July 13, 2012*)

When Vic Snyder considers our American political system today, he is optimistic. What some consider gridlock in Washington, he describes as democracy in action. He compares the political climate of 2012 to two previous eras of great unrest in our country: the late 1960s, when we were bitterly divided over many things, including the war in Vietnam; and the period following World War I, when we were struggling with questions regarding immigration and there was great prejudice against the Germans. Having served in the Arkansas Senate and the U.S. House of Representatives, Vic expresses great confidence in and respect for our governmental institutions.

Vic was born in Medford, Oregon, and his parents were divorced before he was three years old. His mother had only a high school education, and she supported Vic and his younger sister by working as a bookkeeper. Vic attended public schools and then went to Willamette University in Salem, Oregon, for two years before enlisting in the U.S. Marine Corps. He calls his decision to enter the Marine Corps the "first adult decision" of his life. He knew when he enlisted for a two-year stint that he would be sent to Vietnam. As one of the young officers explained, "There are two kinds of Marines: those who are going to Vietnam, and those who have already been to Vietnam." Looking back, he appreciates his time as a Marine because of the culture of the Corps. They considered themselves unique and special, and they acted accordingly. They treated each other with respect.

After completing his service in the Marines, he spent four years traveling solo throughout the western United States, supporting himself with odd jobs. He worked at a school for children with mental-health problems, pumped gas at a filling station he leased, and helped finance a restaurant in Santa Fe. Back in Oregon, he supervised VISTA volunteers and got some training as an Emergency Medical Technician. That's when he decided to complete his undergraduate degree in chemistry and go to medical school. Following graduation, he came to the University of Arkansas for Medical Sciences to do his residency in family practice in 1979. He liked Little Rock and has lived here ever since.

As a family practice physician, Vic also made several medical mission trips during the 1980s. He served in Cambodia, Thailand, Honduras, El Salvador, Ethiopia, and for six months during 1983-84 in Sierra Leone, West Africa. Often he worked in refugee camps, and he once witnessed the devastation of a cholera outbreak within a camp. Those experiences along with his tenure in public office have prepared him well for his present position as a medical director at Arkansas Blue Cross Blue Shield, where his job is to focus on the "big picture" of how insurance companies and health-care providers can work together to improve health outcomes for all our citizens. Vic is also optimistic that we are moving in the right direction within our health-care systems, and he is glad to be informing those efforts.

Vic first ran for public office in 1990, winning an Arkansas Senate seat against a long-time incumbent Doug Brandon. Vic credits his victory to "retail politics," which he learned about while working on political campaigns in high school. Retail politics refers to a campaign in which the candidate focuses on meeting individual voters face-to-face. Vic went door-to-door throughout his district to 12,000 homes. Six years later, in 1996, he defeated Bud Cummins for the U.S. House of Representatives. He was elected for seven terms in Congress and chose not to run again in 2010.

When asked about his accomplishments in the state legislature, Vic recalls his work with Republican Senator Doyle Webb and activist Stacy Sells (Humanitarian Award Honoree, 2012) on legislation regarding underage drinking, administrative license revocation for drunk driving, and

interlock devices. Others are quick to cite his support of conservation issues, his efforts to overturn anti-gay laws in Arkansas, and his challenge
to the power of the Arkansas Highway Commission.

The online Encyclopedia of Arkansas sums up Vic's time in
Washington this way:

> In Congress, Snyder has served on the House Committee on
> Veterans' Affairs, the House Armed Services Committee, and the
> Joint Economic Committee. In 2007, he was elected chair of the
> House Armed Services Subcommittee on Oversight and
> Investigations. Snyder was the only member of the Arkansas dele-
> gation in the House to vote against the 2003 resolution authorizing
> the use of military force in Iraq. In 2009, he was also the lone
> Arkansas congressional delegate to vote in support of climate-
> change legislation. He defended his willingness to support health-
> care legislation in the 111th Congress in various "town hall
> meetings" in his district in 2009.

Vic won't bring it up, but his reputation as a legislator is one of
honesty and integrity. Everyone seems to agree that Vic could always be
trusted to do what he said he was going to do, whether or not it was popular or politically expedient.

Vic and the Reverend Betsy Singleton were married in 2003. In
2006, their son Penn was born, and in 2008, they had triplets, Wyatt,
Sullivan, and Aubrey. In 2010, Betsy returned to work as the senior pastor of Trinity United Methodist Church. With two full-time jobs, Betsy
and Vic share the parenting duties for their active brood.

Vic Snyder has a tendency to expect the best in others and to see
the best in things. But he is certainly not starry-eyed. Otherwise, he never
would have knocked on those 12,000 doors in his first campaign for office. And he is concerned about the effects of the recent "Citizens
United" decision by the Supreme Court. Vic feels that if citizens start

thinking that "it's all about the money," and not about their involvement and vote, then we might do fundamental damage to our democratic system. Vic says, "The key to a successful democracy is not how good legislators are, but the continued confidence of the public in the election process." Vic has always put his optimism to work to make "the best in things" become reality. It's what he did in the state legislature and in Congress, it's what he is doing at Blue Cross Blue Shield, and it's how he is raising his four boys.

Henry E. Spitzberg
Humanitarian Award, 1976
(October 23, 1902–October 13, 1990)

Henry Spitzberg, 87, lawyer, retired senior partner, dies
By Arkansas Gazette *Staff, October 14, 1990*
Reprinted with permission from the Arkansas Democrat-Gazette

Henry Spitzberg, eighty-seven, of 1205 Garfield St., retired senior partner of Spitzberg, Mitchell and Hays law firm, died Saturday.

Mr. Spitzberg was a past president of the Pulaski County Bar Association, a lecturer at the University of Arkansas Law School, past president of the Community Chest and Council of Little Rock, past vice president of the United Fund of Pulaski County, past chairman of the Health and Welfare Council of Pulaski County, past president of the Board of Pulaski County Guidance Center, past president of the Senior Citizens Activities Today Inc., and a past president of the Arkansas chapter of Christians and Jews.

In his spare time, Mr. Spitzberg enjoyed fishing, hunting and playing golf.

Survivors are his wife, Mollie Lindenberg Spitzberg; two daughters, Betty Taylor of Lexington, Va., and Lynne Rosenfield of Jackson, Mississippi; two sisters, Louise Rosenberg of Dallas, Texas, and Marie Spitzberg of Little Rock; five grandchildren; and five great-grandchildren.

Edward L. Wright, a Little Rock attorney and 1969 honoree of the National Conference of Christians and Jews, made the award presentation to Henry Spitzberg, citing his "outstanding contributions to the cultural and corpo-

rate life of our several communities." According to the Arkansas Gazette *article on Friday, April 30, 1976, "Spitzberg professed himself unworthy of the award, which he said 'places me in a charming magic circle.' He said that the presentations of the awards to people of different races and religions would have been 'socially impossible' twenty-five years ago." (That same year, the humanitarian award was presented to Annie Mae Bankhead, Dr. Dale Cowling, and, posthumously, to Raymond Rebsamen.)*

Mary Steenburgen

Humanitarian Award, 2006

Biography provided in 2006 by Mary Steenburgen's staff

Mary Steenburgen is an Academy Award and Golden Globe winning actress who has appeared in more than fifty films and television programs. She recently completed work on three films that will be released over the next year, including *Marilyn Hotchkiss' Ballroom Dancing and Charm School, Nobel Son* and *Elvis and Annabelle*. Her film credits include *Melvin and Howard, Parenthood, Philadelphia, What's Eating Gilbert Grape, Back to the Future III, Elf*, and *Life as a House*. Partial television credits include *Gulliver's Travels, About Sarah, Tender is the Night*, and CBS's acclaimed series, *Joan of Arcadia*.

Some of Mary's theatre credits include *Marvin's Room, Holiday, The Beginning Of August, Candida*, and *The Exonerated*. Most recently, David Mamet directed her in his play *Boston Marriage*. Mary is a member of the Atlantic Theater Company in New York.

Mary has also spent the last thirty years working as a social and political advocate on issues she cares deeply about. In 1989, Mary and fellow actress Alfre Woodard founded Artists for A Free South Africa to call for sanctions against the apartheid government in South Africa. This group is still alive today under the name Artists for A New South Africa. In 1996, Mary and her husband, Ted Danson, were presented with Liberty Hill Foundation's prestigious Upton Sinclair Award for their work in human rights and environmental causes. She has also worked closely with the Elizabeth Glaser Pediatric AIDS Foundation and was honored to serve as the National Spokesperson for the organization. Mary also works with the Progeria Research Foundation in their search for a cure for the disease.

Mary has tried to focus as much of her energy as she can on her beloved home state of Arkansas. She feels that everything she's been able to accomplish in her life is due to the incredible community in which she grew up, and it is important to her that she never forget it. Some of the Arkansas-based groups she has worked with include Arkansas Children's Hospital, Arkansas Public School System, THEA Foundation, CareLink, Heifer International, Arkansas Repertory Theatre, Clinton School of Public Service and the Democratic Party of Arkansas. She has honorary doctorate degrees from UALR and Hendrix College.

Mary was born in Newport, Arkansas, and raised in North Little Rock, where she attended North Little Rock public schools. She is the daughter of a railroad conductor and a secretary. She began her career at the age of nineteen when she went to New York to study with the legendary Sanford Meisner. She was discovered in 1978 by the actor Jack Nicholson when he cast her as his leading lady in a film he directed, *Goin' South*. Mary currently lives in Malibu, California, with her husband, Ted Danson. They also enjoy spending as much time as possible in their apartment in downtown Little Rock. Mary and Ted are the proud parents of four children—Kate, Lilly, Charlie, and Katrina.

Charles Stewart

Humanitarian Award, 1999
(Interview conducted July 10, 2012)

When Charles Stewart talks with students, he reminds them, "Sometimes life isn't fair. But it's how you react to your circumstances that counts, not the circumstances themselves." He knows what he's talking about, because when life handed him a lemon, he took that lemon and made not only lemonade, but a lemon icebox pie. That's how he became an executive banker—the first African American in Arkansas to do so.

While going to night school at UALR, Charles worked as an audit clerk for First National Bank, traveling throughout the state to audit smaller correspondent banks. His immediate boss wanted to promote his "favorite female" employee into Charles's position, so he moved Charles into the role of "Trust Auditor." Charles was hurt and angry when he saw the room full of files that were now his responsibility. However, he decided to do the best he could, and after thirty days of making that proverbial lemonade, the bank Chairman, Finley Vinson, invited Charles to lunch. Vinson told Charles that if he would commit at least three years to the bank, they would give him the opportunity to learn the business and make it "very difficult for him to ever leave." That luncheon led to a thirty-seven-year career in banking, and Charles has enjoyed the whole—sometimes wild—ride.

Charles survived numerous mergers and acquisitions, aided along the way by mentors such as Jack Fleischauer and Bill Cravens. When he retired in 2008, he was an executive vice president of Regions. One of the highlights of his banking career occurred when he was called to Birmingham, Alabama, to present to the board of Regions Financial

Corporation about how to set up a Community Development Division—something that Charles had done successfully for many years in Arkansas. Charles knew that any new division had to be a profit center. Remembering the adage "Doing Well by Doing Good," he proposed ways to offer banking services to low- and moderate-income markets as a business strategy. He remembers being a nervous wreck as he prepared and finally presented his ideas. The board members embraced the idea, and Charles became Senior Vice President and Director of the new Community Development Division for 16 states.

Charles was born in the parsonage in Sweet Home, Arkansas. His father, Frank James Stewart, an AME pastor, and his mother, Ola Fay Stewart, an elementary school teacher, raised eight children. Tired of moving, his parents bought a home at Twenty-ninth and Louisiana Streets in Little Rock, where Charles's mother, now 85 years old, still lives. Charles describes his childhood as "living in *Happy Days*." Their community was intact and the institutions were strong—families, schools, churches and, happily for young Charles, the William Thrasher Boys Club at Thirty-third and Izard Streets. The kids were safe and could walk anywhere. They couldn't misbehave, however, because everyone within their community knew them and their parents. Charles attended segregated schools, including Washington Elementary, Dunbar Junior High, and Horace Mann Senior High School, where he says he got an outstanding education with teachers such as Morris Holmes, Odessa Talley, William "Sonny" Walker, and Bill Hamilton. One teacher in particular made an impression on Charles. It was Mrs. Edna Douglass, his eighth-grade civics teacher, who told the class one day, "You little black boys and girls are going to learn because I'm going to *make* you learn." Charles notes that happened before anyone called African Americans "black." Mrs. Douglass also gave Charles a job mowing her large, beautiful yard. To do that, he had to also clean up after her two large dogs. He often mentions that chore, too, when he talks with students...he wasn't always a banker who wears a suit every day!

Along with his outstanding banking career, Charles has made a difference for Arkansas, too. During the 1990s, Charles chaired the Paint Your Heart Out project, which was jointly sponsored by the United Way of Pulaski County (now Heart of Arkansas United Way), the City of Little Rock, and area businesses. The City of North Little Rock later joined the partnership. Paint teams were provided by churches, organizations, businesses, and neighborhood groups. At the program's height, more than eighty homes were painted on one Saturday by 1,600 volunteers. The Paint Your Heart Out program had an undeniably positive impact on low-income homeowners and whole neighborhoods. The sight of one house on a block newly spruced up often motivated other neighbors to do the same. Some Paint teams also planted flowers, and some practically adopted homeowners. The success of Paint Your Heart Out also led to the City of Little Rock receiving an All American City Award in 1992. Then-president George Bush, in a heated battle with Governor Bill Clinton for the presidency, postponed the awards ceremony, not wishing to present an award to Clinton's home city. In 1993, Mayor Sharon Priest invited Charles to accompany her to the belated awards ceremony in Washington DC, and they were treated to a tour of the West Wing of the White House by President Clinton.

In 1992, Charles, with Patricia Goodwin, co-founded the Arkansas Black Hall of Fame. Each year the Hall of Fame holds a gala honoring outstanding individuals with strong Arkansas ties who have achieved national or international acclaim in their chosen field or endeavor. Charles continues to chair this project, and in 2012, the Black Hall of Fame Foundation awarded $55,000 in grants to eighteen organizations. Since 2004, ABHOF has awarded more than $316,000 to organizations serving African Americans and other underserved populations in Arkansas.

Motivated by his belief in the value of education, Charles also helped found the Little Rock Preparatory Academy in 2008. Its mission is to provide a quality education for inner city children and to prepare those children for college and other forms of higher order careers. What began as a fifth-grade school with eighty students now serves children from kindergarten through eighth grade at two sites. For the 2012-13 school year, they have an enrollment of 432 students with others on a waiting list. The children are ninety-three percent minority and eighty percent eligible for free or reduced-price lunches. LRPA's "no excuses" approach upholds the belief that "children of all races and income levels can meet high academic standards." And that is exactly what is happening with their students.

After retiring from banking, Charles was available to serve for one year as the interim CEO of Heifer International after his good friend Jo Luck stepped down. For several years, he has been leading Heifer International Study Tours to countries throughout Africa. If you want to join one of his study tours, you'd better hustle—his last tour to Kenya was booked up in three days.

Charles has two children, Sherri, a teacher, and Christopher, an engineer, and one grandson, Lawrence Daniel Anderson III.

Reverend Hezekiah Stewart

Joseph H. Biltz Award, 1988
Humanitarian Award, 1995
(Interview conducted June 25, 2012)

In 1987, a tornado ripped through College Station destroying homes, busting every gas line, and downing every power line. Reverend Hezekiah Stewart opened Mt. Nebo AME Church that night and placed a candle in every church window. Those candles were the only light in the entire community, a symbol of help and hope to all who saw them. That's exactly what Hezekiah Stewart has been doing for more than thirty-four years: offering help and hope to those in need.

Hezekiah was the oldest of five children born to Hezekiah Sr. and Edna Abraham Stewart. They lived in Liberty Hill, a part of Charleston, South Carolina, that had been settled by his relatives. Although the townspeople were all poor, they didn't think of themselves that way. Everyone in the town helped everyone else. His grandfather had a small grocery where anyone could get credit. When someone butchered a hog, they shared the meat all around. As a boy, Hezekiah cut wood and raked yards for others. There was a culture of hard work and helping in their highly religious community. One of the things he treasurers most are the memories of his grandparents' house, where he and his siblings and cousins played, mostly on the wrap-around porch.

Hezekiah's parents separated when he was only four, and he determined that he would help his mom look after his younger brothers and sisters. His dream was to protect her from his dad, who had been abusive, and to buy her a home and a mink coat. He accomplished all.

Hezekiah was aware of many racial indignities during his childhood. His cousin was executed after being found with a white girlfriend. His mother was once hit with a potato, and he still remembers being pelted with an egg, ruining his brand new shirt. At thirteen years old, he asked his uncle Julius what it was all about, and he remembers his uncle saying, "You need to grow up and make a difference."

Hezekiah got his high school diploma at Bonds-Wilson in North Charleston. They wore suits and ties every day, perhaps a testament to the value they placed on education and the high expectations that their teachers set for them. Following graduation, Hezekiah went to work at whatever job he could find. His younger sister Deloris was the first to attend college. She left home with a borrowed $13 and graduated from Allen University, a small, coeducational, private institution in Columbia, South Carolina, founded in 1870, by the African Methodist Episcopal Church. He had been helping to support their family, so it was against his mother's wishes that Hezekiah followed Deloris to Allen University in 1965. To make ends meet there, he took $26 to buy a #2 tub and a small grill to sell sodas, hamburgers, and hot dogs. He turned that $26 into $500. He laughs that he should have kept that business going because he's been poor ever since.

Out of money again during his junior year, he was sleeping in the park every night, when his basketball coach Jim Davis offered him a job at a nearby school for boys. He didn't even ask the salary when he learned that the job included a place to sleep and meals. Following graduation, Hezekiah was public relations director of Allen University for three years. Then he entered the Interdenominational Theological Center in Atlanta to prepare himself for ministry in the AME Church. Hezekiah was assigned to a church in Madison, Georgia, for his first call. In 1976, he left Georgia to come to Mt. Nebo AME Church in the College Station neighborhood near Little Rock.

Hezekiah drove around the neighborhood and saw complacency, poverty, crime, and fear. He remembered his uncle Julius's advice, and the Watershed Human & Community Development Agency was born, and it became that place of help and hope so needed by the community. Operating originally out of the basement of the church, it is now housed in the former Gillum School, which was given to Watershed by the Little Rock School District. The agency will celebrate its thirty-fifth anniversary in 2012.

Because Hezekiah is a master at sharing his vision, Watershed has received enormous help from the city, county, state, and federal government, from the business community, and from individuals. Every day, Watershed provides food, clothing, housing, job counseling, and crisis intervention, all with the aim of encouraging self-sufficiency in those it serves. And when disaster strikes, they are there, just as they were after the 1987 tornado.

Hezekiah took advice from his good friend Walter Smiley, who said, "We've all got to work together, because there's *nothing* we can't accomplish together." With partners too numerous to list, last year the Christmas Coalition, led by Watershed, provided fourteen to twenty-one days' worth of food, along with toys for the children, to between 6,000 and 8,000 families in Arkansas. Hezekiah dreams of a time when there will be Watershed sites all around Arkansas, lifting up the outcast, the poor, the sick, the unwanted, the alcoholics, the drug addicts, and the convicts. Helping them all to help themselves.

Hezekiah thinks that all our problems can be solved if we "love one another as Christ has loved us." He certainly demonstrates that every day.

Grif Stockley
Father Joseph H. Biltz Award, 2011

Grif Stockley grew up in a conservative family in racially segregated Marianna, Arkansas. His father was a business man. His mother stayed at home to care for Grif and his two older sisters. At T. A. Futrall High School, Grif played football, acted in the senior class play, and served as the student body president, before heading to Southwestern at Memphis (now Rhodes) to earn a college degree. Dr. C. Calvin Smith, the first African-American faculty member at Arkansas State University, also grew up in Marianna, just four blocks from Grif's boyhood home. The two historians, only one year apart in age, had much in common, probably even as boys in their hometown, but they never met until shortly before Calvin Smith's death in 2009—a clear example of the cost of segregation based on race.

Grif credits his sister Sally with influencing his moral and educational development and broadening his world view. She had preceded him in attending Southwestern and returned to Marianna, where she was his English, world history, and Spanish teacher. Grif thought he might like to be a diplomat, but failed the Foreign Service exam. Though he had been accepted as a graduate student at the University of South Carolina, he signed up for the Peace Corps and spent two years on the northern coast of Colombia where he served as a rural community development volunteer. He helped identify community leaders, identified the residents' felt needs, and assisted in building a cemetery wall, a latrine project, and a three-room school. In Colombia, he saw real poverty and eventually realized that the plight of African Americans in the Arkansas Delta wasn't that much different than the situation of the villagers in Colombia. This was something he hadn't understood as a child of white privilege in Eastern Arkansas.

After the Peace Corps, Grif was drafted into the Army a week before he was to go to graduate school. After two years in the Army, Grif entered law school and quickly joined the Law Students Civil Rights Research Council. He embarrassed his mother by writing a letter to the editor of the *Arkansas Gazette* about the racism he saw in eastern Arkansas. Following the death of his father, his mom had become a sorority house mother at Ole Miss, and Grif says by the late 1960s her attitudes about race were beginning to change, just not as fast as his.

Right out of law school, Grif joined the Center for Arkansas Legal Services as a staff attorney. During his thirty-two years there, he served as counsel on cases that routinely resulted in upholding the rights of some of our most vulnerable citizens, particularly those suffering from mental illness, children in foster care, families who are eligible for Aid for Dependent Children benefits, and those who were involuntarily committed to the state hospital. Grif also did a stint as staff attorney for the Disability Rights Center in Little Rock and the ACLU of Arkansas, continuing to fight for justice. Grif also made time to serve non-profits as a board member and volunteer, and he has been recognized with awards by the Pulaski County Bar Association, as Lawyer-Citizen of the Year in 1991; by AACF with the "Friend of Children" award in 1986; as Public Citizen of the Year, by the Arkansas Chapter of the National Association of Social Workers in 1992; and as an "Honorary Uppity Woman" for service to children, by the Arkansas Women's Political Caucus in 1992.

Today, Grif is best known to many Arkansans for his writing, which includes the Gideon Page series of mysteries, plays, short stories, articles, and essays. His most recent non-fiction work documents the history of race and race relations in Arkansas and the life of civil rights leader Daisy Bates. *Ruled by Race: Black/White Relations in Arkansas from Slavery to the Present* was published in 2008. He actually began writing that book in the 1970s and wrote many novels and non-fiction over a period of nineteen

years before he got anything published. Grif credits his three-year opportunity as the first Dee Brown Fellow, at the Butler Center for Arkansas
Studies, Central Arkansas Library, with making it possible for him to finish the research and writing of *Ruled by Race*, a most important work for
all who want to truly understand Arkansas and our heritage.

Grif has not slackened in his commitment to our community nor
in his aim to help us all understand the pathology of prejudice and the
enduring damage of white supremacist attitudes for both blacks and
whites. He is a past president of the ACLU of Arkansas and of AACF,
he currently serves on the Little Rock Racial and Cultural Diversity
Commission, and he is a devoted member of the New Millennium
Baptist Church. He is also working on a book about the fire that killed
twenty-one children at the Negro Boys Industrial School in Wrightsville,
Arkansas, in 1959.

Grif Stockley is determined to help us confront our past with the
aim of improving our collective future.

William H. Buddy Sutton
Humanitarian Award, 2002

Buddy Sutton's life and work could be the stuff of cinema; perhaps the title could be "It's a Wonderful Life." Just like George Bailey in the original, Buddy has had a profound impact through his dedicated and loyal service in the many roles he has filled and upon the many lives he has touched.

Buddy attended the University of Arkansas in 1949 and played football as a Razorback. As a beneficiary of the GI Bill, Buddy felt he had a debt to repay, and through his service to our state, he has been giving back for many years.

As a partner in one of our state's leading law firms, Buddy has served his clients with integrity; in 1991, he was named Outstanding Lawyer by the Arkansas Bar Association.

At his church, Immanuel Baptist, Buddy has taught Sunday School and served as a deacon, and he was recognized with the Brooks Hays Christian Citizenship Award in 1991. Buddy served as chair of the Arkansas Billy Graham Crusade, served two terms as president of the Arkansas Baptist State Convention, and chaired the Pulpit Committee, which called Rex Horne as pastor of Immanuel.

As a board member of Baptist Health, Buddy has been one of the visionaries who has seen that institution become one of the premier providers of health, preventive, and rehabilitation care in our state.

Buddy has served on the board of Ouachita Baptist University for more than twenty years, and as board chair eight times, watching the addition of sixteen campus buildings and fifteen new endowed chairs.

Buddy continues to support the University of Arkansas's Razorback athletics and the law school, with service on the University of Arkansas 2010 Commission and on the steering committee for the Campaign for the Twenty-first Century. Buddy has also chaired the law school's fund-raising efforts.

Buddy and his late wife, Peggy, had three children, Rebecca, Richard, and Wesley. Buddy is now married to Susan Overton.

Adolphine Fletcher Terry

Humanitarian Award, 1971
(*November 3, 1882–July 25, 1976*)

Adolphine Terry

Arkansas Gazette *editorial, July 27, 1976*
Reprinted with permission from the Arkansas Democrat-Gazette

Adolphine Fletcher Terry was a great lady and a true heroine, one who left the imprint of her spirit, her character, and her intellect, upon the twentieth-century history of Arkansas. Certainly she was one of the leading Arkansans of her time.

She died Sunday at ninety-three, and her life was one of those that people regard as paradoxical, for she was an aristocrat magnificently concerned with the needs and cares of the deprived and downtrodden. She was to the manner born and bred, a Vassar graduate presiding over the grandest ante-bellum mansion in Arkansas; her husband was a member of the Congress, her brother a Pulitzer Prize-winning poet, a first cousin the (Catholic) Bishop of Arkansas. She might have easily settled for a life of ease and comfortable distinction but soon after the turn of the century she developed instinctively an affinity for causes—human rights education and racial equality became her passionate concerns, along with a wide range of less controversial enterprises. Her public interests were catholic, ranging from the community chest to public libraries to homes for delinquent children; her courage was inspiring, as all of us learned in the historic school confrontation of the late fifties. Other distinguished women in America have served their society in the same kind of way, and a parallel that comes to our mind is that of Eleanor Roosevelt, who had the same kind of background, courage, and compassion.

It is recognized that Mrs. Terry's time of critical test and singular achievement was in the years of the Little Rock school crisis. In this time of turmoil and rampant unreason, she went forth to battle against the bigots and demagogues. While many of Little Rock's leading men were conspicuously silent and inactive, Mrs. Terry assembled a group of leading young women to a meeting in her home and in this fashion the famous Women's Emergency Committee was born. The WEC fought valiantly and successfully to save the public schools and prepare the way for the civil rights that black citizens enjoy in Arkansas today as a matter of course.

Adolphine Terry was a magnificent figure and her record will adorn the histories of our state. In any state it is only once in, let us say, a hundred years, that an Adolphine Terry comes along, and the lives of all of us are enriched for her coming.

Dr. Billy Thomas
Father Joseph H. Biltz Award, 2013

One of the first things you notice about Dr. Billy Thomas is that he is soft-spoken. But he doesn't need a big voice; he has big plans. He wants the University of Arkansas for Medical Sciences Center for Diversity Affairs to be nationally known for its work to "enhance the education of our students, reduce racial and ethnic health disparities in our state, and provide an environment in which all employees and views are welcomed." To accomplish this mission, he leads a staff of ten that strives to interact with and serve all components of UAMS, including the six academic departments, the seven institutes, and the University Hospital.

Billy was born the eleventh of twelve children of Jake and Clyde Tyler Thomas. His parents were sharecroppers in the small town of Tyronza, in the northeast corner of Arkansas. Billy said they knew most everyone in their town of 600 residents. And until he was in the sixth grade, he attended the "colored school." He remembers those as good years, and after his grade school burned down, he learned firsthand the downside of integrated schools. He said many of the African-American children were unable to assimilate in the integrated schools, and there were some teachers who didn't think the African-American students were smart enough to succeed. He still mourns what he calls the loss of people with enormous potential who could have gone on to contribute a great deal to society.

Billy graduated from high school in Tyronza, and with the constant encouragement of his high-school principal and his stepmother, he decided to attend college at nearby Arkansas State University in Jonesboro. He majored in science and finished his degree in December of 1975. After graduating, he enrolled in graduate school to pursue a masters' in zoology, and was later offered a graduate assistantship by the chair of the ASU science department. Billy became the only African-American student in the graduate school pursuing a science degree. He took anatomy and biology classes, and he found that he was often held to a different standard than his white classmates. Billy considered pursuing a PhD in basic science, but he knew that would be a difficult field. So, when his best friend from ASU applied to medical school at UAMS, Billy thought, "If he can do it, so I can." Billy was admitted to UAMS in 1976. Following graduation from medical school, he did his residency in pediatrics at Arkansas Children's Hospital, and he completed a three-year fellowship in neonatology in Cleveland, Ohio. Along the way, he married Beverly Dean, and subsequently they had three children, Aaron, Billie Jean, and Jesse. They also have one granddaughter, Ionia.

Billy was still interested in doing scientific research, and when a position opened for a faculty member in neonatology at UAMS, with a lab for research at Arkansas Children's Hospital, he gladly returned to his home state. Since returning to Arkansas, he has been able to do some important work in the field of rickets (bone disease) and vitamin D in infants, in addition to teaching and seeing patients.

When associate dean of Minority Affairs, Dr. Phillip Rayford, was ready to retire in 1999, Dr. Dodd Wilson, chancellor of UAMS, asked Billy to head up the Office of Minority Affairs. Wilson assured Billy that he would still be able to do some research and see patients. It didn't take Billy more than a few months in his new position to realize that there was great value, to UAMS and to himself, in making his efforts in minority affairs more of a full-time commitment. The importance of the office was also recognized when it was renamed the Center for Diversity Affairs, and when Chancellor Dan Rahn broadened its mission "in recognition of diversity as an institutional core value, critical to the fulfillment of the mission of UAMS."

The focus of the Center for Diversity Affairs is fourfold: diversity, inclusion, equity, and cultural competency. Dr. Billy Thomas and his team are addressing each one.

The campus of UAMS is home to more than eighty different nationalities. So what does diversity mean at UAMS? According to Dr. Billy Thomas, "Diversity is not just about race and ethnic background, but also personality, learning styles, and life experience." Recent presentations for students, faculty, and staff have included topics such as "The Health of Lesbian, Gay, Bisexual, and Transgender (LGBT) People," and the "Myers-Briggs Type Indicator" about personality. In a recent article regarding the importance of recruiting a racially diverse student body, Billy wrote,

> It comes down to whether we as a society and as a health care institution believe in the educational benefits of diversity—that it enriches the quality of education for everyone (students and faculty) because individuals with unique personal differences and life experiences contribute to and are part of the learning community. The outcome is a cadre of health care workers who are more open and wiser about the diversity of patients that they are trained to care for. Our job is to accept, promote and embrace diversity so that we as a society may reap the benefits in the future.

It's easy to see that Billy believes this about all facets of diversity too.

About inclusion, Billy says, "Inclusion is creating an environment where everyone feels comfortable. Not just our foreign nationals, but all of our in-state students need to feel welcomed." Only in an inclusive environment can we expect all employees to be "seriously committed to assuming personal responsibility for contributing to achievement of organizational goals," according to a recent article in *Diversitas*, the Center's online newsletter. For more than twenty years, the Center has also offered summer enrichment programs for kindergarten through college students, particularly from minority groups, to introduce them to the possibilities of a career in health care.

To promote equity, UAMS is pursuing the following strategies: a review of current admissions processes so that disadvantaged students of promise are not excluded; investment in student support services, such as mentoring, tutoring, wellness, and "an early warning system" to identify and help students in academic distress; and development of a post-baccalaureate program for students aspiring to enter the College of Medicine who might have failed to make the first cut on admissions but who have the capacity to make fine medical professionals with some investment by the university.

About cultural competence, Billy has written, "Cultural competency extends well beyond the race, ethnic background, or gender of a health-care provider, but rather is a gestalt of knowledge, skills, and attitudes that every health-care provider—regardless of training or degrees after one's name—should aspire to attain. To that end, UAMS is in the midst of myriad initiatives—revamping curricula, training for providers, programs to better engage patients in the health-care system—to help us all become more culturally sensitive and aware."

Billy remembers what he discovered in his time as a resident at Arkansas Children's Hospital and in Cleveland. It was that the most important skill for a doctor is the ability to communicate with patients, both listening and talking. Billy says, "If you will listen, patients will usually tell you what you need to hear to be able to treat them effectively." Billy clearly has the ability to listen, and he is using that skill to make UAMS a more diverse, inclusive, equitable, and culturally competent institution. Chances are good that he will realize his vision of UAMS receiving national recognition for the important work being done there every day.

Ray Thornton

Humanitarian Award, 1986
(Interview with Julie Baldridge, October 8, 2012)

It's difficult to find a "theme" for Ray Thornton's life because he has served and excelled in so many areas.

Ray was born in 1928 in Conway, Arkansas. His parents were educators: Raymond Thornton Sr. was the superintendent of schools in Grant County, and Wilma Elizabeth Stephens Thornton was a teacher. Ray graduated from high school at age sixteen. He then enrolled at the University of Texas, but the Korean War quickly interrupted his college education. However, after his military commitment was completed, he was able to attend Yale University with the benefit of the GI Bill. He couldn't afford to come home for holidays, and one Thanksgiving he had to sell his clarinet to have enough money to feed himself since the dorm's dining hall was closed for the week. He graduated from Yale in three years, earning a BA in international relations and engineering in 1950.

Ray moved back to Arkansas to attend law school in Fayetteville. As a law school student, he was elected president of the University of Arkansas student body, an honor usually reserved for an undergraduate student. Following his graduation in 1956, he married Betty Jo Mann of Sheridan, Arkansas, and they subsequently had three daughters. He had a law practice downtown, representing Arkansas Louisiana Gas Company (Arkla). He and Arkla employee Ed Handy designed a small, fuel-efficient automobile that was shaped like a truck and called a Handy-wagon. Arkla ordered 100 of the vehicles at $1,250 each, but large-scale production plans were scrapped because of costs. Soon after, new Asian-manufactured vehicles entered the U.S. markets, which caused some second-guessing about the decision to stop production.

In 1965, Ray successfully sued Southwestern Bell Telephone Company (now AT&T) on behalf of Allied Telephone (later Alltel). Southwestern Bell had cut Allied from its lines, and the court ruled against Bell on the basis of anti-trust and monopoly actions. Ray's win allowed Allied/Alltel to become a multi-state telephone provider.

In 1969, Ray told his uncle, Witt Stephens, that he wanted to run for Attorney General of Arkansas. Mr. Witt advised Ray that he could make more money in the private sector. He further admonished him that if he did run for office, he should never use that public office for personal gain. Ray respected Mr. Witt's advice and subsequently removed himself from benefitting from the Stephens Family Trust. Ray served one term as state attorney general and then was elected to the U.S. House of Representatives, where he served the fourth congressional district for three terms.

As a congressman, Ray chaired the Subcommittee on Science, Research, and Technology. One significant accomplishment of that committee was the establishment of the Experimental Program to Stimulate Competitive Research (EPSCoR), which helped spread government research grants more evenly among state universities. In his spare time, he headed the Recombinant DNA Advisory Committee. He also served on the House Judiciary Committee, and hand-drafted the original articles of impeachment which ultimately led to the resignation of President Richard Nixon in August of 1974. Throughout his career, beginning with his time in Congress, Ray had a strong history of hiring women and African Americans as top staff members.

Ray left the House in 1978 to run for the U.S. Senate, and after he lost that race, he began to make his mark on higher education in Arkansas. Serving as executive director of the joint Educational Consortium, he helped Ouachita Baptist and Henderson State Universities to share resources to better serve students from the two schools. In 1980, he became president of Arkansas State University in Jonesboro. After the sudden resignation of the president at the

University of Arkansas in 1984, Ray was hired two days later without a national search. At Fayetteville, Ray championed the drive to preserve the oldest campus landmark, Old Main, which now houses the J. William Fulbright College of Arts and Sciences.

After five years as president of the University of Arkansas at Fayetteville, in 1990 Ray made a successful run for the U.S. Congress as the representative for Arkansas' second congressional district, the district where he was born. He served three terms but was disheartened by the partisanship and lack of civility that emerged following the 1994 elections. During his tenure, he was part of a Supreme Court case in 1995 that overturned an Arkansas effort to place term limits on its U.S. senators and representatives. And he again headed the House Subcommittee on Science, Research, and Technology.

Instead of running for Congress again after three terms, Ray announced his bid for a seat on the Arkansas Supreme Court. He drew no opposition, and served one eight-year term, which was completed in 2006. As a justice, Ray engineered an agreement that requires every death penalty case to be reviewed by the Supreme Court. After his retirement from the Supreme Court, Ray was the first Public Service Fellow for the University of Arkansas at Little Rock William H. Bowen School of Law.

About Ray Thornton, his colleague Justice Robert L. Brown says, "No one has been more dedicated to public service than Ray Thornton. Wonderfully committing himself to a legislative career, academics, and finally the Arkansas Supreme Court, he has done as much, if not more, than anyone to mold the future of Arkansas. When I served with him as a justice on the Arkansas Supreme Court, I learned the secret of his success. It was not only his ethic of hard work, but a well-honed sense of fairness and irrepressible good humor."

Ray often mentions a guiding principle in his life: "It's amazing what you can accomplish when you don't care who gets the credit."

Sanford Tollette IV

Father Joseph H. Biltz Award, 2007

First and foremost, Sanford Tollette says his life has been a spiritually enlightened journey.

He graduated with a degree in early childhood education from the University of Arkansas in 1975, moved his family to Little Rock, and reported for his "promised" job at the Little Rock School District. He was despondent when that job fell through, because he had given up an offer to manage a  pizza parlor for $30,000 a year, twice as much income as a beginning teacher. In his desperation to support his family, he took a weekend job as a camp counselor and became a long-term public school substitute. It was within those two experiences that he found his calling.

Sanford had been a scout and grown up in a rural area, but through Aldersgate and Pfeifer Kiwanis Camp, he really learned what outdoor education could accomplish. He was active in the regular camps, the medical camps for children with disabling conditions, the camps for disabled Vietnam vets, and in the first *integrated* camp, which was held under the leadership of Ray Tribble. He attended training across the United States, and recounts being frozen, dunked, bitten, and exhausted during his many camping experiences. With his education major and his minor in elementary science, he soon realized the potential of the "Alternative Camping Experience."

Sanford Tollette serves as executive director of Pfeifer Kiwanis Camp and remembers when Buddy Coleman, on behalf of the Downtown Kiwanis Club, named him director (one of the few African-American camp directors then and now) with a yearly budget of $15,000 and the expectation that he would hold one two-week summer session. Sanford Tollette had a bigger dream.

Sanford was one of the first people to identify "at risk" children—those children who are not in trouble, but who need some extra help to make good choices. He got the attention of the Winthrop Rockefeller Foundation's Bob Nash, and in 1978, the foundation funded the first Alternative Camping Experience for at-risk youth in the nation. From that beginning, Pfeifer Kiwanis Camp has become a model for creating academic and social change in children in the third through sixth grades.

The results are amazing. A student's average grade-level improvement is one half grade level in reading or math in only five weeks, and the parent meeting attendance rate is more than ninety-five percent. Today, in 2007, Pfeifer Camp holds five month-long sessions and serves 500 children each year. Those "at-risk" kids come from sixty-four schools in Little Rock and Pulaski County. They are boys and girls, approximately fifty-five percent African-American, forty-three percent White, and two to three percent Hispanic and Asian.

Sanford and Pfeifer Kiwanis Camp have been recognized, and copied, by the U.S. Dept. of Education, the Honda Corporation, and America's Promise, among others. Sanford is a member of the American Camp Association and the International Association for Experiential Education.

Dr. William H. Townsend

Humanitarian Award, 1994
(July 30, 1914–September 15, 2005)

Black Optometrist Stood Up for Rights

Featured obituary, September 18, 2005
Reprinted with permission from the Arkansas Democrat-Gazette

William H. Townsend, the first black licensed optometrist in Arkansas, opened his clinic in 1950 and provided services to patients for fifty years. Before then, blacks could only go to places where they had to sort through ready-made eyeglasses, trying on pair after pair until they found one they could see with, said his wife of fifty-three years, Billy Gene Townsend.

William Townsend died Thursday at the Arkansas Hospice Inpatient Center at St. Vincent Infirmary Medical Center in Little Rock. He suffered from Alzheimer's disease and various hearth problems. He was ninety-one.

Townsend was the oldest of eleven children and grew up on a farm in Earle. His father was strict and instilled in his children a strong work ethic, something that stuck with Townsend his entire life, his wife said.

Unable to afford college after high school, Townsend enlisted in the U.S. Army and served overseas during World War II. Townsend was wounded by shrapnel in his knee.

"It gave him trouble sometimes," his wife said.

After the war, Townsend received his Bachelor of Science in agriculture from Tuskegee Institute in Alabama. He then studied pre-medicine at Howard University in Washington DC, where he decided to go into optometry.

"He had a college professor who was an optometrist, and he encouraged him to pursue that field," his wife said.

Townsend graduated from Northern Illinois College of Optometry in 1950. That same year, he married Billy Townsend at the Bethel AME, church in North Little Rock and opened the doors of his first clinic on East Ninth Street in Little Rock.

Incorporating with other doctors, Townsend formed Professional Services Inc. in the late 1950s and moved his office to Wright Avenue. Townsend retired in 2000 after fifty years of service.

During the 1960s, Townsend participated in several civil-rights demonstrations, including sit-ins at restaurants that refused to serve blacks.

"They went back every day until they got service," his wife said. "It was very important to him, because at the time our oldest daughter [of three] was in kindergarten. And he wanted all of our children to have freedoms."

In 1972, Townsend was elected to the Arkansas House of Representatives and served District 65 for twenty-four years. He was the first black man to become chairman of the Aging and Legislative Affairs Committee, his wife said.

Townsend often spent his evenings attending meetings in the community to try to see what he could do for people.

"He was proud of the fact that he came from being an underprivileged boy from a rural farm in Earle to being a member of the Arkansas House of Representatives," his wife said. "He was a politician through and through."

After retirement, Townsend dedicated his time to serving in various positions at Mount Zion Baptist Church.

"He enjoyed helping out wherever he could," his wife said.

Townsend stood five feet three inches and liked to wear brown suits and newsboy caps, the flat-topped caps newspaper boys used to wear. He was also known for his tendency to speak to a stranger as if the two were already good friends, his wife said.

"The first words to a stranger were always 'And how is your family,'" his wife said.

Obituary submitted by his family, September 15, 2005

Dr. William H. Townsend, ninety-one, departed this life, September 15, 2005. Preceding him in death was his daughter, Yolanda Gene Townsend. Survivors are: his wife of fifty-three years, Billy Gene Townsend; two daughters, Terezenha Booty (Michael) and LaJuan Julun (Ron); three grandchildren, Akelah Booty, and Darian and Joseph Ronald Van Julun.

Dr. Townsend was born July 30, 1914, in West Point, Mississippi, and grew up in Earle, Arkansas. He was the oldest of eleven children, all of whom preceded him in death. He earned a BS in agriculture from Tuskegee Institute. He served in the U.S. Army during World War II, and was able to study at Nottingham University, England, for nine months during his tour of duty. He attended Howard University for pre-medical studies. He graduated from Northern Illinois College of Optometry in 1950. He was in practice in Little Rock and retired after fifty years.

Dr. Townsend was the first African-American licensed optometrist to practice in Arkansas. He was a member of the Arkansas Optometric Association and a former member of the Board of Directors. In 1981, he was Optometry Doctor of the Year. He and other doctors formed the Professional Service, Inc. He was a member of Mt. Zion Baptist Church, where he served on the Deacon and Trustee Board; Men's Bible Class; and Library Committee.

He was a life member of the NAACP; life member of the Urban League; and former member of the Board of Directors. He was on the Little Rock and the Central Arkansas Board of Health. He was an executive member of the National Conference of Christians and Jews; a member of Pi Lambda Chapter of Alpha Phi Alpha fraternity; and the Arkansas Black Caucus.

During the Central High crisis, he was one of the founding members of the Council of Human Relations, and served as its president. In the 1960s, he was a civil rights activist. The fight for equality and desegregation was aided by the Council on Community Affairs, of which he was a founding member. In 1972, he was elected to the Arkansas House of Representatives, District 65 where he served for twenty-four years, authoring several bills in the Legislature. He served as vice-chairman on the Education Committee and was the first black to chair the Aging and Legislative Affairs.

Henry Tuck

Father Joseph H. Biltz Award, 1987
(*Interview conducted June 18, 2012*)

When Henry Tuck was invited to accept the very first Father Joseph Biltz Award in 1987, he was reluctant. For one thing, he had to ask "What is the NCCJ?" For another, the FBI agent and "card-carrying introvert" was accustomed to keeping a low profile. However, his good friend Mimi Dortch (then president and director of the Arkansas Interfaith Conference, and a later Biltz Award winner, in 1995) persuaded him to accept. And Henry had another reason: he was a friend and great admirer of Father Joe, who had just died earlier that year.

About Father Biltz, Henry says, "Joe Biltz was a thorn in the side of the Arkansas Catholic Bishop at the time, always bringing up some problem that Biltz felt the Diocese should be working on." According to Henry, "Biltz was brilliant. Half the time he was way ahead of the rest of us. His consciousness had been raised by working with migrant Hispanic laborers in California, and we Arkansans were hard-pressed to keep up with him."

Henry entered the FBI almost by accident. His father had been an FBI agent, but he never talked much about his work. During his final year in law school in Fayetteville, Henry was trying to figure out which branch of the military he should join because everyone his age and status was getting sent to Vietnam, and he expected that to be his path, too. When the FBI changed some of its admission requirements, Henry's father suggested that Henry take that route, and Henry thought, "Why not?" After training, Henry's early post was in Detroit working organized crime and monitoring the Black Panthers organization. Henry says they recognized that the Black Panthers were doing a lot of good in the community, but they were also responsible for some "really bad stuff," too. For example, through sources within the Black Panthers, Henry and his partner were able to save the lives of several police officers who were targeted for ambush by the Panthers and other organizations associated with them; this also resulted in the capture of a member of Students for a Democratic Society (SDS) who was among the "top ten most wanted" at that time. When Henry was re-assigned to Little Rock as a legal advisor for the local FBI office, he says they were working cases that would have been ignored in Detroit as minor.

At the age of thirty-two, Henry had what he calls "a conversion experience." After several months of study, he decided that if you were a follower of Jesus, then your responsibility was to do everything you could to help others grow: "When you see a need and a gap in services, then that's the place to work." With that as his guiding principle, Henry was a driving force in establishing several non-profits. He calls himself a "start-up man." Often working through his Catholic Church, Henry helped found all of the following:

> **Our House,** a family housing program that offers long-term assistance including such things as child care and job skills training. Founded in 1987, Our House programs have been replicated in thirty-nine states.

> **We Care,** with a mission to give hope and assistance and promote the empowerment of the poor and disadvantaged in the communities of southeast Pulaski County. We Care continues as a mission of Christ the King Catholic Church and it aims to give the youth of these communities direction, to assist the elderly, and to promote self-sufficiency.

> **Centro Hispano,** an organization built to support Spanish-speaking immigrants with such things as a medical clinic, counseling, job

training, and referrals. Centro Hispano also translated public documents and helped hospitals, public schools, and the State Police to better serve the growing Latino population.

Catherine's House, a center designed to assist young (mostly high school-age) single mothers in earning their GEDs and to provide early childhood programs such as Head Start for their children.

After Henry learned about NCCJ, he later became a board member and served as chair for three years. His biggest accomplishments? He persuaded the board to hire a second staff person and he secured a $50,000 grant from the Wal-Mart Foundation to open an office in Northwest Arkansas.

Henry married his college sweetheart, Ginger Hamner, who died in 2006. They had two children, Carey and Brent, and three grandchildren. In 2009, Henry married former Arkansas Supreme Court justice Annabelle Imber. They spend a lot of their time with grandchildren and traveling.

When you ask Henry how he got started fighting for human rights, he says, "I really don't know why. I just got it." He must have been like the kid who's never been swimming, but who sits on the side of the pool all summer long—and then one day dives in and swims across the pool. The amazing thing about Henry is that he seems to pick the deepest and most dangerous end of the pool to swim across...always carrying a lifeline to those who need it most.

Honorable Jim Guy Tucker
Humanitarian Award, 1978
(*Interview conducted June 29, 2012*)

On November 9, 1989, hearing that the Berlin Wall would be opened, thousands of residents of East and West Berlin began to tear down the wall. Betty and Jim Guy Tucker were in London when they saw what was happening on television. They looked at one another, packed a bag, got on a plane, and flew to Berlin in time to help tear down a portion of the wall. A fellow offered Jim Guy a sledgehammer, which he used for all of fifteen minutes. He said it was very hard work—but then, Jim Guy Tucker has never been afraid of a little hard work.

Jim Guy was the son of James Guy and Willie Maude White Tucker. Both of his parents worked. Jim Guy learned about social security from his father, who was manager of the system in Arkansas. His mother started a small chain of cosmetic studios. She let Jim Guy help her take inventory and do the bookkeeping every night on their dining room table. He considered his childhood idyllic—camping, hiking, and hunting with classmate friends.

Highly motivated even as a youngster, he earned an Eagle Scout rank at the age of twelve and remembers traveling to the National Scout Jamboree in 1956. Starting that same year, he worked as a counselor at Boy Scout Camp Quapaw and as a laborer shoveling gravel for the Pulaski County Road Department. His high school years were marked by the start of integration, including Army troops and then the closings of Hall and Central high schools by the Governor. Despite that disruption, Jim Guy did well. His friend Irving Spitzburg and his two older sisters encouraged him to apply to Harvard. He did, and he entered

Harvard in 1961. He joined a U.S. Marine Corps Reserve officer training program in 1962 while continuing college.

Jim Guy's father was disabled by tuberculosis, and he died in 1964. Therefore, Jim Guy's education presented his mother with a tremendous financial burden. To do his part, Jim Guy worked as a "food man" delivering mostly brown bread and bagels to Radcliffe College dorms in a used car that he bought for less than $100. Despite frequent hospitalizations from developing autoimmune diseases, he took extra courses and graduated a year early, in 1964.

America was at war in Vietnam; John F. Kennedy was president. Reverend Martin Luther King gave his "I Have a Dream" speech, which Jim Guy watched from his summer job at the U.S. Capitol, and America mourned the assassination of President Kennedy. Jim Guy says it was an amazing time to be alive in America. On graduation he went on active duty with the Marines, but the doctors at Quantico ruled his autoimmune condition disqualifying.

Not one to be sidelined, Jim Guy worked his way by cargo ship from San Francisco to Asia. He spent most of 1965 in Vietnam as an accredited freelance war correspondent. He reported for the *Saigon Post* and ABC news. He returned to Vietnam in the summer of 1967 reporting for Arkansas newspapers and radio stations.

In 1968, Jim Guy received his law degree at Fayetteville, began work with the Rose Law Firm, and was one of the founding board members of the ACLU branch in Arkansas.

He was elected as prosecuting attorney of the Sixth Judicial District in 1970 at age twenty-seven. He made his first mark in the political arena by cleaning up a back log of over 1,000 felony cases and helping set up the County Public Defender system. He was then elected to two terms as attorney general of Arkansas. As attorney general, he served as co-chairman of the Arkansas Criminal Code Revision Commission from 1973 to 1975, making the first revision and codification of the state's criminal laws and procedures, and he began aggressive challenges to utility rate increases.

Jim Guy was elected to the U.S. House of Representatives but was then defeated for the U.S. Senate in 1978 in a run-off with David Pryor. He spent the next twelve years as a trial lawyer and partner in the Mitchell Law Firm. In 1990 he was elected Arkansas's lieutenant governor, and then governor.

As governor, Jim Guy led successful fights to create a state trust fund financed by a soft-drink tax to support Medicaid programs in Arkansas, revise school funding, and establish mandatory summer programs for children not achieving at grade level. He tried without success to get a new state constitution and a new roads program. Jim Guy loved the art of governing, but he resigned from office in 1996 after becoming enmeshed in the Whitewater investigation.

While Jim Guy was attorney general, his friend Wayne Cranford introduced him to Betty Allen Alworth. They were married in 1975. Together they have four children—Lance, Kelly, Anna, and Sara—and five grandchildren.

Jim Guy has witnessed first-hand that women can do anything ... beginning with his own family and his mother's cosmetic studios. His sister Frances Tucker Kemp was an Equity stage actress performing in professional theaters across the United States (and frequently at Arkansas Repertory Theatre), and his sister Carol Tucker Foreman was assistant secretary of agriculture during the Carter Administration and later was director of the Consumer Federation of America.

His wife, Betty, formerly a school teacher, earned her law degree in 1982, and they've been developing far-flung businesses ever since. They built and operated cable television systems in Arkansas, Texas, and Florida. They later formed public companies in London and Hong Kong that built cable and Internet systems in England and Indonesia. While living in Hong Kong, they were instrumental in establishing Heifer International–Hong Kong, of which Jim Guy was a founding board member.

Back in Arkansas, Jim Guy is director of a company working with researchers at the University of Arkansas at Fayetteville on development of a new vaccine technology for diseases such as E. coli, salmonella, and avian influenza.

Jim Guy Tucker has made a tremendous impact on lives in Arkansas and around the world. Maybe that's why he got two second chances along the way. He recovered from colon cancer in 1989, and had a liver transplant on Christmas Day 1996. One gets the sense that Jim Guy takes nothing for granted.

Honorable John W. Walker
Father Joseph H. Biltz Award, 2005

Looking back, it is clear that John Walker didn't have much chance of *not* becoming involved in civil rights.

As a youngster growing up in Hope, Arkansas, he learned from his school teacher grandmother, Alfaretta Walker, that he must get an education and he should "stick with things" that he started. She also advised him not to come back to Hope but to look for greater opportunities. Sure enough, he was the first black student to be admitted to the University of Texas in 1954. But when he and the five other black students showed up for school that fall, they were not allowed to enter. The school was not willing to let one of the students play football, so all were denied enrollment. John filed a lawsuit against the University of Texas and entered Arkansas AM&N in the second quarter of that year. He lost that first case, but he has never stopped fighting for equal rights for blacks, women, and anyone else who faces bigotry.

He cites as mentors and teachers such leaders as Dr. Lawrence Davis, Chancellor of AM&N, who encouraged his scholarship and involvement in the larger world. John especially remembers being editor of the campus newspaper and being allowed to write and publish strong editorials that a less-brave chancellor might have censored.

Another important friend was Nat Griswold, director of the Arkansas Council on Human Relations. As assistant director, John said he was afforded his first significant interaction across racial lines. He also learned the necessity of confronting injustice.

John continued his education, earning a masters degree from New York University and a Law degree from Yale Law School. He worked as a lawyer-intern with the NAACP Legal Defense Fund in New York for two years before he returned to Little Rock to establish one of the first racially integrated law firms in the South.

His firm has been responsible for handling a great majority of civil rights litigation in the State of Arkansas since 1965. Seven of his cases have been heard by the U.S. Supreme Court, and his practice has been far ranging and across legal discipline; much of it involves the making of law in the field. The list of companies and organizations John has sued reads like a "who's who" of Arkansas.

John has worked with some of the best and brightest in our nation, including Wiley Branton, Martin Luther King Jr., Whitney Young, and Dorothy Height, and he was even accused of being a Communist by Arkansas Attorney General Bruce Bennett during the Faubus years.

Something we can learn from John is something that he has said himself: "You don't always have to agree with someone to trust them."

We have certainly learned to trust John Walker. We know that he will speak up for the children just as he has for more than forty years now. We know that he will speak truth to power just as he has for more than forty years. We know that he is concerned about who is in prison, who is in special education, and whether or not we are making progress for the poor and disenfranchised.

What John didn't know is that we would all still be working on civil rights in 2005. He said when he left Yale, which he described as a hotbed of activism, he thought we'd have all this civil rights stuff worked out and an end to segregation by the early '70s. We all must join John Walker to create a more just world for our children and for John's own five children and thirteen grandchildren.

Thank goodness for all of us, John really learned from his grandmother to "stick with it."

Honorable Kathy Webb
Humanitarian Award, 2011

Representative Kathy Webb was a sixth-grader at Williams Elementary when she got her first tastes of activism, negotiation, compromise, and victory. Told by her teacher that a girl couldn't be the safety patrol officer for her class, she asked to petition the principal to change the "boys only" rule. Accompanied by her teacher, she pled her case, and the principal decided that she could serve as the first female fire marshal for her class. That was just the first of many "firsts" in Kathy's life.

Kathy and her two older siblings had passionate parents; her father was a United Methodist Minister, and her stay-at-home mother, Kathy jokes, would begin bedtime stories with, "Once upon a time there was a man named Franklin Delano Roosevelt." Her parents' encouragement helped forge Kathy into an agent for change, but she became truly galvanized during her college years in the late '60s at Randolph-Macon Woman's College in Lynchburg, Virginia. She admits that she wasn't much of a scholar at Randolph-Macon because while others were in the library, she was making trips to nearby Washington DC to take part in anti-war and civil rights activities. She along with African-American classmates integrated a Lynchburg restaurant in 1968, and as junior class president, she led the seniors into the hall for graduation ceremonies with a black arm band prominent on her white robe.

After college, Kathy returned to Little Rock and got involved with the National Organization for Women (NOW), establishing the Little Rock chapter and serving as its first president. In 1980, she helped to establish Arkansas Gay Rights, the state's first activist group for gay and lesbian rights. Having always felt embraced by her faith community, she helped to establish two gay-friendly churches in Central Arkansas so that all people might feel similarly accepted and supported. In 1982 she was elected national NOW secretary, breaking a powerful slate, another first. While based in Washington DC, her responsibilities included nationwide leadership and chapter development. She was in San Francisco when Geraldine Ferraro accepted the nomination for vice president on the Mondale ticket. At that moment, Kathy thought, "I can be anything I want to be."

After six years with NOW, Kathy joined the corporate world as the first woman to serve as a regional store manager for the largest Domino's Pizza franchisee. She was also the first woman named National Store Manager of the Year out of 6,500 stores. She moved to Chicago as a Regional Vice President with Bruegger's Bagels, but never abandoning her passion for civic engagement, helped establish the Gay and Lesbian Chamber of Commerce and started a Susan G. Komen Affiliate in Chicago, serving as president for three years and organizing the city's inaugural Race for the Cure.

Kathy returned to Little Rock in 2002. She and Nancy Tesmer opened the restaurant Lilly's Dim Sum, Then Some and immediately got involved in the community, most notably in the area of hunger relief. Rice Depot is one recipient of Kathy's talent and commitment. She has developed two popular rice mixes for the Depot: Lilly's Fried Rice, which she created to honor the memory of her mother, and Presidential Rice, to commemorate the opening of the Clinton Presidential Center. Kathy serves on the board of Arkansas Foodbank Network and supports animal-rescue organizations Central Arkansas Rescue Effort for Arkansas (CARE for Animals) and Feline Rescue and Rehome (FuRR). At a recent birthday party for Kathy, guests brought over 2,000 pounds of pet food to be donated to these organizations. Kathy also helped organize a local chapter of the Stonewall Democrats, and it was in the political arena that Kathy soon saw new opportunities to effect positive change. When the Arkansas House seat in her district became open due to term limits, she pulled together a talented campaign team, took fifty-seven percent of the vote in a Democratic primary against three highly qualified candidates, and was elected to the Arkansas House of Representatives in 2006. She is presently serving her third term in the House.

She well remembers those sixth-grade lessons, and she has accomplished a lot for Arkansans. Two of the things she's most proud of are chairing the Task Force on Global Warming, which yielded legislation such as the Energy Conservation Act for State Owned Buildings and Higher Education; and the Legislative Hunger Caucus, which has raised awareness about hunger and effected positive policy change. One awareness initiative, the Food Stamp Challenge (to live off of $3 a day for three days), has been replicated in several other states.

She's as committed as ever this session to positive outcomes for Arkansans, and she's still racking up those firsts: first openly gay elected official in Arkansas, first woman in the history of Arkansas to chair the joint Budget Committee. It makes you wonder what "first" will be next on Kathy Webb's list.

Dr. Josetta Edwards Wilkins
Humanitarian Award, 2001

Dr. Josetta E. Wilkins's leadership serves as an inspiration to all of us who wish to make a difference for ourselves, our families, our neighbors, our communities, and our state. She served four terms in the Arkansas House of Representatives, and now serves on several state commissions and local and state committees.

Dr. Wilkins was the author and lead sponsor of legislation that created the Martin Luther King Jr. Commission in 1993, and of the life-saving legislation that became the Arkansas Breast Cancer Act of 1997, among many others.

Dr. Wilkins graduated with a bachelor's degree from Arkansas AM&N, earned her master's degree from the University of Arkansas, and after her youngest of five children graduated from high school, she earned her doctorate in higher education administration, counseling and adult education from Oklahoma State University.

Josetta Wilkins has been honored with several awards named for her. Among them are the Josetta Wilkins Courage Award, given annually by the Martin Luther King Jr. Commission, and the Josetta Wilkins Award for outstanding contributions in the area of breast cancer awareness given by the Arkansas Breast Cancer Control Advisory Board.

Josetta was married to the late State Representative Henry Wilkins III. In addition to her five children, she has seventeen grandchildren. Josetta is a tireless worker, and just two of her recent volunteer involvements are teaching third through fifth graders "How a bill becomes a law" and leadership in Bosom Buddies, a support group for breast cancer survivors in Pine Bluff.

Grainger Williams
Father Joseph H. Biltz Award, 1999
(*Interview conducted August 7, 2012*)

The Grainger Williams family had a birthday celebration in late July, 2012. Grainger
turned 101 years old on July 23, and his
wife, Frances Bulwinkle Williams turned
100 three days later on July 26. At this stage,
neither Grainger nor Frances gets out any-
more, and they don't have many visitors.
However, their children, Ann Williams
Wedaman and Alfred L. Williams, arranged
for me to have a short visit with them. When we were introduced,
Grainger said, "I think I know you." I responded, "I know you because
you are famous." "Oh, really?" he responded with a great big grin.

There is certainly a lot for Grainger Williams to remember about
his long, eventful life. If you ask him a question, you can hear him sifting
through the memories as he begins with the name of a street, trying to
place that memory somewhere in space and time. Although he can't always catch that memory, he is still just as affable and charming as he has
always been. Maybe that's how he got so much done throughout his
many years of service.

Grainger was born in Little Rock, attended public schools, and
then Little Rock Junior College (now the University of Arkansas at Little
Rock). He graduated cum laude from Davidson College in North
Carolina in 1933. You might say that he "married well" when he persuaded Frances McKean Bulwinkle of Gastonia, North Carolina, to be
his bride in 1939. Frances was the daughter of Bessie Lewis Bulwinkle
and the Honorable Alfred Lee Bulwinkle, a U.S. Congressman from
North Carolina from 1921 to 1929 and from 1931 to 1950. Frances and
Grainger had children Ann and Alfred, and they also raised three nieces

and a nephew, Brownie Williams Ledbetter, E. Grainger (Bish) Williams II, June Hoes Williams, and Quendrid (Quendy) Williams Veatch, after both of their parents had died.

Grainger and Frances were outstanding for many reasons, not the least of which was that they raised such fine children. Emblematic of their leadership is what they did to help heal our community during the late 1950s, when we were torn apart by the world-renowned 1957 crisis at Central High School.

The story of how Governor Orval Faubus manipulated the fears of Arkansans regarding school integration for his political purposes has been widely reported. At that time, even progressives were often intimidated by the tension that pervaded not only Little Rock but all of Arkansas. The 101st Airborne Division may have dispersed the angry crowds from around Central High School during 1957, but the fear and uncertainty in the community remained. After Faubus closed the schools during the 1958-59 school year, everyone began to realize what damage this crisis was doing to our state's economy and reputation, and the toll it was taking on our residents. Among those who stood up were Grainger and Frances Williams.

Frances had been an active member of the Women's Emergency Committee to Open Our Schools. The WEC met in secret so that their husbands wouldn't lose their jobs, and much of their work was behind the scenes. Grainger supported Frances's involvement in the WEC and says, "We wouldn't have gotten a thing done if it hadn't been for the women, because I think the women were a force to get the men to look at some things they didn't want to look at. I think they really played a role in it."

Grainger was to become president of the Chamber of Commerce in December of 1958. According to Sara Murphy's book *Breaking the Silence*, "Those who preceded him as president had been heads of Southwestern Bell Telephone Company and the Arkansas Power & Light Company and because of their positions did not dare oppose the governor." (Grainger was vice president of the Williams & Rosen Insurance

Agency.) Aided and abetted by Frances, Grainger took the opportunity of his president's address at the annual chamber banquet to make a point. His remarks had been written by the chamber staff, but the night before, he and Frances decided to insert the following:

> I cannot keep faith with myself...as your newly elected president, without a frank statement to you, and a plea in the interest of public education...
>
> It is neither my purpose nor desire to discuss any of the political or sociological aspects of our school situation—nor do I have any solution to offer. But it is my feeling that the time has come to evaluate the cost of public education—and the cost of the lack of public education.
>
> I would urge that no matter what our personal feelings might be—each of us encourage the reestablishment of all areas of communication....To achieve this climate of communication would be one of the greatest contributions we could make, and to that end I am dedicated.

The chamber audience was at first deathly quiet. Grainger had mentioned the unmentionable. After a few seconds, they broke into loud applause, and Grainger was both surprised and pleased. He later said, "It was something I had to do regardless," according to Sara Murphy. Chamber members were still hesitant and willing to go only so far as allies of the WEC. However, in February of 1959, the majority of members voted in favor of reopening the schools with limited, controlled integration. According to Murphy, "The chamber executive board, acting on the strength of the poll, recommended that the schools be opened, using a pupil placement plan, and that there continue to be private, segregated schools."

Grainger and Frances Williams's values of seeking understanding and reconciliation obviously made a lasting impression on their children. Their daughter Ann Williams (Wedaman) was a student at Central during 1957, and she was one of very few students remembered by Elizabeth Eckford, one of the Little Rock Nine, as being friendly. And their niece Brownie Williams Ledbetter was recognized with the Father Joseph Biltz Award in 1991 for her many contributions to the community.*

The City of Little Rock will forever be indebted to the leadership of brave individuals like Grainger and Frances Williams, who stood up for what they believed. Their son, Alfred, tells the story that early in the history of the NCCJ Annual Dinner, Grainger was invited to accept the Humanitarian Award, but he turned it down, saying, "A person shouldn't be recognized for simply doing what is right to do."

*The only other "father-child" pair on our honoree list is Grif Stockley, Biltz Award 2011, whose daughter Erin was recognized as part of the "Accept No Boundaries Founders, Little Rock Central High School" in 1990.

Townsend Wolfe
Humanitarian Award, 1998
(Interview with Brooks Wolfe, August 23, 2012)

Although naturally shy, Townsend Wolfe's personality will fill any room that he enters. The only thing more vibrant than his personality is his love of art and his understanding of the power of art in our lives.

Townsend Wolfe received twenty awards for painting between 1958 and 1968, so he likely could have made his living as an artist. Instead, he chose to share his love of art with others. As director and chief curator of the Arkansas Arts Center from 1968 to 2002, Townsend accomplished what every leader dreams of: achieving phenomenal growth at the Arts Center, both in the facility and in the collection and programming; establishing a firm financial base; and developing a committed board of trustees. Townsend left his personal mark on the museum through acquisition of the AAC's nationally recognized holdings of twentieth-century drawings and sixteenth–twentieth-century European drawings.

When he was interviewed for the Arts Center position in 1968, Little Rock real estate man Billy Rector asked him what made him think that he would succeed. Townsend replied, "I'm too young to fail." At the time, the board was running a deficit of $400,000 to $700,000 a year, and Jeannette and Governor Winthrop Rockefeller were making up the difference. Five years into his tenure and following Winthrop Rockefeller's death, Townsend turned down a million-dollar gift from Winthrop Rockefeller's trust (a move he characterized as youthful exuberance) to begin weaning the AAC off the life support of Rockefeller money. He proposed instead to raise $500,000 from the people of Arkansas if the trust would match that three-to-one. They agreed, and the Arts Center would finally become the property of Arkansans.

The significant accomplishments during Townsend's thirty-four years at the AAC are remarkable by any standard: annual attendance at exhibits rose from 80,000 to 393,000; an operating budget growth from $384, 000 to almost $4.5 million; foundation endowment growth from $37,000 to $21 million; collection appraisal growth from $313,000 to more than $35 million. In addition, the exhibit spaces and other areas were greatly expanded, the Decorative Arts Museum was opened in the nearby Pike-Fletcher-Terry Mansion, and the theater was restructured as a Children's Theatre in 1974, modeled after the Children's Theatre Company of Minneapolis. But above all, Townsend Wolfe taught us how to appreciate art.

Former AAC board member Curtis Finch says that because of Townsend, he has amassed a fine collection of drawings of self-portraits and faces, including works by many Hungarian artists. "Wolfe gave me confidence, made me comfortable. I have no problem going in any gallery in the United States and asking to see what they've got in the way of drawings. He has given me the ability to buy what I like." Warren Stephens, also a benefactor of the Arts Center, says, "I doubt I would have nearly the interest (in art) if it were not for Townsend. If you had told me twenty years ago that I'd be as involved in the Arts Center and the arts as I am, I don't think I would have believed you." And judging by a typical Townsend Wolfe schedule, he has often shared his understanding and love of art. During 1971, for example, he made presentations to groups as disparate as the Little Rock Rotary, the Central District Dental Auxiliary, Little Rock Model Cities, Junior League of Little Rock, Arkansas Federation of Garden Clubs, Little Rock Community Concert, Little Rock Women's Chamber of Commerce, Little Rock Second Church of Christ, Arkansas State University, Arkansas State Chamber of Commerce, and the Governor's Conference on Leisure Time.

According to those who worked most closely with him, Townsend's strengths are: "He's honest. He's got a great eye. He's decisive, confident. He knows what he wants. And he works like a dog." Those qualities have built an Arts Center of which we can all be proud. However, our Arkansas Arts Center is known beyond Arkansas, too. Will Barnet, who at the age of 100 was awarded the 2011 National Medal of Arts by President Barack Obama, said this about Townsend in 2001: "Townsend is unique in today's museum world. He has his own ideas, he doesn't go by trends, but what he believes in and feels is important. And therefore his collection is perhaps the most encompassing of American art, with various views and statements. It's remarkable, because so many museums are not that way."

By all accounts, Townsend could explain every line of the multi-million dollar Arts Center budget and was a stern taskmaster with his staff. But he also knew how to have fun. In conjunction with a 1996 ex-hibition of photographs by William Wegman, well-known for his Weimaraner dogs, Townsend dreamed up a contest called The Great Arkansas Dog Hunt. More than 500 photographs were entered, includ-ing a photo of Townsend's own pet, a miniature dappled dachshund. He then hosted a Sunday afternoon reception for people—along with their dogs—who had submitted photos. More than a thousand people and their dogs attended.

At the party that AAC trustees held for Townsend upon his retire-ment in 2002 from the Arts Center, he said, "You have treated me as family, as a sibling, as an infant, as an adult, as a leader, and most of all a friend and an Arkansan. You have given me a spirit, a liberty, to do what I believe in—the arts. There is important art in this city and state. I will protect it until my grave. I thank you with all my heart."

Since his retirement, Townsend has continued to curate exhibits, write essays, and install collections for public spaces. Most recently, in 2011, he and his wife, Brooks, curated and installed the permanent ex-hibit for the 66,000 square feet in the new Donald W. Reynolds Health

Science Building on the Arkansas State University campus in Jonesboro. Townsend and Brooks were delighted that almost sixty percent of the artists represented in the collection are from Arkansas.

In summing up Townsend's impact on Arkansas and its people, Brooks explains his influence this way: "Good art grows your soul. It transforms you—much like religion. Townsend brought good art to the people of Arkansas. He transformed Arkansas! He transformed me! It's been one hell of a ride!"

Edward L. Wright Sr.

Humanitarian Award, 1969
(July 16, 1903–February 1, 1977)

One of Most Honored Lawyers In State, Ex-head of ABA, Dies
February 2, 1977, Arkansas Democrat
Reprinted with permission from the Arkansas Democrat-Gazette

Edward Ledwidge Wright Sr., aged seventy-three, of 5011 Hawthorne Road, one of Arkansas's best known and most honored lawyers, collapsed and died about 12:30 p.m. Tuesday at the offices of Wright, Lindsey & Jennings, the Little Rock law firm of which he was the senior partner.

Mr. Wright reached the pinnacle of his profession in August 1970 when, without opposition, he became president of the American Bar Association, in whose councils and committees he had been active for forty-five years. He also was a prominent Roman Catholic layman, having been invested as a Knight of Malta by Pope Paul VI in 1965, the only Arkansan ever to be so honored. He had played a significant role in the state's political life, and his counsel was sought by at least two presidents. Colleagues had once urged his appointment to the U.S. Supreme Court.

Mr. Wright had spent Tuesday morning appearing before a legislative committee on behalf of the Catholic Diocese of Little Rock, with representatives of other denominations, in opposition to a bill to tax certain revenue-producing church-owned property.

In 1971, while attending a meeting of the American Bar Association at London, he was stricken with a serious kidney ailment, but after two years of intensive treatment had overcome the disease and had regained relatively good health, putting in his usual seven-day work week.

Mr. Wright was born July 16, 1903, at Little Rock, the son of B. B. Wright and Mrs. Kate Ledwidge Wright. He took an undergraduate degree at Little Rock College and his law degree at Georgetown University at Washington DC. He was admitted to the bar in 1925. He served in numerous capacities in the American Bar Association before assuming the presidency. He was elected to the ABA House of Delegates in 1946 and became the first Arkansan to be elected chairman of the House, a position he held from 1962 to 1964. He was only the second Arkansan to head the ABA, the first being U. M. Rose in 1901-1902.

In 1964, he became chairman of an ABA Special Committee on Evaluation of Ethical Standards, which under his leadership prepared a new Code of Professional Responsibility to replace the Canons of Professional Ethics that had been adopted in 1908. Most states since have adopted the new Code.

State Bar Head

Mr. Wright was president of the Pulaski County Bar Association in 1948 and as president of the Arkansas Bar Association in 1957. From 1938 to 1941, he was chairman of the Arkansas Board of Law Examiners and in 1948 he helped to draft the Arkansas Probate Code.

Among other professional activities, Mr. Wright was Arkansas' representative in the National Conference of Commissioners on Uniform State Laws from 1945 to 1957; a member of the Second Hoover Commission Legal Task Force in 1954-55; a trustee of the Southwestern Legal Foundation at Dallas; president of the American College of Trial Lawyers in 1965-66, a fellow of the American Bar Foundation and American College of Probate Lawyers; and a member of the American Judicature Society, the American Law Institute, the International Association of Insurance Counsel and the International Academy of Trial Lawyers, whose membership is limited to 500 trial lawyers. The Law Society of Britain made him an honorary life member in 1971, at the conclusion of his term as ABA president, the ninth person to be so honored by British lawyers' association in 150 years. He also was made a bencher of Middle Temple, one of the ancient Inns of Court in England.

In 1963, Mr. Wright was one of some 244 lawyers called to the White House to discuss civil rights problems with then-President John F. Kennedy. The following year he was a member of the National Lawyers Committee for President Lyndon B. Johnson and Vice President Hubert H. Humphrey.

In the mid-1960s, after the assassination of President Kennedy, Mr. Wright was appointed by the ABA to serve on a committee that prepared an amendment to the U.S. Constitution to make explicit the line of succession to the presidency, an amendment that was ratified by the states.

Mr. Wright received an honorary doctor of laws degree from the University of Scranton (Pennsylvania) and Georgetown University, whose Student Bar Association also presented him a distinguished alumni award. In 1963, Mr. Wright was an alternate delegate to the First World Conference on World Peace Through Law at Athens, Greece, and was a delegate to the Union International Des Avocats at Bonn, Germany and the International Bar Association's biennial meeting at Mexico City, both in 1964.

The Arkansas Bar Association presented Mr. Wright its "Outstanding Lawyer" award in 1963, and the Southwestern Legal Foundation two years later gave him the Hatton W. Sumners Award for contributions to the improvement of the administration of justice and preservation of democratic form of government. The Arkansas Chapter of the National Conference of Christians and Jews, of which Mr. Wright was the Catholic co-chairman in 1965, honored him with its Brotherhood award in 1969.

In 1975, Mr. Wright was elected president of the state Constitutional Convention that later was aborted by a state Supreme Court ruling. A year earlier he had been chairman of the inauguration committee for incoming Governor Pryor.

Urged for Court

When two vacancies occurred on the U.S. Supreme Court in 1971, then-President Richard M. Nixon was urged by the Arkansas Bar Association and numerous individuals to name Mr. Wright to the Court.

Mr. Wright held several directorships, including those of Arkansas Blue Cross–Blue Shield, Worthen Bank and Trust Company, Pulaski Federal Savings and Loan Association, and Winburn Tile and Manufacturing Company. He also was a former trustee of Little Rock University, forerunner of the University of Arkansas at Little Rock.

Survivors are his wife, Mrs. Rosemary Tuohey Wright; a son, Edward L. Wright Jr., a member of his father's law firm; three daughters, Mrs. Philip S. Anderson and Mrs. James H. Atkins of Little Rock and Mrs. Bridget W. Warner of Albuquerque, New Mexico; and eight grandchildren.

Appendix

Bomb Threat Breaks Up Dinner
as Grundfest Accepts Amity Award

(*Printed Tuesday, April 6, 1965, in the* Arkansas Gazette)
Reprinted with permission from the Arkansas Democrat-Gazette

An anonymous bomb threat abruptly ended a National Conference of Christians and Jews dinner at the auditorium Monday night in the middle of an acceptance speech by Dave Grundfest Sr., the recipient of the 1965 Brotherhood Award.

The police said that a woman called police headquarters about 8:10 p.m. saying that a bomb would go off in about a half hour at the auditorium where more than 1,000 persons, including Governor Faubus and Senator John O. Pastore (Democrat, Rhode Island) were attending the second Brotherhood Citation Dinner of the NCCJ's Arkansas Region. No bomb was found.

E. Grainger Williams, the dinner chairman, interrupted Grundfest's talk to announce the bomb threat and said that the building had to be cleared. Williams and other NCCJ officials had just finished talking with police and firemen at the side of the speaker's rostrum.

Evacuation was orderly, and after the dinner guests had cleared the large downstairs room, police and firemen searched the building.

This was Little Rock's second bomb threat within three days. A memorial service for Mrs. Viola Liuzzo and others killed during the civil rights drive in Alabama at St. Andrew's Catholic Cathedral Saturday was delayed by similar calls to police headquarters and the Cathedral rectory.

Happily, the Monday meeting was about coming to its conclusion when Williams made his announcement about 8:35 p.m. Police said later it took time to line up the officers to patrol the building and confer with auditorium personnel and Conference officials about evacuating the building.

Channel 7 started a telecast of the program at 8 p.m. and it was to have ended at 9 p.m. The station said that it stopped the broadcast after Williams made his announcement and joined the network but that its cameramen stayed in the balcony and shot films of the search.

The threat ended the meeting of many of the city's most prominent citizens and their wives at which all of the speakers had spoken of the need of tolerance and justice in a misshapen world and Grundfest, president of Sterling Stores, Inc., had received the award for his contributions to the growth of good human relations.

Grundfest had just finished mentioning the need for such organizations as the NCCJ to fill a void "in a world torn asunder—the Congo, Vietnam, or you don't have to go that far—there's the Bronx and Selma, Alabama." He had said he was happy to be part of an organization which works "to make a better way of life for all people, all creeds and all colors."

He had been given the award by Dr. Marshall T. Steel, the president of Hendrix College.

Earlier, Senator Pastore had said that he was somewhat surprised, a little confused and curious why "a liberal Yankee from up North" would be asked to speak in Arkansas but, he said, he decided it would be good to exchange ideas "in the hope that out of this meeting we can better come to know each other."

The world is in turmoil, he said, and all the depressed people are looking to the United States for help. "We have it in our power to guide the destiny of civilization. It may be inadvertent but the responsibility is ours and we must accept it," he said.

The people are looking for an example and that example is morality in our time, he said. There can be no rationality or sanity, he said, unless everyone is directed by the concept and spirit of brotherly love and that it makes no difference in the sight of God whether a man is Catholic, Protestant or Jew or whether the color of his skin is black or white.

"The eternal law is the same, 'Love thy neighbor as thyself.'" He declared.

"We came together to break bread, rub elbows, and look each other in the eye with respect and regard for each other, and that is the America I love," he said.

Pastore said he had been asked to come to Arkansas by Governor Faubus, Senators John L. McClellan and J. William Fulbright, and Representatives Wilbur D. Mills and Oren Harris.

He was introduced by former representative Brooks Hays, now a consultant to President Johnson, who served with the Catholic senator and leading Democrat at the 10th session of the United Nations.

Bob McGrath, a singer with the Mitch Miller television show, sang, and the invocation was given by Rabbi Elijah E. Palnick of Temple B'nai Israel.

All that remained on the program after Grundfest's response were some closing comments and the benediction by Bishop Albert L. Fletcher of the Diocese of Little Rock.

The Speech the Bomb Threat Delayed

During the second National Conference of Christians and Jews Brotherhood Dinner, in 1965, the police received a bomb threat and all the guests were evacuated from the building just as Dave Grundfest Sr. began his speech to accept the Humanitarian Award. Grundfest later went to a local studio and recorded his speech, naming the record "The Speech the Bomb Threat Delayed," and distributed copies of it to those to whom he wanted to thank for the honor bestowed upon him. Following is a transcription of that recording:

Let me say at the outset to those of you who came because of your friendship and devotion to me, I am and shall be eternally grateful. And to those of you who came because of your friendship and tremendous interest in the work of the National Conference of Christians and Jews, I am equally grateful. For here is an organization filling a void that long needed to be filled in America. With the world torn asunder, whether it be Vietnam, Turkey, the Congo, the Bronx, or Selma, Alabama. With literally thousands of people throughout the world each day being trained in the art of destruction, I, for one, am pleased and happy to be a part of an organization dedicated to building a better way of life in America for all people, all creed, all religion, all color.

Now I mentioned earlier that this is a beautiful thing, and it really is. And if one is inclined to be emotional, and I am, and if one is inclined to be sentimental, and I am, then I am sure that you can understand that it is with a great deal of difficulty that I stand before you outwardly composed, and I hope I do. For deep down within me just now, there are being shed warm tears of gratitude to all of you for your thoughtfulness. I guess I've written a half a dozen speeches for this evening. Each one better than the other, but none I felt justified the occasion. And certainly anything I might have to say following Senator Pastore's magnificent address would go for naught.

Hence I thought I'd just tell you a couple of stories that I think are pretty cute. One has to do with a dinner something akin to this, that several of my good friends and I gave for a very deserving citizen, a great Arkansan, Mr. Hamilton Moses. It was a beautiful dinner and he was tremendously impressed as I am this evening. And then about two months later it was my good fortune to be the master of ceremonies at a dinner where Mr. Moses was the principle speaker. And with his permission then, and I'm sure I have his permission now, I told this story. I told the audience about this beautiful dinner, about 600 of his friends from all over that state being present. And then following the dinner he was riding home with his wife sitting on the back seat of the car. And Mr. Moses was in deep thought. And she said to him, "Ham, why are you so pensive?" And he said, "Honey, I was just thinking. Do you realize how few, how very few great men there are in the state of Arkansas?" Without a moment's hesitation, she came right back and said, "Ham, I've never given it much thought. But I'll tell you this: there's one less than you think there is."

Now I tell you that story for a particular reason. The reason being that I promise you despite this beautiful dinner that you have here tonight in my honor, that come another day, I will never let myself get into the frame of mind, so that little ol' Maureen Grundfest can say to me that there is one less great Arkansan than I think there is.

As this is the most beautiful tribute ever paid me as a citizen of Arkansas, let me tell you about the most beautiful compliment ever paid me as a businessman. It came from a little four-year-old girl in the small town of Lonoke, Arkansas. And when I heard about it, I wrote the child's mother, and in subsequent correspondence, she wrote me. She said: Mr. Grundfest, we are Baptist, and my little four-year-old girl had just joined the church. And she was tremendously imbued and impressed with the spirit of heaven as it was told to her by her preacher, her Sunday School teacher, and her parents. And with this fresh in her little mind, her mother went to town one day and took her into Sterling

Store where her mother wanted to do a little shopping. And as her
mother went over to the notion counter to buy some needles and pins,
and buttons and bows, the little child wandered over to the toy department. And there she saw all the beautiful toys made, packaged, and designed to appeal to little girls. And with this fresh in her little mind, the
spirit of heaven, she stood there longing for each one of them. She called
her mother and said, "Momma." And her mother didn't hear her. And
in a loud voice, she called, "Momma!" And her mother said, "What is
it, honey?" And the child said, "Momma, will there be a Sterling Store
in Heaven?" Now if I live to be a thousand years old, I never expect to
have a more beautiful compliment paid me as a businessman.

Senator Pastore, sir, many of us have known for a long time that
you are a great American and a great statesman. But your coming to be
with us this evening, leaving your busy schedule in Washington, gives further evidence of your tremendous interest in human values. Your message
was fraught with tremendous interest. It did not fall on deaf ears. We are
richer because you came. On behalf of the people of my town, and my
state, as well as those connected with the National Conference of
Christians and Jews, I thank you sir. I thank you very much.

Governor Faubus, it's always a joy for me to sit on any dais with
you and Mrs. Faubus. I know of your interest in the work of the National
Conference. You know my friendship. You've dignified our meeting with
your presence, and I'm grateful for your being with us.

Marshall Steele, Dr. Marshall Steele, dear, sweet friend, president
of Hendrix College. You sir, being an ordained minister of God, could
not have stood before this beautiful audience and said all the nice things
you said about me unless you felt, at least, some of them were true. You
made my family and me very happy. You know of my friendship to you
and my tremendous interest and devotion to your school.

Bob Lowery, Jim Penick, Ed Wright, Bill Pharr, you, who I think
were, in the main, responsible for my being honored this evening, I
thank you. I don't know that your judgment was good. I don't know but

that you made a mistake. But if you made a mistake, I'm glad you did. I shall always be indebted to you for your thoughtfulness.

Bob McGrath, I think it would be a bit trite for me to say to you that you have a beautiful voice. You've added a great deal to our meeting. The ovation you received tells better than I how grateful we are for your company and how much we enjoyed your songs. Please take back to our mutual friend Mitch Miller our thanks, our greetings, and our good wishes.

Grainger Williams, Mr. Chairman, Mr. Toastmaster, having trod your path just one short year ago when we paid tribute in a dinner just like this for a truly great Arkansan and a great American, Brooks Hays, no one knows better than I, the tremendous amount of effort, and time-consuming hours it takes to bring into being a dinner of this sort. And to you and your whole committee, I offer my thanks. My thanks to the press, the radio, the TV, and all people who helped to bring into being this delightful evening.

It's pretty hard to thank everybody without being a complete bore, and if I've overlooked anyone, and I'm sure I have, please be understanding. Please be sympathetic, and please know of my gratitude.

And now my friends, I'm going to tell you about thirty years ago when it was my good fortune to meet and to know a great American. He started in life in the work of the YMCA. He was secretary of the Y in Tulsa for many years, and then came over to the National Conference, and served as the southwest regional director with headquarters in Dallas. Upon his retirement, he went with my good friend, the president of Southern Methodist Univeristy, and he has made a terrific contribution to the welfare of that college. I'm sure you know that I'm talking about Hastings Harrison. If ever it was my pleasure to know a man entitled to wear the mantle of a true Christian gentleman, Hastings Harrison is that man. Hastings, I wonder if you would honor me by standing and sharing the spotlight with me for just one brief moment. Hastings Harrison, ladies and gentlemen, from Dallas, Texas.

At the expense of reiteration, let me say again to those of you who came because of your friendship and devotion to me, I am and shall be eternally grateful. And to those of you who came because of your friendship and tremendous interest in the work of the conference, I'm equally grateful. It is my fervent prayer for each of you that your years will be many and bountiful. And as you go through life from day to day, henceforth, the good Lord will continue to hold you by your hand. My special thanks to my many friends from out of the state who came to be with us this evening.

A thousand thanks to a thousand friends. This is a beautiful thing.

JCA's Humanitarian Dinner

The National Humanitarian Award is granted each year to provide pub-lic recognition and honor to civic leaders for meritorious achievements in building community and advancing opportunity for the common good. By focusing each year on outstanding citizens, JCA not only draws attention to the good works of the honorees but seeks as well to stimulate others to similar achievements which will strengthen and deepen what President Abraham Lincoln called "the better angels of our nature." That is why in 1964, JCA choose the Humanitarian Dinner as a fitting way to raise money to support our mission.

1964
Honoree: Honorable Brooks Hays
Dinner Chair: Dave Grundfest Sr.
NCCJ Chair: Robert. D. Lowry
Speaker: Eugene McCarthy, U.S. Senator

1965
Honoree: Dave Grundfest Sr.
Dinner Chair: E. Grainger Williams
NCCJ Chair: Steele Hays
Speaker: John Pastore, U.S. Senator

1966
Honoree: Most Rev. Albert Fletcher
Dinner Chair: Frank Whitbeck
NCCJ Chair: Henry E. Spitzberg
Speaker: Ray Lindley, University of Americas

1967
Honorees: Hon. and Mrs. Winthrop Rockefeller
Dinner Chair: B. Finley Vinson
NCCJ Chair: John A. Healey
Speaker: John Charles Daly

1968
Honoree: Dr. Ira Sanders
Dinner Chair: Frank Lyon Sr.
NCCJ Chair: Richard Butler Sr.
Speaker: William Gossett, GM President

1969
Honoree: Edward Wright Sr.
Dinner Chair: A. Allen Weintraub
NCCJ Chair: James Binder
Speaker: Thomas Paine, NASA Director

1970
Honoree: Dr. Lawrence Davis
Dinner Chair: Sidney McMath
NCCJ Chair: Phillip Carroll
Speaker: Mrs. Lenore Romney

1971
Honorees: J. N. Heiskell and Mrs. David D. Terry
Dinner Chair: Hon.Wilbur Mills
NCCJ Chair: Herbert McAdams
Speaker: John Volpe, Transportation Secretary

1972
Honoree: Hon. Wilbur D. Mills
Dinner Chair: William L. "Sonny" Walker
NCCJ Chair: Alan Patteson Jr.
Speaker: Edward Kennedy, U.S. Senator

1973
Honoree: James H. Penick
Dinner Chair: Hon. Dale Bumpers
NCCJ Chair: Margaret Kolb
Speaker: Simcha Dinitz, Israeli Ambassador

1974
Honorees: Hon. and Mrs. Dale Bumpers
Dinner Chair: Phillip Back
NCCJ Chair: Philip Parker
Speaker: Howard Baker, U.S. Senator

1975
Honorees: Frank Lyon Sr. and Msgr. James O'Connell
Dinner Chair: Edward M. Penick
NCCJ Chair: Philip Parker
Speaker: Richard Gerstenberg, GM Chairman

1976
Honorees: Annie Mae Bankhead, Dr. Dale Cowling, Raymond Rebsamen,
     Henry E. Spitzberg
Dinner Chair: William H. Bowen
NCCJ Chair: Steele Hays
Speaker: Elliot Richardson, Commerce Secretary

1977
Honoree: Margaret Kolb
Dinner Chair: Hon. Bill Walmsley
NCCJ Chair: Walter Davidson
Speaker: Hubert H. Humphrey, U.S. Senator

1978
Honorees: Rev. and Mrs. Richard Hardie
Dinner Chair: Sheffield Nelson
NCCJ Chair: Walter Davidson
Speaker: Dale Bumpers, U.S. Senator

1979
Honoree: Fred K. Darragh Jr.
Dinner Chair: Hon. Bill Clinton
NCCJ Chair: Arnold Mayersohn
Speaker: Gary Hart, U.S. Senator

1980
Honoree: Ben N. Saltzman, MD
Dinner Chair: Louis L. Ramsay Jr.
NCCJ Chair: Terence Renaud
Speaker: Andy Rooney, CBS News

1981
Honoree: Alan Patteson Jr.
Dinner Chair: Jerry L. Maulden
NCCJ Chair: Joseph Bates, MD
Speaker: Paul Tsongas, U.S. Senator

1982
Honoree: Dr. E. E. Palnick
Dinner Chair: James H. Atkins
NCCJ Chair: Joseph Bates, MD
Speaker: Alan Dixon, U.S. Senator

1983
Honoree: Sheffield Nelson
Dinner Chair: D. Eugene Fortson
NCCJ Chair: Philip Kaplan
Speaker: David Pryor, U.S. Senator

1984
Honoree: Hon. David Pryor
Dinner Chair: Ray Thornton
NCCJ Chair: Philip Kaplan
Speaker: Andrew Young, Mayor of Atlanta

1985
Honoree: Sister Margaret Blandford
Dinner Chair: Terence Renaud
NCCJ Chair: Dr. Anthony Dube
Speaker: Gene Jankowski, CBS Broadcasting CEO

1986

Honoree: Ray Thornton
Dinner Chair: Warren Stephens
NCCJ Chair: Dr. Anthony Dube
Speaker: Charles Bolden, NASA Astronaut

1987

Honorees: Louise H. and Hugh Patterson Jr.
Dinner Chair: John Flake
NCCJ Chair: Ben Saltzman, MD
Speaker: Walter Mondale, U.S. Vice President

1988

Honorees: Hon. Bill and Hillary Clinton
Dinner Chair: Senator Dale Bumpers, Senator David Pryor, (Banquet Chair:
    Skip Rutherford)
NCCJ Chair: Ben Saltzman, MD
Speaker: Andrew Young, Mayor of Atlanta

1989

Honoree: Jerry L. Maulden
Dinner Chair: Herschel H. Friday, Hon. Lottie Shackelford
NCCJ Chair: Charles Stewart
Speaker: Coretta Scott King

1990

Honoree: Louis L. Ramsay Jr.
Dinner Chair: William H. Bowen
NCCJ Chair: Charles Stewart
Speaker: Ernest Green, Little Rock Nine

1991

Honorees: Daisy Bates, Donna and Mack McLarty
Dinner Chair: Mac Geschwind
NCCJ Chair: A. Jack Reynolds
Speaker: William Gray III, U.S. House Whip

1992
Honorees: William H. Bowen, E. Charles Eichenbaum
Dinner Chair: Walter Hussman Jr.
NCCJ Chair: Lottie Shackelford
Speaker: David Mullins, Federal Reserve Board

1993
Honoree: Hon. Jim Guy Tucker
Dinner Chair: W. Jackson Williams
NCCJ Chair: Charles Stewart
Speaker: Jerry Jones, Dallas Cowboys

1994
Honorees: Robert L. Brown Sr., Dr. William H. Townsend
Dinner Chair: Jerry F. Hamra
NCCJ Chair: Louie Caudell
Speaker: George Stephanopoulos, White House

1995
Honorees: Sen. Jim Keet, Rev. Hezekiah Stewart
Dinner Chair: H. Maurice Mitchell
NCCJ Chair: Henry Tuck
Speaker: Andrea Mitchell, NBC News

1996
Honorees: Cora Duffy McHenry, H. Maurice Mitchell, James (Skip) Rutherford
Dinner Chairs: R. Drake Keith, Mary T. Manning
NCCJ Chair: Henry Tuck
Speaker: Itamar Rabinovich, Israeli Ambassador

1997
Honorees: Jo Luck, Sidney Moncrief
Dinner Chair: Lunsford Bridges
NCCJ Chair: Cora McHenry
Speaker: Deborah Mathis, White House Correspondent

1998
Honorees: Marian Lacey, Jim Shelley, Townsend Wolfe
Dinner Chair: Michael Means
NCCJ Chair: Dale Nicholson
Speaker: Terrence Roberts, Little Rock Nine

1999
Honorees: Kay Kelley Arnold, Hon. Vic Snyder, Charles Stewart
Dinner Chair: Everett Tucker III
NCCJ Chair: Dale Nicholson
Speaker: Mayor Brent Coles, Boise, Idaho

2000
Honorees: Ron Lanoue, Dale Nicholson, Larry Ross, Amy Rossi
Dinner Chair: Mike Maulden
NCCJ Chair: Dale Nicholson
Speaker: David Pryor, U.S. Senator

2001
Honorees: Dr. Josetta Edwards Wilkins, Hon. Winthrop Paul Rockefeller
Dinner Chair: Gus Vratsinas
NCCJ Chair: Mike Maulden
Speaker: Oliver "Buzz" Thomas, Esq., National Council of Churches

2002
Honorees: Dr. Sybil Jordan Hampton, William H. "Buddy" Sutton
Dinner Chair: Bob Cabe
NCCJ Chair: Mike Maulden
Speakers: Morgan Miller, Junior, Central High School; Lino Cerda, Junior, Hall High
School; Katherina Yancy, Senior, Mount St. Mary's High School; Christopher
Love, Senior, Parkview High School; Molly McGowan, Senior, Central High
School

2003
Honorees: Bishop Steven M. Arnold, Charles E. Hathaway III
Dinner Chair: Sharon Priest
NCCJ Chair: Marla Johnson Norris
Speaker: Loretta Sanchez, U.S. Representative

2004

Honorees: Clarice Miller, Dr. Raymond P. Miller Sr., Jim Pickens
Dinner Chair: Russ Harrington
NCCJ Chair: Marla Johnson Norris
Speakers: Grace Deacon, Senior, Mount St. Mary's High School; Justin Warren, Junior,
    Episcopal Collegiate School

2005

Honorees: Bob Cabe, Keith Jackson
Dinner Chairs: Dora Jane and Greg Flesher
NCCJ Chair: John Bel
Program: The Nubian Theatre Company, Memphis

2006

Honorees: Hon. Joyce Elliott, Dean Kumpuris, Mary Steenburgen
Dinner Chairs: Kathy and Jack Grundfest
JCA Chair: John Bel
Speaker: Justin Warren, Hendrix College

2007

Honorees: Senator Jim Argue Jr., Thomas A. Bruce, M. Joycelyn Elders, Oliver Elders
Dinner Chair: Walter M. Kimbrough
JCA Chair: The Right Reverend Larry E. Maze

2008

Honorees: Joel E. Anderson, Bruce T. Moore
Dinner Chairs: Brad and Debbie Diner
JCA Chair: Sue Weinstein
Speaker: Katya Lyzhina, Senior, NLR West High School

2009

Honoree: Governor Mike Beebe
Dinner Chair: Sharon Heflin
JCA Chair: Sue Weinstein
Speaker: Chris Love, Arkansas Coalition for Excellence

2010
Honorees: Henry L. Jones Jr., Rabbi Eugene H. Levy
Dinner Chair: Byron M. Eiseman
JCA Chair: Jay Barth
Speakers: Shayna Levy, B.S. Sociology, College of Charleston, Cameron Jones,
    Director, National Public Radio

2011
Honorees: Bobby Roberts, Rep. Kathy Webb
Dinner Chair: Nate Coulter
JCA Chair: Jay Barth
Speaker: Muhammad Abu-Rmaileh, Junior, Central High School

2012
Honorees: Dr. Fitz Hill, Dr. Eddie Ochoa, Stacy Sells
Dinner Chair: Marla Johnson Norris
JCA Chair: Oscar Washington
Program: Video: Why JCA Matters and Lawrence Hamilton

2013
Honorees: First Lady Ginger Beebe, Colette Honorable
Dinner Chair: Bill Paschall
JCA Chair: Oscar Washington

Father Joseph H. Biltz Award
Given Since 1987

Father Joseph H. Biltz was a native of
Little Rock who received his bachelor's degree in philosophy from St. John's Seminary
here. He earned three graduate degrees and
served as a pastor at churches in Arkansas
and Oregon before returning to work in the
Arkansas Catholic Diocese as the director
of its refugee resettlement program. In
Little Rock, he directed the federal legaliza-
tion program, under which undocumented immigrants who had lived
in the state a certain number of years might gain lawful resident status.

Father Biltz was a passionate fighter for peace and justice. His actions often sparked controversy, but the Most Reverend Andrew J.
McDonald, bishop of the Roman Catholic Diocese, at the time of
Biltz's death in 1987, said he supported Father Biltz "because he was
a prophet, and prophets are always on the cutting edge; prophets call
for us to do better."

Father Biltz worked with an array of people and issues, including
the poor and the elderly, the repeal of the death penalty and the reduction of nuclear arms. He was a board chairman of the Urban League
and a board member of the Arkansas Peace Center. He was committed
to social justice, and all who knew him were inspired by his example.

The Biltz Award has been presented each year since 1987 to individuals or groups who work for social change.

Biltz Award Winners

1987   Henry Tuck

1988   Rev. Hezekiah Stewart

1989   Dr. Raymond V. Biondo

1990   Accept No Boundaries Founders,
        Little Rock Central High School

1991   Brownie Ledbetter

1992   Ourtown Founders

1993   Jane Mendel

1994   Freddie Nixon

1995   Mimi Dortch

1996   Anytown Founders

1997   Elizabeth Eckford and Hazel Bryan Massery

1998   Irene Gaston Samuel

1999   Elijah Coleman and Grainger Williams

2000   Senator Jim Argue and Imam Johnny Aleem Hasan

2001   Members of The Panel of American Women

2002   LaVerne D. Feaster and Willie D. "Bill" Hamilton

2003   Col. Dutch Dorsch (Ret.) and Rev. William H. Robinson Jr.

2004   Annie Abrams, Bishop Kenneth Hicks, and Nina Krupitsky

2005   Dr. Betty Lowe, Bishop Larry Maze, and John Walker

2006   Rev. Stephen Copley, Sister Catherine Markey, and
        Albert J. Porter

2007   Dr. Sunny Anand, Jean Gordon, and Sanford Tollette IV

2009   Rev. Wendell Griffen, Ted Holder, and Rev. Ed Matthews

2010   Gerald Cound, Beverly Divers-White, and Pat Lile

2011   Joyce Hardy, Freeman McKindra Sr., and Grif Stockley

2012   Anna Cox, Rev. Dr. Logan Hampton, and Susan May

2013   Dr. Estella Morris, Renie Rule, and Dr. Billy Thomas

Bibliography

Bowen, William H. *The Boy From Altheimer*. Fayetteville, Arkansas: The University of Arkansas Press, 2006.

Bumpers, Dale. *The Best Lawyer in a One-Lawyer Town*. Fayetteville, Arkansas: The University of Arkansas Press, 2004.

"Director Goes Out in Style: After 34 Years, Wolfe Deserves Party," *Soiree*, November 5, 2002: 18-19.

Encyclopedia of Arkansas History & Culture. http://www.encyclopediaofarkansas.net.

Margolick, David. *Elizabeth and Hazel: Two Women of Little Rock*. New Haven: Yale University Press, 2011.

Moncrief, Sidney. *Moncrief: My Journey to the NBA*. w. Myra McLarey. Little Rock: August House Publishers, Inc. 1990.

Murphy, Sara. *Breaking the Silence: Little Rock's Women's Emergency Committee to Open Our Schools, 1958–1963*. ed. Patrick C. Murphy II. Fayetteville, Arkansas: The University of Arkansas Press, 1997.

Peacock, Leslie Newell, "Fine Art: Arkansas Arts Center Director Townsend Wolfe Embraced the Community and Has a Monument to Show for 32 Years of Work." *Arkansas Times*. January 26, 2001: 12-21.

Pryor, David. *A Pryor Commitment: The Autobiography of David Pryor*. w. David Harrell. Little Rock: Butler Center Books. 2008.

Schwartz, Marvin. *In Service to America, A History of VISTA in Arkansas, 1965-1985*. Fayetteville, The University of Arkansas Press, 1988.

Index

About the Author

Ruth D. Shepherd was born, raised, and educated in Oklahoma. Since moving to Arkansas in 1970, she has been a high school English teacher, a college writing teacher, and a community volunteer, including serving on the Little Rock school board from 1984 to 1987. She took some time off to raise her children: Stephanie Shepherd, a professor of geology and environmental science, and Paul D. Shepherd, currently a PhD student in electrical engineering.

Since Shepherd returned to full-time employment, she has worked in the not-for-profit sector as a fund-raiser, a communications and public relations specialist, and, since 2000, as executive director of Just Communities of Arkansas (formerly the National Conference for Community and Justice). She lives in Little Rock with her husband, Steve.

CPSIA information can be obtained
at www.ICGtesting.com
Printed in the USA
FFOW03n1456020315
11425FF